2002

HUMAN RIGHTS IN THE
INTERNATIONAL PUBLIC SPHERE:
CIVIC DISCOURSE
IN THE 21ST CENTURY

CIVIC DISCOURSE FOR THE THIRD MILLENNIUM

Michael Prosser, Series Editor

HUMAN RIGHTS IN THE INTERNATIONAL PUBLIC SPHERE:
CIVIC DISCOURSE FOR THE 21ST CENTURY

by
William Over
St. John's University

Ablex Publishing Corporation
Stamford, Connecticut

Printed in the United States of America

Library of Congress Cataloging-in-Publication Data

Over, William.
   Human rights in the international public sphere : civic discourse for the 21st century / by William Over.
            p.   cm. — (Civic discourse for the third millennium)
            Includes bibliographical references and index.
            ISBN 1-56750-446-9 (cloth)—ISBN 1-56750-447-7 (pbk.)
            1. Human rights.   2. International law.   I. Title.   II. Series.
        K3240.4.O89   1999
        341.4'81—dc21   99-17575
                                                                                                      CIP

Ablex Publishing Corporation
100 Prospect Street
P.O. Box 811
Stamford, CT 06904-0811

For Terry, my wife and inspiration, who has supported me throughout these chapters

Contents

Part IV.   Global Issues and Dilemmas

Preface

Beginning a project as vast as international human rights can be daunting. There is, unhappily, no shortage of material throughout history to draw upon. As my project was futuristically oriented—to examine and define human rights discourse for the new century—I needed to concentrate only on the most recent decades, particularly the 1990s. Still, there was no shortage of human rights issues, problems, and dilemmas challenging the world's conscience. As I moved from Part I of the book, which deals with the history and development of human rights at the United Nations, into Parts II and III, which deal with human rights in the field among particular cultures and class structures, I came to realize how much particular social settings influence not only issues of social justice and human well-being, but also the discourses about them.

At the same time, though the particular social and economic circumstances of the individual chapters are always unique and unrepeatable, they also always include universal features, commonalities with other contemporary examples. This, I feel, is not only because all of us live in a globalized culture from which it is impossible to escape in either time or space (cf. Buell, 1994), but also because of the common needs facing human beings and the limited resources of a single and perhaps unique planet. I was particularly drawn to human rights as discourse because it remains a relatively neglected area of communications, cultural studies, regional, and international studies. I hope this book bridges the gap between these fields and social justice. Research in current human rights topics inevitably reveals lives at the bottom in vivid detail; nonetheless, such disclosures can only clarify and inform the most advanced thinking on human progress, justifying democratic values for the future. One of Shaw's characters once quipped that the upper classes need the lower classes to keep them in line. This is perhaps more true in a different way that even Shaw in his typical understatement meant.

Human rights discourse takes many forms. I have included many of the more influential arguments and justifications in the era of globalization. To take one example, still photography has tremendously influenced public opinion for social and political issues. Although Susan Sontag (1977) in her seminal study *On Photography* questions the value of photography for the exposition and understanding of reality, she also acknowledges its tremendous evocative power through images of world events brought home. Since the publication of her essay, photography of current events has achieved a new level of acceptance, particularly as thematically based photo collections. A new generation of photographers with little or no ties to mainstream journalism have challenged her contention that the photographic image can inspire but not inform. I feel that television has been similarly underestimated by many critics, but that is perhaps another book.

My interest in human rights and cross-cultural concerns has developed over the years, but was given particular direction by the three annual conferences on intercultural communication organized by the noted scholars Michael H. Prosser and K. S. Sitaram. These meetings brought together a wide variety of academics, activists, and advocates with broad agendas and concerns. The resulting mix has been tremendously vital to my focus on social justice and cross-cultural concerns. I am especially indebted to Michael Prosser for his confidence and understanding. A founder of intercultural communication studies in the United States, his contribution to the emergent field is only matched by his nurturance and attention to new scholars and advocates in the discipline.

The cover photograph, taken in Pakistan by Thomas Haug, on his many travels as a world photographer of remote areas, evokes an image of human rights needs, all the more compelling for being concealed from most of us in the First World. Finally, my interest in human rights history and accountability has been enhanced by the presence of the United Nations headquarters, only a 10-minute subway ride from my residence in Queens. Its programs, bookstore, and conferences have been an important research source and inspiration. The huge sculpture of a modern-day Saint George slaying the dragon in the form of a broken Pershing missile is ignored by most guidebooks in New York, but its placement in the UN lawn along with other monuments to international cooperation has brought aesthetic inspiration to my studies.

Human Rights in the International Public Sphere has an interdisciplinary focus and can be used as a text in communication studies, cultural studies, political science, current events, discourse analysis, area and international studies, and other courses in the social sciences and humanities.

William Over
St. John's University

Introduction: Human Rights for a New Century

During his visit to the United States in November 1997, China's president Jiang Zemin prepared to talk with President Clinton on a number of issues concerning increased trade between the West and his country of 1.2 billion citizens. What he was unprepared for was a confrontation in Washington and later at Harvard University over human rights in China. The Clinton/Jiang dialogue at the Washington Conference had planned to stress similarities, but took an unscripted turn from trade issues to human rights. Later, the Harvard student audience bombarded Jiang with direct questions on China's dubious social justice record. Jiang's quoted response at Harvard is an all too familiar defense in the post-modern era: Human rights is a relative term: "Concepts on democracy, on human rights and on freedom are relative and specific, and they are to be determined by the specific national situation of different countries" (Faison, 1997, p. 14). By absolutizing culture in the debate over human rights, the Chinese president effectively cut off further dialogue. If China is culturally difference in a significant way, its incommensurablility with the West—and other cultural traditions—offers a screen behind which any and all social practices are allowable.

Jiang's Chinese exceptionalism is, of course, not unique. An American exceptionalist rebuttal is commonly used by journalists to defend U.S. involvement in empire-building across the globe, specifically the argument that, unlike all previous empires of the past, the U.S. desires only freedom within its spheres of influence (Zakaria, 1996). Like the now common "national security" defense, radical relativist arguments have been used by modern world powers to justify both domestic and international suppression. Nonetheless, Jiang's relativist defense of domestic oppression did not prevent his later attempts to jump on the commonality bandwagon, as in his repeated claims in Washington, Philadelphia, and New York that Chinese philosophers supplanted the Greeks as the original democrats. Jiang's two-sided argument typifies the discourse of international relations in the New World Order, where hegemonic speakers have been willing to use both universalizing and particularizing language to justify the status quo. Despite Jiang's pluralist assertions of different cultures/difference values, augmented by an appeal to "democratic" roots, he represents a power whose "political system is built on suppressing people's rights," as Xiao Qiang, executive director of Human Rights in China, observes (Erlanger, 1997, p. 14).

The Jiang/Clinton talks had as their chief objective to change the American public's negative image of the Chinese government. "They're trying to build a broader constituency in the American political mainstream for the relationship itself," according to Richard Solomon, Director of the Institute of Peace in Washington (Erlanger, 1997, p. 14). But can political leaders alone be trusted as caretakers of human rights at home and abroad? Ziao Qiang represents one of a growing number of non-governmental organizations (NGOs) that have formed in response to the relative withdrawal of state-centered rights and regulatory groups in the post-Cold War era. United Nations human rights conferences in the 1990s have felt the increasing participatory power of the NGOs, which generally have been welcomed as the most effective agents for domestic and international human rights. Especially regional NGOs, Second, Third, and Fourth World groups that monitor conditions within their own country or cultural entity, have proven capable (Azzam, 1997, p. 99). By contrast, government-directed organizations are frequently regarded with wariness, as in the case of the U.S. State Department's attempted *rapproachement* with China, which must be compromised by the tremendous pressure from U.S. transnational corporations (TNCs) that seek new markets and profits from the world's largest population. Indeed, the feeder-frenzy attached to such "neo-colonial" enterprises in recent years must be viewed very closely by outside observers. Moreover, internationally formed organizations, foremost the United Nations, have been criticized in the 1990s for offering an ineffectual and half-hearted approach to human rights issues. NGOs in particular have called for more "results-oriented" fact-gathering methods and programs at the UN, and often express impatience with the style of "quiet diplomacy" associated with the UN's newly appointed office of Commissioner for Human Rights (Bauer, 1997, pp. 1-2).

The significant rise in the number and effectiveness of human rights NGOs over the last decade, together with the increasing involvement of TNCs in issues that involve international human rights (witness the recent interest of the Harvard Business Review in "the new internationalism"), and renewed government-initiated treaties such as NAFTA, all contribute to what has been described with some anticipation as the beginnings of a true "international public sphere" (Robbins, 1997, pp. 225). Certainly, from the point of view of social justice, the incipient development of nongovernmental agency must be cause for hope. Such organizations and instumentalities hold out the possibility that human rights agency can function relatively free from the more directly repressive hegemony of states, on the one hand, and on the other, the more indirect but perhaps even more influential power of globalized capital, which has increased its bases of operation in the Third World as well as its institutional apologetics (information centers and services) in the First World.

NGOs, of course, have not proven immune from the social and economic conditions that have resulted from governmental social policy and the corporate restructuring of Third World economies. Indeed, international human rights agency is perhaps most realistically seen as functioning within a social and economic hegemony that is largely alien to social justice values. As Pheng Cheah observes, "The normative force and effectivity that human rights have are given by the force-relations that make up the global capitalist system" (1997, p. 264). Happily, Cheah does not find transnational corporate power an unassailable totality, for the nature of the global profit motive creates "points of weakness" that allow for "radical alterity," and thus the "positive points of human rights arise from these unpredictable points" (p. 265). For instance, the globalization of finance and production requires a technologically educated class in the Third World, which in turn leads to the formation of a strata of social justice activists. Thus the New World Order seems to require for the moment a dominant corporate globalization that is challenged by a variety of critical voices, offering degrees of disinterest and involvement in international development through the profit motive. Local and international interest in human rights and social justice issues remain strong, despite the increased spread of capitalist motives, even in the remaining "communist" world (China, Vietnam).

In the following chapters, I will explore human rights discourse as situated within this new international public sphere, a realm that comprises four wide areas: 1) the numerous NGOs; 2) proto-governmental institutions (the UN, the World Court, the World Bank, etc.); 3) TNCs and their affiliates (Organization for Economic Cooperation and Development (OECD), business school "think tanks," etc.); and 4) governmental agencies and information services. The complexity of discourse within the new sphere is augmented by the fact that many advocate groups fall between the categories of these four general areas by virtue of their complicated provenance and the varied backgrounds of their personnel. For example, some organizations may have members who are partially or fully supported by their home countries, as in the case of the UN Commission on Human Rights. Moreover, considering the Internet with its various cyber offspring, many voices in the human rights debate have partial or complete anonymity, and therefore little accountability.

Since each of the four realms comes with its own orientation, and hybrid orientations abound in the overlapping areas, discourse within the international public sphere appears to produce the kind of contradictory argumentation and strategizing that is hardly unique to China's president. This study will give particular attention to two of the most common, and most reductive, modes of discourse used in recent decades: arguments that absolutize particularity in some way; and the persuasive orientations that present a facile universalization of cultures and polities. As we have seen, both forms of argument were used by Jiang in his American tour, not without notice from critical observers. Unfortunately, the human rights discourse of our own (U.S.) leaders of business and government are far less likely to be reported in the domestic media, and perhaps less likely for that reason to be noticed by the private citizen. The same, of course, could be said for the reporting of Jiang's arguments in the official Chinese media.

My own perspective finds the radical relativist argument, that absolutizes cultural difference, the most potentially harmful for human rights progress. Empowered in recent decades by the trajectories of various Western intellectual movements—especially post-structuralism, deconstructionism, and the general orientation of post-modernism—relativism is no longer used simply as a rebuttal to ethnocentric attitudes projected onto the international sphere. As in the case of Jiang, relativism has become an easy way to avoid human rights issues. If culture can be absolutized, can automatically trump in a reductive manner all objections to its praxis, than there is little hope for change and progress in human history. Universal notions come to our rescue at this point, for they can demand accountability of all cultures and nations, within their own societies and between conflicting sovereign states. What relativists often overlook is that particular societies are not homogeneous, but comprise numerous subcultures, identities (gender and religious differences), and histories of persecution that prevent their uncritical consideration as essentialized entities (United Nations, 1994). Certain universal notions call forth human "dignity"—a term that has achieved a unique status in the 50-year refinements to the UN Declaration of Human Rights. As an anonymous journalist recently remarked, "Either life is always and in all circumstances sacred, or intrinsically of no account; it is inconceivable that it should be in some cases the one, and in some the other" (Dillard, 1998, p. 56).

While unexamined universalizing notions have been used in the past and continue to be used by hegemonic enterprisers to force value systems onto other cultures for their own predatory, or simply indifferent, purposes, this does not preclude the use of *other* universal notions to identify and pursue intracultural and intercultural violations of human rights and social justice. Indeed, universal concepts have been used to expose predatory universalizing ideologies. This is the contradiction of extreme relativism today—in its pursuit of harmful universalizing notions it enlists universal concepts and appeals, such as "all cultures have the right to self-determination." When used thoughtfully and with good will, *certain* universal concepts can be successfully applied to rights and justice issues worldwide. Chapter 2 charts the 50-year struggle for this realization in the language of UN human rights agreements and protocols, a history that has not been without conflict and dissent among member nations (Horowitz, 1985a). Before then, however, I would like to explore more directly the question of universal applications to intercultural human rights issues.

UNEQUAL POWER AND UNIVERSAL PRINCIPLES

While observing the storytelling methods used at the 1993 UN Conference on Women's Rights in Vienna, Bruce Robbins (1997) remarks that universal thought on abuse was often needed to overcome the inconclusiveness of storytelling. "For it is only more universality, not less—for example, attention to what Etienne Balibar calls the 'real universality' of capitalism—that can widen our view, returning us to such questions as 'poverty and development' that the sad stories of violence left undiscussed" (Robbins, 1997, p. 227). Although capable of vivid illustration, stories, as instances of particularity, are often inconclusive or ambiguous. What connects the reality of particular occurrence to social agency, and finally to meaningful international policy, is the enlistment of universal principles brought onto the common ground of intercultural decision-making.

The search for connectivity does not exist in a social vacuum. State dictatorships, transnational capital in its First and Third World originative forms, and ethnic hatreds all have reasons to keep commonality at bay. Of these forces, global capital seems predominant in the present world arena. Even the growing influence of the NGOs are partially due to recent campaigns for "privatization" in First World countries such as the United States and Britain. The requirements of unequal global power tend to encourage either a divide-and-conquer strategy within the Third World—and between elements in the First World and the Third World—or an extreme relativist position that minimizes cross-cultural ethical claims. In this regard, the current privileging of cultural incommensurability in Western theory has its function. As Robbins (1997) notes,

> The assertion of cultural difference is often understood as an all-or-nothing proposition that offers no substance for further debate. The assertion of unequal power, on the other hand, opens out into a continuing discussion with more than two sides, indeed with a profusion of tactical and principled complications to attend to. It relativizes the universal on a common ground of assumptions—from within universality itself, as it were. (p. 228)

The common ground of Robbins's claim must remain a dynamic, not a static, goal. For, in order to accommodate the advocacy of disparate cultural and subcultural groups, commonality must enable new visions and revisions for constructive change. Such a task requires a notion of culture that remains detachable and at the same time adaptable. It is unnecessary for all of the abundant life forms of culture to be detached in this way, because it is only particular aspects of any culture that function to enable the drawing forth of those universal human values so recognized over the course of the 50-year formative history of the Declaration of Human Rights. Of course, different cultures will interpret universal human values uniquely, perhaps giving priority at various times to some against others. When cultures are absolutized in such a way that each culture is hermetically sealed from the wider playing fields of common concern—and language averring such an orientation seem rife today in education, business discourse, national histories, identity politics, and diplomacy—conflicts and hatreds will prevail. By insisting that cultures are not absolute entities that sever all dialogue at their borders, the notion of culture's detachability offers avenues to other cultures. Such cross-cultural explorations are akin to Lawrence Doyle's (1997) idea that the scientific method allows for truly international participation, pursuits that are non-partisan and democratic. The notion that science is detachable from particular cultural traditions and can be introduced into any culture, even for purposes of enhancing cultural self-determination, can be expanded to include the discourse of human rights and social justice. These value systems are methods of understanding human identity, and, like the scientific method, are predicated on certain, often complex, assumptions, one of which is their commensurability with other cultures. Human rights for some implies human rights for all—a statement that can be understood transculturally, if not always accepted in practice by all nations today. The half century of UN dilation on the universality of certain human values bears witness to their cultural exportability.

The translatability of culture has been recognized only reluctantly in much academic discourse, and then often with some ambivalence. For example, in order to recognize the efficacy of human identity and universal standards for human rights discourse, the post-colonial and post-structuralist critic Gayatri Spivak presents a puzzling argument, offering a double gesture that reconsiders "essentialist" notions, but only for purposes of "political action" ("Strategy, Identity, Writing" [1990] and "Subaltern Studies" [1988]). While maintaining an anti-humanist post-structuralism, Spivak endorses a "strategic essentialism" for purposes of political action. As a post-colonial critic, Spivak recognizes the need to give back to the former colonial subject "his own history," an endeavor that requires such humanist assumptions as subjectivity and identity. Rejecting in theory the identitarian approach of Enlightenment humanism, Spivak nevertheless requires it for political purposes. Likewise, the feminist critic Diana Fuss (1989) incorporates "essentialist" language into her political strategy "not to imprison women within their own bodies but to rescue them from enculturating definitions by men" (p. 61). Justifying such critical ambiguities, Ann Snitow (1990) remarks, "feminism is inevitably a mixed form, requiring in its very nature such inconsistencies" (p. 9). Thus the tension between reaffirming the identity of "woman," and the need to eliminate the category "woman" as a originative construct of patriarchy, forces many Western feminist critics into a "double gesture."

If the identity of gender has such positive pragmatic ends, and is inscribed so deeply in human history, then how can the category "woman" be eliminated so completely at the theoretical level? Such thinking suggests a disturbing split between theory and practice, as Amanda Anderson (1992) observes; but even more, it calls into question the verity of anti-humanist constructs. Gender categories and identities are more than tools of male oppression; the fact that hegemony incorporates the use of gender, racial, and other human identities does not confirm that such notions are inherently harmful or negative. As Spivak (1988, 1990) recognizes, such identities become vital in the struggle for human rights and social justice, where a group's culture may have been suppressed or relegated for hundreds of years. If culture has in fact a detachable aspect, as I am arguing, then human categories and identities are not inherently negative or positive, but become associated with certain agendas, hidden or overt, that assist or resist power relationships, social structure, economic organization, and so on. At the same time as these human identities are doing service for entities beyond the personal, they also abide to direct the inner life of individuals, where they may represent very different orientations.

In partial response to the "enabling practical lie" of these post-structuralist critics, Amanda Anderson (1992) offers a reconception of intersubjectivity, utilizing Jurgen Habermas's theory of communicative reason for democratic and plural politics. Habermas argues that norms for ethical discourse be validated through a process of public argumentation. However, Anderson rejects his stipulation that only norms that bring about consensus have validity. Arguing that Habermas accounts only for the "generalized" and not the "concrete" other, he "fails to recognize the affective specificity of reciprocal recognition, which in turn provides the basis for the principles of need as opposed to justice" (1992, p. 83). With an overemphasis on reason, he overlooks empathy and compassion as key ingredients in mutual understanding between cultures. Hence, his norms of mutual understanding must be broadened to include affective forms that bring about recognition and respect. Moreover, Anderson feels Habermas slights intersubjectivity by giving priority in his theory to the principle of justice and to moral stages of development. Ignored is the significance of intersubjective tension, brought about by social plurality. "The regulative ideal of mutual understanding must be enlarged and recast so as to embrace both the concreteness of otherness and the indeterminacy of social identities and relations" (1992, p. 86). Political change is made possible by the indeterminate nature of social relations, which relies on mutual understanding and dialogue.

Anderson conceives the ideals of an enhanced communicative reason—respect, understanding—only as a "procedural model," in hope of avoiding essentializing concepts of identity. "A regulative ideal of mutual understanding does not render identity determinate, it merely renders politics possible" (1992, p. 89). Yet, in Anderson's scenario more is asked than "understanding." Since questions of rights are always negotiated with subjects who inhabit the same social relation, equality must be augmented by a freedom that recognizes differences—a pluralism. This is the problem of the global public sphere, where empathy and compassion are not always present, indeed perhaps are seldom present in everyday practice.

If it is true, as Asad Latif (1994) has charged, that appeals to human rights issues are often used by First-World hegemony to keep down emergent powers, then

Third World response has often been to appeal to universal principles rather than to exceptionalist values (p. 2). Thus, Cuba's 1985 UN resolution asserted the principle of nonselectivity, impartiality, and objectivity in dealing with human rights; the proposal was opposed by most Western powers until its passage in 1991. Certainly, double standards have been practiced by the First World, even against non-Western First World and emerging Third World economic powers. For example, current U.S. media criticism of Japan's practice of "dumping" lower-priced goods onto Western markets ignores the economic boost given the U.S. economy when it undersold entertainment goods (TV shows and Hollywood films) and massed-produced technology to a recovering Europe after World War II. Singapore recently rebutted U.S. media criticism of its legal system (the Michael Fay caning punishment) by pointing out the inadequacies of the U.S. criminal justice system. Here recourse to incommensurable cultural differences are passed over in favor of universal appeals to fairness. Such cases support the view that ethical criteria can transcend cultural particularity. Even arguments supporting cultural self-determination presuppose self-determination as a universal principle.

Whether scales of normativity are perceived as overlapping other cultures, or as detachable, able to be attached to other, broader communities, their significance thereby transformed, are questions for further discussion. When particular cultural values are used to indict violations outside of that cultural sphere (fraudulent labor practices by transnational corporations in the Third World, for example), the original values (fair labor practice) are not so much altered as reapplied to other cultural settings. The still commonly sounded argument that Third World workers somehow deserve such treatment—because of a presumed rigorous traditional lifestyle, or because better pay and benefits would somehow "spoil" their family structure or village life—relies not upon arguments of universality but upon relativist notions of incomprehensible cultural difference. Such relativism is fueled by racial stereotyping and dismissive assumptions about the nature of Third World poverty.

THE *REALPOLITIK* OF HUMAN RIGHTS

Some postmodern critics foresee a politics beyond what they take to be the disabling effects of human identity. They advocate a politics of difference on the way towards a "politics of indeterminacy" (MacNeil, 1997, p. 394). Such views reduce perceptions of difference to democratic sensibilities. But history offers a far less certain picture. Perceptions of difference have often, perhaps most often, led not to democratic agendas but to ethnocentric rigidities; instead of openness toward the perceived other, indifference or aggression usually follow. Those who ground their politics in human indeterminacy point out that ahistorical and universalizing forms of human rights—and of human identity in general—estrange other (non-Western) cultures from their social and political milieu. When contextualized within the current world of Realpolitik, such universalist thinking serves as pretext for intervention on the military, economic, and cultural/ideological levels. Thus United States foreign policy has been viewed as using the UN Declaration of Human Rights to reduce "all human beings across nations and cultures into an abstract universal community of which the U.S. government is the champion" (Lazreg, 1979, p. 34). Such arguments point to a long history of hegemonic aggression that incorporates moral arguments as pretense. It is true that contemporary world powers like the U.S. often "sell" their universal moral principles to their own publics when their hidden agendas include less altruistic goals. Even so, given a compliant domestic media, such societies frequently find it unnecessary to offer moral arguments as pretext for military intervention and predatory economic expansion. Thus, in the aftermath of the Nestle Corporation scandals over the marketing of infant formula in Africa, when the U.S. became the only country not to sign the 1981 World Health Organization's code for milk substitutes, the U.S. media failed to point out its government's noncompliance (Sklair, 1995).

Corporate power also has self-serving reasons to profess universal principles of justice and fair play, often by means of sophisticated discourse and bureaucratic deception. Nestle, for example, preempted the language and methods of its boycotting opponents by creating the Nestle Coordination Center for Nutrition, Inc. and the Nestle Infant Formula Audit Commission. Using Orwellian language to confuse public discourse, Nestle successfully beat back the opposition. Later, when it was discovered that Nestle had hired (at great expense) an advertising firm to pursue a "Proactive Neutralization" campaign to infiltrate their opponents, the boycott was resumed. Nestle, along with other infant formula companies, have representatives on the Codex Alimentarius, the international food regulatory agency run jointly by the World Health Organization and the Food and Agriculture Organization. At the 19th session of Codex (1989–1991), Nestle had 38 representatives, versus only 8 from all public interest groups. Industry had far more representatives than any other group on the Codex (Avery et al., 1993).

The Nestle example illustrates the limitations of the current preoccupation with the binary opposition of universal versus particular in intercultural and postcolonial discourses. For their vested interests, private corporations and governments are willing to use universalizing language and particularistic arguments concurrently. High-sounding rhetoric about industry fairness and health safety appear alongside orientations that assume significant cultural difference, as when such corporations argue that Third World sites allow for different (less strict?) hygienic practices. Faced with the highly pragmatic discourse of contemporary hegemony, the insular focus of the universalism/relativism debate becomes more and more apparent. Thus the Bangkok Declaration, signed at the 1993 Vienna Conference by Asian states in opposition to Western imperialism, uses universal notions to argue its particularism. Although opposed to what they perceive as the stifling unanimity of Western-inspired universalism, Asian representatives nonetheless argue within a human rights framework of global dimensions. Often, human rights standards have provided Third World peoples with useful tools for condemning colonialist and neocolonialist forms, and for envisioning a new international economic order (see Becker, 1997; Nickel, 1987). Moreover, as Pheng Cheah has noted, human rights is not a monolithic concept, since it has evolved into three "generations" of rights (1997, p. 235). The first generation contain mainly "negative" civil and political rights; the second generation involve "positive" social, economic, and cultural rights; and the most recent generation concerns the right to development, generally affirmed by Third World countries and least supported by developed countries. Since the right to development is predicated on the universal right to self-determination, the Bangkok Declaration upholds universal principles, despite its stance against them.

Moreover, states and regional polities that argue an unqualified "respect for difference" ignore their own multicultural makeup, since nation states—signers of the Bangkok Declaration, for instance, whose indigenous groups experience rural displacement for profit motives and are discriminated against educationally, economically, and legally—promulgate their own centripetal actions. Under these circumstances, only delimited, contextualized arguments for difference can have validity. The Bangkok Declaration must be seen within the text of a Western and transnational corporate threat (which includes significant cultural elements), not as an absolute injunction. However, human rights and social justice need to retain their universal potentiality, since violations of these principles can appear anywhere. Human rights advocacy does not stop at national borders, since state leaders and other forces can conspire against minority groups—or even the general population—within a country or region. Hence President Clinton's attempts to ally with President Suharto for market-opening motives in Indonesia must be critiqued within the context of the latter's genocide in East Timor. As Cheah (1997) points out, the prominent journalistic coverage of Western versus Eastern cultural difference, Northern economic imperialism versus Southern cultural difference, is not accurate. "The two poles of that binary opposition are complicitous. The fight is between different globalising models of capitalist development attempting to assert economic hegemony" (p. 237).

Such considerations lead away from the question of whether universal human rights exist or not. Human rights claims should instead be contextualized, judged within the particulars of global and local relations of power. Most often, such judgments will be difficult, involving investigative approaches that require regional and global knowledge of a critical kind. Too often, for instance, Western news media and academic observers alike are quick to point to rights and justice violations in other cultures while ignoring the complicity of their own governments and business groups. Jiang Zemin's visit to the U.S. is a case in point: *The New York Times* featured detailed coverage of Western objections to the Chinese government"s human rights violations, but overlooked the negative influences of Western corporate practices in China, actions that include anti-union requirements and inadequate worker benefits in its Special Economic Zones (Sklair, 1995).

The contextualization of international human rights may imply, as Cheah argues, that an international public sphere, grounded in a rationalist conception of morality, may be indefensible. How, then, to uphold international human rights without constructing the unwieldy scaffolding of a transnational political morality? Cheah (1997) proposes a middle way of normative choice between "historicist relativism and rationalist-teleological conceptions of history" (p. 240). His crucial point is that, unlike particular rights that can be challenged by one culture or transnational power, the right to rights "is not contestable because it has no specific historical, political or cultural content" (p. 241). Connecting the right to rights with the dignity of the human person expressed in the Preamble and Article One of the UN Universal Declaration of Human Rights, Cheah argues that, since "dignity" is a contentless abstraction, "reason," also prioritized in Article One of the Declaration, serves to flesh out human rights and justice situations. Cheah next links reason with "freedom," also uplifted in Article One: "Freedom is the ideal state of being unconstrained and reason co-belongs with freedom because it is the persistent ability to question and transform the external situations in which we find ourselves. In other words, human rights are the enterprise by which we find ourselves" (p. 242). Hence, the open-ended nature of the justice and rights pursuit embodied in the Declaration and its offspring call upon all nations for a "nonexhaustive common standard."

Perhaps Cheah's most challenging point is that human rights are not automatically available in any given age for all political agendas, whether retrogressive or progressive. This is because "the normative force and effectivity that human rights have are given by the force-relations that make up the global capitalist system" (1997, p. 264). However, while transnational corporate power is the present structure determining our human condition and relationships, it is not a totalizing hegemony, because history is always a "shifting global force field," where relations of power are always changing. Happily, there is a randomness to global relations that creates "points of weakness," which allow a "radical alterity" to the global capitalist system. Human rights advance from this unpredictability. However, since the alternatives advocated remain part of the dominant structure, subject to its historic determinations, they cannot offer a system beyond the present structure from which they arise. In other words, human rights movements cannot transcend the particular power structure they seek to overcome. They are instead "contaminated" by the forces they oppose. Cheah uses the example of how sustainable development, environmental projects, and "international civil society" have been co-opted by the IMF and the World Bank, their original visions subsumed by an all-encompassing global capitalism. His conclusion may also be controversial: The validity and effectivity of any human rights intuition "depends on the constellation of forces at a given conjuncture rather than an ideal or imagined horizon of all-inclusive universality which that vision has managed to grasp" (pp. 265–266). Thus a constellation of forces (transnational capitalism, state power, transnational "comprador" classes) determines both the nature and degree of success of any human rights and justice endeavor. Claims to human rights are without absolute rational justification, since such views spring from the "radical alterity" of the "force field" of global power. Because current human rights concepts are inscribed in the text of transnational power, they can never be coterminous with reason and presence.

By claiming that human rights are without absolute rational justification, Cheah forgets his own belief that human "dignity" is the abstraction that allows for the "right of rights"—also an abstract notion—to ground all rights and justice issues. Moreover, Cheah's reconception of international human rights, although forthright in its attempt to overcome the realities of a dominant world capitalism, can nonetheless become a prescription for half-measures. It is wise not to jettison universal principles of rights and justice in favor of the vague "enabling force" (1997, p. 266) of human rights. Successful advocacy doesn't work that way. Rights advocates conceive "the way the world ought to be" not "in this situation" but, to use Cheah's own word, "inexhaustibly"—with the unlimited possibility of change. Anything less falls into a complacent pragmatism. Moreover, Cheah's argument seems to confuse "validity" with "effectivity" when he perceives human rights as dependent on a constellation of forces (p. 266). Simply because human rights are never completely won does not deny their truth claims. Certainly, the relative success or failure of rights issues depends upon the particularities of the historic situation, given that all human action is historically based. However, this historic determinism does not affect the truth claims of human rights, since such abstractions are necessary to allow for the goal of unlimited possibility and to maintain a horizon of broadening options. If all social movements and causes may eventually be reinscribed to the text of hegemony, this does not invalidate the continued effort to reach beyond the grasp of pragmatic settlement. Without a continually expanding vision of the way things ought to be, how they could be better, Cheah's "conjuring with and against the inhuman force field of global capitalism" (p. 266) may lead to the all-too seductive argument that "this is as good as it's going to get." Hence *dialogue* with the devil, necessary but never sufficient for social change, must be followed by a *dialectic* with the devil. Social criticism in any given age requires a stepping back from the particularities of historic determiners, where perspectives wider than the pragmatic can be applied.

The following chapters explore the appropriate degrees of universality needed to apply human rights standards in an effective way. Other questions follow from this goal: 1) How does our analysis of culture connect with the concrete social, political, and economic situation of each society? 2) To what extent do international power relations influence governments, given that in most cases such influences are hidden or ignored? 3) How do questions of rights vary from one cultural sphere to another and how does this affect an international understanding of such rights? Such questions will remain quite relevant as globalization in its many forms will continue to develop in the twenty-first century. By exploring the particulars of a variety of problems and issues world wide, I hope to advance our comprehension and appreciation of universal human rights principles.

QUESTIONS FOR FURTHER THOUGHT

1. Which conflicts around the globe today are significantly affected by the cross-cultural assumptions of both the participants and those international organizations attempting resolutions? What are the particular assumptions in each case?
2. Do the participants in these conflicts use universalizing notions, exceptionalist notions, or both to justify their actions? What motivates these strategies in each case?
3. Do you agree or disagree with Cheah that international human rights agency today is most realistically seen as functioning within social and economic power systems that are largely alien to social justice values? If so, how do these power systems affect human rights organizations?
4. To what extent can ideas and practices from particular cultures be "detachable" to either assist or resist power relationships in other cultural settings? If so, trace instances of this in recent history.
5. How successfully can such "detachable" notions resolve human rights violations, given the hidden agendas of most international and intranational power structures? Give a recent instance in which universal notions were applied successfully.

Part I

The United Nations Develops Human Rights

1

DEFINING HUMAN RIGHTS AT THE UNITED NATIONS

From the very beginning, United Nations planners recognized that the creation of a universal human rights statement would involve much debate. The cultural diversity of the proposed UN was felt to be an area of contention and uncertainty for the formulation of normative standards. The United Nations was accurately perceived as a growing institution; in fact many more countries joined as the decades advanced than had signed the original Charter. Moreover, these new Member States, most of them post-colonial and non-Western, would represent greater cultural diversity than those in the original charter. To meet the challenge of institutional pluralism, UNESCO in 1947 organized a series of conferences and seminars on the theme of universality versus cultural difference (United Nations, 1995b). Nongovernmental organizations (NGOs) also quickly produced statements, recognizing the dangers of ethnocentricity and misguided standards applied across cultures for political and economic motivations. For example, the Executive Board of the American Anthropological Association (1947), influenced by relativist understandings of cultural differences that were gaining recognition in American academe, published a "Statement on Human Rights," which questioned the undertaking. These interpretations remain debated today, with individual scholars and movements falling on either side of a dividing line that separates the universalists (with "weak" and "strong" gradations of foundational beliefs) from the relativists (who also divide themselves along "weak" and "strong" lines).

Beginning in the 1980s, attempts to resolve the relativism/anti-relativism opposition greatly increased, perhaps impelled by a growing sense of cultural and economic interdependence—or dependence—brought on by the rapidly developing marketplace of Global Capital, as well as by the recognition among intellectuals and advocates alike of the inadequate absolute statements derived from both approaches. What has become apparent is that the classification of strict relativism and universalism are extreme positions in a continuum, with various "strong" and "weak" forms of these notions in between. Donnelly (1984), for example, has proposed "some form of weak cultural relativism," by which he means "a fundamental universality of basic human rights, tempered by a recognition of the possible need of limited cultural variations" (p. 419). This seems more of a qualified universality than a form of relativity. However, whichever terms are used to categorize this approach—"weak universality" or "weak relativity"—the point here is that both ways of thinking are needed to qualify and legitimize human rights standards. The following section will explore more fully some recent attempts to overcome the binary impasse of cultural difference verses commonality in a world that continues to shrink through technology and the increased contact of peoples.

THE MOVEMENT FOR CROSS-CULTURAL CONSENSUS

Although few advocates today seriously envision worldwide cultural unity in the near future, and many consider such a goal undesirable, some important work has been done to move beyond the type of minimalist thinking that posits only "the lowest common denominator" approach to global cooperation. Such approaches may prove inadequate to meet the realities of an increasingly competitive world where social understanding and cultural legitimacy take a back seat (it seems they always have) to quarterly profits and individual prosperity. Abdullahi A. An-Na'im (1992) has taken a more proactive approach to this increasingly limited and redundant discussion by proposing a "constructive element...to broaden and deepen cross-cultural consensus on a 'common core of human rights'" (p. 22). While his constructive approach is, as he admits, only beginning to unfold, it promises a more secure locus from which to uphold human rights standards. His main concern is to persuade thinkers not to ignore differences, but to focus their efforts on the common ground between cultures and nations.

Conceding that a level of ethnocentricity is unavoidable for survival in any given culture, An-Na'im nonetheless affirms the flexibility of culture, to the extent that it can adapt itself to meet the demands of history, both cross-culturally and within cultures. Both radical relativists and rigid universalists of human rights tend to view culture as a static, unchanging, and monolithic arrangement. This is to discount perhaps the most significant feature of human culture for the purposes of affirming human rights standards, which is its ability to change and modify itself in the face of contingency. The mechanisms of change within culture need to be identified and applied to evolving issues of rights and justice. An-Na'im cautions that such processes must be culturally legitimate to that culture, not imposed or applied artificially from without. The idea, however, is to broaden and deepen common values for global consensus. Universal standards are necessary because powerful self-interest groups would challenge their protection.

Instead of total global cultural unity, which he regards as both unattainable and undesirable, An-Na'im seeks "a certain minimum cultural consensus on goals and methods," in short, an applied consensus (1992, p. 27). What enabled this approach is the nature of culture, which he agrees is subject to change over time. Moreover, it affords its subjects a range of choices in the present. This flexibility allows for qualified universal consensus. As Melville Herskovits (1964) observed, "to recognize the values held by a given people in no wise implies that these values are a constant factor in the lives of succeeding generations of the same group" (pp. 49–50). We could add that neither does it imply that these values are a constant factor in the lives of every individual, or subgroup, of the same group. Although all cultures must obey internal criteria of legitimacy, all cultural values are subject to a range of interpretations. An-Na'im finds this aspect of culture the most important for intercultural agreement. This ambivalence allows for the development of internal cultural discourse, which will result in more adaptive "alternative" interpretations within cultures.

Internal discourse and cross-cultural dialogue, for An-Na'im, must work together towards establishing a body of beliefs to "guide action" for human rights, despite differences over the *justification* of those beliefs (p. 28). Going beyond Herskovits, then, An-Na'im recognizes not only that the values of any given culture change over time, which is Herskovit's belief, but that within the present, alternative views are present, or perhaps at the very least potentially present. The space for alternative interpretation within cultures is not explored by An-Na'im beyond this point. More, perhaps, can be said about this dynamic. It is generally true, for instance, that small, well-organized or motivated minorities can sway large majorities to accept new viewpoints and actions, or at least modify existing cultural practices. Quite often, the young are more motivated for change than the middle-aged or older. Moreover, certain cultural groups may be more impressionable and malleable than others. Also, certain individuals within any culture—perhaps those who perceive their lives as changing, or who want change, for upward mobility or nontraditional careers, and so on—may seek alternative views, or at least may be more open to them. Of course, outcasts, the disenfranchised, and minority cultures may be more willing to hear alternative propositions. While these groups and individuals may well seek values and practices that go against human rights, they may also lean towards universal views of justice and dignity.

An-Na'im urges the development of "techniques" and "general conditions" for both internal cultural discourse and cross-cultural dialogue about human rights (1992, p. 37). These approaches require commitment at all levels of contact. Commitment in one country will inspire commitment in others, and the efforts of international organizations such as the UN will inspire other international bodies as well as individual states. Surely, agreement in the abstract always proves easier than agreement in particular cases. An-Na'im's example of this are the differing views of legal punishment between Western and Islamic countries. Muslims may feel that corporal punishment, such as arm amputation for the crime of theft, may be more humane (in addition to being prescribed by *Shari'a*, Muslim law) than the Western prescription, imprisonment. These are arguments that may not be resolved easily. To add to An-Na'im's example, and further complicating the matter, many Western groups may regard the current state of Western prisons, particularly in the U.S., as punishment too severe. In addition, the new practice in the U.S. of prison privatization may eventually render the objective of rehabilitation inoperative. On the other hand, these recent complications may eventually serve to open new avenues of dialogue between the West and the Islamic world for alternative forms of punishment.

Building towards global concord on human rights involves, at least initially, a reinterpretation of cultural concepts and practices within specific cultures. This has been understood and urged by most cross-cultural thinkers today. Richard Falk (1992) gives priority to this demand: "To be effective at local and community levels, the imposition of the universal must be by way of an opening in the culture itself, not by external imposition on the culture" (p. 49). Hence, rethinking and reinterpretation must develop, along with the kind of internal dialogue that fosters wider understanding of human rights and social justice. Of course, such dialogue and strategizing must be authentic and sincere, otherwise local power structures, as well as more globally based systems, can build a provincial legitimacy that allows tyrannical and abusive actions. Dialogue must continue then at the cross-cultural level, regionally and globally, applying what has been discovered and reinterpreted within individual cultures.

Advocate groups today have discerned the need to move beyond the current discussion of universal human rights, which they regard as too legalistic and nationalistic in its presuppositions, if not in its agendas, and call for a politically based discussion of human rights, one based upon transformative notions of social structure. Groups as diverse as the Third World Christians, influenced by contemporary Liberation Theology in Latin America, and Hindu writers such as Smitu Kothari and Harsh Sethi (1989) have urged this approach. They contend that without the transformation of the political base, the social structure of cultures, human rights cannot be obtained by most Third World peoples. Such goals will meet with far greater resistance on all levels of discourse, especially from the affluent countries. Yet, social change is assumed on some level in all human rights discourse. Quite often, these assumptions are hypocritically denied by those countries representing powerful economic and military systems with global postures. There is no doubt that many of the human rights standards of the Universal Declaration, covenants, and agreements coming from the UN since the 1960s assume, or at least strongly suggest, fundamental political change within member states. Such directions are discussed in Chapter 2.

Taking their inspiration from Mahatma Gandhi, Kothari and Sethi recognize that Indian cultural traditions have been responsible for human rights violations, but that they also have the capacity for promoting progressive and liberatory undertakings. Gandhi's own career, they remind us, has demonstrated that a reinterpreted Hinduism can transform cultural practice as well as power structures (British imperialism) profoundly. Their point is that different cultures are ethically rich enough that appropriate responses to democratic and social justice movements can be undertaken. The agenda of human rights is closely bound with democratic movements of all kind around the world, actions that are increasingly recognized as necessary with the advancement of "modernization" in the Third World. First World postmodern thought has also challenged modernization as a progressive given—the automatic assumption that capitalistic development of rural regions will lead to liberatory opportunities for all classes. With the effects of unrestrained transnational capitalism increasing, especially in the Third World, human rights discourse will remain vital well into the 21st century. So far, the actions of transnational corporations, and many local businesses as well, have demonstrated that democratic motivations are ignored for the sake of profit for the few (Chomsky, 1993). Although European colonialism has long denied democratic priorities, the scale and rapidity of Global Capital in the technological age has recently increased anti-democratic trajectories. International nongovernmental organizations (NGOs) have proven more willing to confront such formidable business activity than have states, which are often compromised by their own corporate and military influence. Under such circumstances, consensus between cultures becomes a vital, perhaps the chief, means of combating the few and the powerful worldwide. It must be remembered, also, that not all forms of modernization have demonstrated negative results in Third World countries. In fact, cross-cultural judgment must take account of the full effects of technology, public health improvements, medical assistance, education, improved infrastructure, and so forth, on indigenous and post-colonial societies. This is a matter of not falling into the binary impasse of modernization/anti-modernization, a road that surely leads to harmful oversimplification.

The Bangkok Declaration: Difference Declared

As a response to the UN World Conference on Human Rights at Vienna in 1993, a group of Southeast Asian states signed the Bangkok Declaration, which urged the international community to recognize regional difference in their approach to human rights. This action was significant in so far as a faction of UN states formalized what had long been discussed unofficially. In fact, the American Anthropological Association's 1947 statement had equated the idea that human rights were universal with anti-relativism. The language of the Bangkok Declaration is somewhat more qualified. It only urges the recognition of regional differences in decision making. There is in its formulation perhaps some recognition of cultural convergence theory, which postulates that cultures become more similar over time as a result of the exchange of information (Becker, 1997). With the advent of the information age, together with the increased mobility of the industrial revolution, cultures would converge much more quickly and perhaps profoundly. This phenomenon may be viewed negatively—especially by more militarily vulnerable nations, former colonial societies, economically weaker societies, such as those of Southeast Asia, China, and Somalia—or positively—by more dominant nations and cultures, such as the U.S. and Europe. Certainly, cultural convergence theory needs to take account of political power relationships, economic dominance, and military force when considering the movement towards similarity. In the actual world, no two cultures would converge in an absolutely even way; one would tend to dominate over the other; another would remain the primary receiver of the other's culture, and usually with ambivalent feelings. With one culture giving more information than receiving, cultural dominance follows, given the fact that information is never completely "value neutral," and often has overtly ethnocentric characteristics. The members states who formulated the Bangkok Declaration were in part motivated by the primary inequality of cultural convergence.

To uphold difference as the primary arbiter of human rights and cross-cultural issues, however, leads to special problems. Many relativist treatments of cultural difference assume a closed system. The assumption is that cultural values and practices exist within a stable society where social and class conflicts do not exist (Becker, 1997, p. 81). But culture is generally regarded by communication scholars as the result of recurring interactions, and thus must be conceived as more dynamic than static (Fischer & Hawes, 1971). As with convergence theory, relativism must take account of relations of power both intraculturally and interculturally. Quite often, as with the example of Jiang Zemin, President of China in the Introduction of this book, cultural difference and exceptionalism can be exploited to justify repressive practices.

Human Rights and the Dynamics of Culture

Acknowledging the dynamic rather than static nature of culture is a key to successful negotiation of international human rights covenants. To move beyond rigid notions of cultural difference, however, has continued to be difficult at the end of the 20th century. For example, Hui-Ching Chang and G. Richard Holt (1997) point out the problem of absolutizing difference in their study of current intercultural training programs designed for expatriates in new cultures. Most of the programs stressed unexamined and stereotypical cultural differences. They also failed to "recognize the importance of power and politics in forming the substructure of meaning for any international encounter" (p. 208). Moreover, trainees were usually presented with unalterable means of approaching the cultural other. Instead, cultures should be recognized as adaptable, within degrees, and subject to negotiation for meaningful communication and action. Although the Chang and Holt study mainly concerns business trainees, its findings can be applied positively to the international human rights encounter at all level of discourse. Comparing their recommendations for cross-cultural understanding with UN practice can help understand the UN approach to international human rights.

Examining the current academic influence on practice-based research in intercultural training, Chang and Holt (1997) find that a consistent theme runs through the literature of these training manuals: they place an "emphasis on cultural differences at the expense of a dynamic, contextually sensitive view of intercultural communication" (p. 209). Furthermore, their survey of the training-manual literature finds an overemphasis on the anecdotal at the expense of theoretical grounding, and a reliance on popular literature and media contributions, which include lists of "do's and don'ts" (p. 214). Most significantly, most training programs today assume people *of equal status* who attempt to overcome intercultural difficulties. With emphasis on manners and encounter procedure, appropriate and inappropriate behaviors, "do's and don'ts," and appreciating "how others behave differently," little consideration is given to the dynamics of the cultural situation, or to the sociohistorical factors underlying the power struggles between cultures (p. 217). This "anthropology of manners" approach, with its focus on overt behaviors, lacks contextual understanding and remains ahistorical and abstracted (Irwin, 1993, p 75).

Chang and Holt recommend less emphasis on unexamined normative differences and more understanding of the negotiation of meaning within a dynamic process. They offer the advice of Armstrong and Bauman, "Sociolinguistic theory suggests that it is more productive to look at communication as a process in which social identities are negotiated rather than seeing communication as following a fixed set of norms and rules" (1997, p. 218). Most significantly for human rights discourse, "contact between representatives of different cultures always involves inequality between interactants and hence makes more important issues of power and struggle" (p. 219). The overemphasis on abstracted differences implies that "culture" is unidimensional and unchanging, hermetically sealed from historical forces, classism, racism, sexism, discriminatory practices, and so on. Permission to stereotype, prejudice, status and power between individuals in special context, are all influenced by political and historical conditions not associated with "culture" in these programs. In response, Chang and Holt offer a revised program of intercultural training, one that moves from Level I, discussion of differences, to Level II, which asks, "What do people do about these cultural differences and why?" Decisions by expatriate and host participants in real-life situations of intercultural contact are conditioned by power, politics, and other factors that need to be acknowledge in the program. Going further, these "are less matters of cultural difference (such elements are generally acknowledged to be universal) than outgrowths of historical conflict and struggle that are worked out in the contexts in which interaction takes place" (p. 225).

Chang and Holt's (1997) Level I of intercultural training, "Cultural Differences," is static, linear, and unchangeable:

1. Presenting only one view;
2. Fixating the image of the cultural Other;
3. Creating stereotypical thinking; and
4. Devoid of contextual implications.

Level II, however, moves beyond such rigidities, and is dynamic, changeable, and contextually sensitive:

1. Situational specificity
   a) Physical, sociopsychological context
   b) Emergent, depends on interactants

2. Sociohistorical impact
   a) Sociohistorical context
   b) Laden with power implications

3. Multiple voices
   a) Unique perspectives
   b) Equal degree of legitimacy

Level II could be usefully applied to the cross-cultural discourse of human rights, where progress is often stymied by perceptions of absolute or unalterable difference. As in Chang and Holt's program, human rights participants would move from "We are different!" assumptions to "What can be done about the differences?" Here, for instance, the situational dilemma would be emergent, depending on the interactants (1.b), rather than absolute and unchanging. The unique perspectives of the participants (3.a) would be sought, not frozen out by claims of exceptionalism or cultural disparity. And each nation involved would have equal degrees of legitimacy (3.b), rather than powerful ones outarguing weaker ones.

This perspective has long been implied, at times overtly stated, in the UN agreements on human rights beginning in 1948. The assumption has been, as Becker (1997) contends, that culture is dynamic, not static, able to adapt to new challenges and evolve progressively. The UN language is also consistent with An-Na'im's (1992) goal, to "broader and deepen cross-cultural consensus" for a core of human rights, has been assumed (p. 22). It is now necessary to examine more closely the language of these early agreements to better understand UN perspective on human rights.

UNDERSTANDING HUMAN RIGHTS
AT THE UNITED NATIONS

The United Nations originally conceived human rights in ways that went beyond mere legalism. Unlike international law, elements of which were adopted by the UN, the newly formed organization saw human rights and social justice as a *cause*, not merely law. This is apparent in the language of the UN Charter, adopted before the formulation of the Universal Declaration of Human Rights (UDHR). (The UN human rights texts mentioned in this chapter are collected in Langley, 1992.) The Charter, signed by the founding Member States on June 26, 1945, speaks of faith in the concept of human rights and "education" for its realization. These are attitudinal approaches to human progress, involving the identity of human beings. Human beings are *defined* in part as deserving of human rights, along with other qualities that would be clarified in the decades after World War II. The Preamble of the Charter requires the member states "to reaffirm faith in fundamental human rights, in the dignity and worth of the human person, in the equal rights of men and women...." (Levin, 1981, p. 19). Thus, faith, an inner quality, is given focus, along with the "dignity" and "worth" of each individual human. The latter two terms seem to go beyond the purely subjective locus of "faith" and would be clarified in the language of subsequent agreements to include both material aspects (living conditions, treatment under the law, etc.) and subjective qualities. Especially the idea of dignity, as a quality necessary to be fully human—that is, to live in a manner appropriate to a human being—would receive much attention in later decades and remains today a chief operative term in human rights discourse.

Education was also perceived as central to progress on human rights. Like faith, this idea associates with attitudes and other inner qualities of the person, but also to material progress. The UDHR (1948) states that "education shall be directed to the full development of human personality and to the strengthening of respect for human rights and fundamental freedoms" (Article 26, para. 2). Furthering the educational orientation of the UN is UNESCO, whose constitution obliges further universal respect for justice, the rule of law and human rights, and basic freedoms. To promote this goal, UNESCO adopted in 1974 a normative instrument, the Recommendation Concerning Education for International Understanding, Co-operation and Peace and Education relating to Human Rights and Fundamental Freedoms. Three major international meetings were held to further the educational goals of this statement. The International Congress on the Teaching of Human Rights at Vienna in 1979 had both theoretical and applied aims: to foster *attitudes* of tolerance and openness; and to offer political *means* of translating human rights concepts into reality. The most recent education congress, held in 1993 in Montreal, Canada, made for the first time the intrinsic link between human rights and democracy. It adopted The World Plan of Action on Education for Human Rights and Democracy, which asserts that education for democracy is an integral part of education for human rights. This was a crucial step in the educational orientation of the UN, since the World Plan went from making international law to associating human rights with social systems. Whereas the law rarely questions the social structures in which it operates, but instead looks for internal coherence through precedents in court judgments, the UN—and many NGOs— include the law but look beyond it to question social and political systems and arrangements. UN human rights activity thus involves as much on-going fact-finding projects, the dissemination of information and theory, and exploratory approaches to discourse as it does the passage of binding international law. These approaches are matters of general education, not solely legal enactment.

Understanding human rights at the UN in terms of "faith" and "education" requires an adjustment of our notions of legislative bodies. While many national and regional legislatures (for example, Washington, D.C., and the 50 U.S. states) regularly commission fact-finding teams and organize investigative commissions, the UN and its various instrumentalities formulate their ideas and information into the legislation. Approaches, theories, standards, and reports are voted on and proclaimed. The UN organization works through informative persuasion more than overt force or threat of law. This fundamental orientation makes the UN a unique creation of the 20th century, holding out new possibilities for the next century. A significant product of this educational approach is the Vienna Declaration and Programme of Action, adopted by 171 Member States at the World Conference on Human Rights in 1993. It also articulated the link between democracy and human rights made at the Vienna congress the same year and underscored the universality of human rights: "the international community must treat human rights globally, in a fair and equal manner, on the same footing and with the same emphasis" (para. 5). This language is insistent and forceful, perhaps in partial response to exceptionalist groups who claim particularistic priorities and many postmodern thinkers in the First World who have challenged universality. With the educational approach of the UN in mind, the Vienna Conference recommended a Decade for Human Rights Education (1995–2004), proclaimed by the General Assembly in 1994 (Resolution 49/184). Other educational programs include UNESCO's Associated School Projects, which affects 3,300 schools in 125 countries (1995); the UNESCO chairs, which are established at universities worldwide; and the UNESCO publication of over 200 books on human rights since 1949.

The UN approach to human rights centers on education, publicity (public exposure of abuses), and moral suasion, less on enforcement and legal obligation. This method is overtly normative and symbolic:

> The ultimate goal of these actions is the creation of a culture, the very core of which is adherence to the basic values of human rights and democracy and readiness to defend them in daily life....Such a culture of human rights and democracy can only be constructed by the combined efforts of educators, families, the mass media, and intergovernmental and non-governmental organizations, in other words by all social actors and by civil society as a whole. (Levin, 1981, p. 9)

The United Nations thus functions largely as a symbolic theatre where human rights are researched and analyzed, taught, broadcast, and monitored (every Member State must present a human rights progress report and answer charges against it). Although this approach has been attacked regularly as a mere "debating society," and certainly its enforcement arm would be more significant if the powerful Member States chose to support it, the UN has from its beginning explicitly called for persuasive means to change the underlying causes of human rights abuse, what Levin describes as "the creation of a culture." Although Levin (1981) does not define this UN culture, it must be inherently pluralistic and universal, with, for the first time in human history, a vision of global harmony based on a shared communicative understanding. This vision needs to be seen in historical context to appreciate its uniqueness and futuristic orientation.

A Brief History of Human Rights Organizations

Early international treaties that concerned human rights were the products of war, and thus were intended as much to safeguard the status quo as to allow individual (or at least family and community) freedom. Freedom of religion was promised in Europe in the Treaties of Westphalia (1648), which ended the extremely bloody Thirty-Years War between Protestant and Roman Catholic states. Slavery was condemned by the Congress of Vienna (1815), which ended the Napoleonic wars and, paradoxically, largely reestablished and reaffirmed the class structure of Europe. International slavery was legally abolished in the British Empire (1835), in the U.S. (the Treaty of Washington, 1862), and in later European conferences (Brussels, 1867, 1890; Berlin, 1885). Also in the 19th century were regulations for more humane war practices, the Geneva Conventions (1864, 1906); and Henri Dunant's founding of the International Red Cross (1864). The League of Nations, the international peacekeeping organization created in the wake of World War I, did not mention human rights in its mandate. Although many of the above treaties and organizations were inspired by world powers intent on maintaining the status quo by granting concessions and regularizing commerce, the symbolic significance of these treaties was profound.

Except for the establishment of the International Labour Organization (ILO) in 1919, which set standards for labor conditions, no human rights laws were passed in the inter-war period. Articles I, 55, and 56 of the UN Charter specifically mention human rights, while Articles 13, 68, and 76 concern their study and implementation. However, the 1945 Charter does not specify what human rights are, or give examples, nor does it stipulate the mechanisms to safeguard human rights in the Member States. The International Bill of Human Rights took several years to develop. Its creation was the responsibility of the Commission on Human Rights, founded in 1946 and presided over by the powerful personality of Eleanor Roosevelt. The Commission remains under the Economic and Social Council (ECOSOC), a main UN organ. Thus, from its inception, the UN has associated human rights with economic and social causes, a connection developed by nineteenth and twentieth-century thought. The evolution of human rights at the UN is discussed further in Chapter 2.

Sold to the public during World War II as an international body that would promote cooperation to prevent future wars, and galvanized around the trauma of devastation and genocide of that war—destruction so vast that even the victors were frightened—the UN was viewed as, 1) a humanitarian response to the holocaust and similar atrocities in Asia; 2) a means of preventing war by establishing social justice. However, the UN, through the structural feature of the Security Council and in *de facto* ways, was dominated by powerful Western countries—initially, the U.S., France, Britain, and the Soviet Union. Each of these countries had recent histories of imperialist ambitions, that is, aggressive postures towards Third World countries. Thus, an inherently conservative trajectory was built into the UN, a feature hard to circumvent. Senator Arthur Vandenburg, a prominent conservative U.S. Senator in the 1940s, commented on the Charter:

> The striking thing about it is that it is so conservative from a nationalist standpoint. It is based virtually on a four-power alliance...This is anything but a wild-eyed internationalist dream of a world State....I am deeply impressive (and surprised) to find [Cordell] Hull [U.S. Secretary of State, 1933–1944] so carefully guarding our American veto in his scheme of things. (qtd. in Zinn, 1998, p. 147)

For Vandenburg and Hull, the UN would remain a nationalist organization, with the most powerful Western countries in control. Throughout the 1940s and most of the 1950s, this arrangement would hold, but the U.S. and the Soviet Union would come to dominate the UN, creating a binary opposition with the remaining world falling in between. In the 1990s, with the fall of the Soviet Union, the U.S. has become the single dominant power at the UN. While nationalism has remained operative in the structure of the UN, economic developments, chiefly the transnationalism of Global Capital, has influenced this statist arrangement. Transnational corporations (TNCs) influence their governments more than ever, and this influence is felt at the UN, albeit indirectly. These power arrangements influence the promotion, reporting, and enforcement of human rights worldwide, affecting not only national and international governance, but mainstream media journalism as well (now increasingly owned by fewer and fewer corporations). Under these conditions, the UN perception of the connection between social and economic conditions and human rights remains imperiled, and its effectiveness as a regulating organization is challenged.

QUESTIONS FOR FURTHER THOUGHT

1. What steps can be taken that would allow the United Nations to function more democratically and equitably in response to human rights abuse?

2. What are two recent international or national examples of how particular cultures can change and modify themselves to broader and deepen their values for global consensus in human rights?
3. Do you believe most societies can apply mechanisms of change for the evolving human rights issues of the 21st century? If so, which issues will need to be addressed by traditional cultures in the world?
4. Do you agree or disagree with Kothari and Sethi that human rights can be realized in many cases only by changing the political structures of societies? Give examples for or against.
5. What are some recent examples of how cultural convergence theory is affected by the relations of power between cultures?

2

THE EVOLUTION OF HUMAN RIGHTS AT THE UNITED NATIONS

From its very formation, the United Nations recognized the connection between human rights and the social, political, and economic status of any culture. The Preamble of the UN Charter gives high priority to economic and social concerns: "to employ international machinery for the promotion of the economic and social advancement of all peoples." Responsibility to promote and encourage respect for human rights is also stated quite early in the Charter (Article I, para. 3). Moreover, the Economic and Social Council (ECOSOC) was given responsibility to promote human rights and to create an International Bill of Human Rights (Article 68). These associations placed human rights within a political and economic perspective that is still being realized and applied at the beginning of the twenty-first century. This chapter will explore the evolution of human rights thought as it appears in UN conference language over five decades.

THE INTERNATIONAL BILL OF HUMAN RIGHTS

Created by ECOSOC in 1946 and headed by Eleanor Roosevelt, the Commission on Human Rights drafted the Universal Declaration of Human Rights (UDHR), which was adopted by the UN General Assembly in 1948. Structurally, the Commission was unique among UN agencies. With the official members of the body are seated many nongovernmental organizations (NGOs) with consultative status. Of the original membership of 43, Western states held 10 seats. In 1989, however, the General Assembly passed a measure that would broaden the geographical, cultural, and economic diversity of the Commission by including 10 new states, all from Africa, Asia, and Latin America. The effect was to both diversify and universalize the representation. Although not legally binding, the UDHR has set an unofficial common standard of achievement worldwide and has greatly influenced obligatory international law. As a result, over the decades since its adoption, international law has given more attention to the rights of individual people than solely to matters of state (Baehr & Gordenker, 1994, p. 101). It remains a seminal work, influencing subsequent UN resolutions on human rights and self-determination as much as human rights legislation within countries.

The 1948 UDHR offers a comprehensive list of human rights. Three categories of its rights have been defined. The first relate to the physical and mental (psychological or spiritual) wholeness of the person: freedom from inhuman or degrading treatment or punishment, arbitrary arrest and detention. Guaranteed are freedom of thought, conscience and religion. The second category are political rights: freedom of opinion and expression, peaceful assembly, participation in government. The third, social, economic and cultural rights, has proven the most contentious since 1948; it includes social security, choice of employment, protection against unemployment, fair conditions of work, rest and leisure, education, and participation in the community. While these categories are for analysis only and don't assume a priority, they seem arbitrary to a degree. For instance, most of the rights listed in category three also relate to the physical and mental wholeness of the person, category one. Since the original 1948 list, increasing emphasis has been placed on development and self-determination as rights that have significance for the life of individuals as well as groups. In fact, both became cutting-edge issues at the UN by the 1990s (United Nations, 1995b).

Some non-Western states have given more emphasis to social, economic, and cultural rights than to civil and political rights. One argument is that developing societies need to satisfy the basic human needs of food, shelter, and clothing before other rights, such as freedom of expression and participation in government, can be granted. While Baehr and Gordenker (1994) dismiss this argument as irrelevant to economic advancement, offering a theoretical example to point out its absurdity, they overlook the dominant influence of transnational corporate power, which, backed with sophisticated military and diplomatic power from their mother countries, can adversely affect both the civil and economic life of Third World majority populations. The global reality is perhaps more complex. Certain Third World governments may use exceptionalist language as a mean simply to retain ethnic and class systems, whether Communist or capitalist led, while other Third World governments may express the sincere conviction that so-called "democratic" measures—free trade, deregulation, and privatization—are only substitutes for uncontrolled corporate exploitation and control. Such charges are being made at the grassroots level in Mexico, Guatemala, Nicaragua, Malaysia, and other economically dependent nations. Pivotal in this debate is the definition of "democratic," which some advocates seem to interpret merely as free-trade capitalism, while others have attempted to implement the two-way approach of the UN, which associates civil and political rights with both economic and social realities. While it is true that civil and political rights cannot be withheld indefinitely, the reality is that these rights seem unobtainable in countries with tiny economic elites and huge majorities of impoverished.

The right of peoples to self-determination is mentioned in the UN Charter only in principle, not as a right. The UDHR does not mention this group right at all. However, self-determination became legally binding in the two landmark human rights covenants of 1966, the International Covenant on Economic, Social, and Cultural Rights (ICESCR), and the International Covenant on Civil and Political Rights (ICCPR). Their passage was enabled by the then recently admitted states from Asia and Africa. Thus, they became the first fruits of the post-colonial era (United Nations, 1993). Moreover, whereas the UDHR carries no legal obligation, the 1966 covenants are legally binding for all signatories. Both covenants begin with the same two paragraphs:

> All peoples have the rights of self-determination. By virtue of that right they freely determine their political status and freely pursue their economic, social and cultural development." (Article 1, para. 1); "All peoples may...freely dispose of their natural wealth and resources without prejudice to any obligations arising out of international economic co-operation, based upon the principle of mutual benefit, and international law. In no case may a people be deprived of its own means of subsistence." (Article. 1, para. 2; in Langley et al., 1992)

The self-determination of a people is clearly connected with their economic and social choices—the rights to "freely pursue...economic, social and cultural development." In particular, economic development has become a contentious focal point for human rights, as First World industries increasingly choose Third-World sites because of their unregulated labor, environmental, and civil conditions, and "favorable" (that is, undemocratic) local enforcement. Proclaiming the end of European colonialism, both documents remain pivotal as the post-colonial period takes on the characteristics of a neo-colonial era under transnational corporate capitalism. Also, the special mention of women in ICESCR, which promises them conditions of work not inferior to men, has remained a salient area of advocacy. Together, these 1966 convenants remain normative blueprints for the next hundred years, enunciating a comprehensive and universal understanding of human well-being.

Both convenants require their signatories to present periodic reports of human rights violations. Since many, perhaps most, Member States are reluctant to pursue their own human rights violations forthrightly, human rights reporting has become an important discourse of the NGOs. Reports are constantly submitted by Amnesty International, the International Commission of Jurists, the watch committees: Helsinki Watch, Asia Watch, Africa Watch, Americas Watch, and so on. This system has often placed the independent international organizations in opposition to national governments and transnational corporations. Since both covenants have no means of enforcement, their fact-finding reports and recommendations can only serve to publicize violations in hope that the offending country will comply for the sake of its reputation. However, this system of international cooperation affirms that national borders do not limit human rights, but that "by their nature human rights represent transboundary values" (van Boven, 1997, p. 5). We might add that the system also implies that for human rights there are no limits between private and public, evidenced by the participation of the NGOs as progress reporters and as official representatives on the Human Rights Commission.

The UDHR and the two 1966 human rights covenants with their two optional protocols comprise The International Bill of Rights. It constitutes a normative frameworks through which function regional organizations, such as the Council of Europe, the Organization of American States, the Organization of African Unity and the League of Arab States. They are quoted in international legal instruments, such as the Council of Europe's Convention for the Protection of Human Rights and Fundamental Freedoms (1950), and the Constitution of the Organization of African Unity (1963). This history of international cooperation, regardless of the success rate in particular cases, has demonstrated that the international community—both private and public—is a legitimate venue for human rights concerns.

In the ICESCR, the term "dignity" is given special prominence, placed in a single paragraph of its Preamble. This concept has had far-ranging applications for human rights and fundamental freedoms since its drafting. Its usefulness can be seen when applied across a broad spectrum from the abuse of prisoners and legal punishment, to women's rights issues, to labor practices. Its breadth applies to cases as diverse as elderly issues, family relations, minority rights, child labor, poverty conditions, rules of war, and many others. Dignity was uplifted in Article 1 of the 1948 UDHR: "All human beings are born free and equal in dignity and rights." This proposition is more specific than Thomas Jefferson's famous statement in the U.S. Declaration of Independence, "all men are created equal." Dignity addresses not only specific material freedoms and rights, such as just punishment, but subjective conditions as well, such as freedom from fear, defamation, and disrespect. It has been recognized as a central concept of human rights by 20th century secular as well as religious thinkers. Ronald Dworkin (1984) places the concept centrally in his ethical thought: "Anyone who professes to take rights seriously...must accept, at the minimum...the vague but powerful idea of human dignity" (p. 198). Recent Christian theological movements, such as Liberation Theology, have associated human dignity with the biblical notion of being created in the image of God as moral beings. Therefore, each human beings must be regarded, in Kantian terms, as ends in themselves: "For when God broke bits off himself he brought into existence creatures with a real independence" (Harries, 1991, p. 2). Similarly, Dworkin (1994) finds that human rights are political "trumps" that take precedence over all human collectivities: "Individual rights are political trumps held by individuals. Individuals have rights when, for some reason, a collective good is not a sufficient justification for denying them what they wish, as individuals to have to do, or not a sufficient justification for imposing some loss or injury upon them" (p. xi). Dworkin's statement is too vague and underdeveloped for the new internationalism, where individuals in the form of business interests can cry for a "free market" ethic in which individual rights to property, investment, and action can "trump" the rights of the collective good, such as the rights of the economically vulnerable to a fair wage and a clean living environment. Such ethical limitations need to be further clarified in the language of UN resolutions, which contain rights that may come into conflict with each other. In particular, the UN Declaration on the Right to Development has attempted to deal with such contradictions.

UN human rights agreements subsequent to the International Bill of Rights underscore the comprehensiveness of these rights, but articulate more accurately the connections between human rights and other areas of human action, such as social and political conditions, social structure, regional and global influence, environmental impacts, and so on. What has been recognized is the connectivity of all human action and the limitations of pure legalist and statist approaches to human rights. One dilation has been the notion, now made into a slogan, "No peace without Justice." Peaceful cooperation—the original motivation for the founding of both the League of Nations and the UN—is only possible when justice for all is achieved. Although the opening words of the Preamble to the 1945 UN Charter connected world peace and stability with social justice—"to save succeeding generations from the scourge of war, which twice in our lifetime has brought untold sorrow to mankind, and to reaffirm faith in fundamental human rights"—and recognized the conscientious promotion of social conditions by the UN—"to employ international machinery for the promotion of the economic and social advancement of all people"—more specific language that linked social conditions, human rights, and world peace was needed (qtd. in Levin, 1981, p. 19).

Never mentioned in the Charter were other world forces that also sought stability, although not for democratic reasons, most especially Global Capital, which depends upon stable currency exchange and "stable" political conditions within countries to maximize profits (Herman & Chomsky, 1979; Manley, 1991). In fact, UN agencies, the International Monetary Fund (IMF) and the World Bank (IBRD), were formed to maintain just such forms of stability. The IMF is "to promote exchange stability"; the IBRD is "to promote private foreign investment"

(Baehr & Gordenker, 1994, pp. 38, 37). Neither the IMF nor the World Bank follows the "one state, one vote" practice of other UN agencies. Rather, voting strength is determined by capital investment, not democratic procedures. This money priority extends to the standing executive bodies of both agencies, which make decisions on loans. The 1966 covenants, passed by a UN that had become increasingly Third World in its membership, would become benchmarks for succeeding UN instrumentalities and NGOs that address, directly and indirectly, the realities of foreign capital investment.

One approach to altering the investment pattern of Global Capital began in 1964 with the First UN Conference on Trade and Development (UNCTAD), which was subsequently established as a permanent UN agency, UNCTAD. It has come to act as an interest group for Third World Member States. Influenced by Paul Prebisch's analysis of underdevelopment, it has led to the creation of the Group of 77 (now much larger), the original Third-World state parties who attended the first UNCTAD in 1964. Prebisch, who was Executive Secretary of the UN Economic Commission for Latin America, contended that advanced development takes place in certain economic centers, forcing countries outside these areas into dependency. These dependent societies are harmed by unfair trading practices. The solution for such dependency, Prebisch proposed, was to alter the terms of trade in favor of the developing countries (Baehr & Gordenker, 1994). These views sought to counterbalance the "rich man's club" of developing countries by proposing alternative economic practices and by opening critiquing the financial policies propagated by the developed countries. The conferences of UNCTAD have resulted in sharply drawn dialogue between the developed and underdeveloped countries over the specifics of the UNCTAD resolutions:

- The promotion of international trade so as to encourage development;
- Multilateral agreements to stabilize commodity prices; and
- To serve as a center for harmonizing trade and related policies of governments and regional groupings.

While offering an alternative, often critical view of the UN orthodox financial agencies, the IMF and the World Bank, UNCTAD also presents critical assessments of negotiations under the General Agreement on Tariffs and Trade (GATT). Behind this factional approach is the recognition that self-determination is directly related to particular forms of economic development. UNCTAD's approach to human rights is through the alteration of economic structures and policies. As such it attempts a three-way discourse at the UN between developed countries, socialist-oriented countries, and underdeveloped countries. More than any other UN agency, it has sought to articulate and apply the connection between economic well being and human rights.

The Declaration on the Right to Development (DRD, 1986) clarified the interdependence of all human rights. One aspect of this was the recognition that individual rights also involve the rights of peoples. The latter includes the rights of minorities and the rights of post-colonial (and neo-colonial) peoples to function free of outside interference. Self-determination is also mentioned in Article 1 of both 1966 human rights covenants and reaffirmed in the World Conference on Human Rights in the Vienna Declaration and Program of Action (1993). The dialectic relationship of individual and group rights are also recognized in the African Charter on Human and Peoples' Rights (1981), which became the first document to include a listing of the rights of peoples. This direction in the discourse of human rights, its interdependence and group aspects, points out the universal nature of human rights, a feature still under attack as the new century begins. Another indication of universality is the rise of regional institutions of human rights. Initial fears that regional human rights institutions, such as the Council of Europe, the Organization of American States, the Organization of African Unity, and so on, may challenge the validity of global instruments such as the UN, asserting alternative truths to these human rights, have proven unfounded. "The view now prevails, after many years of experience with the coexistence of global and regional instruments, that they are complementary and that they mutually reinforce each other" (van Boven, 1997, p. 11). Human rights, at least at a certain general level, has been accepted by diverse groups worldwide.

The type of applied discourse established for UN human rights work is the reporting system. Originally adopted by the International Labor Organization, it created a basic tripartite committee of ILO representatives of governments, employers' and workers' organizations, with representatives of the governments involved. The reporting system, also described as a regular supervisory system, has been adopted by several human rights treaties, including the two 1966 covenants. As discourse, it is noncontentious and aims at constructive dialogue. Typically, independent experts review and assess progress in human rights, functioning as control mechanisms for change. One obvious limitation of this method is that, without an enforcement arm, it can be nonproductive. As discourse, however, it can be effective in publicizing the abuses of particular nations. Instrumentalities using the reporting method have recognized that more can be gained from creating a descriptive and nonadversarial approach, especially given the current UN's inability to enforce its standards by military means. The use of constructive dialogue assumes that "every state is an actual or potential violator of human rights (no matter how good its intentions may be) and second that a degree of routine international accountability is in the best interests of the State itself, of its citizens, and of the international community" (Alston, 1997, p. 20). Van Boven (1997), Director of the UN Division of Human Rights in Geneva from 1977 to 1982, has cautioned, "international supervisory procedures and control mechanisms can never be considered as substitutes for national mechanisms and national measures with the aim of giving effect to human rights standards" (p. 16). While human rights have succeeded in gaining universal acceptance in principle and with regard to particular rights, they remain dependent upon positive intra-cultural dialogue and implementation.

The conference and reporting method of the UN has been criticized for being ineffective in promoting change for human rights. Large world conferences have been described as "one-time spectacles" that lead to false hopes, their programs of action "dead letters" (Baehr & Gordenker, 1994, p. 130). Another criticism is directed at the information-gathering methods. The UN is currently dependent to a degree upon governments for statistics on human rights progress and abuse, which can mean the fox is guarding the hen house. Can offending governments—which perhaps includes all governments—be unbiased sources? Their methodology, motivations, and thoroughness are always open to question because no outside institution monitors their reporting, and there are no standards which are universally, or even regionally, accepted. While there is no rebuttal to this obvious weakness in the UN system, a weakness that falls in favor of the perpetrator rather than the victims of human rights abuse, the solution may lie in the growing importance of the NGOs, which have increasingly proven confrontational in dialogue with offending governments at the UN and which supply their own prodigious share of facts, often of an investigative nature. In fact, the investigative approach of the NGOs generally stand in stark contrast to the more passive, "bureaucratic," approach of most governmental reporting, including at times that of the UN itself. As to the criticism of the conference method of human rights, it seems largely misdirected. UN conferences and summits only become "one-time spectacles" and "dead letters" in proportion to the degree of motivation of the Member States. When large states fail to pay UN annual dues and prove under-motivated or narrowly nationalistic for geopolitical reasons—a common criticism about UN commitment—ideas and programs will remain underapplied.

DISCERNING HUMAN RIGHTS AT THE UNITED NATIONS

The right of self-determination, omitted from the UDHR in 1948, but uplifted as a right with legal obligation in the two 1966 covenants, has moved to the center stage of human rights as the 21st century begins. The 1986 UN Declaration on the Right to Development (DRD) states that development is a human right. This direct equation was undergirded by the Declaration of the World Conference on Human Rights (1993), and reconfirmed unequivocally at the UN International Conferences on Population and Development (Cairo, 1994)) and Women (Beijing, 1995), as well as at the World Summit for Social Development (Copenhagen, 1995). The language of human rights has become increasingly associative, as international and regional bodies have recognized that human rights discourse cannot be treated in isolation, but only has meaning when placed contextually (United Nations, 1992). In addition to becoming more associative, the rhetoric of human rights has become more operative—one may say more reality-based—in that it is increasingly directed towards particular structural and bureaucratic strategies for success. This aspect is perhaps the result of decades of trial-and-error tactics dealing within an international institution with much responsibility and too little power. NGO and governmental advocates alike tend to be more directional in their description of human rights goals when articulating specific strategies for specific human rights loci. Moreover, strategizing human rights resolutions at regional conferences is different from national and intra-cultural, "grassroots" approaches, a distinction that was rarely discussed in the earlier decades of the UN.

A recent instance of the associative language of human rights is by J. G. Speth, administrator for the UN Development Program (UNDP):

> The UNDP advocates the realization of human rights as part of sustainable development, an approach that places people at the centre of all development activities. The central purpose is to create an enabling environment in which all human beings lead secure and creative lives. Sustainable human development is thus directed towards the promotion of human dignity—and the realization of all human rights, economic, social, cultural, civil and political. (United Nations, 1998, p. iv)

Speth's language also serves to humanize development agendas, placing the "dignity" of human beings first when approaching investment, infrastructural planning, environmental concerns, and so on. This connection is, it hardly needs stating, harder to achieve in practice. First World dominance of Third-World labor forces and landscapes is not at present directed towards the creation of an "enabling environment" for "secure and creative lives." Many examples of the low priority given Third World labor forces appear in the following chapters. While the language of the UN is nothing short of revolutionary in terms of the current status of Global Capital and domestic oligarchy in the Third World, the UN will be greatly challenged for the foreseeable future to put these goals into practice.

Also associative is the current tendency to place human rights within the structural realities of particular societies. Mary Robinson, UN High Commissioner for Human Rights, typically makes this connection in strong and explicit words:

> The 1993 World Conference on Human Rights and the 1995 World Summit for Social Development highlighted the importance of an integrated approach to social advancement. Lasting progress depends on respect for human rights and effective participation of citizens in public affairs. Nevertheless, we also know that democracy and human rights will prove elusive without social justice and sustainable development. Poverty deprives millions of their fundamental rights. Societies, in turn, are deprived of these people's contributions. Achieving sustainable progress requires the interdependence between respect for human rights, sustainable development, and democracy. (United Nations, 1998, p. vi)

Robinson makes the "no peace without justice" connection in language that is far more direct and polemical than the style of the UN Charter, UDHR, and even the 1966 covenants—"Poverty deprives millions of their fundamental rights." Moreover, Robinson clearly integrates—a new verb used by the UN—democracy and "sustainable development" with human rights. This new thinking about development has become part of the action plans of the 1990s world conferences. UN language has become increasingly operational in nature, a trend that often clashes with another strong and long-standing UN principle, the sovereignty of nations:

> Development requires that governments apply active social and environmental policies, and the promotion and protection of all human rights and fundamental freedoms on the basis of democratic and widely participatory institutions. Goals of economic growth and social progress in larger freedom must therefore be pursued simultaneously and in an integrated manner. (United Nations, 1997, p. 4)

Far less proactive statements have been attacked as "social engineering" by conservative commentators, and "socialist" by reactionaries worldwide. Certainly, the "integrated manner" called for in such language must assume that economic growth and social progress will be regulated by some sort of "state planning" to insure democratic and fair distribution of resources, labor, and investment. This position, somewhat paradoxically, has been the consistent position of the socialist Members States of the UN since its founding—states that have since experienced "the fall of Communism" around the world. Indeed, Marxist commentators may find their political philosophies undergirded by recent world conference approaches:

> An open and equitable framework for trade, investment and technology transfer, as well as enhanced cooperation in the management of a globalized world economy and in the formulation and implementation of macroeconomic policies, are critical for the promotion of sustainable economic growth. While the private sector is the primary motor for economic development, the importance of an active role for governments in the formulation of social and environmental policies should not be underestimated. (United Nations, 1997, p. 4)

This language is somewhat guarded and ambivalent. The last sentence clearly foresees "the private sector" as the main generator of wealth, but the "formulation and implementation of macroeconomic policies" must depend upon "social progress," a goal notoriously difficult to implement through Global Capital.

These and other problems in the UN plans of action fall upon ECOSOC, as the UN body responsible for overseeing, coordinating, and integrating major international development plans. Perhaps apprehending these dilemmas, ECOSOC has recently created the Administrative Committee on Coordination (ACC), headed by the Secretary-General, which will organize the autonomous UN agencies—the

IMF and the World Bank—into specific task forces. Unhappily, the latter two agencies have been criticized as interested more in foreign investment—which is indeed their official function—than in social equality and fair economic distribution. The ECOSOC bureaucratic scaffolding seems to accommodate strange bedfellows, an unfavorable sign for future human rights progress through the UN.

When the UN General Assembly issued the DRD in 1986, it attempted to clarified the vague and equivocal language of earlier human rights resolutions. Whose rights are secured, the entrepreneur's or the laborer's, the husband's or the wife and children's? The ethical position that individual rights "trump" all others proves inadequate in these all-too-common instances. Absolutizing individualism by placing the individual over common social needs ignores the dominance of international finance in economically weak societies. The DRD's trajectory offers a response to such prioritizing. Reaffirming the human right to development of Article 1 of the Vienna Declaration, Principle 3 of the Cairo Program of Action, Commitment 1 of the Copenhagen Declaration, and Article 213 of the Beijing Platform of Action, it offers several component rights designed to clarify the UN position as a challenge to late 20th century economic realities.

According to Article 20 of the DRD, people-centered human development must be a universal goal. People and their well-being come first, before other development objectives: People have the right to be "the central subject of development," which "aims at the constant improvement" of human well-being. (All quotations from the DRD are found in United Nations, *Integrating human rights with sustainable human development*, 1998, Annex 3.) This is premised by the far-ranging provision that all development must enable a "fair distribution" of its benefits (Preamble). Article 1(2) upholds the importance of group rights over the private investment of enterprisers and multinational corporations by linking development with self-determination: "The human right to development also implies the full realization of the right of peoples to self-determination, which includes...their inalienable right to full sovereignty over all their natural wealth and resources."

Despite its renewed attempt to connect human rights with economic and social structures, the language of the DRD does not always escape legal ambiguity and overgeneralization. Its statement in the Preamble, "The promotion of, respect for and enjoyment of certain human rights and fundamental freedoms cannot justify the denial of other human rights and fundamental freedoms," can be taken both to support "free enterprise" zones, where the rights of the enterpriser are upheld, and to go against it. Such occasional ambiguities are reconciled, however, by the overall intent of the document, which remains clearly a preferential option for the vulnerable and disenfranchised. This preference is made possible in the DRD by its universal language: Every person and all peoples have the right to "the implementation, promotion and protection" of "all human rights and fundamental freedoms...civil, political, economic, social and cultural." Open to interpretation, then, is the relative amount afforded to the individual, based on the total wealth of the society. While the document never takes a straightforward socialist stance, that the equality of economic wealth undergirds and assures fundamental human rights, it does go in by the back door by requiring people-centered development and guaranteeing life-enhancing goals to all. Moreover, it specifically features obligations of states, that is, governments, one of which is to eliminate "all social injustices" (Article 8[1]). Its right of nondiscrimination implies an egalitarian distribution, although the language falls short of saying so outright: "without distinction of any kind such as race, color, sex, language, religion, political or other opinion, national or social origin, property, birth or other status" (DRD Preamble). Such universal statements can be open to contradictory interpretations, such as the statement that all are entitled to "active, free, and meaningful participation in development" as an "active participant" (Article 2), a statement that ignores the prohibitive facts of poverty and lack of education. Nonetheless, the "fair distribution" (Preamble) of development benefits is clear from the overall document.

The UN understanding of human rights has moved from overgeneralized statements that circumvent the economic realities of the Third World and much of the First World, to an appreciation of the "holistic" and "interdependent" nature of human rights. Along the way, UN and NGO advocates alike have discovered through trial and error that their aims can only be achieved by affirming the intracultural rootedness of human rights—their dependence upon interpretation and acceptance within individual societies.

QUESTIONS FOR FURTHER THOUGHT

1. What ways are necessary to assure that future development planning is people-center rather than motivated by profit?
2. Following from Question 1, are there basic differences in the approach to First World economic development from Third World development? What differences might be operative?
3. How might future world conferences on human rights address the stubborn and growing gap between First World and Third World wealth?
4. How might the right to business interests be reconciled with human rights as defined by the DRD?
5. To what extent do you agree with van Boven that "by their nature human rights represent transboundary values"? Does this statement justify more assertive action on the part of international human rights groups? What kinds of actions would be appropriate?

3

THE HUMAN
RIGHTS CHALLENGE

The dilemmas that seem so formidable for United Nations human rights initiatives will continue to exist into the 21st century. The selectivity, slow pace, and bureaucratic complexities that characterize UN actions in human rights and social justice are only partially the result of problems inherent in the structure of the UN organization. Given the extent of its responsibilities, the scope of its vision, the diversity of its membership, and the geopolitics of its members, it would hardly seem surprising—except to the merely cynical and the nationalistic—that the UN would experience major problems of cohesion and implementation. This chapter will begin by examining the more recent attempts to manage the intracacies of human rights at the UN, then attempt to offer constructive criticism of its various deliberations, executive stances, and actions as they affect social justice issues. I by no means claim to have "solved" these problems, which in any case are too various to be covered adequately in one chapter (Righter, 1995). Rather, by examining the discourse of human rights as the UN in the final years of the 20th century, it may be possible to discern important shortcomings as well as virtues of the current organization and practice. While the UN by itself can never hope to eliminate human rights abuse and social inequality, it may function as an important standard-maker, source of inspiration, and seat of knowledge for human rights advocacy worldwide.

THE UNITED NATIONS DEVELOPMENT PROGRAM

As Secretary General, Kofi Annan supports new initiatives in human rights, recent UN resolution language has begun to concede its past limitations and striven to redefine its basic approaches. Whether these new developments will offer more opportunity for improving both the extent of UN influence and its practical understanding of the root causes of human rights abuse is open to question. A major step in this direction has been the World Summit for Social Development, which produced the Copenhagen Declaration and Program of Action in 1995. The signatories pledged "to put people at the centre of development" and "to make the conquest of poverty, the goal of full employment and the fostering of stable, safe and just societies their overriding objectives" (United Nations, 1995c, p. vii; all Copenhagen Declaration references are to this source). The agreements included ambitious commitments to "eradicate absolute poverty by a target date to be set by each country"; "support full employment as a basic policy goal"; and "ensure that structural adjustment programmes include social development goals" (p. vii). Nevertheless, a key problem remains. Not discussed are the particular means through which state-supported and monitored human rights initiatives are to be implemented through the current system of Global Capital and "free trade" approaches to wealth accummulation. Although the Summit Follow-up conceded that "closer links" were needed between the Bretton Woods international financial institutions—the IMF and World Bank—and the UN system with respect to its social development agendas, the language remains quite vague. Certainly, these special agencies of the UN have been criticized over the decades for their disregard of cultural development in favor of profitable foreign investment (see Chapter 2 in this volume). Moreover, the official purposes of these two institutions place obvious priority on long and short-term profit for the few rather than for the many. This contradiction seems all the more obvious since there remains no straightforward acknowledgement of this discontinuity, at least not in the official commitment language and follow-up literature. Nonetheless, the sheer size of the Copenhagen Summit—14,000 participants representing 186 countries, 2,300 representatives from 811 NGOs, and 2300 journalists, in addition to 12,000 NGO representatives at a parallel conference called NGO Forum '95—is perhaps indicative of worldwide recognition of the "people-centered" approach to development. Moreover, the Social Summit took seriously the recommendations of earlier 1990s UN conferences on sustainable development, especially the Conference on Environment and Development (Rio de Janeiro, 1992); and the International Conference on Population and Development (Cairo, 1994). Subsequent to the Social Summit, the UN General Assembly in 1996 reviewed the specific progress made on implementation of its goals to eradicate poverty. Finally, in the year 2000, the same body will review the overall implementation of the Copenhagen Declaration. These events indicate a significant and sincere interest in the connection between poverty, social development, and human rights.

Paragraph 1 of the Copenhagen Declaration gives "the highest priority" to "social development and human well-being" for the future. Paragraph 2 acknowledges the "underlying and structural causes" of "poverty, unemployment and social exclusion." This admission of fundamental social change goes further than previous UN resolution language, but it stops short of offering particular social systems to replace existing unregulated Third world capitalism, in fact it avoids discussion of "free trade" transnational capitalism altogether. Instead of language that presents the particularities of a manifesto, of agendas for change, its language often seems confessional in nature: "We acknowledge that our societies must respond more effectively to the material and spiritual needs of individuals..." (Paragraph 3). The interdependence of economic, social, and environmental development is reconfirmed (Paragraph 4), and the allusion to the UN Charter's incipient recognition of this interdependence is made (Paragraph 5). Criticism of the harmful effects of prominent geopolitical agendas appear, but infrequently, and the names of complicit Member States are withheld: "the negative impact on development of excessive military expenditures, the arms trade, and investment for arms production and acquisition must be addressed" (Paragraph 21). Overall, the discourse of the Copenhagen Declaration continues the UN tradition of offering reform measures in abundance with little or no attention to the mysterious "structural causes" occasionally alluded to. For this reason, UN human rights discourse seems to follow only meliorative aims, despite repeated insistence in its language that profound, permanent change is necessary. Overall, the UN discourse of the 1980s and 1990s has shown a slight inclination to offer more explicit implementation measures and more articulate discussion of the nature and magnitude of human rights issues, with occasional hints at underlying causes (Robinson, 1998).

Organizationally, the Copenhagen Declaration and Program of Action seem more pragmatic than previous UN resolutions, perhaps as a response to increasing worldwide impatience with the UN's relatively nugatory effect on global conditions. Its Program of Action, for example, includes chapters on An Enabling Environment for Social Development, Eradication of Poverty, Expansion of Employment and Reduction of Unemployment, Social Integration, and Implementation and Follow-Up. Also, Paragraph 26d of the Declaration uses operative language to set an agenda for its Principles and Goals section (B): "Integrate economic, cultural and social policies so that they become mutually supportive, and acknowledge the interdependence of public and private spheres of activity." At least part of its agenda seems to be self-education for the Member States involved: "Recognize that the achievement of sustained social development requires sound, broadly based economic policies" (26e). Such language indicates that many, if not most, of the signatories are unsure of the current causes and solutions. The Articles at times seem only a sort of thinking out loud, descriptive cogitations on social injustices rather than firm convictions and visions. Occasionally, extremely radical phrases stand out: "Promote the equitable distribution of income..." (26g). Such demands seem nothing short of social leveling, a movement beyond the class societies fostered by most Third world governments. The verb "promote" is in this regard ambiguous, perhaps intentionally. Does this mean that a classless society must be achieved, or that the type of horrendous inequality that exists throughout the Third World needs to be alleviated to a degree through *promotion* of egalitarian thinking and social interaction? Such demands are perhaps intended to be left open for future exploration on all levels. In any case, the World Summit and other 1990s UN human rights resolutions place a great deal of emphasis on education, presumably at all levels—from the illiterate farmer displaced from his traditional landscape by newly arrived foreign industries to NGO advocates searching for means to eradicate poverty conditions in their assigned areas. Thus, the World Summit trajectory can be characterized positively as an ongoing, in process commitment to further education along certain lines, and negatively as an overly descriptive exercise in stating the problems without offering solutions.

A prime example of explicating the problem while offering vague remedies is Paragraph 27 of the Declaration, which mentions the principle players in human rights conditions and charges them with appropriate goals, but leaves unsaid how this is to be accomplished:

> The international community, the United Nations, the multilateral financial institutions, all regional organizations and local authorities, and all actors of civil society need to positively contribute their own share of efforts and resources in order to reduce inequalities among people and narrow the gap between developed and developing countries.... Radical political, social and economic changes in the countries with economies in transition have been accompanied by a deterioration in their economic and social situation.

Such statements risk stating the obvious—that Global Capital and nationalistic oligarchies have contributed to increases in poverty and the breakdown of traditional social identities—but also calls into question the Declaration's basis in reality. The hope that "multilateral financial institutions" will "positively contribute" voluntarily their resources to eliminate poverty and human indignities denies the long tradition down to the present of corporate efforts to keep labor politically and economically weak and to exploit the environment for profit.

Despite such quixotic stances, the Copenhagen Declaration and Program of Action does include comprehensive listings of aims and achievements. A brief selection of these will quickly demonstrate just how socially radical these ideas are:

> To ensure that people living in poverty have access to productive resources...and participate in decision-making on a policy and regulatory environment that would enable them to benefit from expanding employment and economic opportunities. (Commitment 2c)

To remove any political, legal, economic and social factors and constraints that foster and sustain inequality. (Commitment 2f)

Promoting and strengthening capacity-building in developing countries, particularly in Africa and the least developed countries. (Para. 9i, Program of Action)

To ensure that the benefits of global economic growth are equitably distributed among countries. (Para. 10, Program of Action)

Supporting the efforts of developing countries, particularly those heavily dependent on commodity exports, to diversify their economies. (Para. 10e, Program of Action)

Improving...fair competition...through complementing market mechanisms and mitigating any negative impacts posed by market forces. (Para. 12b, Program of Action)

Considering measures to address inequalities arising from accumulation of wealth through...the use of appropriate taxation at the national level. (Para. 13d, Program of Action)

Clearly, the Program of Action necessitates strict regulation of economic activity by governments "to promote eqitable distribution of the benefits of growth" (12b). At the same time, it assumes the transformation of "economies from centrally planned to market-oriented one" (17h). This contradiction becomes more glaring in Chapter 2, Eradication of Poverty, where planned social transformation sits uneasily with free market policies for sustainable development:

The eradication of poverty cannot be accomplished through anti-poverty programmes alone but will require democratic participation and changes in economic structures in order to ensure access for all to resources, opportunities and public services, to undertake policies geared to more equitable distribution of wealth and income....(Para. 23, Program of Action)

Once again, the "changes in economic structures" are left unspecified. While the goals are specific and ambitious—becoming at times completely unrealistic and visionary, such as ensuring primary health care everywhere for a "socially and economically productive life" by the year 2000 (36g)—the specifics of implementation are vague or completely avoided. Just how free-market Global Capital, which is now openingly gloating over the "collapse" of Asian "planned markets" (Lewis, 1998), is expected to join in voluntarily, or even under threat of regulation, is not determinable from the literature of the World Summit. Rather, the influence of Global Capital and national corporate power in the Third World is barely mentioned in the Paragraphs. While the military/industrial complexes and "excessive investment for arms production and acquisition" around the world are plainly described as negative (Para. 70, Program of Action), the realities of retrogressive social development are acknowledged only briefly and then only in context of a wider progressive economic evolution (Paras. 67, 68).

UNITED NATIONS HUMAN RIGHTS IN PERSPECTIVE

As a culturally diverse, universally focused international organization, outside criticism of UN human rights efforts has been both abundant and extremely varied, from the cogent to the transparently cynical, sectarian, and reactionary. This section will offer a selection of the more constructive commentary with the purpose of improving the promotion and implementation of human rights standards worldwide.

Frustrations with UN gradualism, the hidden agendas of its Member States, and the highly selective and tendentious nature of its responses can be placed in perspective when it is realized, as Ramcharan (1989) finds, that it is much easier to promote human rights than to protect them (Schemo, 1998). The chief UN instrumentalities involved—ECOSOC, the Commission on Human Rights, and the General Assembly—have promoted human rights much better than they have implemented specific solutions. Commenting on the extremely inconsistent and highly selective performance of human rights efforts at the UN, Alston (1992b) remarks:

> The evolution of the regime has reflected specific political developments. Its expansion has depended upon the effective exploitation of the opportunities which have arisen in any given situation from the prevailing mix of public pressures, the cohesiveness or disarray of the key geopolitical blocks, the power and number of the offending state(s) and the international standing of their current governments....Pragmatism, rather than principle, has been the touchstone of the UN's evolution. (p. 2)

Alston's examples of this "pragmaticism" include the UN's reluctance to offer normative arguments in specific condemnations; the lack of a theoretical framework that would assure objective fact-finding efforts; and the absence of consistent means to determine when assistance and advice should be offered. Alston states a common objection, that the main organs of the UN have applied *ad hoc* approaches and avoided efforts at consistency (p. 3). Certainly, lack of consistent and acknowledged performance standards can inhibit the progressive development of human rights efforts in any institution. When consistency is lacking, there is nothing to build upon, only much to react to. Alston attributes these incongruities partially to the UN's extremely disparate bureaucracy, the medley of agencies, commissions, and committees often at odds with one another. In response to such criticism, the position of High Commissioner for Human Rights was established in the 1990s. Its recent creation prevents a suitable assessment. The office is designed to introduce a personal management and authority style in hope of unifying the complex bureaucracy.

Another problem with UN human rights is its tremendous accountability as a global and centralized institution, a circumstance which can overwhelm its practitioners. The 1966 General Assembly directive to the Human Rights Commission requires it "to put a stop to violations of human rights wherever they may occur" (GA Res.2144 A (XXI). If the statement is taken at face value without qualification, this goal has obviously never been met. March and Olsen's general observation clearly applies to UN human rights organs: "Institutions develop and redefine goals while making decisions and adapting to institutional pressures, and initial intent can be lost....[A]ctions taken (for whatever reasons) become the source of a new definition of objectives" (March & Olsen, 1989, p. 66). The *ad hoc*, highly selective, and inevitably compromised history of UN human rights actions brings one to conclude with Donnelly (1986) that the UN is strong on promotion and weak on monitoring. This is an appropriate circumstance for some critics, who see the primary goal of the UN "to socialize and educate actors into changing their views and policies over time towards a cosmopolitan (universal) human rights standard as defined by UN instruments" (Forsythe, 1991, qtd. in Alston, 1992b, p. 18). Here, the UN becomes primarily a centralized educational institution whose outlook becomes a resource for regional and local advocacy. In fact, this position has been affirmed all along in UN resolution language, along with, of course, other envisioned goals.

The charge that UN human rights has been overly influenced by geopolitical maneuverings is clearly valid. Examples are myriad. The U.S. launched a resolution on human rights violations against Cuba at the 1986 General Assembly. Cuba responded by offering resolutions on U.S. human rights violations against blacks, American Indians, and Puerto Ricans. No UN action was taken on either Member State. In 1987, Chile offered a retaliatory resolution on human rights violations against Mexico, which cosponsored many UN resolutions against Chile (Quinn, 1992). Besides being overly politicized, the General Assembly human rights initiatives generally have taken second place to actions by more motivated NGOs and to direct contacts between two or more governments. This supports the view mentioned earlier, that the UN functions primarily as an educational body, where cutting-edge discourse becomes influential through a global "trickle-down effect."

With the change in composition of the UN in the 1960s, attention to human rights began in earnest (O'Donovan, 1992). Western countries generally proved more responsive to racial issues after their divestment of colonies in the late 1950s and early 1960s. "The relative indifference of Western opinion to the civil war in the Congo at the beginning of the [1960s] gave way to major debate on the rights and wrongs of the Biafra revolt in Nigeria at the decade's end" (O'Donovan, 1992, p. 119). Apartheid became the first well-known UN cause, beginning in the late 1960s. This was helped by the African/Asian group of Member States, who initiated debate on self-determination as a locus of human rights, and by the Teheran Conference on human rights, which emphasized anti-colonial and economic development agendas. The African/Asian group formed effective committees on

Apartheid, De-cononization, and Palestinian Rights, which reported directly to the General Assembly, bypassing the Charter bureaucracy. Such thematic committees have proven far more productive than ECOSOC, which has generally failed to respond to human right issues and to relate human rights to the economic and social areas (O'Donovan, 1992). Far more NGOs attend the Commission on Human Rights than attend ECOSOC, which seems to function now only as an ineffective holding operation.

The Commission on Human Rights has proved the most active and responsive instrument of the UN (Alston, 1992a). Its role as the premier standard-setting international body remains its legacy, but it has had some success responding to particular violations and in providing a modicum of protection to actual and potential victims. It continues, however, to provide inadequate protection to human rights advocates and reporters on location, as the recent murders in Colombia demonstrate (Schemo, 1998). A catalyst for the new activist attitude in the Commission was the passage in 1965 of the Convention on the Elimination of All Forms of Racial Discrimination (CERD), which included a clear mechanism for submission of complaints (Article 14, Langley, 1992). This event marked the emergence of the new Third World majority at the UN, which was determined to give racism major focus.

Generally, however, the Commission has hesitated to move except in clearly documented cases of widespread heavy suppression. Alston (1992a) comments on the geopolitical sources of this selectivity:

> The "mere" suppression of democracy, the violation of economic and social rights, the denial of the cultural and other rights of minorities and indigenees, and comparable violations were not deemed sufficient to warrant the creation of a special procedure. As a general rule it seems that blood needed to be spilled, and in large quantaties. The main exceptions (such as Cuba and Poland) resulted from the investment of massive political capital (especially by the United States). (p. 163)

The consistent reporting of the Inter-American Commission on Human Rights in the late 1970s and early 1980s, the involvement of churches in Latin America, and the general new emphasis on human rights at the UN prompted the U.S. Representative to the UN, Jeanne Kirkpatrick, to tell the General Assembly, "[H]uman rights has become a bludgeon to be wielded by the strong against the weak, by the majority against the isolated, by the blocs against the unorganized...The activities of the United Nations with respect to Latin America offer a particularly egregious example of moral hypocrisy" (qtd. in Alston, 1992a, pp. 163–164). Alston doubts the sincerity of such discourse, since the source did not argue for an expansive across-the-board approach to human rights violations, but only for more sanctions against the ideological adversaries of the U.S. To this may be added the observation that Kirkpatrick's speech language remains self-referential in a truly

Orwellian way, an example, of unintentional verbal irony. Just who are "the strong against the weak" and "the majority against the isolated" with respect to U.S. involvement in Latin America? One wonders how the speaker assumed her words were received and who her intended audience was.

Despite internal attempts at reform in the 1980s, the acknowledgement of the connection between social and economic conditions and human rights, and the decision to place the Commission as coordinator of all human rights issues, the UN has moved very slowly towards an appropriate proactive stance for human rights. NGOs have provided the major impetus for the progressive evolution of human rights at the UN. This influence occured not without bureaucratic resist- ence. In fact, before 1980 NGOs were restricted from naming names to the Commission (Kamminga & Rodley, 1984). Over the decades, the vast majority of evidence for violations has come to the UN from NGOs, and UN thematic rapporteurs have kept a close relationship with NGO fact-gatherers. As the most active and respected human rights entity outside the UN, the NGOs helped pushed procedural reforms through the Commission in 1990.

The Commission has functioned best as a forum for consultation and a dis- course-provider for human rights. As such, "[i]t provides a degree of personal interaction which can greatly enhance the effectiveness of subsequent bilateral and multilateral discussions on related issues" (Alston, 1992a, p. 205). The Com- mission has functioned relatively well as a legitimator rather than as a generator of norms, subsequent to their adoption. In this regard the originative work has been the 1948 UDHR, the universalization of which has been the key to the Commis- sion's success. Thus it has functioned as an indirect means of global progressive change. While geopolitical battles have dominated the General Assembly—and distorted the mainstream Western media—regional intergovernmental organiza- tions, such as the Council of Europe and the Organization of American States, have proven more efficient at human rights fact-gathering. Within this dynamic, the Commission's capacity to mainstage certain kinds of violations has remained unsurpassed. Its publicity value has presented important opportunities for interna- tional discourse to affect national governments.

LOCATING HUMAN RIGHTS FOR THE NEW CENTURY

Just as human rights remains a goal very much unclarified within the UN, notions of international human rights remain unsettled among academics and advocates outside the UN. Complicating the dialogue are the contradictory realities of Third World aims and achievements. Of such countries Adamantia Pollis (1992) com- ments, "The articulated goal for most is rapid industrialization, which symbolizes modernity and advancement; but the reality frequently continues to be structural dependence on the industrialized countries and concomitant restraints on auton- omous, self-sufficient development and the continuance of underdevelopment"

(p. 153). Perhaps it would be hasty to conclude that Third World societies will undergo the same evolution from industrialization to economic and political development as Western nations have. Further complicating the issues are debates over cultural differences as they relate to political and social goals. Radical relativist find cultural differences between East and West, North, and South so profound as to challenge universalized concepts of rights. Thus, inherent individual rights are judged meaningless concepts for non-Western, pre-industrial societies (Zvobgo, 1979, pp. 92–103). Some recent theorists have gone so far as to call human rights a luxury only for rich countries (Vatikiotis & Delfs, 1993). "Traditional" attitudes towards group cohesion is often claimed to justify the preeminence of the state in Third World nations. The secondary position of individual rights in socialist as well as nonsocialist Third World countries is attributed to the conception of the state as an organic whole, which takes precedence over the individual (Pollis, 1992, pp. 152–153). How "organic" states differ from authoritarian and dictatorial states with regard to human rights is not clear in this line of thinking.

Moreover, serious doubt has been placed on the consistency of normative relativism. Westerners who argue either that non-Western cultures don't need individual rights (left-wing), or that non-Western cultures are too backward and inferior to need individual rights (right-wing, reactionary), express elitist views by prejudging other cultures and denying individual status. Marxists who see the human rights movement as a duplicitous bourgeois conspiracy to assure power to dominant "free trade" transnational capitalism overlook the popularity of human rights agreements among Third World societies (Teson, 1992, pp. 48–50). It is true that the right to property and the valorization of "free trade" has been a long-term strategy of transnational corporations and their governments to keep open-door policies in Latin America—and now perhaps in Africa and Asia. However, arguing that human rights, including fair-labor practices, are completely conspiratorial is reductive. Characterizing non-Western societies as not interested in the individual or individualism substitutes gross-generalization and distortion for empirical argumentation. What evidence is presented that confirms the absolute statement that, in non-Western societies, "[t]he individual has identity and a self only in terms of her or his relations with others in the reference group" (Pollis, 1992, p. 152)? Moreover, such statements can be shown to apply to Western societies as well, since all individuals are products, to various degrees, of their culture, class, gender, age, race, religion, and so on. Also, the psychologically and socially conformist nature of highly competitive Western societies—much discussed effects of advanced capitalism—lends support to the view that individual and group identity commingle as well in Western societies. In this respect, cultural difference may be a far more nuanced—and less reliable—influence than present dialogue about Western versus non-Western human rights may assume. Is self-expression really welcomed in powerful Western societies, dominated by corporate conformism and militaristic expenditures, or are only certain sorts of nonpoliticized license permitted?

The seldom questioned tenet that Western culture encourages individual critical expression is further undermined by a glance at the recent history of European political and social thought. Communitarian sentiments were systematically expressed in 19th-century German idealism as well as Marxism. In 1894, the British philosopher F. H. Bradley observed, "The rights of the individual are today not worth serious consideration.... The welfare of the community is the end and is the ultimate standard" (qtd. in Weston, 1989, p. 16). In the U.S., the atomistic pursuit of "the American Dream" is balanced by a long tradition of religious conformism and evangelical moralism. Theory, field research, and terminology have yet to replace superficial anecdotal evidence and stereotypical reaction in the study of individualism and cross-cultural behavior. Finally, at the UN and elsewhere, Third World countries quite as much as First World countries have demonstrated their support for first-generation political and social rights. Accordingly, the relativist belief that Third World countries discard the rights of the individual in favor of vaguely expressed notions of cultural organicism can no longer be assumed. In fact, such views may be questioned as self-serving and exceptionalist strategizing.

On the other hand, the lack of centralized, compulsive judicial procedures represents a major shortcoming of current international human rights law. Despite exceptionalist strategies by both First and Third World governments, nothing in the UN human rights conventions, accepted by nearly all countries, suggests that respect for human rights depends upon local cultural conditions. Neither is their evidence of such relativism in the African Charter on Human and Peoples' Rights of the Organization of African Unity (Teson, 1992). Cross-cultural solidarity for human rights standards are needed more than ever, as the implementation of Global Capital proceeds from wealthy to poor nations, and the governments of the wealthy nations attempt to enforce an economic hegemony that affects human rights in the Third World. Michael Haas (1994) observes, "support for authoritarian dictatorships by internally democratic countries has given rise to such phenomena as subfascism, under which human rights are violated by illegitimate dictatorial regimes that are kept in power by means of arms provided by democratic governments" (p. 3; see also Duvall & Stohl, 1988, p. 247). That internal democracies are capable of systematically promoting undemocratic societies abroad is historically verified, from the city states of ancient Greece to U.S. support for "banana republics" in Latin America.

To meet this powerful transnational influence, human rights standards that are clearly universal in language and practice, while sensitive to cultural difference, must be advanced. Moreover, First World populations must be made aware of the dynamics of the current human rights struggle, the two-edged effects of Third World "modernization" and development, and the paramountcy of corporate profit over basic rights and social justice issues in highly deregulated, privatized societies. Thus far, the many human rights agreements have not moderated the effects of First World investment, consumerism, and military buildup on Third World societies, despite half a century of detailed exposition and reaffirmation.

A sceptical attitude towards the discourse of international diplomacy needs to be developed through education and media exposition. The increasing "deregulation" of the media has often resulted in fewer rather than more alternative voices. Privatization has led to fewer and fewer corporations controlling more and more of the news in many First World societies. This trend is easily transferable to the Third World. Moreover, the public discourse of government representatives needs to be placed in context of their countries' foreign policy agendas. Frequently, this involves critical discernment of their salient terms of persuasion. For example, Jeanne Kirkpatrick's (1979) distinction between "authoritarian" and "totalitarian" states needs to be placed in context of her country's support of the former, which she considers more likely to become "democratic" than do "totalitarian" countries. But the real distinction between Kirkpatrick's authoritarian and totalitarian regimes may simply come down to which countries allow deregulated transnational corporations and support U.S. policies uncritically, and which do not.

An outlook for UN human rights success in the twenty-first century must acknowledge the continued tensive relation between universalizing values and radical relativism. This expresses the bifercated history of twentieth-century political thought. Whereas H. G. Wells affirmed in 1930 that "the battle for the peace of the world is a battle for cosmopolitan ideas," and Franklin Roosevelt would observe confidently that "civilization is not national—it is international," thus supporting the sentiments for a people-centered internationalism, the same decade Adolt Hitler would rise to popularity with the tribal slogan, "nothing else but to think as Germans and to act as Germans" (qtd. in Iriye, 1997, pp. 93, 95). The market place of ideas in the international sphere must be kept open and vital to avoid a monolithic foundationalism on the one side and a self-serving exceptionalism on the other. Collectively, the agencies of the United Nations remain a symbol of that open market place, and a focus of global progress for the future.

QUESTIONS FOR FURTHER THOUGHT

1. Do you agree or disagree that sustainable and egalitarian development in Third World countries is possible without strong government regulation? Are there other possible solutions?

2. How are economic and cultural globalization related? Is it possible for a Third World country to retain its distinct culture under heavy economic transformation? What are the usual consequences of rapid development?

3. How can First World public opinion influence UN efforts to improve its human rights commitment? What is the role of education in this regard?
4. How might the UN change its institutional structure to create a more responsive and consistent human rights organization?
5. How true is the common conception that Western societies favor individual rights and lifestyles, while non-Western societies favor consensual, group-oriented rights and lifestyles? Give examples to support your views.

Part II

Other Channels
of Discourse

4

PURSUING HUMAN RIGHTS: THE NGOs

By far the most numerous organizations in pursuit of human rights in the era of globalization have been the nongovernmental organizations (NGOs). Their initiative and comparatively high level of motivation have also made them the most effective human rights grouping. NGOs often face opposition not only from local governments, onsite corporate contractors, and internal paramilitary and terrorist groups, but from other international organizations as well, including intergovernmental organizations (IGOs), such as the UN's instrumentalities and financial institutions (World Bank, IMF), many of which are to different degrees self-serving or serving nondemocratic interests. Moreover, NGOs face the formidable forces of corporate globalization and unilateral national power, which at times have threatened their effectiveness and capacity for independent action. This chapter will consider the continued viability of NGOs for the new century and identify areas of fruitful change and adaptation. Whether NGOs should continue their relatively independent status or rather undertake closer cooperative relationships with other human rights organizations and institutions, as seems likely in the near future at least, is an important consideration. Taking history as a guide, many NGO advocates have remembered the old query, "Can success kill us?" Maintaining their formula for success while adapting to newer developments in human rights advocacy will challenge NGOs throughout the next few decades.

TOO MANY COOKS, NOT ENOUGH MEDIA ACCESS

Inherently, human rights advocacy in the international political sphere has involved interorganizational contact. The associative aspect of NGO work can only increase in the decades ahead, as organizations such as the UN continue to increase their bureaucratic structures in the human rights area while downsizing their employees. The organizational structure of the UN expanded during the 1980s and 1990s with the introduction of such offices as Human Rights Commissioner—a position intended to make effective the top-heavy structure of which it has become a part—and the ever-increasing number of sub-commissions and working groups intended to address specific areas of human rights controversy. The continued development of UN structures has meant greater participation of NGOs in the UN, since the latter's centripetal pull as a world media platform and locus of moral conscience obliges international organizations to cooperate significantly with its agendas.

An example of the ambivalent nature of such cooperation is the Working Group of Indigenous Populations, founded in 1982. It comprises five members representing the five global areas officially recognized by the UN (Africa, Asia, Eastern Europe, Latin America, and "Western Europe and others"). The five are drawn from the membership of the Sub-Commission on Prevention of Discrimination and Protection of Minorities. Often regarded as the most open body in the UN system, the Working Group has allowed indigenous individuals and groups to speak before it, along with NGOs, IGOs, and member states. Its purpose is to draft international standards, such as the Universal Declaration on Indigenous Rights. However, the presence at the UN of the many NGOs representing indigenous people also attracts host state participation and subsequent monitoring of the Working Group's indigenous groups. While the UN may seem at first a positive locus for dialogue between host governments and their indigenous groups seeking self-determination or self-identification, in practice, many indigenous NGOs refuse to participate lest they attract the unwanted attention and consequent scrutiny of their host governments. In such instances, governmental and NGO participation can be less than satisfactory. Many meetings of the Working Group become closed debates in which each side repeats defensive arguments and no progress is achieved (Corntassel & Primeau, 1995).

NGOS NOT COMMONLY RECOGNIZED

The American Indian Movement (AIM), an activist tradition begun in the early 1970s and expanded to include international indigenous groups from Central and

South America, does not fit neatly into the prevailing category of NGO. As an NGO whose membership often takes an antigovernment approach, refusing even to use its host nation's passports when traveling to international conferences by substituting indigenous identifications, AIM and its many associates constitute an alternative approach to nongovernmental activism. Despite its lack of funding and nonrecognition, it has become increasingly international in its reach. AIM and its affiliate groups believe that there are alternatives to traditional European concepts of individual rights and the priority of property. Their approach would replace even "liberation" governments that continued to export natural resources and food to First World markets. Instead, AIM activists often emphasize the traditional indigenous regard for the natural environment and its intrinsic relation to human culture. Their alternative to the prevailing Western stress on individual rights has been echoed by many recent Western theorists of human rights. Penna and Campbell (1998) recognize that non-Western approaches to human rights, although ignored by Western advocates and theorists alike, have special value in that such optional approaches to social justice may often prove more effective for progressive change than the Western stress on individualism with its demarcations of rights and property.

This unique merging of ecological, local economic, and human rights found expression at the 1977 Conference on Discrimination Against the Indigenous Populations of the Americas in Geneva, Switzerland. There was an initial clash between mainstream NGOs sponsoring the conference and the indigenous delegation over speaking procedures. Still, the 130 delegates—representing Aymara from Bolivia, Guami from Panama, Mesquito from Nicaragua, and Hopi from Arizona—brought a unique message of energy conservation and indigenous rights for self-determination based on economic localism, and ecological preservation. The initial clash between traditional NGOs and indigenous delegates revealed the different degrees of recognition each movement experienced from the international public sphere: "This is *our* conference. We came here, for the first time, to present our case to the world and now we are told that we have to sit and give half our time to some damn white speakers to tell us how nice it is to have us here" (Geneva, 1977, 1978, p. 40).

The indigenous message of economic self-sufficiency and ecological conservation cut across the traditional Western binaries of capitalist versus socialist values, an approach that seems to have affinity with many postcolonial theorists, including Homi Bhabha's notion of the location of culture and Edward Said's developed view that allows greater space for non-Western approaches to social justice issues. Sotsisowah's (1981) thesis was typical of the American indigenous approach:

> The development of liberation technologies, many of which already exist but have been largely ignored by the political movements (even the anti-colonial political movements) are a necessary part of the decolonization process. Liberation technologies are those technologies which can be implemented by a spe-

cific people in a specific locality and which free those people from dependency upon multinational corporations and the governments which multinational corporations control. Liberation technologies are those which meet people's needs within the parameters defined by the cultures which they themselves created (or create), and which have no dependency upon the world marketplace. Windmills can be a form of liberation technology, as can water wheels, solar collectors, bio-mass plants, woodlots, underground home construction—the list is very long. (pp. 115–116)

This approach appropriates some of the vocabulary of Global Capital, converting its presuppositions to define a locally based, anti-colonial, conservationist value system that assumes a process leading to self-sufficiency. It is consciously against transnational corporate power, which it associates with neocolonial methods of conquest, displacement of cultures, and environmental ruination.

Ignored in the American indigenous approach, at least in the formative years of the 1970s, was an adequate means of dealing with its host governments, the reality of whose power and legal dominance could not be denied. While the Swiss government accepted the presentation of indigenous passports as superseding those of the host governments, its *ad hoc* openness to the indigenous delegations did not presage a general acceptance of such anti-host government movements in the international public sphere. In fact, Sotsisowah's method of self-determination assumes an internal approach, requiring the wide enlistment of indigenous communities, who will demand local methods to achieve human rights progress and economic equality. However, there is no sign that such internal movements have begun in the 1990s. Rather, a generation after the Geneva Conference, most Native American groups are struggling over issues of identity and cultural preservation, not developing an internal organizational structure with significant economic and ecological agendas. This is not due to lack of need. Throughout much of the Americas, indigenous peoples remain imperiled economically, medically, and politically, as the unfortunate example of the Guayaki Indians of Paraguay has demonstrated.

In one public arena, however, indigenous groups have achieved a new level of economic autonomy. In Canada's British Columbia province, a treaty was signed between the federal government and the Nisga'a, a West Coast Indian group. The large tract of land came with legal rights to a certain degree of autonomy in 1998. Joseph Gosnell, president of the Nisga'a Tribal Council, exclaimed, "Today we join Canada and British Columbia as free citizens, full and equal participants in the social, economic and political life of this country" (DePalma, 1998, p. A10).

The Nisga'a land decision was the result of indigenous NGOs negotiating with a host government rather than through litigation. However, a look at the 500 tribes and councils within the U.S., granted the right to govern themselves to varying degrees a hundred years before, raises concern that the Nisga'a new grant of autonomy may prove disappointing. Although U.S. indigenous groups consider themselves sovereign nations, non-natives living on their land are often not taxed, and the indigenous right to levy taxes has been challenged in court. The U.S. tribes remain the poorest ethnic group within their society, as are the Canadian tribes. Canadian indigenous groups remain hampered by lack of money for social projects, since banks have been reluctant to lend money to them. Nonetheless, economic independence is still a goal of indigenous activists, who point to evidence that tribes who have achieved greater degrees of political independence also achieve the most economic independence.

Some indigenous NGOs in the United States have recently used litigation to press their land claims. The Native American Rights Fund, which graduates 20 to 30 advocates a year, has recently argued a case before the U.S. Supreme Court that would expand indigenous lands throughout much of Alaska. Although the Court ruled against the Fund in 1998, claiming that the lands could not fall under Indian jurisdiction, the organization continues to fight disputes over traditional indigenous concerns such as cultural ecology, fish, and game. In New Mexico, the Isleta Pueblo group went to court claiming that the federal Clean Water Act, which gave indigenous groups the right to regulate water standards, permitted them to set water standards that were higher than the rest of New Mexico. The tribe wanted cleaner water for religious as well as health reasons, but the city of Albuquerque, which shares the Rio Grande River with the Iselta Pueblo, contested the indigenous standards, claiming costs of $300 million to meet the new water requirements. The Supreme Court ruled in favor of the indigenous group in 1997 (Egan, 1998).

Long-term and consistent advocacy by indigenous NGOs has positively affected the economic independence of many groups within North America, although many tribal lands remain underdeveloped and many tribes are overdependent upon host government bureaucracies. Forceful and articulate advocates for North American indigenous groups, such as Ward Churchill (1992), one-time codirector of AIM and currently professor at the Center for Studies of Ethnicity and Race in America, and bell hooks (1992), cultural critic and activist, have brought activism into the sphere of ideology by influencing scholars and theorists of human rights and public policy. While such efforts remain primarily a North American phenomenon, they constitute a model for Third World indigenous discourse and activism. Above all, sustained advocacy and united movements that transcend tribal and continental borders are needed for significant progressive change. Art Solomon, a delegate to the 1977 Geneva Indigenous Convention, expressed this view succinctly, "We not only delivered our message on unity—we not only told them about unity—we showed them" (Geneva, 1977, 1978, p. 36).

Indigenous NGOs face the persistent disagreement over the definition of indigenous people. Host governments and private vested interest groups have often used the ongoing confusion over indigenous identity among IGOs, local governments, and NGOs to deny discriminatory policies and intrusive actions. The discourse of definition remains controversial. In the early 1980s, the World Council of Indigenous Peoples (WCIP) adopted the following statement as a working definition of indigenous peoples: "The term…refers to people living in countries which have a population composed of differing ethnic or racial groups who are descendant of the earliest populations living in the area and who do not as a group control the national government of the countries within which they live" (Fourth World, 1998, p. 2). Its definition is broader and less problematic than that adopted in 1972 by the UN Sub-commission on the Prevention of Discrimination and Protection of Minorities, which includes a stipulation that requires the indigenous to live as culturally distinct peoples: "who today live more in conformity with their particular social, economic and cultural customs of traditions than with the institutions of the country of which they now form a part…" (The Fourth World, 1998, p. 2). Under such definitions, indigenous groups must prove in a court of law that their lifestyles constitute distinctly different cultures from the host majorities. Moreover, other IGOs, NGO, and host governments utilize their own working definitions of indigenous people. Although both the WCIP and the International Indian Treaty Council have received consultative status as NGO within the UN system, and the right to self-determination is mentioned frequently throughout the UN human rights covenants, the question of who qualifies for indigenous status hinders the work of indigenous NGOs and their mainstream NGO supporters.

MAINSTREAM NGOS

The UN High Commissioner and NGOs

Despite the official observation of the new UN office of High Commissioner for Human Rights (1997), that "the primary responsibility for protecting human rights rests with Governments" (p. 1), NGOs remain the most committed group to uncover abuses worldwide. In fact, the office of High Commissioner has disappointed many NGO human rights advocates, who see the Commissioner's emphasis on "quiet diplomacy" as an ineffective, if not feckless, response to economic and political oppression, particularly in Third World settings. "The net result of this approach has generally meant that information on the nature of discussions held with governments, the issues covered and the results, if any, have remained largely unknown" (High Commissioner, 1997, p. 1). Some NGO spokespersons have even concluded that the new office of High Commissioner, although intended to break the bureaucratic encumbrances of the former UN system of too many agencies with too little specificity and even less power for enforcement, has instead joined an inner circle of diplomats rather than stand apart as a strong advocate of human rights promotion and protection. However, other NGO activists have been appreciative of the High Commissioner's points of recommendation made to them, particularly those dealing with the language of human rights resolutions.

Among these recommendations were: 1) To craft the resolutions in more "result-oriented" language so that progress from one year to the next can be more clearly measurable; 2) Condemnations of governments, private institutions and corporations are at times necessary, but should only be a means to an end, which is "part of the process of identifying durable solutions to serious human rights problems"; 3) Human rights resolutions should analyze and clarify certain questions, such as: a) Have specific human rights problems been identified? b) Have remedial human rights actions been suggested or taken? c) Have durable solutions been considered? and d) What is being budgeted for these actions? (High Commissioner, 1997)

Above all, the 1996 Report of the High Commissioner (Mary Robinson) recommended for human rights NGOs deeper social and economic analyses that go beyond merely meliorative approaches to abuses: "[NGOs] will also have to develop more fully skills that move well beyond the traditional approach of enumerating symptoms and deal more directly and consistently with causes" (High Commissioner, 1997, pp. 2–3). The High Commissioner's emphasis on causal relationships in human rights and social justice issues has perhaps been a result of the greater attention given to the connectivity between social, economic, and political rights at the 1993 World Conference on Human Rights and the 1995 World Summit for Social Development. Regarding these insights, Mary Robinson (1998) has remarked, "Poverty deprives millions of their fundamental rights" (p. vi).

This integrative approach to human rights activism has been further articulated in such UN policy documents as *Integrating Human Rights with Sustainable Human Development*, by the UN Development Program. The new perspective encourages human rights NGOs to probe more deeply into international abuses to discover the interdependency of democratic standards and economic/cultural development. Thus, reports on violations cannot be surgically removed from the wider contexts of trade policy, land use and management, policing methods, labor rights, and gender rights, to name a few areas of influence. Cross-cutting themes will be more and more expected in the decades ahead, as second-generation human rights issues are increasingly associated with first-generation rights issues. Moreover, the relationship between the High Commissioner and human rights NGOs—only a few years old—holds the promise of mutual critique and focused cooperation that alone can replace the preference for procedural norms over substance that has often debilitated UN human rights mechanisms in the past.

A Prominent NGO: Maximizing Success with Little Power

Amnesty International (AI), based in London, has major branches throughout the world. It has become one of the few human rights organizations that has gained recognition from the mainstream media of most societies. One of its activist strategies is to focus on a single-issue campaign in one country at a time. In 1998, the United States became the focus of one such campaign. For most of its 37-year existence, AI has monitored societies far from home, usually in the Third World. However, its selection of the U.S. sent an additional message to the international public sphere—that First World states, even the world's only superpower with unilateral global ambitions—can be subject to human rights scrutiny (Amnesty in America, 1998). By so doing, it questioned a basic assumption of the post-Cold War era—that a country that perceives itself as a global policing power by virtue of its economic and political success (see Chapter 17) cannot itself be challenged on the moral ground of human rights and social justice.

AI's 153-page report, *Rights for All* (1998), collected a wide variety of instances of police brutality throughout the U.S., from local police departments to prisons. Among the more alarming findings of the study are that the prison and jail populations tripled between 1980 and 1996 to 1.7 million, with the majority of inmates (60 percent) minorities. In violation of international standards, more than 3,500 children are housed with adults. Pregnant prisoners in labor are routinely taken to the hospital in fetters, also a violation of international law, as is the common practice of transporting prisoners in chains and leg irons. Other international violations include: the sentencing to death of the mentally retarded; the widespread use of electroshock weapons of various kinds, some emitting as much as 50,000 volts; the use of pepper spray, which has killed 60 people; and the indefinite detainment of political asylum prisoners. Moreover, the U.S. government has imposed hobbling reservations on certain international human rights treaties it has signed, including the Convention Against Torture. It has also failed to sign other treaties, including the Convention on the Rights of the Child (Amnesty in America, 1998). The mainstream U.S. press has not given this AI report as much coverage as earlier reports—when other countries were involved, particularly those without U.S. client state relationships. True to its custom, AI has included a series of reform proposals in its U.S. report. However, whether the 1998 AI report on U.S. prisons and police brutality will be recognized and acted upon by the U.S. public very much depends upon the extent of media coverage in the years ahead.

Less Successful NGOs

Other NGOs have proven less effective, not because they have failed to develop a sufficient grassroots base, but because they have not discovered a successful entree to the international public sphere. One instance was the petition of the International Women's Tribunal Centre. It began when women of the World Council of Churches met with women from the UN to discuss the commemoration of the 50th anniversary of the UN Commission on the Status of Women. Their decision to petition for a 5 percent reduction in military spending worldwide eventually garnered over 100,000 signatures. The result, however, proved a political dead-end when the signatures were delivered to Hennadiy Udovenko, president of the UN General Assembly, who pledged his support in vague terms. Its overly simplistic request—surely some countries need to reduce their military budgets more than others—and its vagueness about holding the UN in some way accountable for accepting their petition probably rendered their considerable efforts at the grass roots level ineffective.

Although it could of course be argued that such grass roots contact has its own value in consciousness raising among those participating in the petition, it could equally well be argued that the isolated efforts of NGOs serve only to relieve guilt without really affecting the status quo. Little coverage of the petition effort was given in the mainstream press, which may indicate a lack of attention to coordination efforts with the media. Moreover, in that the petition's overly simple request did not associate with other issues and problems in the human rights/social justice areas, it failed to heed the wisdom of the High Commissioner and most of the major human rights conventions over the past decade, which has stressed the interdependence of democratic conditions, economic development, and cultural issues. To be more effective, NGOs need to be better informed about the causal connections between undemocratic agendas and human rights violations.

Human rights NGOs on the other end of the financial spectrum, with prestige and institutional influence, can also prove ineffectual. Here, the problem may not only be misdirected efforts but also lack of motivation within the foreign policy establishment for substantive change. One example is the recent 257-page report *Preventing Deadly Conflict* (Carnegie Commission, 1998). While the subject was timely—more than four million people, 90 percent of them civilians, have died in conflicts worldwide since 1989—the three-year, $9.5 million study, like the Women's Tribunal Centre petition, received little press attention and perhaps even less commitment from dominant First World states. This did not surprise John Mark, founder of the NGO Search for Common Ground, which has been trying to reduce global strife since 1982. He generally supports most of the Carnegie book's conclusions, but finds it "a bit elementary" because conflict prevention has not yet become "our conventional wisdom." Citing Washington as an example of a government that seems unmotivated to discuss the multilateral approach to conflict resolution recommended by the study, Marks notes the inconsistent thinking among its foreign policy officials. They recognize the conventional wisdom that an ounce of prevention is better than a pound of cure, but "[i]t's hard to get their attention until the crisis occurs" (qtd. in J. Miller, 1998, p. 39).

Many established U.S. analysts were critical of the Carnegie study. Barry Karl of the Hauser Foundation found it "has no shape beyond the moral direction it wants the world to take." Leslie Lenkowsky, former director of the conservative Hudson Institute, dismissed the report as a "classic example of 'false philanthropy,' or aspiring to do what cannot be done instead of spending the [money] on small but doable things" (qtd. in J. Miller, 1998, p. 39). Judith Miller, journalist for *The New York Times*, laments such observations from the report as "decent living standards are a universal human right," seemingly unaware that these and other statements have been generally accepted as international human rights goals—second-generation rights—for some time (1998, p. 39). Such dismissive cynicism accompanying the report's release underlines the difficulties such efforts face. The multilateral approach of *Preventing Deadly Conflict* goes against the prevailing unilateral mood in Washington, which looks askance at international cooperative efforts such as mobile peacekeeping forces and improved mechanisms for human rights enforcement.

NGOs with Obligations Back Home

Other human rights organizations, though not governmental in the strict sense, still labor under a complicated polity with extenuating obligations to their home countries or distant seats of power. These NGOs often alter and even reverse their approaches from year to year. One instance is the Special Synod of Roman Catholic Bishops from North and South America. Convened in 1997 by Pope John Paul II to survey the moral, social, and economic challenges facing the Americas, from the effects of foreign debt to broken families, its month-long meeting, though broad in scope, focused on regional human rights standards. The *ad hoc* nature of the synod would seem to help its effectiveness. However, the meeting's final 76 proposals and final collective message fell short of expectations. Clearly, the bishops from North and South agreed on many significant issues and problems, such as the burden of foreign debt, globalized economies with their resulting social and economic dislocations, securing the rights of minority groups, and the "cry of the poor for justice" (qtd. in Bohlen, 1997, p. 26). Still, the bishops were not addressing many of the most controversial issues, and the synod's concluding message did not include any new departures.

Some onlookers attributed the lack of focus at the 1997 synod to the mixing of North and South American bishops, which may have diluted debate. Others concluded that the preparation time for the Americas Synod was much shorter than the more productive and focused 1994 African Synod, which was in preparation four years. However, the political motivation of the First World bishops may have clashed with that of the Third World bishops. At this time, North American bishops may be unwilling to prescribe remedies that take account of the social and economic causes of human rights violations, since such approaches remain out of favor with Washington. Moreover, the results of the finding heavily depend for their effectiveness on the direction of the papal document that will follow one year later, a statement that is presumed to be based on the proposals of the American bishops. The hierarchical nature of this type of NGO heavily determines the effectiveness of its proposals, a polity that can work for or against the cause of human rights. Given the conservative nature of the current Roman Catholic pontificate, the extent to which new pathways for social justice and structural reform can be undertaken with constancy and force remains doubtful. Moreover, certain bishops and advocacy movements within the Church of Rome—such as liberation theology and its community-based activism for human rights throughout Latin America—will face opposition from the political elites within their individual countries.

At the same time, the various Protestant churches in Latin America demonstrate an even wider diversity of political and social interest. Mainline liberal and progressive churches, such as the United Church of Christ, The Episcopal Church USA, and their advocacy organization, The World Council of Churches have even pursued policies that oppose official U.S. foreign policy, as many mainline churches did by supporting the Sandinista government in Nicaragua during the 1980s. On the other hand, this often effective method of gaining the empathy of the U.S. public for causes that are unfashionable with the mainstream media is counterbalanced to an extent by the often extremely regressive social and political posture of U.S. fundamentalist and evangelical Protestant denominations in Latin America and elsewhere. Despite such lack of unity, the general effect of the great number of North and South American NGOs active in the Americas is progressive and especially capable of uncovering human rights abuses and unjust social systems.

The Essential Ingredient: Advocacy Networks

As borders between states become more and more porous, with networks of human rights NGOs operating across national demarcations, a new political orientation has challenged state sovereignty arguments. NGOs have engaged in the new international sphere in a way formerly assumed to be only the prerogative of national governments. As such, they are at once political insiders—working within the borders of state governments, and outsiders—working outside state borders. NGO insiders rely on international allies—particularly in the First World—for their political voices, access to the media, and entree to the important IGO platforms. NGO outsiders are noncitizens who form a vital link between local NGO activists on the front lines and the powerful and influential IGOs and dominant states. For example, human rights NGO insiders and outsiders in El Salvador and Guatemala during the 1970s and 1980s eventually drew sufficient international pressure on both governments to lessen or eliminate the widespread repressive practices of those countries. The insider NGOs in these countries furnished outsider NGOs with the "symbolic imagery" needed to enlist international public opinion (Burgerman, 1998).

The shift in normative standards from "home rule" authority to a more influential international public sphere can only help human rights causes. The improved responsiveness and influence of international human rights organizations, however, depend upon the ability of First World and Third World NGOs to work cooperatively and consistently over the long-term. Their cross-border connectivity has proven the key to overcoming the formidable power of national governments, who have often established their own connections with other national governments, such as Guatemala has done with the U.S. As S. D. Burgerman (1998) notes, "the category of rights itself has been internationalized by the establishment of a global regime in discourse that delegitimized the efforts of governments to justify violations by claiming their actions to be an 'internal affair'" (p. 923). While particular governments usually still claim sovereign rights in rebuttal to international human rights criticism, such discourse has lost a great deal of legitimacy among IGOs, other governments, and general world opinion.

QUESTIONS FOR FURTHER THOUGHT

1. How can human rights advocacy networks continue to improve their connectivity and strengthen lines of communication between "inside" and "outside" NGOs? How could the new office of UN High Commissioner for Human Rights strengthen and regularize such networks?
2. What are the present obstacles to inter-NGO cooperation? How could the various religious-based NGOs work more closely together?
3. The new office of UN High Commissioner for Human Rights has focused on the link between second-generation and first-generation rights. How can this new emphasis improve the discourse of human rights at the grassroots level?
4. The office of High Commissioner has also recommended results-oriented language for human rights NGOs. How could this improve the documentation and advocacy of human rights at global and regional IGO assembles?
5. Will the new tendency to disregard the absolute sovereignty of state governments in matters of human rights help or hinder the implementation of human rights standards? What will be the effects on human rights enforcement of this new assertiveness?

5

THE MEDIA AND HUMAN RIGHTS: KNOWLEDGE AND POWER IN THE GLOBAL VILLAGE

The essential connection between an independent media and the promotion and sustainment of human rights has always been a primary concern of postcolonial thought. Hans-Dieter Klee (1993) responds succinctly,

> The media can play a key role in this aspect of the reform process. Who will observe and control the power of the state if an independent legal system does not yet exist or is still fighting for its independence? Only the media can fulfill this watchdog function. Who else can inform the public about human rights abuses, corruption, political scandals and the abuse of power? (p. 181)

Until quite recently, Third World civic discourse has been threatened by dictatorial governments of political elites who have controlled media access. What African and other nations of the south face in the coming century is the possibility of transnational corporate dominance of the airwaves and print media. Local political elites may be gradually assisted, and perhaps dependent upon, large TNCs with intercontinental control of information (Herman, 1988, 1998). This chapter will examine both the dangers and the contributions of the media in international human rights discourse, and offer an outlook with recommendations for positive change.

THE AFRICAN CONCERN

Fearing the further marginalization of Africa within the emerging "global village" of technological development, when its societies face increasing dependence on international information networks, representatives from several African nations met at the Intergovernmental Council of Communication (ICC) at Khartoum in October 1992. The final report made specific recommendations that comprised a declaration for the self-determination of Third World media. Interested in strengthening their technological capability and the control of information on the regional and continental levels, African representatives called for their own information network and the creation of a communications strategy. Initially, they pledged to construct an African satellite project and to found an institute that would encourage the open exchange of information and experience between African countries.

Africa sought to break free from the increasing effects of media globalization before the ICC conference in Khartoum. Earlier attempts established the Panafrican News Agency (PANA) and the radio and television union (URTNA), efforts that aimed to reverse the continued technological marginalization of the continent. However, as the 1990s went on, the privatization of the public sphere increased worldwide in the wake of the fall of Communism. This movement affected all continents North and South, resulting in a discourse of "deregulation," a project proclaimed as a virtue in the face of the victory of transnational capitalism. According to deregulation theory, the marketplace would replace the pernicious effects of government controlled electronic and print media. With the airwaves no longer "public" but open to the dynamic of the free-market, censorship and tendentious governmental regulation would end. In its place the forces of consumer demand would determine programming and editorial policy, enabled by a fair system of private competition between news services and entertainment networks. The rhetoric of deregulation in communication systems was attractive in its simplicity. However, the result, predictable to historians of the industrial age, was not the removal of censorship and dictatorial policy, but the replacement of one system (governmental control) that narrowed the spectrum of opinion represented on television, radio, and in print with another (free-market competition) that also limited the representation of opinion and the voices of civic discourse.

Deregulation did not lead to the free and open playing field of free-market utopianism, but instead opened the door to the eventual re-regulation of the media by giant corporate communication networks, each one attempting to devour all competition to form one or two large systems of ownership. The resulting information "spin" would parallel the tendentious versions of reality offered by government dictate in many Third World countries (Buell, 1994). Newscasters and journalists would receive their salaries and pensions from large TNCs rather than from governments. Information that did not support the transnational corporate enterprise would receive little or no air time and print space. The so-called "free market" would once again become a closed marketplace of ideas.

In Africa in the 1990s, TNC involvement in the public airwaves has not advanced as far as it has in North America and Europe. However, to counter the anticipated "cultural imperialism by invitation," African states have sought careful planning and support for their media from among their own governments and donor countries of good will (qtd. in Klee, 1993, p. 180). At one African symposium, Paul Ansah (1992) expressed the urgency of local media control:

> We should try to get our people solidly moored in their own culture as a countervailing force to any undesirable external cultural influences. In the past, it was possible to isolate people from such foreign influences, undesirable though that action might have been, but with the current developments in information technology, such isolation is no longer possible and we have to draw the necessary conclusions and take appropriate, concrete and positive actions instead of remaining passive and limiting our reaction to denouncing the cultural imperialists who come to us at our own invitation, more or less.

Behind this plea is the recognition that the huge forces of globalization threaten to turn the prospect of a Global Village into a single Global Restriction Zone wherein even feverish corporate competition is eventually subsumed by knowledge systems representing one powerful interest.

Africa's private electronic and print media have often furthered the promotion of democratization in several postcolonial countries. However, the trend towards dependence on large domestic or foreign economic interests has begun (Klee, 1993). Within this context, the viability of national radio and television for democratization in Africa is problematic. In African nations, with borders in many cases arbitrarily established and with high illiteracy rates, educational programming about democratic practices has been crucial for reform. Generally, civic discourse in the Global South has given greater emphasis to monitoring and reforming social institutions than civic discourse in the Global North. For example, southern NGOs have placed greater emphasis on involvement in national judicial processes, have been more active in devising national legislation, more likely to promote national implementation of human rights standards, and more active in monitoring elections than are First World NGOs (Smith, Pagnucco, & Lopex, 1998). This greater-felt need to construct and maintain democratic systems is evident in the responses of Third World NGOs to reform of the UN human rights bureaucratic structure. For example, NGOs from the South had greater involvement in the campaign to establish the High Commissioner for Human Rights (established during the 1993 Second World Conference on Human Rights in Vienna) than northern GNOs (High Commissioner, G.A. Res. 48/141). One of the NGO recommendations to the new High Commissioner was to focus its office's activities on "media campaigning on [human rights] violations" (Smith, Pagnucco, & Lopex, 1998, p. 399). Thus, southern human rights advocates find the media at least as essential to progressive human rights development as do northern advocates. The perilous existence of national media that respond positively to social justice issues has made the High Commissioner's new agenda all the more vital.

African advocates of human rights are keenly aware that democratic behavior patterns and ideas must be taught if democratic processes are to remain uncorrupted. However, they also know that African democracy begins at home and cannot be imposed from outside the continent, even by well-meaning Northern advocates and certainly not by TNCs with self-serving commercial agendas. Klee (1993) finds that African democracy must come through "decentralization":

> Who tells the citizens in rural regions how one practices democracy at [the] local level, or how one should combine African consensual practices with modern patterns of political behavior? Perhaps an army of instructors and technocrats from the capital cities? Do they know what democracy mean—not as it is described in school textbooks, but as it should be lived in practice? This task must be executed by radio (in the first place) and by the press, in dialogue with the people. (p. 182)

Klee's understanding that the unique capacity of the media to discover means through which traditional African "consensual practices" can be combined with "modern patterns of political behavior" presses him to require an open and free "public broadcasting corporation" that receives government funding but remains free from government control. He mistrusts national news agencies that become instruments of censorship and monopolize domestic and international news. The African news and commentary agencies must realize they have "a service function" for the development of democracy. Klee's combination of private and public news services would also be decentralized, to reach the grassroots level and respond to their particular needs.

While Klee's program of media involvement in democracy building and community development may be tailored to the particular requirements of postcolonial societies, it is not invulnerable to the huge global forces that have affected poor nations during the past 30 years. What is to prevent, for instance, his independent broadcasting system from going the way of the PBS stations in the United States, which are now financed mostly by business corporations and reflect that bias in their selection and treatment of the news and in the narrow spectrum of opinion commonly presented? Moreover, Klee's assumption that donor countries, whom he calls upon to support more fully the national news services in Africa, will not attempt to apply their own agendas to the broadcasting of information seems overly optimistic. The connection between powerful First World states and their often predatory TNCs cannot be forgotten.

THE THIRD WORLD FIGHTS BACK

During the 1970s, debate began in the United Nations over the dominance of U.S. television programming around the world. Many critics termed U.S. programming "cultural imperialism" and demanded its restriction. In response, U.S. advocates offered the view that free market capitalism in the media constituted a "free and open" exchange, which should not be discouraged (Davis, 1997, p. 9). When the debate continued in many UN forums, especially UNESCO, the result was the McBride Report (1980), which demanded a New World Information Order, an action that led to the eventual withdrawal of the U.S. from UNESCO (Stevenson, 1988). The prolonged struggle over the global airwaves received scant attention in the mainstream U.S. media, but became a rallying cry for many national groups throughout the Global South.

First World dominance of Third World programming continued throughout the 1980s and into the 1990s. However, the situation was not as one-sided as it at first appeared. In some parts of Latin America, the U.S. contributed upwards of three-quarters of the imported material (Varis, 1984). However, beginning in the mid-1980s in the Middle East and Latin American, there was an increase in regional programming. Often, the regional replacements for U.S. dominance were also transnational corporations, such as TV Globo (from Brazil) and Televisa (from Mexico). Third World political and economic elites will continue to pose the most immediate threat to an open media. Under such circumstances, the question of whether First World corporate media will control Third World notions of social verity, and by so doing inhibit human rights and social justice discourse, becomes less relevant. In the decades ahead, as powerful regional media corporations compete with First World TNCs throughout the Global South, human rights questions become less transcultural and more class-based: Who controls the media and for what purpose? How does it want its "consumers" to think and behave?

CHINA'S CONCERN

In China in the 1990s, most issues of human rights and the media have not reached the point of controversy. For Chinese critics of the media, many of whom are young and educated in the West, the sudden incursion of Western, (particularly U.S.) entertainment industries into China's developing broadcasting system has raised issued of cultural identity and the loss of social values. For most Chinese critics, these human rights concerns are more general and long-term, threatening Chinese culture chiefly through the suddenness with which they arrived.

Before 1980, Chinese people had little or no exposure to Western media. After the government adopted a new open-door policy in 1979, China increased its Western importations, particularly in such culturally significant areas as fast-food restaurants, clothing, film, children's toys and games, and television programming. Whereas in 1970 China had six programs from abroad, by 1990 the number of Western programs had increased to 202 (Wang & Chang, 1996). Chen and Amienyi (1997) observe, "The most observable reflection of this penchant for Western lifestyles among Chinese can be found in their preference for Western fast foods, their celebration of Western holidays, the practice of giving names with western flavor to new-born children, and the negative attitudinal changes toward Chinese life" (p. 5).

While such new habits may seem relatively superficial, China's altered cultural superstructure has begun to change the personal values of its young. On the sudden popularity of McDonald's hamburger restaurants in urban China, one observer remarked that parents often felt that if their children can eat at McDonald's, they can go out in the world and succeed. The association of Western, particularly U.S., lifestyles with success in the new globalized world, available to Chinese people only within recent years, has left ambivalence and uncertainty. Many Chinese lament the loss of family life that fast-food eating has brought about: "Eating was a social activity that was enjoyed with friends and family and involved talking, arguing, and the sharing of a common experience.... Now, food consumption has become a solitary activity as individuals purchase fast food, consume it as fast as they can, and go on their way" (Chen & Amienyi, 1997, p. 7). The new lifestyles, advertised widely throughout the new imported media, ignore traditional Chinese conceptions of family life, consensual relationships, and self-identity. Western news coverage has also troubled and angered many Chinese. NBC coverage of the 1996 Summer Olympics in Atlanta, broadcast throughout China, was widely criticized for its negative treatment of Chinese athletes, teams, and training methods.

Criticism of the global dominance of U.S. television programming has not been solely a Chinese concern. In June 1983, European television executives met in Italy to discuss the global success of U.S. television. Erik Barnouw remarked that it is "a homogenized product that represents no one culture. It is formula fiction that endlessly recycles a mythology of its own, a mythology that can be understood anywhere but is really of nowhere" (qtd. in Werber, 1983). For its part, the Chinese government has set programming policies to control the globalized media. It plans to double its domestic program production during the 1990s (Ai, 1991). China will also attempt to sell its media products abroad and position satellites for television broadcast to other countries.

The worldwide concern with the dominance of Western values in the global media led to the first UN World Television Forum in November 1996. It agreed that television should play a major role in promoting unbiased information, in preserving cultural diversity, and in promoting international understanding. Television should also present a multiplicity of cultures and viewpoints. At this formative stage of worldwide telecommunication systems and programming, Chinese human rights advocates have stressed the need in China to present a variety of cultural viewpoints and class orientations. The government should actively pursue program exchange and cooperation so that a balanced flow of information becomes available (Chen & Amienyi, 1997).

Another option that has become apparent to the Chinese is the cooperation with Western TNCs to produce indigenous programs. There is already, for example, a Chinese version of Sesame Street. The option for cultural hybridity has already been apparent in a different guise, since television programming from Hong Kong and Taiwan reflects Western values within an Asian context and has been distributed in China for some time. However, such attempts to assure the cultural integrity of China in the next century does not also guarantee the promotion of human rights standards and democratic concerns. Chen and Amienyi (1997) recommend the formulation of consistent policies to give China's domestic media producers and journalists autonomy. They see journalistic independence and other free press issues primarily as goals for cultural self-determination rather than as a protection and monitor of human rights issues in general:

> More importantly, Chinese media should make potential use of their infrastructure to educate and enlighten people to love Chinese history, culture and tradition. Building immunity against foreign influence will be the most effective way to deflect cultural invasion, and maintain Chinese cultural identity. It should be seen as a minimum duty for a nation to preserve its culture from the loss of its heritage, soul, and identity. (p. 15)

Autonomy for the media will only serve the cause of human rights promotion in China and other emerging economic powers if there is a consistent and long-term commitment at the grassroots and national levels for social justice issues. International non-governmental organizations outside these countries must also support and cooperate with the domestic media networks, autonomous agencies, and internal NGOs. Media watch dog organizations, such as the U.S.-based associations, Accuracy in Media, The Advocacy Institute, Alternative Press Center, American Civil Liberties Union, The Anti-Censorship and Deception Union, Asian American Journalists Association, and Project Censored, can function as external monitoring and supporting organizations for the internal independent media organizations, which may be under pressure to conform to governmental or corporate agendas. Project Censored, a 20-year-old organization of U.S. university students who monitor the U.S. news and bring into the public sphere news events censored or downplayed by the corporate media, may be an effective model for similar organizations in China, the African states, and other struggling democracies. Finally, IGOs must demand greater media accountability from their member states. The UN, for example, must press China not only for such civil rights as free expression but also for an open news and entertainment media. Such international efforts, however, must remain sensitive to a nation's cultural identity(ies).

THE FIRST WORLD MEDIA AND HUMAN RIGHTS

In the First World, media ownership has fallen into fewer and fewer hands. With the passage of the 1996 Telecommunications Act in the U.S., heavily supported by such media lobbying organizations as the United States Telephone Association and the National Cable Television Association, corporate control of the U.S. mainstream media was reconfirmed. The National Association of Broadcasters (NAB), a powerful Washington political action committee (PAC), was credited with helping broadcasters gain extra TV channels and pushing for few restrictions on ownership of radio and TV stations. It also lobbied successfully to stop regulation of liquor ads and argues that free air time for political candidates is unconstitutional. The NAB also coordinates its member stations to influence Congress (Jaquet, 1998). Moreover, Washington regulators often receive lucrative jobs in the corporate media lobbying sector. Dick Wiley, for example, left as Chair of the Federal Communications Commission in 1977 to build the largest communications law firm, Wiley, Rein, & Fielding, which has giant media clients such as CBS and Gannett. Such closeness is commonly acceptable, as evident in Wiley's own blasé attitude toward his move; he found it "perfectly acceptable" to work for the firms he once regulated (qtd. in Jaquet, 1998, p. 27).

Adding to the crisis of media openness is the vertical integration of media conglomerates forming even larger economic entities within the U.S. "These companies now create films and television programs, and distribute them through partially or fully owned theatre chains, broadcast television networks, stations and cable networks. These works are then directly disseminated through video distribution companies, in both the domestic and foreign markets" (Masur, 1998, p. 30). Films can become books, television shows, games, toys, hit songs, even a ride. Such integration results in less diversity. Such cross-marketing leads to fewer works that have only the most general appeal. Space for human rights and democratic concerns has been greatly reduced by such corporate uniformity. The move toward "deregulation" in Europe and North America may result in the next century not in greater competition and the airing of alternative views, but in even greater uniformity and control. Such tendencies have been evident for decades in the U.S.

The U.S. public in the main is not aware of such media control, as it relies upon the institutions that are responsible for civic information. According to a recent survey, the vast majority of U.S. respondents did not know that the airwaves were publicly owned and that media corporations paid nothing for their use (M.C. Miller, 1998). Several U.S.-based NGOs have attempted to inform the public of the true nature of media control. For example, the Media Education Foundation produces videos and print literature that attempt to inform the public about threats to freedom of speech and information, but their efforts are hindered by the daunting scale and outreach of the information producers they seek to expose. When one viewpoint—extremely narrow in terms of democratic measurements—dominates public consciousness and determines social verities, then general grassroots movements, although never impossible, become more difficult to sustain.

Much of the responsibility for the exposure of human rights violations in the globalized public sphere rests, not surprisingly, with NGOs and independent journalists, who often function as worldwide watchdogs and whistle blowers. Quite often, however, their work is not easily brought to public notice, and then often only after a dramatic incident involving an international personage. For instance, by 1995, Human Rights Watch—Africa had gathered hundreds of reports of the rape, torture, and murder of civilians by Nigerian Army forces. Entire villages were burned to the ground. Yet few observers outside Nigeria noticed the mounting human rights and ecological crisis there until the noted activist and playwright Ken Saro-Wiwa, along with eight others belonging to Nigeria's Movement of the Survival of the Ogoni People (MOSOP), were murdered on false charges in 1996. The murders motivated a wide coalition of environmental, human rights, and labor groups such as Greenpeace, the Sierra Club, and Human Rights Watch, which demanded a boycott of the Royal Dutch/Shell Group, a TNC widely regarded as supporting the oppression.

Of the Sara-Wiwa incident, Stephen Mills, campaign director for the Sierra Club, remarked, "I've never seen this level of outrage on an international issue. People now see the insidious relationship between Shell and a murderous regime, and the extreme measures a multinational corporation will use to protect the bottom line" (qtd. in Bielski, 1997, p. 352). TNCs, however, rely on public relations (PR) to sell their corporate agendas, using media methods so seamless that local protest movements like MOSOP find it difficult to penetrate mainstream broadcasting systems. Moreover, the relationship between corporate PR firms and the mainstream media has become closer as a result of the increasing homogenization of the international news and public opinion industries.

Many PR pros think that the media, both national and local, are easier to handle than the public...the media itself is a huge, profitable business, the domain of fewer and fewer giant transnational corporations. Not surprisingly, these transnationals often find that their corporate agenda and interests are compatible with, or even identical to, the goals of the PR industry's biggest clients. While this environment may be demoralizing to responsible journalists, it offers a veritable hog heaven to the public relations industry. (Stauber & Rampton, 1997, p. 363)

According to a senior vice-president with Gray and Company PR, "[m]ost of what you see on TV is, in effect, a canned PR product. Most of what you read in the paper and see on television is not news" (qtd. in Stauber & Rampton, 1997, p. 363). With vast amounts of financial resources, the PR industry hire private detectives, lawyers, and spies in mass, generate letters, send out faxes, affect editorial opinion and reportage, launch phony "grassroots" movements, and use high-tech methods, such as satellite feeds and Internet sites. With billions of dollars, the PR pros can usually win any battle for public attention from the local to the international levels.

Corporate Ideology in the Public Sphere

Fewer and fewer corporations own the mainstream print media and airwaves in the First World. Corporations have telecom channels with common carriers globally privatized. Besides news programs and "magazine" exposes, media advertising, funding almost 100 percent of U.S. television, are loaded with ideology, selling "free market" capitalism and consumerism along with products. As a result, the hope of creating a truly public sphere is neutralized by corporate money. Also, it has become more difficult to contest the contemporary media system because of its seamless ubiquity. Corporate public relations and commercial underwriting almost completely blend into media's exposition of reality (Herman, 1998). With the advent of computer hardware and software systems, the Bill Gates-style communications revolution will offer a "friction-free capitalism." As a result, ideology and communication are now pressed into the same space. Bill Gates's political orientation—that government action distorts reality and hinders social effectivity, while corporations present the "bottom line" truth—is increasingly assumed without comment by mainstream journalism. "Ideology and communication are now pressed into the same space" as the corporate media and corporate advertisers increasingly work together (Foster, 1998).

Corporate domination of the media commonly leads to a truncated journalism that bypasses the investigative reporting necessary to uncover human rights abuses in the world's "trouble spots." Robert Fisk, a courageous investigative reporter of international events, recipient of the British International Journalist of the Year award seven times, feels that the First World media, especially U.S. mainstream media journalists, lack the commitment to human rights concerns:

> The conformity of American journalism is going to be one of the nails in its coffin. All American journalists write in the same style, and there is a kind of sickness among a lot of Western correspondents in that they have this dreadful reliance on their own governments, their own embassies...an American journalist arrives in town and they go to the U.S. embassy, the French embassy, the British embassy. They get their accreditation from the ministry of information and maybe ask for a couple of interviews. (qtd. in Rothschild, 1998, p. 39)

Believing that U.S. journalists in particular tend to uncritically accept U.S. foreign policy, he finds a general reluctance to go out into the field to do the kind of research necessary for human rights vigilance.

The steady consolidation of broadcast and print commentary that favors First World dominant groups sends a message supportive of their assumptions of power. According to K. Sue Jewell (1993), social policy in the media—always an unspoken ideology—is grounded on the definition and characterization of the character, values, lifestyles, and behaviors of the intended beneficiaries of that social policy. In the other direction, "[n]egative imagery purveyed by the mass media can adversely affect the formulation of social policies that can enhance the quality of life for certain segments of the population" (p. 16). The groups within society whose interests the corporate media most favor are directly determined by self-serving economic interests: "on balance, the mass media have historically demonstrated a propensity for purveying the materially privileged more favorably, while those with access to, and in possession of, meager resources experience relative devaluation based on images projected by the mass media" (pp. 18–19). The power of the media to affect both cultural and economic well-being can work either for or against human rights.

The decision of the U.S. Federal Communications Commission (FCC) in 1987 to annul the 1949 "Fairness Doctrine" in the media was the result of a decade-long U.S. trend that merged the ideology of privatization with freedom of expression, the latter right given the peculiar interpretation of the right of corporations and other money interests to project upon the public airwaves their own opinions while minimizing other viewpoints (Harvey, 1998). Feeling the erosion of the public interest in the media, the U.S. Supreme Court in a 1973 judgment offered a "posture of flexibility" that was intended to balance private and public interests, democratic and profit-oriented values: "Congress, and the [FCC] as its agent, must remain in a posture of flexibility to chart a workable 'middle course' in its quest to preserve a balance between essential public accountability and desirable private control of the media" (Ramberg, 1986, p. 21). This balance between private control and public accountability in the media remains a chief concern of political policy in the new century.

Jurgen Habermas lamented that public communication and the exchange of ideas in the First World was being replaced by the exchange of commodities. The suspension of the Fairness Doctrine gave legal sanction to what had in effect resulted from the overemphasis on commercially supported programming over not-for-profit programming. "The Fairness doctrine provided some limited ability for the poor side in a referendum to answer the organized interests on such issues as smoking bans or nuclear power safety; that lever is no longer available....Those who have the wealth to own stations or buy time on them will dominate television's contributions to issue discussion" (qtd. in Entman, 1989, p. 123).

Crucial to the promotion of human rights in developing countries, who remain far more dependent upon the media for the education and promotion of democratic values and practices, is the commitment to democratic standards and issues of social justice. The danger that predatory commercial broadcast systems will overwhelm the financially limited national media of poorer countries remains great. Although the Third World has not yet experienced the privatization and deregulation of the media that is apparent in Europe and North America, there is no reason to assume that these developments will not become global in future decades. Some Third World media scholars feel that, although the threat from transnational media capital has not yet arisen in the poorer countries, its day will come (Pratt, 1998). International human rights must offer a system where control of the media is dominated neither by private commercializing interests nor by state tyrannies. As the contemporary examples of Nigeria, Haiti, and scores of other Third World countries reveal, state tyrannies and transnational capital often work together, indeed may often depend upon one another. This is a significant difference between First World and Third World political systems. The latter do not generally possess an oppositional system between private and public, but generally have state systems that control business planning and practices. This system may easily be corrupted by the economic wealth of Global Capital, or it may gradually develop a democratically oriented media based on a truly independent broadcasting authority that regulates programming to those ends.

QUESTIONS FOR FURTHER THOUGHT

1. What measures can be taken to assure a truly independent Third World media, given the power, reach, and technological advancement of the TNC media?
2. In what ways can IGOs like the United Nations help to assure self-determination for the media of poorer nations? How might they work effectively to that end with Third World organizations like the ICC?
3. How can the media retain its independence and still rely upon external funding?
4. Is it possible for countries such as China to collaborate with First World media TNCs and still retain their own cultural integrity?
5. Is it possible to retain a balance of for-profit media and government regulated systems? Why are some countries (such as Britain) more successful at not-for-profit television than others (such as the United States)?

6

WHEN CELEBRITY DOES HUMAN RIGHTS

A BRIEF HISTORY

Since the 18th century, when modern celebrity developed, individuals have used the public good as a means to enhance and sustain their status as public figures. One of the earliest figures to recognize the value of altruism in the advancement of individual fame was David Garrick, who attached his name and reputation to another English actor and playwright, one who had only a few generations before achieved the status of cultural icon, William Shakespeare. Always in the name of the public good (the word *public* had become an 18th-century coinage), Garrick sustained Shakespeare's and his own reputations by associating them with national pride. Shakespeare was Britain's cultural gift to the world, and now Garrick was giving Britain its reincarnated genius by embodying his "correct interpretation" on the stage. Unlike all previous actors of Shakespeare, who abused and exploited the Bard's truth, Garrick sold himself to the public as the faithful embodiment of that genius (see, for example, Davies, 1808). His stage productions proclaimed a "new acting style" of simplicity and truth, a proposition that was largely accepted by the British public. Going further, Garrick devised the first Shakespeare festival, to be presented at the 200th anniversary of the Bard's birth at Stratford, England. Heavily criticized for its extravagance and poor planning, the first Stratford Shakespeare Festival was a grand publicity success for Garrick, making him the first super-celebrity (England, 1964). An actor, whose profession was heretofore viewed with suspicion, became associated with truth, simplicity, patriotism, and altruism. Garrick's public personality and lifestyle seemed to his contemporaries equally conscientious, as he was known to manage London's great Drury Lane Theatre with sagacity and discipline and to treat friends with modesty and civility. In fact, Garrick managed to avoid the risks of political alliance and religious controversy throughout his public career. He set a trend that continued as the effects of the industrial revolution throughout the 19th century quickly replaced aristocratic indifference to the public good with middle-class respectability and hard work. Personal effort and altruism became the chief ingredient for celebrity and respectability.

POST-MODERN RESPECTABILITY AND
THE PACKAGING OF HUMAN RIGHTS

In the final decade of the 20th century, celebrity status has developed into many forms, expressing various ethical and aesthetic values. Madonna, for example, achieved fame initially as "the material girl," one whose music videos were conscious and meticulous imitations of an earlier female cultural icon, Marilyn Monroe. Later, her reputation gained more respectability as she projected an image of the hard-working, demanding, and "serious" businesswoman, not unlike Garrick's reputation for theatre management. Other postmodern figures have gone beyond respectability to achieve reputations for benevolence; still fewer have achieved higher ethical reputations, largely by their willingness to "go the second mile," to reflect kindness when faced directly with human misery and injustice. If kindness, as a human quality uplifted by the sensibility of European Romanticism, became a replacement for indignation as a response to social injustice, then such recent celebrities as the late Mother Teresa, the late Lady Diana, Princess of Wales, and the international supermodel Iman, represent this tradition to their publics. Two of these women, Lady Diana and Mother Teresa, have achieved the status of near sainthood for their representations of kindness within the locus of social injustice and indifference. Both were repeatedly chosen as among the most identifiable as well as the most respectable personages in the world. Following Garrick two centuries before, they sought to alter or enhance their reputations through altruistic projects. A universalized good, beyond individual self-aggrandisement and the particularities of group identification, is now associated with their names. The remaining chapter will analyze their particular discourses of human rights as projected onto the stage of the world media, and evaluate the particular shortcomings of celebrity as it distorts, perhaps inevitably, the reality of human rights conditions. Finally, this chapter will compare the celebrity approach, the haves, with their counterparts on the other end of the current civic discourse spectrum, the have-nots, those largely anonymous—and usually invisible—filmmakers who produce unauthorized or illegal films and videotapes of human rights abuses around the world. Unhappily, although the have-nots (the poorly funded filmmakers) reveal far more details of such abuses and depict many more inidividual victims, often allowing them to tell their own stories through follow-up questions and interviews, they are presently able to capture only a small fraction of the audiences commanded by the big celebrity names.

Iman: Return to Africa

In the world of the supermodel, the name of Iman has special significance. First promoted as an exotic—over 6 feet tall, posed wearing what appeared to be African tribal dress within a typical (to Western eyes) African landscape of broad savanna—she eventually overcame negative publicity that charged her with ethnic inauthenticity and criticized the racist underpinnings of her white image-makers. Currently, Iman remains a top model, more than ever in worldwide demand. As a Somali, she has associated herself with the social, and perhaps with the political, struggles of that war-torn country. However, the U.S. media has severely restricted the representation of this altruism by concentrating almost entirely on the figure of Iman at the expense of the Somali famine and war victims.

Driving through the dust of African back-country roads, bumped back and forth by the heavy-duty Range Rover suspension system, Iman and a colleague, a white model, arrive at the village site. An extremely abbreviated sequence of camera long shots shows Iman touring the ravaged village, or refugee camp ("Iman in Somalia," 1998). The voiceover commentary does not bother to distinguish the setting. Instead, what is given is a brief summation of the significance of this tour for Iman's personal life and career. The model is shown led by an unidentified guide, shaking hands with emaciated victims of an unidentified action, and posing with a fellow model in front of unidentified huts, or perhaps temporary refugee shelters. Iman's own voiceover mentions that she herself is Somali, leaving the viewer to surmise the necessary connections between her tour and this particular human rights crisis. No interview of a victim or helper at this site is attempted. There is not even the rudiments of conversation, or exchange of greetings, heard between Iman and any of the victims. Moreover, no shot within the video sequence for Entertainment TV shows Somalis by themselves, or in fact anyone other than Iman and her traveling suite of reporters, friend, and guides.

There is no attempt in the Somalia videotape to:

1. Offer the necessary background exposition that would reveal the significance of the setting for human rights and social justice discourse;
2. Represent the victims themselves through interviewing, dialogue, or solo shots; and

3.   Discuss with Iman or an onsite authority the specificity of the tragedy as a
     human rights problem, its causes, outcome, and outlook.

Instead, the video for Entertainment TV was clearly intended to focus on the
glamorous supermodel's recent career decisions and lifestyle, a trajectory that
placed human rights and world events in a decidedly secondary, in fact insignificant position.

The use of the tragedy in Somalia was employed as romantic background for the
figure of Iman, whose image as an exotic is still promoted by the fashion industry.
Such exploitation depends upon colonialist perceptions of non-Western cultures.
At the beginning of the new millenium, colonialist systems have been replaced by
what academics have defined as "neo-colonialism" and "post-colonialism," terms
which may greatly misrepresent the widening economic and cultural gulf between
much of the First and Third worlds. Iman remains a "borderland" figure, that is, an
African, non-Westerner, who appears as a bridge between cultures, a hybrid
whose hybridity—her Westernization and Africanness—is both the source of her
appeal as a supermodel, a figure of glamor, and the glue that binds her as identifiable in European-based culture. As such, she becomes a comfortable representation of the "politics of difference," a non-Westerner for whom Westerners can feel
affinity and even attraction. However, as Arif Dirlik (1994) has pointed out,

> Borderlands may appear on the surface as locations of equal cultural exchange,
> but they are products of historical inequalities, and their historical legacy contin-
> ues to haunt them.... It is necessary to underline that [non-Westerners] do not all
> live in the same borderlands and that the affirmation of difference does not imply
> that all differences are equal. As long as drastic inequality persists, the cultural
> exchanges that take place across unequal positions, too, must bear upon them the
> mark of inequality. (pp. 97–98)

Can Iman's identity as a borderland figure represent her first culture accurately
and fairly when she is packaged by her industry as a non-threatening bridge
between vastly different cultural and economic spheres? Going further, can
Iman's "cultural exchanges" bear anything but the mark of inequality? In the
Entertainment TV promotional video, the model appears in stylish "safari" clothing, befitting a First World traveler to Third World primitivism. But her Banana
Republic/Eddie Bauer appeal betrays the altruistic pretensions of her promoters.
Such clothing manufacturers insist on using exploited Third World workers and
hiding the fact from their First World customers. In her attempt to "return to
Africa," Iman has allowed the international fashion industry to trespass upon and
distort the realities of Third World suffering and social violations.

As a borderland figure, Iman needs to become more aware of those forces
within Global Capitalism that foster inequality. Perceived in her professional life
as a figure—a woman and black—who has achieved a level of gender and racial

liberation, Iman nevertheless remains an articulator of the *status quo*, the contemporary situation of transnational capital. From this standpoint, her efforts to uncover human rights situations remains feckless and even misleading. A more ingenuous approach for broadcasting the crisis in her home country must involve her complete break with the promotion arm of the Western fashion industry, whose trajectory remains compromised by the narrow demands of profit, international "development," and business competition. Her altruism, in short, must be divorced from her celebrity, at least as it has been defined until now. This will involve much more individual effort, and difficulty—perhaps even risk to her career and interpersonal relationships—but her position as a borderland figure demands such initiative and independence, a project that would make her a more authentically liberated figure.

Diana: From the Palace to Human Rights

"They don't believe I should help AIDS victims. They think it is not the *right* type of charity for a princess of royal blood to support" (qtd. in Davies, 1997, p. 279). As the Princess of Wales, Diana gave up her life as an upper-class single woman to become wife to the heir apparent of Britain, only to find her personal independence threatened by "the palace." This intentionally vague term is used by both courtiers and journalists alike to signify the authority and demands of the late 20th century British monarchy. The generic character of "the palace" can be manipulated by its user—in print, on the electronic media, or in conversation—to refer narrowly to the person of the Queen, Elizabeth II, Diana's mother-in-law; more widely to the coterie of courtiers and advisors surrounding the Queen; more widely still to the Royal family, the Windsors, Charles, the husband and heir to the throne; and, widest, and vaguest of all, to the often nuanced set of traditions and ideals that determine behavior for British royals as role models to a nation (and perhaps to certain pockets of transnationals within and without the former British Empire). Diana's break with the palace was in stages, but undoubtedly her most significant efforts at personal liberation came about as she became more involved with, at first, unacceptable causes—such as AIDS, which to "the palace" seemed, at least initially, too much associated with homosexuality and perhaps sexual contact in general—then, international human rights.

Diana's move away from the palace was most defined when cameras followed her to international sites. Away from her husband Prince Charles, Diana seemed more comfortable and relaxed. Her particular charisma changed from straighforward glamor—for which she was considered worthy enough to appear on the cover of fashion magazines of the caliber of *Vogue*—to the more interpersonal appeal of hospice and hospital visitor to the sick, dying, and distressed. Her liberation finally progressed to the point of travel to onsite inspections of landmine zones and civil combat areas, often in remote and dangerous locations. Diana's bedside manner and presence at these former battle zones seemed to express through the camera an immediacy and concern for the victims that was compelling, decidedly different from the other British Royals, or in fact any other current international celebrity. Princess Anne, sister of Charles, had long been involved in Oxfam and other relief organizations in Africa and elsewhere, but Anne lacked camera appeal, seemed cold, and, perhaps most significantly, disliked the press and refused to become camera-ready, give interviews, or respond to the media in any positive way. Diana, photogenic, victim of an admittedly adulterous husband, and outcast from "the palace," seemed the most camera-ready for the mainstream media.

Diana's ambition to move beyond the traditional obligations of the British Royal family—chiefly, for a woman, to raise the heirs to the throne—was modest at first. She promoted the British fashion industry by wearing its designer clothing. After venturing into AIDS advocacy, which was mainly a domestic endeavor, Diana took another giant step from the palace through her involvement in international human rights. During the summer of 1996, she got the idea of advocating a global ban on landmines while watching television with her two sons, William and Harry. In January 1997, she contacted Elizabeth Dole, head of a major anti-landmine organization and wife to Robert Dole, Republican candidate for the U.S. presidency. She began pushing openly for the ban. This was a direct political action, one that raised comment from the more traditional wing of the British public. The greatest power in the world, the United States, Britain's chief ally, opposed the UN legislation banning mines under the pretext that such mines were needed to safeguard the border regions of North and South Korea. She traveled with Elizabeth Dole to Angola, site of the heaviest concentration of landmines and greatest number of landmine casualties in the world. In August 1997, Diana toured Bosnia advocating the ban. There she met a young Muslim woman crying for her dead child in a cemetery. The videotape of the encounter was seen worldwide. News cameras captured Diana demonstrating her greatest persuasive qualities. Her empathy for the young mother in a lonely place had an immediacy and reality that standard newscasts of such tragedies lacked. During this tour, she was very aware of the Ottawa Conference to abolish landmines scheduled for December of that year.

Diana's untimely death only helped her cause. Publicity and money poured into the special memorial funds established to sustained the landmine cause and her other projects. What made Diana's contribution to international human rights unique was her willingness to travel to on-site areas and her eagerness to be photographed in conversation with victims and site workers. Her engaging presence on film contrasts with Iman's isolation. Whereas Iman never seems to connect with the victims of human rights, Diana seems almost to need their response and individual stories. Her special brand of human rights advocacy depended upon a few unique qualities that distinguished her success. Princess Anne was not photogenic, shunned cameras, and, perhaps most significantly, openly disliked mainstream journalists. But Diana's ability to enlist media reportage for her causes was honed by years of negotiating positively with papparazzi, tabloid journalists, and well-known interviewers. Her most successful quality, however, was a unique affectivity in world crisis locales, an endowment which she seemed to offer spontaneously. Also helpful to her success was her position as Princess of Wales, albeit estranged wife of the British heir apparent. With this quasi-official identity, Diana possessed great communicative power with less political responsibility. This allowed her to express empathy, engage more freely and intimately with human rights victims. National office holders and political representatives commonly shy from such emotive encounters, mindful of their country's official foreign policy positions.

Soon after her death, Diana was memorialized as an honored internationalist who became more than a good-will ambassador. A sampling of titles for recent best-selling biographies indicates her status: *Diana, The People's Princess* (Davis, 1997), and *Diana, Princess of Wales: Empress of the World* (Chinmoy, 1997), *Diana, the People's Princess: The Story of Diana* (Whitelaw, 1998), and *Princess Diana: Her Life Story, 1961–1997* (Buskin, 1997). Diana's enormous success as an advocate nevertheless came with certain limitations inherent to her position. Her efforts to comfort victims of international injustices fell within the long tradition of European moral domination, a history fraught with hypocrisy, Eurocentrism, and straighforward political deception. As a semi-official representative of a former European imperialist power, Diana symbolized a colonizing nation that still holds economic and cultural dominance over Third World peoples. Her presence in Angola, no matter how sincere and charismatic, must be viewed within the local context of a war that was sustained largely through First World interference in Third World political development. Much of the misery of the Angolan war was caused by a white South Africa's trespass across internationally recognized borders. The landmines themselves were manufactured by Western arms merchants at a profit. From this perspective, Diana's presence must be viewed with ambivalence. To what extent is she the great white savior who gains personal satisfaction helping victims of First World power politics? European nations have offered to helped colonized peoples in the past as pretext to political and economic takeovers. In our "post-colonial" world, the "white man's burden" has a long history.

Although Diana's approach to human rights may be questioned, however ambivalent its ultimate effects, there is no denying that her sincerity and openness to the pain of others quite different from herself has transcended the image of a media celebrity. Her sensitivity before the cameras was based on a genuine conscientiousness: "I am a humanitarian. I always have been, and I always will be" (qtd. in Davies, 1997, p. 281). One biographer's summation of her advocacy work, "She had become a professional at bringing hope and compassion to people from all walks of life" (qtd. in Davies, 1997, p. 281), needs to be rephrased to encompass the reality of world politics. Not by any means a member of mainstream professional journalism, Diana did not so much bring hope to the victims of "hot spots" around the world as draw first-world attention, albeit with neo-colonialist associations, to the plight of those sufferers.

Mother Teresa in the Third World

Leading journalists on a tour of her Calcutta hospice, she stops to comment on an underweight baby in diapers alone in a crib, its body too weak to cry. "Look at her! She holds on to life." Her words carry a dramatic resonance throughout the open courtyard where the crib seems forgotten. Next, Mother Teresa begins ministering to the infant by cleaning the bars of the crib with a rag, as if she were herself a Hindu supplicant worshipping Krishna with offerings of food, perfume, and comfortings. The effect is compelling, and far more dramatic than anything coming out of Hollywood. Here, surely, is a real 20th century saint in the postmodern age. And yet, later, viewers perhaps wonder why there were not more medical attendants in view, why the infant appeared left alone in an open area, what was being given her to reverse her weight loss. The saint in Indian clothing creates a sacred space around the child, but seems to ignore her medical condition. What *was* the rag-cleaning all about? Was the rag disinfected?

Ambivalent thoughts accompanied the international career of Mother Teresa, a woman who proclaimed spirituality over politics, but visited political figures worldwide. Although her numerous hospitals across the globe have attracted large amounts of donation money, the facilities themselves seem spartan, lacking basic pain-killing drugs, antibiotics, and clean, disposable needles. Governmental regulations seem inoperative at her centers, and few have questioned their minimalist standards of health care (Fox, 1994). Nevertheless, the uncanonized saint remains among the most admired celebrities of the twentieth century, sought after by dictators and sincere human rights advocates alike. Michele Duvalier, wife of Haitian dictator "Baby Doc" Duvalier, sought her comforts and inspiration, just as much as Diana, Princess of Wales, who consciously modeled herself after Teresa's example. However, few of the educated who admire her would accept, or even consider, her professed political position, which falls under the category of ultra-right wing. Mother Teresa was strongly and uncompromisingly anti-abortionist, against birth control of any kind, considered sex other than for procreation a mortal sin, and seemed to support, and court, far right dictatorships around the world.

Once again, the ambiguity of the woman: advocate of "the poor," supporter of the status quo in class-based societies. Mother Teresa's advice for those thousands who mourned the loss of their loved ones at the Bhopal Union Carbide site catastrophy was "Forgive, forgive" (qtd. in Hitchens, 1995, p. 87). No mention was made of the gross violations of safety regulations at the plant, the priorities of international corporations, the disparity between the ethos of quarterly profits and the preferential option for the poor of Christ. Other charges made by respected sources against her worldwide Sisters of Charity organization abound: deceitful baptisms of the dying, the acceptance of donations from illicit sources, the refusal to offer even simple treatment procedures to the critically ill (Hitchens, 1995). Since mainstream media coverage has been almost entirely laudatory, investigative journalism seems not to apply to the Mother Teresa phenomenon, and the world public remains enthralled by the saintly image of the nun. But even the most cursory onsite investigations leave questions about the career of Mother Teresa as her movement approaches the 21st century.

Whatever the shortcomings of the relief and advocacy work of Mother Teresa, her movement has doubtless garnered the admiration of communities around the world. Whatever her medical accomplishments, she was brilliantly successful at creating an image of helping kindness among the most destitute communities, particularly in the Third World. She was photogenic in a uniquely dramatic, almost theatrical, way. Her photographic images remain not only among the most identifiable globally, but also among the most arresting. Unlike Iman's presence at Third World human rights locations, Mother Teresa seemed to be in direct physical contact with victims of disease, war, and starvation. In one famous news photograph, she holds the hand of an underweight sufferer at her Calcutta missionary. The composition is at first compelling. The patient, in bed but uncovered, looks directly up at her, while she looks not at him but outwardly and upward, her focus indistinct, as if contemplating the patient's suffering, meditating perhaps on the existential state of humankind under the providence of God. Such a tableau is reminiscent of Western art from the late Medieval through the Baroque periods: the saint looks not at the sufferer but away and up, contemplating the wondrous ways of God. More recently, memorial statuary of Abraham Lincoln freeing the slaves comes to mind. The slaves are below, crouched and huddled, looking up at the figure of Lincoln, who does not make direct eye contact, but rather looks beyond them, as if contemplating their freedom in the abstract. Teresa's left arm is held akimbo, a touch uniquely hers, as if questioning to a degree the ways of God, or perhaps the human condition, a subtle act of protest.

In a well-known video clip, Teresa leads right-wing British pundit Malcolm Muggeridge on an inspection of Calcutta's poor in 1969. Her arm is gesturing towards the long line of Indian poor, palm upwards, as if indicating their condition as well as physical location. Her expression is serious and contemplative, in contrast to Muggeridge's, which is set with the uneasy smile of an outsider. Clearly, she is in her element, neither the poor nor her British companion have focus. Besides photographs and films of Teresa with victims, perhaps the most frequent images of her are with world notables and government leaders, such as Ronald and Nancy Reagan; Margaret Thatcher; Charles Keating, convicted of savings-and-loan misconduct; and Hillary Clinton. In contrast to her demeanor among the poor, she smiles broadly in these photosgraphs, focusing directly on the leader or notable and often pointing her finger at them, as if in mild admonishment, perhaps for their worldly lifestyles. In one revealing photograph, however, she seems to have been caught off guard. She sits with Robert Maxwell in plush surroundings—possibly a hotel suite or home—and holds rosary beads while he converses on the phone. In contrast to other images of her, she appears tired, perhaps bored or anxious, and the focus is clearly on the more dynamic figure of Maxwell, publicity promoter and organizer. Mother Teresa seems unaware of the cameras and remains preoccupied rather than in profound spiritual contemplation. The commonality of the photograph is startling when compared with the usual images of her as a powerful spiritual leader among the poor.

Disturbing criticism from a number of respected sources continued to follow the human rights efforts of Mother Teresa and the Missionaries of Charity, who by the 1990s numbered over 45,000, lay and religious. Her phenomenal success over four decades had led some to attribute her simplicity and fundamentalism to a worldwide postmodern urge to uphold a vague spirituality in a world of radical relativist values and pervasive material cynicism. As Christopher Hitchens (1995) observes:

> The rich world likes and wishes to believe that someone somewhere, is doing something for the Third World. For this reason, it does not inquire too closely into the motives or practices of anyone who fulfills, however vicariously, this mandate. The great white hope meets the great black hole; the mission to the heathen blends with the comforting myth of Florence Nightingale. (pp. 50–51)

Whatever the extent of her misguided benevolence, certainly Mother Teresa's approach to human rights and social justice, like Diana's, was heavily dependent on the cult of personality, which functions as stand-in for more direct, and genuine, empathy towards human misery and injustice. Such personalism functions well in the First World, which remains confused by changing cultural values, institutional mendacity, and impersonal living conditions. Mother Teresa's approach demanded a primarily passive, quiescent response to human rights, where social abuses must be transcended in favor of the contemplation of divine will. This essentially Medieval outlook becomes a cult of nostalgia for First World postmoderns, who tend to idealize the past into whatever is felt as lacking in the present. Should human rights for the new century avoid the temptation to fall into a quietude of transhistorical contemplation, moving instead towards the world of the victim on the streets, rural villages, and urban slums, where justice is neglected for more immediate reasons than divine providence? This pathway involves a strong faith in the human community, a basic affirmation of unity amidst diversity, an eagerness to engage systemic evils to root out its causes, and, finally, a commitment to tolerance. Of religiosity's association with human rights, Walt Whitman's lines seem appropriate: "But not curious about God,/For I who am curious about each am not curious about God" (1891).

THE LIMITATIONS OF CELEBRITY

This chapter has attempted to demonstrate the current overreliance on the power of personality and fame to broadcast social abuse. Although such methods are often successful at bringing initial attention to regional and global conditions, they lack informative content and tend to focus upon the charismatic individual rather than more substantive analysis. The result is that quite often, perhaps most often, international problems come before the notice of First World publics with little examination of the causal connections between the human conditions of suffering and those social and political agencies affecting them. World coverage of Mother Teresa's trip to Bhobal, for example, centered on her saintly behavior, leaving the issues of multinational corporate responsibility unexamined, perhaps even unofficially exonerated by her widely reported remark, "Forgive, forgive."

The influence of Mother Teresa on First World ethical sensibilities has been profound, instanced by Diana Spencer's emulation of her. However, other, unpublicized approaches to international human rights issues usually show more understanding of advocacy for the poor. Theologically, other Western spiritual leaders have emphasized humility of outlook when approaching the poor, just as Mother Teresa has done. Their humility, however, is not directed towards a distant and all-powerful God of mysterious providence; rather they emphasize the humility of learning from the poor. In terms of international human rights, such approaches need to be affirmed by Western missionaries (also heads of benevolent and service organizations, officials of the UN and other international fact-finding organizations) who attempt to understand the basic causes of poverty, civil and human rights abuse *before* rushing to judgment or imposing First World standards on non-Western cultures. Henri Nouwen (1986), the Dutch Catholic theologian, expresses an engaging understanding of humility in international service: "The main problem of service is to be the way without being 'in the way'" (p. 108). Nouwen's understanding of "hospitality" assumes an equality of friendship between healer and healed, helper and sufferer, the affluent and the poor. If the outsider is unable to identify on an egalitarian level with the disenfranchised, no meaningful change will occur. Going further, the American Protestant theologian Cornel West (1993) discerns love and community as necessary ingredients for a transformation of the conditions that foster social and political injustice:

> The politics of conversion is based on a love ethic....It's a cultural renaissance that's needed for persons to believe that non-market values can and will make a difference. And you only do that by generating social momentum. And you generate social momentum by creating networks, later on mobilizing, possibly organizing and, if you're lucky, creating a social movement....What I would argue, for the prospects of democracy, is...creating conditions for the possibility of social momentum and social motion. (pp. 202–203)

West affirms for First and Third World peoples alike "conscientization," which concerns issues of identity for the victim: "persons no longer view themselves as objects of history, but rather as subjects of history, willing to put forward their own selves and bodies to reconstruct a new nation" (p. 134). This is lacking in the current advocacy of celebrity, which promotes the traditional subtext of a uniquely wonderful person (a Westerner) helping defenseless victims (nameless non-Westerners) whose cultural shortcomings have led to their victimhood. True healers, these theologians are saying, must enable others to find their own ways of social and political improvement. Diana, Iman, and Mother Teresa offer primarily a meliorative approach, giving succor to the incapacitated rather than hope for a better life through programs of education, consciousness-raising, and cultural affirmation. Through the cult of personality, they overlook the need for community building as a prime ingredient for social change.

The "have-nots" of international social advocacy today, those on the opposite end of the spectrum from the celebrities, are the journalists who produce "unauthorized" films and videos of abusive conditions around the world. These advocates remain unpaid or underpaid for their efforts, are forced to live in harsh, unhealthy conditions in underdeveloped and hostile areas, usually work without the blessing of corrupted local authorities, and place themselves at great risk by investigating illegal conditions. Such advocates lack audiences for their documentaries because few distributors will show their films. One such filmmaker, David Belle, produced an unauthorized video, *Zoned for Slavery* (1995). It investigates a Korean-managed U.S. corporate clothing factory in El Salvador. The workers, who are mostly poor Native American girls between 12 and 17 years old, are interviewed frequently, asked details of their working and living conditions, are also filmed at their homes with their family members, and are informed of the confidential nature of their interviews. The girls tell of being forced to take birth control pills, which are passed to them as "anti-malaria pills." If they become pregnant, they are given a cheap drug to induce abortion. Twelve-hour shifts are common, some are up to 23 hours. Such detail makes a vivid and accurate case against sweatshops in Latin America and Asia, but few of these filmmakers achieve recognition because few of their films are distributed, even in limited areas. Choosing between a detailed, informative analysis of human rights abuse and a celebrity-centered media event appears to be an easy one for the current First World media. Human rights discourse for the next century must move beyond the attractions of fame to a new appreciation of cross-cultural understanding.

QUESTIONS FOR FURTHER THOUGHT

1. Is there a way of combining detailed, informative documentary with the attention-getting methods of celebrity in human rights advocacy? If so, how would this work?
2. Are there other examples of well-known personalities (in either the first, second, or third worlds) who have managed to present human rights issues and problems in an informative manner? Who are they?

3. Discuss whether First World resources and financing can support indigenous movements that act for successful social change. Which countries or areas of the world can achieve this goal in the near future?
4. Do you agree with the textbook author that human rights advocacy needs to center primarily on this-world actions rather than on otherworldly or divine providence for social change? To what extent could religion play a role in this transformation?
5. By what means could "unauthorized" documentarians have their works more widely distributed in the United States and other countries?

7

THE IMAGE OF
HUMAN RIGHTS:
FILM AND STILL
PHOTOGRAPHY

The power of still photography and film to raise political consciousness was recognized by Martin Luther King (1964) in *Why We Can't Wait*, his book on the 1963 Burmingham, Alabama civil protest movement: "The brutality with which officials would have quelled the black individual became impotent when it could not be pursued with stealth and remain unobserved.... It was imprisoned in a luminous glare revealing the naked truth to the whole world" (p. 39). Current attempts to articulate an international human rights consciousness are clearest and most uncompromising in Third World film industries, in First World "independent" films, and in First World still photography collections. Before discussing films and photographic collections that offer more authentic images of human rights issues and problems, I will discuss mainstream films that have sacrificed clarity and authenticity for the certainties of wide distribution and profit.

HUMAN RIGHTS IN RECENT CINEMA

The film industries of First World nations have remained for the most part preoccupied with distribution of formula film genres, hoping to discover the occasional "blockbuster" production that will attract wide audiences and large profits. The U.S. film industry, today represented by large corporate productions and "independent" films, has avoided social commentary perhaps more than the film enterprises of most other countries. Films about the U.S. civil rights movement of the 1950s and 1960s are very few, and those that have been distributed and promoted have tended to take a distant perspective on the historical forces and groups involved. For instance, the large studio production *Mississippi Burning* (1988), discussed later in this chapter, manages to develop a plot wherein no actual civil rights protesters are featured. Sadly, even the so-called independents have tended to shy from the dramatization of human rights issues and movements; this is especially true of issues involving the Third World. Some of the rare exceptions have achieved a degree of promotion and subsequent popularity. One such film is Oliver Stone's *Salvador* (1985), which includes two actors with box-office appeal. True to form, however, while the film manages to represent the brutalities of the U.S.-sponsored Salvadoran government in the early 1980s, its vagueness and ambiguity dissipates the impact of the death squads and other human rights violations that Stone simulates with typical Hollywood explicitness. While the violence is rendered in the naturalistic fashion typical of Hollywood since the late 1960s—plenty of hi-tech blood explosions off costumes and automatic weapon fire from rented helicopters—the causes of such violence are glossed over, and the human dimension is left largely unexplored.

Salvador: An Outsider's Approach

Salvador stars Jim Belushi and James Woods, actors whose type combines raucous humor and sex appeal. Both qualities Stone employs as much as possible given the human wrights theme, as the plot quickly becomes one about the ruggedly independent American (Boyle, played by Woods), whose failed domestic life forces him on a desperate and unplanned search for a new "story" to photograph. With Belushi, side-kick and drinking buddy, they drive to "Salvador," where they quickly become involved in the crossfire between revolutionaries and government forces. At this point the viewer expects an exposition of the life of ordinary Salvadorans under the harsh military dictatorship. Instead, the film remains focused on Boyle's personal life—he is shown to have an abandoned Salvadoran lover—and never seeks to represent Salvadoran characters in their own right. Even Boyle's girlfriend Maria retains a secondary role, presented in brief scenes as the traditional supportive wife. Stone never attempts to represent Salvadoran characters in their own life setting and thus avoids the human intimacy needed for fully developed dramatic portrayal. Instead, wide camera shots of large crowds (actually Mexican extras and supernumeraries) replace closeups and midshots of Salvadoran characters in the capital, San Salvador. Moreover, instead of focusing on the historic assassination of Archbishop Oscar Romero in the national cathedral, Stone imposes the love story of Boyle and Maria onto this scene. They take communion from Romero because Boyle has promised Maria to "become a good Catholic" before they marry. The film's elements of screwball comedy, apparently inserted to give the film domestic box office appeal, lack credibility and appropriateness. One scene of pure Cary Grant humor involves Boyle confessing to a priest in a confessional of the cathedral only moments before the assassination. Stone's disregard for the tragic aspects of the incident—Romero's murder soon elicited the outrage of the world media through satellite relay—reflects the films lack of commitment, if not irreverence.

Salvador tries very hard to conform to the popular international action film genre, represented by more conventional Hollywood products such as Phillip Noyce's *Patriot Games* (1992) and *Clear and Present Danger* (1994), where the improbable adventures of a CIA agent (played by superstar Harrison Ford) push all cross-cultural contact into the wings while constructing an outdated Cold War atmosphere. By imitating such high-profit films, Stone prioritizes box-office appeal over the political substance of human rights. Political dialogue does appear in *Salvador*, but, significantly, it involves only U.S. nationals: Boyle, a U.S. Army advisor, and a State Department official. Their argumentation goes no further than to underscore the shallow premise of the film, that the brutalities of the U.S.-sponsored government must be tolerated because the other side is far worse. Boyle, who as the iconoclastic photojournalist could presumably argue for the other side, responds with a defense typical of the "opposing view" on U.S. public television: the methods used by the U.S.-backed government won't work and they are driving the people closer to the Communists. Rather than allowing Salvadoran characters (and actors?) to speak for themselves, Stone reduces their political dialectic to a debate between three Anglo-Americans, delivered around a lawn table at the U.S. embassy. Even so, the debate scene is weakened by the interweaving of Boyle's private story, since he begins the debate by giving the U.S. advisor photographs of the resistance's camp, which he does in order to secure a U.S. passport for Maria.

Muddled by a narcissistic focus on U.S. nationals and by the trivialization of human oppression through the use of Hollywood glamor and a slick humor that borders on the xenophobic, the Salvadoran voice in the film is muted by various distancing devices. Stone's government goon squads threaten Boyle and his friends in an overly long scene that U.S. audiences would interpret as dangerous Hispanics molesting whites in U.S. cities. The analogy is clear: these people are violent and disorderly by nature. Instead of presenting an exposition of U.S.-sponsored tyranny in the Third World, *Salvador* is itself reflective of the callousness that perpetuates First World actions against Third World populations.

Mississippi Burning: Missing the Point

More typical of Hollywood's human rights subject matter is Alan Parker's mainstream and popular *Mississippi Burning* (1988). Unlike *Salvador*, this film makes little pretense to represent civil protestors, freedom riders, or freedom summers. Instead of dramatizing aspects of the monumental civil rights movement of the 1950s and 1960s, Parker simply replaces the mass movement of people confronting the social fabric of the American South with an unrealistic, in fact extravagant, tale of two FBI agents whose unorthodox ways within the agency substitute for the hundreds of thousands of human rights advocates whose two-decade struggles gradually changed the Jim Crow laws of the South and border states. Parker's point is clear: bureaucratic reformers become respectable replacements for interracial civil protestors. White, middle-aged males (played by the popular romantic leads Gene Hackman and Willem Dafoe) become comforting substitutes for the direct challenge to cultural values that the desegregation movement represented. The film's thematic complacency perhaps went unnoticed by most U.S. viewers, since the powerful acting, cinematography, and technically superior visual effects of fire bombings and other street explosions drew audience interest at regular intervals. Parker's accurate depiction of local white hatred was mitigated by the fact that the lead character, played by Hackman, was himself from the rural deep South, a circumstance that he discloses in a lengthy expository speech early in the film. Since civil rights leaders, voter registration workers, and integrated freedom marchers were perhaps considered too controvertial—challenging dominant values—for Hollywood audiences, these groups were dropped as normative characters in favor of more acceptable establishment figures.

The focus on two bureaucratically reformist FBI agents serves one further function, to white wash the more negative involvement of J. Edgar Hoover's FBI in the desegregation struggle. Hackman and Dafoe almost single-handedly solve the murders of the three civil rights workers who disappeared in Mississippi during the summer of 1964; but even their reformist sentiments within the FBI are underplayed. Incompetent leadership is seen as a local law enforcement problem. A given within the film is that the FBI is doing an honest job to maintain order, presumably to stop the violence, without a hint of Hoover's long-term strategy to discredit Martin Luther King, SNCC leaders, and other notable demonstrators. *Mississippi Burning* profiles white law enforcement officials confronting other white characters with little attempt to reveal the movement and its leaders, who at all times initiated and defined the course of the struggle. The highly disciplined organization and planning structure of the civil rights movement—surely one of the most impressive attempts as social allignment in modern history, and unquestionably the most significant social event in 20th century American history—went undocumented in the film. In fact, no protest groups of any size are shown in the film. Interracial marchers are a fleeting presence, their numbers confined to half a dozen supernumeraries, who remain generally in the background of Parker's deep-focus shots.

Hollywood Blockbusters do Human Rights

Hollywood has yet to produce a drama about the U.S. civil rights movement in its own right. Spike Lee's *Malcolm X* (1992), with a high production value and a strong cast, emphasizes the biography of Malcolm rather than the issues for which he became a major figure in the 1960s black power movement. Malcolm's emphasis on African-American empowerment had economic and civil dimensions that went unrecorded in Lee's film. Moreover, Malcolm's profound change of outlook after his pilgrimage to Mecca was not explored. His decision to move towards integration and away from the separatist orientation that had made his reputation was not developed, nor were the complexities of the struggle within the Nation of Islam (with possible FBI connections) that led to his death. Instead, the film remains a laudatory portrait of an individual with now mythic dimensions, safely noncontrovertial because no longer a political figure. Lee draws no connections with current domestic and international human rights issues, preferring a private portrait that somehow transcends history. By doing so, he conforms to current Hollywood practice, passing up an unexplored cinematic opportunity to engage civic discourse more directly.

The U.S. film *Forrest Gump* (1994), by Robert Zemeckis, was a major international success, with a feel-good theme of honesty, struggle, and human caring triumphing over selfishness and prejudice. However, its view of human rights, both as a goal and as a means to an end, is disappointingly absent. After Gump returns from Vietnam as a soldier still in uniform, he is asked to speak before a huge antiwar rally in Washington, D.C. Just as he begins to give his views of U.S. involvement in the war, his microphones go out, leaving his Washington audience and real audience confronted with silence. Gump never does comment on his involvement in Vietnam, nor on any other human rights issue or problem in the film. Although his character is established early in the film as one who, like a late 20th century Huckleberry Finn, is able to discern reality behind false surfaces, his abilities are used throughout the film only in private circumstances. When Gump begins to gather a following while running across North America, he tells potential followers that he has nothing to reveal to them, then literally runs home, leaving the joke on his followers. The film shows social movements in an entirely negative light, as comprised either of mindless followers of potential leaders who have nothing to say, or of hypocritical advocates of social justice. The latter appear when Gump's childhood sweetheart is involved in Vietnam War protest, but her protest group includes her current boyfriend who beats her in spite of his political concern for human rights. Thus, peace demonstrators are shown to be violent, while U.S. foot soldiers in Vietnam are shown to be kind-hearted and thinking only about home. The point of this role reversal places conformity above civil disobedience: those who would go against the government are violent and false, those who follow unquestioningly, like Gump and his best friend in Vietnam, are honest and appealing.

Gump's power to see past falsity into the hidden realities motivating human action is completely at the service of a privatized understanding of culture. In this way, Zemeckis is able to present a compassionate man who clearly violates the macho male urge towards social domination, but at the same time avoids the deeper implications of social justice and human rights that such "kinder and gentler" values imply. The film distrusts social organization at the grass roots level, a curious attitude given the commonality of its protagonist and his humility and compassion.

John Sayles: Independent Films Try Harder

In contrast to these Hollywood failures, John Sayles's *Men with Guns* (1998) is much more willing to situate its drama within the lives of people under oppression. Like *Salvador*, Sayles's film is set in Central America, but Sayles chooses to leave the particularities of country and government behind, instead presenting the human face of suffering under social and economic tyranny. Rather than creating a Brechtian alienation effect, however, this strategy brings the viewer closer to the indigenous characters; their inhuman choices and futile anguish become all the more manifest when the particularities of foreign policy, regime, and nationality remain unknown. By removing, at least temporarily, the current political controversy, First World audiences are able to interpret characters and situations freely, without interference from media sloganeering and official Washington information releases. Sayles's lack of specificity does not hinder the credibility of his project, since the particularities of death squads, forced clearances from the land, the systematic matching of particular tribal peoples with certain export-oriented crops for harvesting (throughout the village peoples refer to themselves as "sugar people," "salt people," and so on), and a class structure that prevents news of human rights abuse from leaking out, are all problems apparent in many Central American countries. In fact, the film was made in Mexico with a Mexican cast (except for two American actors playing American tourists), and included some non-actors in secondary roles. Sayles's use of nonactors enhances the reality and immediacy of the film, qualities that contribute to its compelling strength.

By using unknown actors, cast for the most part on location or in the film production's host country, Sayles, himself a U.S. national, breaks the power of the Hollywood production formula. No familiar American box office draws are featured, or even presented in cameo roles. By recasting the cinematic mold in this way, Sayles is willing to resist the centripetal pull of American culture by representing non-white populations within their own culture and polity. The film creates a variety of characters within this setting. Dr. Humberto Fuentes is Creole (of Spanish ancestry) and knows nothing about the students he has trained as doctors in the poorest mountain villages. Although one of his own patients in the capital is a high-ranking general, he knows nothing about the brutalities of the government. When he decides to visit his students in their villages out of curiosity, he begins a journey of discovery that changes his life's priorities. He soon learns that all his students have been murdered by the military. Dying of a heart attack in a secret mountain refugee camp, he realizes that his legacy as a physician will be embodied in the young army deserter, trained as a medic, who has taken his medical bag.

Fuentes's trip becomes a pilgrim's progress where he meets a girl, raped by soldiers, who refuses to speak; the army deserter with a dark past; and a runaway priest who has abandoned his village rather than submit to execution as army reprisals. In his search for his former students, he discovers that they have all be executed by the army. Discouraged, he wants to return to the comfort of his practice in the captial, but his companions convince him to look for the mysterious refugee "city" high in the mountains. The mute girl's faith in the "paradise" of such a place impresses both Fuentes and the guilt-ridden deserter. Before their discovery of paradise, the priest surrenders to the soldiers who will execute him by identifying himself as "a ghost." His sacrifice confirms the truth to Fuentes and his companions that running away from injustice will not work. When at last they enter the refugee paradise, where Fuentes realizes he will die, but the mute girl takes his medical bag and forces the deserter, who was trained as a medic, to become the new doctor for the refugees. The deserter accepts the bag, his remorse overcome by the faith of the girl and the example of Fuentes' goodness. Fuentes dies realizing at last that his vocation has been given new meaning through the legacy of the girl and the conversion of the deserter.

Sayles's idea for *Men with Guns* (the title is purposely generic) came from conversations with many friends over several years. One friend, according to Sayles:

> The novelist Francisco Goldman, had an uncle who was a doctor in Guatemala and got involved in an international health program. A few years later he found that most of his students, whom he had sent off in good faith to serve as barefoot doctors in the poorer communities, had been murdered by the very government that claimed to support the program. Another friend's father was an agronomist for the Rockefeller Foundation—several of the people he trained to increase their corn yield were killed within three years of their return to the countryside. (*Angelika Filmbill*, 1998, p. 18)

Sayles justifies the generic setting of his film by stressing the advantages of universalization when approaching human rights issues: "I didn't want people to say, that can only happen in El Salvador.... This doesn't just happen in Latin America. This kind of thing is happening in Africa, in the former Yugoslavia, and the Soviet Union. And it certainly happened in the United States" (*Angelika Filmbill*, 1998, p. 18). By universalizing his message, Sayles places faith in the connectivity of cultures. His cross-cultural project finds meaning only to the extent that different cultures will apply the theme of his film to their own cultural situations (and foreign policies).

Sayles developed his screenplay with the theme of social denial. Impressed by a Gulf War statistic that showed 65 percent of Americans did not want that war covered with the kind of media explicitness shown in Vietnam. "They didn't want that kind of detail, they didn't want the negative side of the story. They wanted a nice comfortable win to feel good about" (*Angelika Filmbill*, 1998, p. 12). Much of *Men With Guns* was filmed in Chiapus, Mexico, where a recent army massacre had taken 45 villagers, an event that adds a tragic relevance to the film's screening. In Chiapus, several thousand natives were removed from their homes, displaced as forced workers, much as Fuentes encounters on his progress to "paradise." Actual destruction and random shooting also parallel the events in the film. Sayles's comments that the hollowness of the media coverage of Chiapus only confirms his theme of denial: "The media make it sound simple like: Oh, those bad local police have been arrested by the army, as if the army are the good guys, when the native people's main complaint is that the army is still there…their long term aim is not what's good for the people" (p. 12).

Sayles's decision to strategize a less particular setting for the film sprang from his awareness that history is constantly redefined to suit political power. Fuentes's unwillingness to face the truth until it is almost too late is "a much more general story. There are incidents in this movie that happened in Vietnam. There are incidents that happened in the Soviet Union, in America's South, as well as in these Latin American countries" (p. 12) In this way, Sayles is able to articulate a human rights statement that universalizes common oppression while remaining true to the particularities of region and culture.

Sayles has included human rights subjects in previous films. *Matewan* (1987), for example, dramatizes a true incident in 1920s West Virginia, where coal miners resist the mining company's goon squads. His perspective, thus far uncommon in Hollywood, may represent a way of choice for future human rights advocates who realize that part of the problem lies in the unwillingness of most people to criticize systemic power: "I got interested in the idea about how all of us don't want to know everything, and some of us want to know nothing. It's hard if you have any conscience at all. Either you have to invent a way that the world works that allows you to live in the way you do, or you have to try to ignore a lot of what goes on out there" (*Angelika Filmbill*, 1998, p. 14). Like his character Fuentes, most people are invested in the power structures that create human rights abuse. Sayles's sense of irony is telling, as two American tourists are willing to stereotype Fuentes himself as a native Latino, even as the other native characters of his journey perceive him as "white." Such cross-cultural alienation is at the root of what Sayles perceives as motivating our indifference to international suffering.

As a photographic medium, for Sayles film becomes a means to jolt his viewers back into reality. In *Men with Guns*, Fuentes represent Thoreau's people of "quiet desperation" whose conscience finally wins out, offering a role model for those who are in positions to make a difference. Sayles has created a profoundly moral tale that fortify First World audiences (and, like Fuentes, elite groups of the Third World) for the 21st century.

Sembene and African Film

Guelwaar (1992), by the Senegalese filmmaker Ousmane Sembene, offers perhaps an even clearer exposition of Third World oppression. Whereas Sayles alters certain details to suit his North American audiences in *Men with Guns* (such as changing the barefoot physicians that Fuentes trains into middle-class medical students, perhaps to make it easier for First World viewers to identify with their deaths), Sembene's Africa is presented with little or no compromise. The tribal groups, religious factions, disaffected urbanites, rural village types, shunned women, all refer back upon West African culture. White people appear as supernumeraries, and then only fleetingly, in the official grandstand of an agronomy exhibition. Sembene presents a parlous nation seduced by foreign aid programs and Cold War area politics. Still, his broad vision unfolds a drama of intracultural struggle and reconciliation.

The conflict of the main plot centers around the mistaken burial of a Christian political victim in a Muslim cemetery. The two communities are at first resistent to each other's cultural differences, but finally recognize the human need for a dignified burial. The mutual understanding of both groups becomes a paradigm for the broader struggles in the film; tragically, the urge toward reconciliation is not followed by the national and international leaders. When a respected political protestor is killed by a corrupt government faction that cannot risk losing the lucrative foreign aid package, the youth rebel against their elders, threatening social transformation or chaos. Sembene ends his film with the various factions—involving gender identities, age differences, religious sects—uniting to reaffirm the traditional values of dignity and integrity.

As a filmmaker, Sembene is free from the requirements of Western cinematic practice and audience sensibilities. *Guelwaar* conveys meaning largely through a strong storyline, fully developed characters, a rich and complex social setting, and, perhaps most of all, timely political subject matter. When the film was shown on U.S. television as part of "Black Heritage Month" in 1997, audiences responded positively. The cultural hybridity of most of the characters perhaps makes it accessible to many Americans. One character, a woman who has been disowned by her family after leaving for the city years before, is one such cultural hybrid. She has become Westernized in dress and manner, but still retains longings for her roots, a circumstance that elicits sympathy from the village elder and other villagers. Her dilemma of being caught between cultures is one not confined to Africa. The film bridges gaps between quite different cultures and economic spheres. Her modern perplexity is also reflected in most of the film's main characters, including the Christian clergyman, the political advocate, and the soldiers, themselves recent emigrants from traditional rural villages. Sembene's identification of parallel experiences of First World and Third World peoples offers the prospect of meaningful intercultural dialogue for human rights issues in the next century. Sembene, however, also sees himself as a national filmmaker, interested in strengthening the cultural identity of Senegalese society while functioning in part as chronicler of intra-African conflict and the threat from the West. Both goals are complementary in his films, if not dependent upon one another. Sembene has discovered that cultural identity can be secured only through an enlightened engagement of the political and social struggle.

STILL PHOTOGRAPHY: THE IMAGE OF HUMAN RIGHTS

Still photography has retained a somewhat tensive position between, on the one hand, photojournalism—with its requirement of instantaneous reportage, its preference for "hard news" events to the exclusion of more long-term and profound social developments, and its tendency to confuse the visually conspicuous with significant moments of social reality—and, on the other hand, photography as a fine art—museum-worthy, and somewhat removed from social commentary. The demise of such popular photography magazines as *Look* and *Life* has removed photography somewhat from popular consciousness. The void is now filled by the rise since the early 1980s of music video channels and the continued expansion of fashion photography, which now includes a wider range of foreign titles and celebrity-oriented publications. Clearly, social commentary is not a priority in current First World professional photography; neither is it a dominant theme in photography as a fine art. Nevertheless, individual professional photographers, and some who would perhaps be classified as full-time amateur photographers, have found publishers willing to reorient mainstream publishing practices to produce collections of human rights and social justice themes. Among the most vital practitioners in this area are photographers Susan Meiselas and Jacob Holdt, and photo editor Steven Kasher, whose work promises to fill the significant void resulting from mainstream news media practice and the apolitical orientation of much of the post-modern visual arts.

Photographing Human Rights

Killing Fields (1996), edited by Chris Riley and Douglas Niven, with text by David Chandler, is a collection of official identity photographs of Cambodian subjects who have been detained by the Khmer Rouge during the period of its dominance in the early 1980s. The editors have chosen shots that present a certain variety of individuals—young, middle-aged, and old, male and female farmers—who face the camera lens upon orders from their guards. Some face certain death, others will be released after a stay in concentration camps. While the editors show their boldness of conception by producing such a work of stark simplicity, their decision to include only identification photos of victims removes the viewer somewhat from the reality of the Cambodian genocidal campaign. The complexity of social forces, history of international involvement, and culture of Southeast Asia are deliberately left out, a strategy that perhaps diminishes the work as a commentary on human rights abuse. The photo subjects register fear, apprehension, weariness, mistrust, exhaustion, resignation, but the shots have a certain uniformity—perhaps intended by the editors, certainly by their detainers—hat restricts the viewer's empathy. As photo-documentation, the collection has even less value, since these portraits, all mid-shots with the same background and size, reveal nothing about the land, the melange of civil strife, and the environmental details that make social events real. Without such specificity, the book becomes a claustrophobic register of unknown faces, the individual posers isolated figures, removed both from the other detainees and from the events that define their predicament.

Chandler's (1996) text also seems insufficient. The events leading to the rise of the Pol Pot regime are sketched too vaguely. While such minimalism seems to complement the starkness of the volume's layout and photography, it also distances the reader from this turbulent history. Cambodia's humanity remains hidden. Moreover, the role of the Vietnamese expeditionary force, certainly key to the successful removal of the regime, is almost entirely ignored. According to Chandler, the Vietnamese perform this life-saving action only because they are "eager to distance themselves" from the Communist associations of the Khmer Rouge (p. 102). Such remarks put the text in cadence with most U.S. mainstream media interpretations of the Vietnamese action, which downplayed its role in the overthrow. Chandler does not mention the U.S. bombing of Cambodia as a contributing factor in the reactionary rise of Pol Pot, an air action that devastated the country's interior, especially in 1973 (Chomsky, 1994). Chandler in fact ignores entirely the historical developments that find the Cambodians photographed by their killers. By showing human faces divorced from the particularities of culture, politics, and environment, the editors have created an abstract commentary on human victimhood, not a social exposition that elicits the viewer's empathy.

More successful is Graciela Iturbide's *Images of the Spirit* (1996), which combines an expository account of the recent grassroots opposition to government policy in Mexico with an intimate portrait of the people of southern Mexico. Farmers and urban workers are photographed in front of their houses, working places, and churches in a way that reveals the cultural setting of a people in rebellion. Iturbide's "Photo of Chiapas Women" conveys an image of classic Greek tragedy. Both permanence and vulnerability are suggested in the long black robes wrapped around the women's heads and bodies; their pale faces peer through hoods at the camera with the perplexity of a Greek chorus. Unlike the bleak simplifications of *Killing Fields*, such starkness evokes a deep humanity, inviting the viewer to feel at some level the subjects' pain. Iturbide does not objectify the struggle for land reform in southern Mexico, nor does she avoid a political position. Rather, she combines these agendas with an affectivity that draws the viewer closer to the people. Her subjects are not anonymous detainees removed from their living spaces, but individuals and groups empowered by their communities, in spite of the pain of economic struggle and the uncertainties of official violence.

Susan Meiselas: A Career in Human Rights Photojournalism

Exemplary of human rights discourse for the 21st century is the work of Susan Meiselas, through three decades, across different continents and cultures. Her first major collection was *Nicaragua: June 1978–July 1979* (1981), a documentation of the Sandinista revolution that brought her photographs international recognition. Her recent collection, *Kurdistan: In the Shadow of History* (1997), attempts to uncover a chronicle of a people lost between international borders and by the vagaries of global powers. In fact, her own photographs comprise only a minority of the volume's collection, which includes historic photographs of independence movements; "postcard" photos intended for tourists (often mislabeled, as Meiselas discovers); and other exotica, including portraits of "national costumes" and figures who would arouse the curiosity of the outsider. Her selections juxtapose a chronicle of mostly black-and-white images throughout the 20th century with large panoramic color shots through her own camera of the landscape and social trauma of the Kurds. The effect is as much a definition of a people as it is an exposition of massive human rights violations.

Meriselas's own large photographs, each filling two pages, juxtapose the rugged landscape of northern Iraq, shown first as an expansive area void of people, with thousands of Kurdish refugees huddled on an unpaved highway, shown next in a photo filled with people. The effect is to merge land with people in a way that has been denied by international conflict through centuries of history. Other panoramic shots include towns in ruins with only stone foundations remaining, and stone markers of graves from the 1988 chemical bombing of the village of Goktapa in northern Iraq. Meiselas's commentary is personal but unobtrusive. Of the myriad brown stone grave markers, she writes, "First mass graves I've ever documented.... I came in at the end of history" (1997, p. xv). Aware that her photographic collection will function in part to advance Kurdish identity and their right to a living space, she remarks, "Archives are strange lands" (p. xv). Going from house to house, she asks to copy cherished family portraits, too often lost or destroyed during decades of social upheaval and official removal policies.

Social documentation, staple of photojournalism, is presented in *Kurdistan,* alongside a text that personalizes the melange of Kurdish life. Meiselas's conciseness serves to minimize her intrusion as outside chronicler: "Within bare rooms, men sit on carpets with their backs against walls, drinking tea; the women are hidden, along with their stories. Only because we are Western women are we welcome to join the men" (1997, p. xvi). She discloses that the temptation to become personally involved in the Kurdish plight is sometimes overwhelming: "I also feel the need to repatriate what I uncover as I attempt to reconstruct the past from scattered fragments" (p. xvi). Meiselas's subjectivist approach, placed alongside photographs of often brutally objective realism, frames the message in a human voice of concern, making her subject more accessible.

Meiselas includes photos of individuals caught between matters of conscience and the will to survive. Thus Burhan Ozbilici's telling portrait of Leyla Zana (one of eight Kurdish members of the Turkish parliament accused of backing the banned Kurdish Worker's Party) shows a frail but determined woman surrounded by male soldiers, official journalists, and lawyers. Another photo is of a woman in an iron witness box in front of a row of Turkish soldiers, her face showing strength and defiance. The photo, we are told, was printed in a Turkish magazine, whereupon the issue was banned. Meiselas often reveals intimate responses to the most barbarous images. Thus her own photo, appearing on the cover of *The New York Times Magazine* in 1993, depicts a woman mourning the exhumed bodies of her brothers at their grave in Koreme. Perhaps the most visually arresting image is of a mother holding a baby in the doorway of a home as a massive armored vehicle passes only a few feet away. The photo, placing fragile humanity next to the powerful enforcers of inhumanity, was taken by Reza in the town of Cizre, where 100 civilians were killed in 1993.

Meiselas's personal involvement in the Kurdish struggle often includes befriending villagers and rephotographing family pictures that have become too dangerous for the Kurds to carry across borders. Even family portraits are often considered by officials subversive because expressive of national identity. Under these circumstances of ethnic erasure, Meiselas's project of photographic documentation has a special import and urgency.

Innocence Abroad: Jacob Holdt's Photographic Journey

Taken with a single used camera, Holdt's 1,500 photographs of class and race in the U.S. were given final form upon his return to Denmark. His collection appeared as *American Pictures* in the U.S. in 1985, after its publication in several other countries. Like the images of rural poverty, child labor, and racial segregation by Lewis Hine early in the 20th century and Gordon Parks in the 1940s and 1950s, Holdt's photographs explore with an uncompromising naturalism issues of social justice and poverty within a land of plenty. As with Hine and Parks, his collection is partly documentation and partly a study of human despair, neglect, and the false values motivating social inequality. Holdt's ability to present his subject matter at once with objectivity and empathy marks his important contribution to human rights discourse. As such, he is another example to motivate social awareness in the 21st century.

Amazingly, when Holdt arrived in America—a land of fantasy to one who grew up in a post-World War II Denmark dependent upon American movies and television for entertainment—it was only to tour the U.S. with no intention of photographing it. He was, in fact, a novice with a camera. Son of a Lutheran pastor, Holdt was shunned by his father when he painted scriptural passages on the facade of the village church after learning that the congregation was building a spire atop the church during the Biafra famine. Endowed with such independent fervor, Holdt was at first disillusioned with the America of his childhood dreams. Instead of romantic adventure and brave independence, he found inequality, injustice, and lack of opportunity. However, his approach to these conditions was to confront them directly and with an openness that became the key to his success as social critic. Disclosing a love for everyone he met, his universal respect, even for the oppressors, gained him rare access to the private spaces of the poor, the wealthy, the fugitive, and the famous. Holdt explores America with what may seem reckless abandon, but his venturesome nature was supported by a basic faith in human connectivity. After interviewing a white tomato grower, Holdt comments, "I always tried to respect the honesty of these southern racists, so when my tape recorder later revealed that I in the heat of the argument had told him a lie I felt very defeated. I had no idea that my photos would one day end up in a book" (1985, p. 42). At Wounded Knee, he joins the few whites who secretly smuggle food into the compound held by members of the American Indian Movement (AIM). Holdt's ability to participate in social conflict while documenting it gives his photos a unique immediacy. Commenting on his participation in the urban and rural social protest in the 1970s when he was touring, Holdt reveals the balance of opposing drives within him that motivates his social commentary:

> To be a vagabond is just an attempt to give oneself fully to the individual person. But to be a revolutionary is an attempt to give oneself fully to all of humanity.... Human beings are so infinitely weak and small that if they are ever to become fully human they *must* combine these two sides. Although almost all of us suffered defeat at Wounded Knee, Wounded Knee was nevertheless a victory, because it was such an attempt. (1985, p. 51)

Like his compatriot Jacob Riis, Holdt's writing is direct and artless. Riis's monumental work on late 19th century America, *How the Other Half Lives* (1890), also urged social reform. Holdt felt that his identity as a foreigner in the U.S. increased his access to people and places that few professional photographers and journalists have matched, but his faith in human compassion and engaging sociability supplied the motivation for his discernment into race and class within a First World country.

Photography of Eastern Europe and Cuba

Antonin Kratochvil's *Broken Dreams: 20 Years of War in Eastern Europe* (1997) combines artistry with striking symbolic commentary on the Bosnian conflict and on the lingering privileges of power under fallen Communist governments. "Victory Sign: Albanian Gulag" shows a hand gesture through a tiny window of a cement pillbox prison cell. The photo's starkness is heightened by its mysteries: only the hand is visible, its gender and age unknown; the cell is not easily placed within its surroundings; and the narrow range of tones, shades of gray, hide such identifiable marks as time of day and reason. "War Wounded Bosnia" also emphasizes bleakness over human contact, as does "In the Field of the New Gods: Romania," which shows giant stone statues of former Communist leaders that have fallen against one other to the ground. The latter's obvious irony is continued in "More Equal Among the Equal: Russia," which shows a group of new entrepreneurs around a large dinner table filled with various main courses. Kratochvil uses photography for explicit social criticism, the bitterness heightened by ironic titles. Amidst such heavy ideology, the human element is inaccessible, replaced by an overriding sarcasm that almost denies its purpose, which surely is to uphold the value of human life over externally imposed control.

Marcia Friedman's *Cuba: The Special Period* (1998) lacks the artistry of *Broken Dreams* but includes an even more dominant ideological agenda. The author wishes to show the deterioration of her former homeland after decades of Communist rule, but she prefers colonial buildings to people, the vestigial refinements of palace and hotel courtyards to social reality. It is in effect a collection of architectual photographs captioned with sentimental commentary: "yet beauty thrives in Cuba" shows a neatly trimmed foreign tourist hotel courtyard, empty of people; "and in the shadows songs are sung" has a small musical band playing in an otherwise empty hotel courtyard, their clothing intended to attract the tourist trade and their faces obscured; "yet what once was...still is—colonial architecture somewhere" shows a 19th century building facade, again with no indication of current social life. *Cuba: The Special Period* prefers nostalgia over the human presence and avoids present realities in favor of past aristocratic glories. Within this highly restricted view, human rights escapes notice in favor of historical preservation. Much more engaging and comprehensive is Aperture's *Cuba: Image and Imagination* (1995), in which Cubans are revealed without politicized screening in a variety of life situations. The human moment takes focus over glorifications of a mythic past.

THE HUMAN ELEMENT

Recent film and still photography have generally avoided discourses of human rights and social justice in favor of more financially secure projects, especially celebrity, fashion, "hard news" photography, and Hollywood formula films. Nevertheless, there remain some smaller publishers and independent filmmakers who are willing to support politically based themes. This study attempts to demonstrate that those photojournalists and filmmakers who, 1) readily engage the social life of their subjects; 2) have the desire and ability to communicate cross-culturally;

and 3) consistently define a social issue or problem, become the most cogent argu-ers for human rights and social justice. Transcending stereotypical conceptions as well as dominant voices of their country's mainstream media and foreign policy institutions, these artists move within a political framework without sacrificing their focus on the human element of their subjects. Meiselas, Holdt, and Sembene best define this approach to human rights discourse. All three assume a universal basis of empathy and understanding, but do not allow prejudgments to turn their focus from the victims—and perpetrators—of social injustice.

Although Holdt admits to personal prejudices, he carefully turns the focus back to his subjects, always with an elements of humility and candor. It is this willing-ness to risk losing face in confrontations with both victim and oppressor that enables his unique discourse, which is able to communicate both sides perhaps more clearly than any other photojournalist. Meiselas is able to connect with her subject unblinkered by the official foreign policy of her government. Thus her photographic study of the Kurds ("to document the present in relation to the past") was undertaken fully conscious of how Washington foreign policy had exploited their plight: The Kurds "were being used to rev up the American public for the bombing of Bagdad. That's not on their own merits and not taking into consider-ation what's best for them" (qtd. in Metz, 1998, pp. 36–37). Meiselas's photo-graphs of the Nicaraguan revolution in the late 1970s are illustrative of successful intercultural communication. They were seen immediately by Sandinista revolu-tionaries, who identified with, and were influenced by, their own images. Meiselas comments on the ways in which photojournalism can raise public awareness glo-bally: "There are lots of ways in which the process of documenting reverberates. Without question [my] photographs shaped people's perceptions of the Sandinis-tas. The photographs also shaped their images of themselves" (p. 38). Stamps, posters, billboards, even rugs were made from her photographs in post-revolution-ary Nicaragua. Referring to her current project on medical care in the South Bronx, Meiselas reveals her approach to human rights awareness: "Documentari-ans are struggling with how to keep connecting people to people" (p. 39).

QUESTIONS FOR FURTHER THOUGHT

1.   What other recent films and still photgraphs convey images of human rights issues?
2.   How well do these other films and photographs succeed at presenting human rights or social justice issues?
3.   What makes these films and photographs with human rights subjects more authentic and accurate than others?
4.   What international social issues or problems need to be more fully defined for the U.S. public today?
5.   What international social issues are most inaccurately reported, most under-reported, or most ignored today and why?

Part III

The Human Rights Setting

8

NIGERIA: DIVISIONISM AND OIL INTERESTS

Recent events in Nigeria have brought before the international community the deferred hopes of social and economic development in sub-Saharan Africa. That nation's attempt to overcome the cultural and economic divisions within its borders demonstrate the general direction of African unity, which, over the past two decades, has envisioned a program for intra-African political cooperation and "South-South" economic development. This chapter will examine recent political events in Nigeria in order to uncover the particular cultural, economic, and political tensions between its regions and groups. In recent times, perceived as an economic and political leader among the African post-colonial states, Nigeria has yet to transcend its past history of ethnic rivalry as shaped by colonial divisionism and the more recent power of big oil. Nonetheless, given its potential to become an advanced NIC (newly industrialized country) within its continent, it remains an important model for human rights study within the Third World. Nigeria is very much influenced by the general cultural and economic direction of the African continent and also by the current attempts among African nations to form polities that transcend national borders—borders that were in the main established by the European colonizers before independence. For these reasons, it is first necessary to discuss the broader African situation at the end of the 20th century.

SUB-SAHARAN AFRICA

Economy and Society

The states of Africa are at once homogeneous and heterogeneous. They possess among them a heritage of colonial history under European domination. They are, in fact, the last continent to be so dominated and were the most recent group of colonial people to gain independence. As a result of this late colonial past, the African states are also alike in their inheritance of an asymmetrical relationship with First World economic markets—the Global Capital of Europe, North America, and parts of Asia. Here, the similarities end. African countries are quite diverse in culture and geography, but also in population size, per capita income, class differences, and political and institutional development. With colonial independence following World War II, Sudan (1956), Ghana (1957), Guinea (1958), most states of west and central Africa, including Nigeria in 1960, suddenly found relatively unrestricted possibilities for the renewal of identity. A new age was heralded by voices within Africa and around the world.

Unhappily, by the mid-1970s, the euphoria had worn thin. The economic marginalization of Africa began, a trend that has only intensified into the 1990s. As the term "Third World" proclaimed its marginality, massive economic investment went into the African post-colonial states, followed, when the promising agendas for development did not keep pace, by the strictures of structural adjustment programs (SAPs). These endeavors maintained investment dependency, but with increased conditionality. Certainly, the trend of disappointment was more or less global. Between 1970 and 1989, the difference in income worldwide between the richest 20 percent of countries and the poorest 20 percent increased from a ratio of 32:1 to 60:1. Even more discouraging, if allowance is made for income inequality (class disparity) within Third World countries, the ratio climbs to 140:1. The wealthiest fifth of the world's states claim four-fifths of worldwide GNP (gross national product), while the poorest fifth share only 1.4 percent (Adedeji, 1993). Moreover, sub-Saharan Africa remains the Third World's most marginal region.

In the first decade of the post-colonial era, Africa was the continent of choice for First World investment. However, starting in the mid-1970s the situation changed. By the 1980s, African economic growth rates were negative. Adding to the economic disappointment were deteriorating social conditions, armed conflict between traditional and colonial-defined groups, civil unrest, drought, and refugee movements on a large scale. In 1992, the overall GNP growth rate of Africa was only 1.9 percent. When placed in context of a rapid population increase of 3.1 percent in 1992, the effect on per capita income was negative (Adedeji, 1993). As Africa's share of world GNP fell in the three decades following independence, its shares of the total global population and official development assistance (ODA) from the First and Second Worlds have increased. In fact, the threat of external dependence has only deepened in recent decades, creating a quasi-colonial—sometimes called a neocolonial—state of existence wherein political independence is undermined by the actions of international lending and aid institutions. This situation Africans themselves are quite conscious of, as evidenced in Ousman Sembene's films about the general response to First World aid programs in Senegal (see Chapter 7 in this volume). Many states in African experienced overdependence from First World assistance that included food and other basic needs.

Since the end of the Cold War era, Africa has lost its status as a geopolitical region. Although the continent was never a primary "hot spot" for the polarity of East (Communist) and West (capitalist), it was given increased attention during the period, ending abruptly in 1989 to 1990. The West saw no immediate reason to keep Africa in its own camp. Accordingly, aid to Africa has decreased over the past decade. Sweden's recent decision to reduce its heretofore generous foreign aid to Third World countries may be a harbinger of what other First World states, who have not been so generous, may do. According to the Organization for Economic Cooperation and Development (OECD), "sub-Saharan Africa [is] the only major developing region not to have experienced an increase in overall financial flows" from North to South (United Nations, 1991, pp. 8–9). Africa simply lacked the relative economic power to make its voice heard in the new world order, thus its debt crisis persisted.

To an extent replacing humanitarian, educational, and skills-development aid has been loan restructuring programs with their often harsh conditionalities. Thirty of the 43 sub-Saharan countries have formal adjustment agreements with the IMF. The effects of these policies are quite negative. In these countries, real wages have declined sharply by from 30 to 90 percent, and about 60 percent of urban work forces are unemployed. The UN World Food Program (WFP) reports malnutrition affecting about 40 percent of African children compared to 25 percent in 1985 (George, 1993). Moreover, SAPs have altered traditional African social structures to create a small elite (0.1 percent of the total population) who are often alienated from their own ethnic and religious traditions and psychologically oriented toward personal aggrandizement within a new international investment culture. As Adebayo Adedeji has described this African economic strata formed by First World economic policies: "They ride on the restless wave of high-turnover financial capital" (p. 7).

Hybridity and Divisionism

Classism and social estrangement of elite groups within post-colonial African nations have aggravated the economic and political turmoil of recent decades. That these new forms of social distress are originative of a European colonialist and neocolonialist ethic are unmistakable. Typically, the new investment-oriented African elites have been seduced by notions of individual aggrandizement based on global market investment. Thus the "hybridity" of the post-colonial subject—borrowing a seminal term of Homi Bhabha (1994) and other recent post-colonial scholars—is most clearly expressed by the groups at the top of African post-colonial society. The significance of the investment class in African human rights discourse cannot be exaggerated. "Riding the restless wave" of venture capital, they are primarily Western-oriented but often hold dominant political and economic positions in their home countries (Cohen, 1998d). This state of alienation within its ruling population is a structural handicap for the post-colonial African state, as it gropes to find means of meeting mounting debt obligations and confronts major hindrances to success, such as failed infrastructures, overburdened educational institutions, and inadequate public health programs. Unhappily, the very groups that assume direction of national planning programs, aid distribution, and contact with First World aid and human rights organizations are often the ones least able to identify with the people within their borders most in need of these services.

Thus, the problem of the "middleman" has proven a major impediment to progressive change and social equality in Africa. This situation is the indirect consequence of colonialist policies. The current African middlemen may be the successors of the colonial most-favored group or "tribe" that was given preference by the European powers in order to function as a link or even buffer zone between the white colonizer and the less controllable, more independent or resistant indigenous groups. This is the political legacy of Nigeria, where a more manageable, "user-friendly" group, from the north of the country, was favored by the British over the less tractable, more resistant southern groups. The division between north and south within Nigeria had particular religious, linguistic, and cultural origins that predated the colonizers. However, the British, as was often the case in their worldwide empire, sought out preexisting demarcations within Nigeria for purposes of its own domination and control-management. To better understand this situation from the standpoint of human rights, it is necessary to examine the particulars of group divisionism in Nigeria.

NIGERIAN POLITY TODAY

Chosen by the departing British colonizers to lead the country, the northern group has dominated post-colonial Nigerian politics for at least two decades. Actually comprising much of the central region, the area known as northern Nigeria is ethnically mixed, but has been largely united by its Hausa language, its Muslim tradition, and its unwillingness to cede political control to the mainly Christian and religiously indigenous south (Cohen, 1998c). The vast majority of the country's commercial and natural wealth is in the south. The high-grade oil reserves of the south are estimated to remain viable for several decades. Nigeria's southern groups, dominated by the Yoruba people, have been more industrious and business oriented, while the northern Hausa groups have shown less independence from the Europeans, are considered more "conservative," and also more represented in the military high command. Thus, in the case of colonial Nigeria, the group of choice for the British consisted not of the most "enterprising" people—a circumstance perhaps typical of European colonial history—but rather in many ways the more "backward" group. For purposes of enforcement, however, the northerners suited the British occupiers. Domestic divisiveness was more easily arranged by the colonizers because the Hausa and southern language groups are not related in any way. Northerners and southerners cannot understand each when other speaking their native languages. After independence, the north/south cleavage continued to dominate Nigerian social and cultural life, although economic elites—and the poor in abundance—can be found in both groups. As Bashir Ikara, a Nigerian-based political scientist, observes, "What you have [in northern Nigeria] is a group of conservative people who regard power as their heritage. But the fact is that ordinary northerners have nothing to show for this long domination and are simply clamoring, like the rest of the country, for honest government" (Cohen, 1998c, p. A4).

This widespread credibility crisis has prevented northern as well as southern Nigerians from fully expecting that their leaders will support the kind of democratic planning required if the human rights goals of ICESCR are to be honored in the next century. To achieve these goals in a sub-Saharan, post-colonial country requires the kind of creative planning and autonomy to stand up to the powerful forces of the World Bank and the IMF, the "terrible twins" of Bretton Woods, who claim democracy as their goal while functioning as collection agencies for Global Capital investment. The recent sudden death of Nigeria's best hope for positive change, Moshood K. O. Abiola, has left the country once more bereft of leadership, a crisis that will continue unless group disunity can overcome the formidable influences of foreign aid policy and the conditionalities of international business.

Abiola and the Struggle for Unity

Nigeria's recently installed military ruler, General Abdulsalam Abubakar, has been the latest of a long succession of northern generals dominating the country. Succeeding General Sani Abacha, who was perhaps Nigeria's cruelest and most autocratic ruler, Abubaker had greatness thrust upon him when Abacha died unexpectedly from heart trouble in June 1998. Rising to the occasion and perhaps eager to show his moderate inclinations, Abubakar has been careful not to fan the flames of Nigerian divisionism. He appointed Yoruba (southern) officers to key military posts and has promised to deliver his power over to a fairly elected civilian on May 29, 1999. Nonetheless, Abubakar has revealed his northern sympathies indirectly by contributing towards a new political party with decidedly northern sympathies, while discreetly absenting himself from its fund raising rally. However, other former rulers of Nigeria graced the rally for a new northern party: General Yakubu Gowon, who seized power in 1966 and surrendered it in a coup in 1975; and Major General Mohammed Buhari, who seized power in 1983 before being deposed by General Babagida in the coup of 1985. Babagida, in many ways the most memorable ruler of Nigeria, remains perhaps the real power behind the scenes. Thus, the legacy of northern domination continues after the untimely death of Abiola.

It was from this northern dynasty—often described as "the Kaduna mafia," which refers to a region in north central Nigeria—that southern Nigerians were hoping to wrest power in the presidential elections of 1993. When it became apparent that Abiola won the election, southerners and progressive Nigerians everywhere rejoiced. A statesman-like figure who had pledged the unity of all Nigeria despite his southern background, Abiola was capable of broad discernment as well as coalition building (Kaufman, 1998). However, General Babangida annulled the vote, an action that only intensified Nigerian divisiveness along north/south lines. Abiola was eventually placed in detention, where he remained until July 1998, when he suddenly died from causes that have been disputed by family members and many others. This event, happening only moments after Abiola received the U.S. Ambassador and Nigerian officials, made front-page headlines worldwide and has precipitated a renewed factionalism.

The northern domination of Nigeria conforms to the practice of European colonial history in some important ways. Although the south has the economic and commercial power—and perhaps in some respects a culture more adaptable to the new world order of Global Capital—it was the north that dominated Nigeria's postcolonial history. This is the direct result of British colonialist actions, and to a large extent the result of one individual's decisions. Frederick Lugard, the British governor general who formed Nigeria in 1914, favored the northern group in his policies because he regarded it as more malleable to imperialist rule than the more independent-minded south. He founded Nigeria's military academy in Kaduna, which attracted mostly northern Hausa speakers. Consequently, northern officers were used to control southerners throughout the colonial period. Lord Lugard's remarks on southern Nigerians epitomized the association of independence from European rule with lawlessness that colonialist ideology embraced: "The most seditious and disloyal, the most purely prompted by self-seeking money motives of any people I have met" (Cohen, 1998c, p. A4). His description of southerners seems quite self-referential today, since self-interest through individual aggrandizement remained the chief motivation of European imperialist policy.

Colonialist self-interest was directly ceded to northern Nigerians when the British left in the early 1960s. This transfer often took a quite literal turn. Kaduna's regional assembly building is still known as Lugard House; Nigeria's premier Polo Club (a sport emblematic of aristocratic power) and the Rugby Club (a British sport) line Waff Road, a street named after Britain's colonial West African Frontier Force. It is against this brand of "internal colonialism" that Yoruba Nigerians struggle, particularly in the more educated centers, such as Lagos, Nigeria's largest city. However, most northern Nigerians are as poor as their southern counterparts and long for the political stability that will foster social justice. The last democratically elected president took office in 1979, and the last two military rulers, Babangida and Abacha, allowed open elections only to ignored the results. Given the history of this sort of official inconsistency, it is not surprising that General Abubakar's promise for elections is met with widespread mistrust. Opposition forces have demanded a civilian government of unity in place by October 1998, but Abubakar has temporized. The rioting following Abiola's death subsided after a few weeks, but general resentment remains. The fact that Abubakar has not appointed opposition officials to his cabinet and has not overtly encouraged the open and free formation of political parties has been noticed with apprehension. Meanwhile, the army remains out of barracks, a constant presence on the urban streets. Of the credibility gap, Aminu Kani, a high official in the Ministry of Internal Affairs, remarked, "I do not think we will see power being simply handed to a government of national unity" (Cohen, 1998a, p. A5).

General Babangida, known in short as I.B.B., has been regarded by many as the real power behind the current military ruler. After annulling the election of Abiola in 1993, he presented the country with the five-year tyranny of General Abacha, who soon became the worst dictator in Nigerian history. Babangida remained very much in the political spotlight, although he claimed a certain distance from the system of power: "I have no interest in politics, therefore no interest in forming a party, and therefore no interest in elective office" (Cohen, 1998c, p. A4). His personable, perhaps fulsome attitude in public hides a life formed in the northern military elite culture. He went to school with General Abubakar, the present head of state, and grew up in his neighborhood. Years after the election annulment, Babangida congenially claimed he was forced into ignoring Abiola's election by other military officers, and considered Abiola his friend. His son Muhammed Babangida offered more details: "There were other generals, including Abacha, who said that if power was ceded to a southerner like Abiola, the north would have nothing left. They put my father into a corner" (Cohen, 1998c, p. A4). What perhaps threatens the northern military generals is the backwardness of their landlocked region compared to the bountiful south, centered on the commercially advanced Lagos.

Babangida's principal achievements were the suppression of the southern Ibo group during the civil war in which the Ibos seceded and declared the state of Biafra in the 1960s; his attempts to restrain extreme forms of Islamic zealotry in the north; and his defeat of a southern-led coup that would expel five northern regions. Of these actions, the Biafra war was by far the bloodiest, leaving a million Nigerians dead. Thus Babangida's career has been punctuated by violent suppression within his own country. After the death of Abacha, his low-profile efforts to support a new political party for the northern military movement denoted a shift in orientation. Whether this new approach was merely cosmetic temporizing before elections or whether it represented substantive change towards tolerance was uncertain. For this question Nigerian post-colonial history offers only ambiguity.

While it is true that Nigeria has experienced extremely violent civil war and factionalism, always at the expense of the human rights standards it agreed upon as signatory to the UN covenants, the country also registers a degree of tolerance within diversity that seems to contradict its rule by force. There is widespread intermarriage between regions and groups. Nigerians have become quite mobile within their borders, as the presence of various tribal groups in all parts of the country indicate. There have been no large-scale reprisals for the mass killings following the Biafran war. And Nigerians, with a population of 105 million and a prosperous south, have kept their sense of being the great power in Africa. Despite these positive signs, Babangida's decision to disallow Abiola the election (and imprisonment under Abacha in 1994) threw away Nigeria's promise of stable democracy and human rights building.

Events during the riots following the unforeseen death of Abiola on July 7, 1998, indicate that there is more to Nigerian politics than regional divisionism. In Abeokuta, a small city in southern Nigeria, the sacred palace of the current Yoruba king was looted and burned by thousands of angry southern protesters. The king was considered a father figure to Abiola, so the attack seemed, at least on the surface, inexplicable. Two lesser Yoruba palaces were also destroyed. On the other hand, the city's mosques were left untouched. Although it was assumed that the rioting across Nigeria was a direct response to the death under detention of Abiola, the awareness of class disparity seems to have been at least equally important. Nigeria remains a very poor country with a small prosperous elite. In fact, per capita income has declined over the past two decades. The Yoruba king is a traditional leader, but also very wealthy. The Yorubas of southwestern Nigeria are in many respects the most progressive group within the country. Abeokuta is also the hometown of Wole Soyinka, the writer and Nobel laureate. Abiola, who had a tolerant, intercultural orientation, endowing mosques as well as churches, grew up within a Yoruba outlook that stressed cooperation between Nigeria's more than 200 ethnic groups. The Protestant high school that Abiola attended is today headed by a Muslim, Gbolahan Aroyeun, who attends church service each morning and has even preached to the students. When he gets home from the school, Aroyeun attends the mosque. "Here, we have a relaxed attitude to religion. When my daughter said she wanted to marry a Christian, I voiced no objection at all." At another Protestant school, the Patterson Baptist Memorial School, a Muslim student who had recently converted to Christianity commented, "When I told my father that I wanted to become a Christian, he just said, 'God bless you'" (Cohen, 1998b, p. 3). As a student, Abiola attended chapel every morning and continued to sing Christian hymns while remaining a Muslim. Onaolapo Soleye, a former Nigerian Finance Minister and resident of Abeokuta, explained, "Here nearly every home is part Muslim, part Christian, part pagan. What distinguishes us from the north is not our religion but the way we interpret it. In the north, Islam is a very serious business" (Cohen, 1998b, p. 3).

Given the generally tolerant orientation of the southern Yorubas, and the reputation of the current *oba*, Yoruba king, the sudden violence against his office seems inexplicable. Class is the important division within Nigerian society, a condition that remains underreported by the foreign press. For example, teachers at the Baptist Boys High School in Abeokuta make $4 a month, while the principal makes $100. Moreover, the Patterson school library has no books and the chapel ceiling is collapsing. Nigeria's infrastructure is crumbling and the unemployment rate remains stubbornly high. The palaces of the king and other high officials in Abeokuta are known to contain precious objects. With Abiola's death, class consciousness, which has lingered as widespread resentment for decades and was suppressed by the Nigerian ruling elites during the post-colonial period, emerged as sporadic and unforeseen violent outbursts. Abiola always expressed a preferential option for the poor, for whom he endowed many projects. His 1993 election victory offered to Nigerians of all regions and religions the promise of ending the systemic corruption, aggrandizement, and human rights abuse practiced by the military ruling elites. By the time of the elections, Abiola had become the statesman with nationwide appeal, even winning the key northern town of Kano. His popularity has been attributed as much to his largesse and uncommon sensitivity to the disenfranchised throughout the country as to his Muslim faith. With his death under suspicious circumstances in government detention, a class violence that transcended other differences erupted. For example, one attack occurred against the palace of Adedapo Tejuoso, a lesser chief, who was known to travel too often to the capital, Abuja, to meet with Abacha, presumably for favors. The Yoruba king, locally known as the Alake of Egbaland, was resented for not becoming more engaged in demanding Abiola's release from prison.

In fact, regional divisionism in Nigeria may be to an extent actively promoted by the military government as an effective distraction from the glaring class differences and discrimination along class lines in education, employment, business contracts, order of law, and so on. Usually the language of human rights protest in the 1990s, Nigeria is cast with reference to regional or group divisions that thinly disguise resentment of social inequality. For example, Gbolahan Aroyeun, principal of the Baptist Boys High School in Abeokuta, remarked soon after the ransacking of the palaces, "It is impossible to live in a country where only certain citizens can aspire to the highest office. Yet here, one or two ethnic groups feel it is their birth-right to rule over everyone" (Cohen, 1998b, p. 3). Other Nigerians expressed more specific concerns that reflect practical responses to a society that practices comprehensive and profound corruption, nepotism, and official forms of extortion. For example, Ahmud E. C. Agberankhe works for Nigerian Radio for $40 a month, although he possesses a university degree in physics. He spends his time working on jingles for advertisements of luxury items that target the upwardly mobile members of the military ruling class. His economic frustration eventually may lead him into collusion with the reigning power in order to secure a decent living. "In the 1980s a graduate like me would have a car. But now it's difficult to make ends met. You have knowledge, but there are no openings. If you strive, you should be given a chance." A Nigerian architect, who is forced to buy expensive black-market gasoline in a country of vast natural oil reserves, expressed a similar view: "Why work for a pittance when you see a military man making $10 million a month because he has the power to award contracts? What's the motivation?" (Cohen, 1998e, p. 5). Both men perceive their downward mobility as representative of the vast majority of Nigerians, who remain poor in the midst of an abundance of natural resources and an elite opulence that has been created by Western values of consumerism and conspicuous consumption. Per capita income in the late 1990s is a quarter of what it was in the 1980s, mostly because of widespread mismanagement and corruption. The resulting sense of social injustice is extreme. These concerns are often articulated by Nigerians in private conversation, but usually become translated into terms of ethnic divisionism in the mainstream media.

In Nigeria, official abuse of power is most often motivated by the desire for personal aggrandizement. This mafia approach to governance can also extend to First World businesspeople who have focused on the military elite to sell their products. For instance, Theodore Luttwak operates a very lucrative marble tile company in Abuja that caters to the materialistic lifestyles of wealthy government officials. Although he is now aware of what is commonly phrased "the Nigerian factor," that is, the adroit use of bribery to move along all commercial trade, Luttwak once spent a term in jail for refusing to pay an official bribe. He now sells imported marble flooring for the new mansions of the ruling generals and other government officials. Luttwak expresses a political view quite different from most poor Nigerians. He sees the military elite as a disciplined and God-fearing Muslim caste, which stands in contrast to an unruly south. Despite his own abuse at the hands of the military, Luttwak identifies with his former oppressors, seeing his business interests tied to the endurance of the ruling elite. For such foreign business residents, democratic values are of little concern, in fact, moves towards social equality are perceived as harming their commercial connections with the wealthy.

Although Nigeria under the generals offers certain lucrative opportunities for Global Capital, at least within the limits of small to moderate-sized private businesses that target the tiny ruling elites, the country's economy as a whole has been devastated by political policies and costly civil strife. Nigeria has impressive reserves of granite and marble, as it does oil reserves, but official mismanagement has led these domestic industries to stagnation. Since state-owned factories are now practically idle, Nigeria is forced to import costly petroleum, granite, and marble, the latter two commodities supplied by First World middlemen such as Luttwak, whose Nigerian-born wife allows his business to pass as a domestic concern.

Responsible for the pervasive official corruption is the fabulously wealthy military elite. Perhaps the most obvious example of personal aggrandizement has been the Abacha family. Maryam, wife of the recently deceased dictator, was caught attempting to flee the country after her husband's death with eight suitcases full of cash. Estimates of the Abacha family fortune stand at over $3 billion, mostly secured in foreign bank accounts. Sani Abacha pillaged Nigeria for personal riches during his 5 years as ruler, but he was also as zealous as any other Nigerian dictator in violating human rights standards. He imprisoned or forced into exile journalists and advocates across the board, including Nigeria's Nobel laureate. The most publicized instance of such abuse was his execution of the community activist and playwright Ken Saro-Wiwa, who had achieved a sufficient international reputation to gain the attention of the First World mainstream media in 1996. Although Abacha promised new elections in 1994, he soon jailed anyone who spoke out against him or doubted his promise. His vice president and several high-ranking generals were dismissed or jailed, often dying mysteriously in detention. Abiola's senior wife, Kudirat, an outspoken critic of Abacha, was executed on a Lagos street in 1996 by a six-man goon squad (Kaufman, 1998). Such actions were influenced by ideological opposition that went beyond resentment of Abacha's personal rule. For example, Saro-Wiwa's death directly followed his advocacy of social equality and the distribution of Nigeria's oil profits with the people in local communities.

Government violence against freedom of expression permeated Nigerian society. Goon squads were supplemented by spies on every street corner, to the extent that well-known investigative journalists had to keep constantly on the move, preparing their copy in taxis and back alleys to avoid detection (Dare, 1998). Abacha's disregard for basic political rights forced him to maintain his power at all costs, making the proposed elections mere window dressing. Kola Ilori, editor of the weekly *Tell*, commented, "Abacha has desecrated the military, he has desecrated the office of head of state, he has also deeply offended the north. It is hard to see how a man like that could safely retire" (French, 1998a). In fact, two months later, Abacha died suddenly of "heart failure," although conspiracies against his life were frequently discovered originating from the top military command throughout the last year of his rule.

ACHIEVING PROGRESSIVE CHANGE

In the 1970s, Nigerians proudly proclaimed their country "the largest Black nation in the world." Then it ranked 33rd among all countries of the world in per capita income. By the late 1990s, it had descended to the 13th-poorest state. Its infant mortality rate is more than 10 times that of the United States and its life expectancy average is 54 years. More than half of Nigerian women are illiterate, and the 1996 inflation rate is 57 percent. With the death of Abiola, Nigeria seemed once again firmly in the hands of the military elite. Moreover, international organizations and unilateral diplomacy have offered the Nigerian people little hope for progressive change. UN General Secretary Kofi Annan advised Ariola in prison not to run for a second election if he were released, and members of the Nigerian opposition know that Washington's foreign policy is more concerned with Nigeria's oil, which the U.S. invests heavily in, than with democracy (French, 1998c; Reuters, 1998a). Neither the U.K. nor the U.S. has pressed the Nigerian government for an investigation into the 1993 election scandal. Moreover, the 1995 execution of Ken Saro-Wiwa, punished for exposing the relationship between Shell Oil Corporation and the Nigerian regime, and the involvement of Chevron, the giant U.S. oil corporation, in the 1998 killing of two activists in the Nigerian delta area demonstrated to Nigerian villagers that the Nigerian military performs necessary executions for transnational oil in the country ("Drilling and Killing," 1998). Under such circumstances, what efforts can achieve long-term democratic change?

Clearly, what has been categorized by First World journalism as "ethnic" or "tribal conflict" in Nigeria is much more complex, involving issues of poverty, class differences, violations of press freedom, pervasive government corruption, and more. In this regard, descriptions of Nigeria's post-colonial predicament closely parallels recent First World discourse about the Horn of Africa, where Ethiopia's "ethnic conflicts" turn out under scrutiny to be economically based. Although the Ethiopian government has been consistently labeled "Shoan domination," the vast majority of Shoan Amharas were as poor, powerless, and exploited as any other group in the country (Assefa, 1996). Thus, the "ethnic conflict" was really "elite-driven" conflict, to borrow Hizkias Assefa's phrase. This inadequate and misleading reportage was accepted so readily by First World news institutions perhaps because it does not threaten world power relations as much as does journalism that explores the common economic roots of conflict in Africa. Accordingly, the first step for positive change in Nigeria—and in many parts of Africa today—is for the various groups to recognize their common needs, concerns, and complaints. This may involve using discourse that affirms rather than discourages commonality. The second step is to consider critically the sources of information about ethnic divisionism. What Assefa (1996) observes about Ethiopia and the Sudan can be applied to Nigeria's current situation:

> It is true that [the Horn of Africa's] ethnic groups have their own prejudices and stereotypes about each other. But these attitudes have not normally turned into conflict at the people-to-people level unless manipulated and organized by political leaders. Elites find ethnic prejudices and stereotypes fertile ground in which they can easily cultivate support for their political and economic aspirations. Expressing their objectives in ethnic and nationality terms (such as "advancing the interest of our own people" or "protecting ourselves from another ethnic group") ennobles their pursuits and gives them more legitimacy. (p. 39)

Fostering a sense of common rootedness does not preclude the affirmation of the particularities of each group's values and sense of origin. The fundamental question then becomes how to honor the particularities of group values while instilling broader definitions that can accommodate others. How much of the "self" in group "self-determination" is consociational, involving connectivities for all human beings? Perhaps the answer for Nigeria and all countries in the future is a new form of federalism that recognizes unity within diversity and acts towards the building and maintenance of an economic and political commonwealth. The result of such endeavors may well call for the dismantling or fundamental restructuring of existing social structures, such as Global Capital, religious fundamentalism, gender and race hierarchies, and so on. For Nigeria, the most immediate task will involve establishing long-term freedom of expression as a fundamental human right. Such freedom is institutional and must precede democratic change.

QUESTIONS FOR FURTHER THOUGHT

1. How can the African states establish an active and long-term cooperative organization that addresses the particular human rights needs of the continent?
2. What obstacles prevent such an organization from being efficacious and enduring? How much responsibility lies with First World organizational actions?
3. Given the great diversity of ethnic and linguistic groups in Nigeria, how can values that emphasize commonality be introduced? Will such ideals interfere with efforts at group identity and cohesion?
4. How can First World foreign policy change to allow Nigeria to enter a period of prosperity with social equality and other human rights standards?
5. How do the ruling systems of other countries foster an "us versus them" way of thinking that distracts their populace from recognizing the underlying causes of social injustice? Does this work the same way in the United States?

9

CONGO: BOUNDARIES OF HUMAN RIGHTS

As Nigeria and Ethiopia face the ambiguities of class conflict as it has been translated into regional and ethnic divisionism by its political leaders and mainstream media, other African peoples face ethnic conflict along national borders. These demarcations were originally imposed by European colonizers and then retained by post-colonial African governments. The crisis in the Congo (formerly Zaire), Rwanda, and, to a lesser degree, Uganda in the late 1990s is representative of the persistence of internal group conflict as against the yet unrealized goal of pan-African economic and political unity. Attempts at African cooperation, the forging a "South/South" trading agreement, the establishment of a meaningful trans-African higher court of appeals, and greater political and military coordination have reached the planning stage among representatives from most of the African states in recent decades, but thus far the region has not been able to actualize these resolutions. This chapter will examine the current conflicts in the Congo and Rwanda from the perspective of human rights and social equality. The recent progress towards inter-African problem solving will also be discussed, especially as it applies to the current struggle for sub-Saharan Africa's economic, social, and political viability. In doing so, it will be necessary to examine the reasons for

Africa's continued inability to achieve a vital regional commonwealth that will protect human rights and move towards democratic standards. The formidable economic and political forces, both internal and external to the region, which have inhibited the realization of the rights guaranteed by the UN Bill of Rights—the UDHR (1948) and the two covenants, ICESCR and ICCPR (both 1966)—will be assessed as to their continued applicability to African democratic standards into the twenty-first century. The UN human rights response to the Congo/Rwanda crisis, characterized as feckless and lacking authority, is illustrative of the lack of interest among First World nations for the continent in general and the central African region in particular. This chapter will also look at the current performance of human rights IGOs (intergovernmental organizations) and NGOs in central Africa, given the region's low priority among the most powerful UN member nations.

EUROPEAN BOUNDARIES AND AFRICAN CONFLICT

The African interior became the last world region penetrated by the European colonial enterprise. With the Treaty of Berlin in 1884, the powers of Europe sliced the continent into many large and small pieces that conformed to no meaningful lines of geography or demographic distribution. Often the result of quite ephemeral diplomatic squabbles between the European states themselves, or the result of the state of technology at the time—especially such "empire-building" developments as the railroad and telegraph—the African colonial borders were realized without regard to the nature of the indigenous peoples living within and between its lines of demarcation. The result has been political confusion of a kind not evident in any other region of the world, with the possible exception of Southeast Asia, whose numerous cultures, languages, and religions is discussed in Chapter 13 in this volume. However, sub-Saharan Africa in the 20th century has remained the largest and most conflict-ridden region of ethnic diversity in the world.

Although many African political analysts, including recent post-colonialist critics and more traditional scholars, have despaired of African unification, serious attempts to discover strength in unity continue. The example of Mahatma Gandhi remains a source of hope for unity amidst what seems persistent and comprehensive factionalism. His notion of "soul force" as a means of achieving commonality among India's numerous ethnic and religious groups also proved a means to mobilize these groups towards political advocacy. The resulting unification of Hindu, Muslim, and numerous religious sects eventually won the prize of colonial independence. Gandhi's early experiences at mobilizing the disenfranchised in Africa was not lost on African thinkers. Cooperation for social advocacy in African can take many forms, and there has been no shortage of such planning, from crassroots organizations to subregional and regional institutional formations. However, lacking, at least in the early post-colonial period, has been the will to change colonial boundaries—both literal and figurative.

In 1963, the Organization of African Unity (OAU) reaffirmed as inviolate all borders of the then independent African states, frontiers that were established by the European colonizers. Its action was chiefly motivated by the belief that future disputes leading to wars for territory would be avoided. The decision was consistent with the mentality of the African elites who comprised the OAU during the first decade of enfranchisement. Not considered at the time were African cultural boundaries, which had little or no relation to European colonial borders. The question of which Africans would represent the independent African nations came into focus as the second post-colonial decade began. When the first generation of African leaders designed grand social schemes and vast infrastructural projects, progress was clearly achieved in the human rights areas of education, medicine, and increased freedom of mobility (Okigbo, 1993). However, beginning around 1982, the effects of this rapid and often misapplied investment began to fade (George, 1993). The social structure rigidified as foreign debt payments and financial restructuring, accompanied by harsh conditionalities, led to a general disregard for basic human rights standards, as for example in Nigeria (see Chapter 8, in this volume).

First World economic systems were directly involved in the grand investment schemes managed by African governing elites of the early post-colonial period. Europeans were still setting boundaries for Africans, this time along economic lines. To fill the void of successful African-centered polity, more local organizing efforts were begun, not unlike the "small is beautiful" movement in the First World during the 1970s. These efforts appeared more or less spontaneously, in a decentered manner, for very practical and immediate goals. "One finds the striving of countless individuals and collectives towards new types of self-organization—perhaps one should say self-defense?—aimed in one way or another at operating outside the bureaucratic centralism of the neo-colonial state" (Davidson, 1993, p. 26). These grassroots organizations include farming associations, small industrial cooperatives, student organizations at all levels, artistic movements (especially noteworthy in Nigeria), and neighborhood religious benevolent organizations. In short, self-reliance often began at the local level—at the bottom, so to speak—and at times trickled upward, to universities, government bureaucratic planning, and so on. Certainly, these efforts at creating a thousand local lights have not been as successful in overcoming what Pius Okigbo describes as "the all-powerful nation state as the symbol of unlimited power" (p. 38). Still, most African post-colonial regimes in the 1990s received increasing pressure from regional and local human rights organizations. The emergence of democratic awareness—through mass education and growing access to electronic and print media—alongside mounting social debt and governmental misrule has motivated the expansion of NGOs and their networks worldwide. Although many of these nongovernmental initiatives are confined to a limited set of issues and range across the political spectrum from environmentalism to feminism to religous fundamentalism, human rights NGOs have recently been able to challenge regime authority, demanding accountability and forthright disclosure. Thus, the use of civic discourse for democratic change in Africa has been the result both of immediate economic/political necessity and of an increased popular awareness of social alternatives to the colonial legacy of the nation state.

Although post-colonial Africans have had limited successes organizing at the local level, there has been less success organizing beyond the nation state. As the North has moved beyond the age of economic nationalism to the new transnational economic order (Global Capital), and Asia has begun to move in a similar direction of "South/South" economic cooperation, sub-Saharan African economic cooperation has remained nugatory or merely at the theoretical level. In fact, the organizing structure for increasing regional cooperation in sub-Saharan Africa has been in place since the early 1990s. Postcolonial African thinkers have been clear about the direction the continent needs to take in order to overcome its legacy of First World dependence. Adebayo Adedeji (1993) often has articulated this trajectory as it affects democratic freedom, equality, and self-development: "the OAU had to play a much greater role in preventing and resolving conflicts on the continent; also, priority should be given to more effective and immediate subregional and regional integration between and among African countries" (p. 11).

This intra-African integration was conceived within the context of the newly forged treaty of the African Economic Community (AEC), which was adopted by the OAU in Abuja in 1991. The treaty was accompanied by many high-level meetings of scholars, policymakers, and NGO representatives, most importantly at the African Centre for Development and Strategic Studies (ACDESS) Conference, held in Dakar, Senegal in November 1992 and attended by over 80 prominent post-colonial figures from Africa and other continents. The direction of the 3-day meeting was succinctly stated by Mahmood Mamdani (1992), "We must question the assumption that 'self-determination' must mean, in the final analysis, independent states" (p. 317). The conference recognized that centralized national power must give way at once to a devolved power of grassroots democracy together with a regional cooperation that transcended national boundaries. Behind the strategizing was the prioritizing of social and political human rights standards. ACDESS was perceived as playing a significant leadership role in this direction.

The discourse toward greater African cooperation has not been dogmatic about relinquishing the nation states originally authorized by colonialism. Rather, the plan has been to integrate existing national, subregional, and regional power towards more effective regulation of human rights standards:

> Artificially created African nation states are at grave risk of disintegration unless some higher "nationality," in the form of economic integration, is put before them to animate their cohesion. The obvious lesson is that the future of Africa lies in national and collective self-reliance and regional integration, and in popular participation in

political decision making at the national, subregional and regional levels. (Okigbo, 1993, p. 38)

In this regard, focus has been given to economic reform programs that are congruent with long-term development policies at all these levels of polity. This will require changes in the new lifestyles that were adopted by much of the African populace as they have been directed by what Michael Manley (1991) has aptly described as the "hemorrhage of consumerism" (p. 63). These long-term policies would purposefully mobilize higher levels of savings and investment towards human development and indigenous production areas (Rasheed, 1993). In Nigeria, for example, this would mean local investment for educational, health, and housing, but also for the cement, marble, and oil reserves that the land possesses in abundance and that presently remains in the hands of TNCs like Shell Oil and of indigenous ruling elites.

Alongside this movement toward social solutions within the African region by Africans has been the recognition, from bitter experience, that the presence of democratic forms and rituals are not enough without progressive economic and social change. Timothy M. Shaw (1993) sees this change as fundamental to future democratic standards: "[I]nternational concern with 'human rights' as well as human needs, women and development, and sustainable development...has also developed away from notions of formal democracy towards those of democratic development or popular participation" (p. 89). However, "multiparty" national political life, regional and subregional organizations for human rights and standards of social equality, and effective international institutions, such as the United Nations and World Court, can easily turn to a superficial acceptance of business as usual, as in the case of the Congo (Zaire) under Mobutu, who spoke multipartyism but practiced oppression.

In the 1990s, the commitments made within the framework of the UN Program of Action for African Economic Recovery and Development (UNPAAERD) were generally unfulfilled. Given the decreasing interest in sub-Saharan Africa among individual First World nations and the United Nations (Economic Commission for Africa, ECA), the outlook for democratic development seems to depend upon Africans themselves. Following the AEC treaty signing in Abuja, the September 1992 Jakarta Message from the Non-Aligned Movement (NAM) underscored the need for Southern self-assertion. The African Development Bank (ADB) was established to begin a regional economic sphere akin to similar efforts in Southeast Asia (see Chapter 12, in this volume). Also, a crucial noneconomic step has been taken by the ECA and OAU secretariats involving the African Leadership Forum under Gen. Olusegun Obasanjo, which would establish peacekeeping, security, and "stability" on the continent. The use of French troops in the 1990s to stop further killing of Hutu by Tutsi reprisal units, although tardy and undertaken reluctantly, perhaps saved tens of thousands of African lives. The fact the President Clinton was unwilling to send American troops—or even to authorize African soldiers—to a geopolitically insignificant area (Rwanda and eastern Congo) underscored the need for such an African peacekeeping force. Beyond the immediate humanitarian needs for such a more responsive regional force, other human rights standards would also be supported by African peacekeeping actions. National dictators would be less likely to persecute minorities within its borders—or to follow minorities across borders—if a strong regional enforcement presence were available. To this end, the 1992 Summit of the OAU in Dakar worked to eatablish its own security mechanism for "preventing, managing and resolving conflicts in Africa" (Rasheed, 1993, p. 48). It remained, however, only at the planning stage and was unavailable for the genocidal tragedy in Rwanda later in the 1990s. The inability of sub-Saharan African nations to establish such political and military cooperation has thrown them back on the mercy of their former European colonizing states.

On the economic side, the program of the South Commission included developing human resources, coordinating financing with democratic goals, establishing a debtors' forum for Third, Fourth, and Fifth World nations, founding a South Bank, promoting South-South trade, commodities management, business links between Southern nations, and planning for food security and distribution (South Commission, 1990). Other organizations worked along parallel lines in the early 1990s, such as the South Centre (1992) and the Group of 15, which also sought to circumvent the shrinking investment dollars from the North. It is by no means certain whether such institutions will be able to overcome the centripetal pull of Global Capital, and efforts such as the AEC treaty have had notable predecessors, such as the Lagos Plan of Action, that ended in failure. As Sadig Rasheed (1993) observed:

> Progress towards regional economic integration has been thwarted by the dominant outward links of the African economies, the strong sense of affiliation to different monetary zones, unwillingness to relinquish national sovereignty over economic and social matters, adherence to SAPs which make cross-border coordination more difficult, and the similarity of economic structures. (pp. 46–47)

The power of SAPs in Africa is understood when it is realized that institutions such as the World Bank and the IMF have more influence over health and education planning in these countries than do the UN World Health Organization (WHO) and UNESCO. Moreover, while the First World and the NICs has abandoned the era of economic nationalism in favor of transnational capital—through such institutions as the World Bank, IMF, GATT, the Tripartite Commission, and numerous TNCs—the North still insists on retaining this obsolete structure for Africa. To overcome the international economic structures that perpetuate the old nation-state arrangement requires strong national and regional institutions that function as guardians of democracy rather than merely upholders of formal democratic structures. These needs have been forcefully articulated by Africa's most prominent thinkers, discussed and acknowledged at regional and continental meetings, like the May 1991 Africa Leadership Forum in Kampala, where Adebeyo Adedeji spoke of formalizing African cooperation for development. Beyond the need to be vigilant about human rights development is the requirement for an established South/South trading organization, between southern continents but especially within sub-Saharan Africa. These economic and political goals will remain illusive unless the African peoples are able to unite to overcome the group divisionism that has been encouraged by the legacy of colonialism and post-colonial regimes.

At the center of this discourse is the project of defining development, which has been conceived in democratic terms rather than as profit-oriented trajectories. Ian Roxborough (1979) offers a perhaps too succinct definition that approximates this thinking: development in the Third World is "an increase in the capacity for controlled transformation of the social structure" (p. 71). Such transformations, however, must be affirming of human rights and other democratic values, not negative, as in Nigeria, Rwanda, and the Congo during the 1990s. Positive transformation remains part of the decolonization process in these and other African countries.

Overcoming the dictates of Global Capital and its international institutions means for these African countries abandoning the assumption of "Industrialization by Invitation," which assumes that, "if a country has to achieve the necessary capital formation from within its own internal processes, it may wait forever. Therefore, the key to capital formation is the attraction of foreign capital" (Manley, 1991, p. 75). What Africans have proposed for the new century is a middle way between this binary formula. Economic and democratic cooperation between nations within a common region or subregion is this new middle way. Actually, seminal work in transforming the North to South direction of economic power began as far back as the Bandung Conference in 1955, which launched the Non-Aligned Movement (NAM). This association has sometimes been termed the New International Economic Order (NIEO), not to be confused with President George Bush's "New World Order" and other uses of the words "internationalism" and "transnationalism." In 1973, the Algiers Summit's Action Program gave detailed expression to the Southern self-reliance movement. In 1974, these ideas were adopted by the 29th General Assembly of the UN, where it was called The Charter of Economic Rights and Duties of States. Also within the UN at the same time was the formation of the Group of 77, which coordinated Third World interests within the UN decision-making arenas. Efforts at creating the Common Fund for what is now described as the Fourth and Fifth Worlds—groups of countries than have not developed to the extent of certain Third World states—have met with stiff opposition from First World powers—at the Lome Convention in 1975, for example—and has since found little advancement (Manley, 1991).

THE CONGO AND RWANDA: WHITHER HUMAN RIGHTS?

Rwandan leaders have been outraged with the United Nations since 1994, when the United States prevented the UN Security Council from sending peacekeeping forces to prevent the genocide of half a million or more Tutsi by their fellow Hutu Rwandans. In 1998, a UN human rights fact-gathering team in the eastern Congo was so impeded by Congo President Laurent Kabila that it had to leave early. That team, sent by UN Secretary General Kofi Annan, submitted their report to the UN Security Council, which chose to take no action on evidence that thousands of Hutu refugees in the eastern Congo were killed by troops under Congo and Rwandan control. The Hutu had fled Rwanda to avoid reprisals for the Hutu-dominated government's murder of Tutsi and Hutu sympathizers in 1994. Reports of human rights violations on a large scale continue to flow out of the region in 1998. Even more, the United Nations closed its local human rights office at the request of the Tutsi-led Rwandan government, which also snubbed Kofi Annan on his 1998 Rwandan visit.

First World Response: "Stability over Accountability"

This continued inaction led Amnesty International to excoriate the Washington-dominated Security Council in July 1998: "It is extraordinary for the Security Council to have abdicated its responsibility and for it to expect the very authorities which have been identified as being responsible for such horrendous atrocities to bring the perpetrators to justice." Reed Brody, advocacy director of Human Rights Watch, observed that in the Congo, "we see a real regional retreat" by the U.S.-dominated West, which had chosen stability over accountability:

> Concern about security in the region is trumping human rights when in fact the protection of people is the key to stability. Look at the Congo, where you have a United Nations team saying crimes against humanity have been committed. Yet the Security Council can't muster the political will to act. Clearly many members have ties to the governments that are implicated and don't want to see human rights concerns weaken those governments. (qtd. in Crossette, 1998a, p. A4)

International human rights groups soon linked the fate of the UN Congo inquiry to the U.S. position at a 1998 conference in Rome that established the International Criminal Court. There Washington policymakers argued strongly for Security Council control over the selection of issues to be passed on to a court judging those accused of genocide and war crimes. The rights groups pointed out that the aborted Congo investigation was precisely the sort of case the Council may face, and that its inaction in the central African region did not argue well for the U.S. position. Washington has favored the present Rwandan government and appears to place human rights issues behind perceived "national interests."

United Nations reluctance to intervene for human rights causes in the region also happened earlier in the decade, when the Hutu massacres of Tutsi and other sympathizers reached genocidal proportions in Rwanda. The United States had prevented Security Council action then as well. It was a decision for which President Clinton apologized in Rwanda on his 1998 tour of Africa: "We did not immediately call these crimes by their rightful name: genocide" (qtd. in Reuters, 1998c, p. 8). But Herman Cohen, former U.S. Assistant Secretary of State for African Affairs, has charged the Clinton administration with more than incorrect word usage. Before a French parliamentary committee he sharply criticized the failure of the U.S. to intervene in the mass killings in 1994. The U.S. halted the UN from sending 5,000 African troops, who may have prevented most of the killing. "After the earlier killing of American soldiers in Somalia, I could understand there was no question of sending American troops to Africa, but I could not accept the United States opposing the sending of African troops. After all, an African farmer is not going to cut off his neighbor's head if a foreign soldier is nearby looking on." The haste of French troops, although tardy, "was the only effort made to save Tutsi lives" (Reuters, 1998c, p. 8). Cohen estimated that the French 1994 operation had saved from 20,000 to 40,000 lives. In addition, he mentioned a 1990 French intervention in Rwanda that also saved lives.

The lack of interest in central Africa by the world's most powerful geopolitical player has weakened the effectiveness of UN peacekeeping operations and even human rights fact-gathering efforts. When Congo President Kabila prevented further investigation of killing in the eastern Congo refugee camps, the UN was unable to pressure him to allow its team to stay. The unfairness of a Security Council, which remains highly selective about which human rights violations to pursue and which to leave, has hindered progressive development in sub-Saharan Africa as much as in Southeast Asia. The retreat of UN enforcement of its own standards set forth in the International Bill of Human Rights can only be the responsibility of its member states, and particularly the powerful permanent members of the Security Council. Under these circumstances, human rights advocates may well worry that the new UN International Criminal Court will be just as discriminatory in its selection of perpetrators to try. After the Rome organizational meeting for the new court, the Security Council was left with the power to delay proceedings but not prevent them. This was over the objections of Washington, which wanted the Security Council to control which issues of war crimes and genocide would be turned over to the new court. U.S. attitudes towards sub-Saharan Africa again seemed negative, if not callous, after the August 1998 U.S. embassy bombing in Kenya, where U.S. troops sent by Clinton were widely perceived as ignoring the buried bodies of 247 Kenyans in favor of uncovering the 12 Americans who died (Bonner, 1998).

Recent Events: Repeating Postcolonial History

Laurent Kabila, who overthrew the unpopular dictator Mobutu Sese Seko in 1997 to become President of the Congo, still found himself entangled in the political fallout of his victory. In July 1998, he ordered the immediate end to the presence in his country of the Rwandan army, which had played a key role in the Mobutu overthrow and supported Kabila's rise to the presidency. Kabila used the Rwandan military in the Congo to deter external attacks and as a buffer between rival factions in the fragile new Congo army. Kabila's army reflected the ethnic instability of his own regime. Its disparate elements included *Banyamulenge*—Congolese of Tutsi extraction; former separatist "gendarmes" from Kabila's native Shaba province in the southern Congo; reintegrated soldiers from the defeated Zairian army; and a varied group of new recruits from the eastern Congo. Kabila won much needed applause from the local population, who resented what was perceived as the conquering arrogance of the foreign Rwandan troops. Kabila faced an ongoing crisis of support from within the Congo and among the complicated relationships he forged with neighboring countries during his rise to power. Equally threatening his regime was the increasing loss of First World diplomatic support.

The Congo's Justice Minister warned the populace against a Tutsi witch-hunt, threatening severe punishment for anyone inciting ethnic hatred or harming either foreign civilian Tutsi or native *Banyamulenge*. For their part, the Congolese Tutsi resented the lack of gratitude and compensation the Kabila government offered them after their allied victory (Wallis, 1998).

At the same time, ethnic tensions were exacerbated by international tensions in the African Great Lakes district of Rwanda and Uganda. Although the Tutsi-dominated government of Rwanda and Uganda still officially supported the Kabila government they helped into existence, they became increasingly impatient with Kabila's passive behavior towards the numerous rebel groups and refugee bases in Congo's eastern border regions that include Rwandan Hutu fighting Rwanda's Tutsi-led government. The Rwandan government's chief motivation for backing Kabila's defeat of Mobutu was the understanding that he would assist in eliminating the Hutu refugee and rebel camps inside his borders. Apparently, the allied drive against the Mobutu regime spent most of its time destroying Hutu camps in the countryside, often with women, children and other noncombatants. After Kabila's victory, he kept thousands of Tutsi Rwandans in his army, this time to stabilize—or at least balance—ethnic tensions among its rank and file.

Instead of leaving on Kabila's request, the Rwandan soldiers mutinied in August 1998, beginning in eastern Congo cities and even in the capital, Kinshasa. Tutsi elements began the rebellion, but the rhetoric of their leaders included strong human rights language. The commander of the 10th Battalion of Congo's army, Sylvain Mbuchi, identified himself as a rebel leader saying that Kabila must be removed because of "nepotism, corruption and bad government" (qtd. in French, 1998d, p. 1). Rebellious troops entered a prison and freed prisoners jailed in a previous mutiny. The Congolese majority interpreted Kabila's frantic radio talk of "the enemy" as the Tutsi ethnic group, which many consider more Rwandan than

Congolese. Fearing witch hunts against the Tutsi, Kabila's Foreign Minister and the Presidential Affairs Minister, both Tutsi, fled the country.

Kabila's loyalty to the Tutsi, who selected him to head the forces against Mobutu, was the rallying point for many Congolese. Before the Tutsi raised him, Kabila had been for decades an underachieving guerrilla fighter from an obscure area of the Congo. The actual fighting against Mobutu was done mostly by Rwandan army units and Tutsi trained by Rwanda and Uganda. The refugee camps the Tutsi wished to eliminate housed more than a million Rwandan Hutu, who fled to avoid reprisals for the Rwandan genocide of Tutsi in 1994. Hutu groups were reportedly using the camps as bases to mount attacks against the new Tutsi government in Rwanda. Kabila resented being associated with the massacre of thousands of Hutu refugees during the 7-month drive to overthrow Mobutu. Aware of the 1999 elections, Kabila attempted to separate himself from the foreign troops and governments that brought him to power. The Rwanda and Uganda governments became impatient with Kabila's inaction against the Hutu camps and his increasing nationalistic language. One African diplomat remarked, "[The Congo] is the most complicated of African puzzles, and holding the capital is a far cry from governing" (qtd. in French, 1998d, p. A6).

Complicated as it may be, but Kabila exhibited traits of the previous dictator, Mobutu, whose "political aristocracy" reigned in the Congo (Zaire) for over three decades. After discharging his Tutsi military commanders, Kabila appeared for photo opportunities and nationalistic speeches accompanied by the same Mobutu commanders he had fought against for three decades (French, 1998e, p. A5). Once vilified, they were now offered as potential saviors of Congolese nationalism. During his rule of slightly over one year, Kabila has left his human rights promises largely unfulfilled. He has found the legacy of Mobutu hard to shake off, and there was no time to begin fundamental social change as the rebel forces began to encircle the capital in mid-August 1998. Mobutu's rule had become typical of central African polity in the age of transnational capital. As in Nigeria, the Congo's social structure has been defined by a post-colonial political aristocracy centered around a highly centralized state that functions solely for the self-aggrandizement of its elite members. Unlike Nigeria, however, the Congo's centralized state has not been identified with a particular ethnic group, grouping, or region. Instead, a cult of personality became the centripetal force that, on the one hand, melded the country's diverse ethnic groups, and, on the other, channeled the foreign investment and aid capital from a variety of separate but loosely associated First World institutions.

Congolese society has not possessed a class-based politics, (as in Latin America) but rather what might be described as a system of authoritarianism. The political economy of the Congo seems more akin to early modern neomercantilism. That is, its ruling group has not been a multiclass coalition, as in Latin America, but possesses "patrimonial forms of rulership and politics overlaid by pseudoconstitutional forms of government" (Callaghy, 1987, p. 101). Loyalty to Mobutu was the entree to the political aristocracy. His cult of personality was not unlike that of

France's Louis XIV, except that the various groups of elite were post-colonial and outwardly oriented to Global Capital. The political aristocracy of the Congo is transethnic in character, comprising a tenuous collection of competing groups and regions. It has demonstrated little concern for public service and the collective good. In the age of Third World development, the Congolese political aristocracy must have social "projects" for the people of its nominal democracy. However, these have been nothing more than what Frederick Cooper (1981) succinctly describes as "the ruling class's project of self-aggrandizement combined with enough redistribution to maintain its tenuous and vital hold on the state" (p. 46).

Given the renewed urge for democratic values, local governance, and regional cooperation among African human rights advocates, political initiatives in the 21st century must overcome the post-colonial aristocracies that have managed to hold power within a transnational corporate world. This undertaking is formidable and requires above all the enlistment of the populace for democratic agendas and the search for an adequate discourse of commonality in a multiethnic society.

QUESTIONS FOR FURTHER THOUGHT

1. Given Ian Roxborough's definition of development for the Third World, "an increase in the capacity for controlled transformation of the social structure," what steps might be necessary in the Congo to replace its cult of personalism and foreign investment support with democratic values?

2. The Non-Aligned Movement (NAM) vision of South/South trading organizations has had only limited success since it emerged in the 1955 Bandung Conference. How can such cooperation between poor countries of the South be achieved given resistance from First World states and trading associations?

3. The United Nation's lack of response to the mass violence in Rwanda, the Congo, and Indonesia in the 1990s has been tied to the relatively low geopolitical significance of these areas for its important Security Council members. Could there be other reasons as well why the United States and perhaps other First World powers are reluctant to involve themselves with human rights in these countries?

4. To what extent may race (or color prejudice) play a part in the reluctance of the North to respond more quickly to documented charges of genocide and other tragedies in the South?

5. In what ways would it be to the advantage of TNCs to retain a political aristocracy in countries such as Nigeria, the Congo, Angola, and Indonesia?

10

GENOCIDE IN RWANDA: HUMAN RIGHTS RETREAT

In 1994, central Africa's trust in the peacekeeping potential of the United Nations and other international organizations was shaken. Their tardy response to the great numbers who perished during the genocide that year by the Hutu-dominated Rwandan government seemed to reflect an international lack of concern for human rights in the region. The slaughter left at the very least half a million Rwandans dead and far more homeless or otherwise dispossessed. For most African advocates of human rights at the end of the twentieth century, the First World retreat in the face of such obvious wholesale murder brought home the pervasive reality of human rights in the age of Global Capital—the center-periphery paradigm of what used to be dubbed "the West and the rest" and is today more accurately called "the North and the South." The North is at the center of this model while the South remains at the periphery in problematic pursuit of economic development to become self-reliant, if not fully self-sufficient. Thus far, however, as the lack of response of OAU member nations to the genocide in Rwanda reveals, the centrifugal force of the world's marginalized countries has been too weak and disunited to break free their orbit economically and politically.

Chapter 9 examined the continued dominance of Congo's "political aristocracy" as intermediaries of transnational corporations and global finance. Mobutu's long reign and the brief reign of Kabila perpetuated the legacy of exploitation begun by the hierarchy of colonial social structures. If it is true of the world today, as Michael Manley (1991) has put it, that "the centre was built through exploitative relationships with the periphery" (p. 69), and that this central exploitative group of nations left in charge the same aristocratic structure that persists in most of sub-Saharan Africa today, then it should come as no surprise that the former colonizing nations may be reluctant to come to the rescue of what they perceive as a struggle between their anointed successors and other former colonial peoples. The Hutu-led government in Rwanda has been replaced by a Tutsi-dominated government, which has sought violent redress for the 1994 genocide. Conversely, Hutu "rebels" frequently have crossed international borders to inflict retaliatory raids on Rwandan soil. Chapter 9 discussed the criticism by human rights advocates of the UN and in particular the United States in their indifference to the genocides of 1994 and earlier. This chapter will examine other avenues of international human rights advocacy for the region. It will also present the discourse of human rights as it has been shaped by the tragedy within Rwanda, a violent history that remains ongoing at the time of this writing. Ways to overcome the persistent denial of human rights at both the national and international levels will be explored in light of the social and political circumstances of Rwanda in the 1990s.

GENOCIDE AND ITS CONSEQUENCES

Selective Human Rights

When a government favored by First World economic interests is overthrown by a popular revolution—as opposed to a mere rebellion of an elite faction—the First World response is often to change, perhaps reluctantly, in the direction of acknowledging the old regime's human rights abuses that it has heretofore overlooked. A good instance of this delayed response occurred after the fall of the Suharto regime in 1998. When it became obvious to the United States that its former and most-favored ruler was overthrown and the mainstream media was no longer silent about long-term human rights abuses under his control, Washington undertook, however tentatively, a discourse of human rights. What quickly followed was the withdrawal of Indonesian troops from East Timor and the resumption of negotiations for that country's release from its 1975 takeover by the Suharto government (Crossette, 1998b). The UN also renewed its human rights advocacy. Secretary General Kofi Annan went to Portugal to talk with the government of East Timor's former colonizer, which had abandoned its possession in 1974 with no defense against local predatory powers.

On the other hand, member states of the UN can move to economic "most favored" status among First World powers when their policies conform to the needs of TNCs and international lending institutions. A 1990s example of this occurred when the United States changed direction and began playing down human rights violations in China (PRC). As the PRC opened its door more fully to TNCs during the 1980s and especially the 1990s, U.S. foreign policy offered China a Most Favored Nation status, despite loud protests from international human rights groups. Washington was willing to overlook those human rights abuses in China that involved workplace rights and conditions, organized labor guarantees, environmental damage, and safety regulations because an unregulated workforce appealed to Global Capital. During the 1998 China Summit, President Clinton mentioned only political human rights abuses, most notably the lack of freedom of speech, but stayed clear of violations involving worker rights and social equality (see Chapter 13, in this volume). Clinton was even advised to stay away from tours of new TNC factories during the China visit so as not to draw international attention to working conditions in the PRC.

Under such circumstances, international human rights groups remained skeptical about the ability of the new UN International Criminal Court to try perpetrators of war crimes and genocide. In fact, the United States had argued strongly at its 1998 planning meeting in Rome to retain control, through the UN Security Council, in which it had permanent veto power, of who was brought before the new court. In the end, the Rome meeting allowed the Security Council to delay, but not prevent, who should be tried.

If First World powers are influenced by self-serving motives when they consider human rights issues, and if their mainstream media remain largely compliant with their selection of which issues to denounce, can international organizations be relied upon to deal fairly with particular human rights abuses? While events such as the Pol Pot genocide in Cambodia have been given ample—if not accurate—coverage by the First World mainstream media, the genocide in East Timor (estimated at one quarter of the entire population of the country) and Rwanda (well over half a million, not including smaller genocides previous to 1994) have been typically underplayed or dismissed. In the main, investigative reporting, causal analysis, and detailed description of these and similar events unpopular with First World powers has not been attempted, except in academic journals of small circulation (see, for example, Pace, 1995b).

Motivation for Genocide

When confronted with mainstream reportage of the "ethnic fighting" in Rwanda and other parts of the continent, it is important to realize that other sources of group tension and competition may have an even greater motivating role in the genocide. In fact, the class basis of most contemporary African cultures remains a significant source of conflict (Newbury, 1988). Recent post-colonial scholars offer ample evidence of this in their new analyses of particular sub-Saharan ethnic groups and regions. However, perhaps the most compelling demonstration of this appears in the emerging African film industries. Ousmane Sembene, for example, represents deep class divisions throughout his films. In *Borom Sarret* (1962), a poor but hard-working Dakar cart driver has his livelihood confiscated when he wanders into a forbidden part of the city, a district known at the Plateau, built for the white colonizers but now inhabited by their appointed successors, the members of the new African ruling elite. The film's analysis of the bleak realities of urban life place social blame squarely upon the African class system (Sembene, 1972). In *Xala* (1974), Sembene directly confronts the rapacious mentality of the African petty bourgeoisie. In the Chamber of Commerce scene, resplendently dressed African businessmen convene around a table where white businessmen, who appear as mere advisors, offer them briefcases bulging with money. Visually, the political aristocracy of *Xala* are separated completely from the masses of Africans. Class differences are also evident in the scene where beggars are driven away from the doorsteps of the rich. In *Guelwaar* (1975), the heroic leader of a new democratic Senegal transcends cultural and religious boundaries. The theme of cross-cultural commonality is also evident in the voluntary cooperation of Christian and Islamic Senegalese at the end of the film (see Chapter 7, in this volume). Med Hondo's *Soleil o* (1970) depicts the harmful differences among Africans alongside typical justifications for racial segregation offered by white settlers. In these films, class hierarchies appear more significant than ethnic identities in the formation of post-colonial African society.

The significance of class in contemporary African society is compounded by the intermediary function of African elites within the world of transnational capital and First World aid programs. The programs of lending institutions like the World Bank have often increased class differences in the Third World (Payer, 1982). Also, the class with government power in Africa can directly determine the plight of refugees, many of whom, as in Rwanda, are not as purely of one ethnic group as the First World media often declare (Kibreab, 1985). Generally, the post-colonial ruling elites throughout much of Africa seem unable or unwilling to reduce the huge disparity in living standards between new urban and traditional rural dwellers (Nafziger, 1985).

Traditional agrarian practices in Africa have also been adversely affected by an enduring class inequality throughout the post-colonial period. Richard Franke (1987) found that among the Bouzou and Dogon societies, "the most positive environmental developments were maintained in societies where the producing classes had the greatest power and the ruling classes were either absent (Bouzou, Dogon) or had their power checked (Serer) or where their power was in process of disintegration (Dina)" (p. 275). Certainly, a disregard for the laborers of the land was characteristic of French colonial rule in West Africa, but groups such as the Hausa, Bambara, and Wolof sacrificed their fixed capital assets for the needs of a largely unproductive exploiting class. Franke concludes that a new way must be found to retain traditional methods of food production while incorporating new technology for greater yield. Such efforts have begun at the grassroots level in parts of Africa.

Africans have identified themselves as wage laborers and organized accordingly since the early decades of the 20th century. In Ghana during the 1930s, for example, workers began demanding not just wage increases but more favorable conditions of employment, sick leave, annual leave, and retirement provisions (Grier, 1987). African workers saw their occupations as long term and full time; they lived in adversarial relationship with their employers and in competition with the increasing numbers of rural poor who were seeking urban jobs. Similar forms of class competition has existed in parts of sub-Saharan Africa for most of the 20th century. In 1948, Ghana's Local Councils consisted of members elected from among local farmers and hereditary members, while the State Councils remained mostly hereditary. Such "reforms" within the colonial system gave limited recognition to the lower classes. Under this system, pawning continued as a form of debt payment and labor control. Ghana's committee on constitutional reform wrote blithely that it was important to retain "the existing community of interests" and the dominion of "customary law." Furthermore, "the social structure of a society should not be disturbed unduly" (qtd. in Grier, 1987, p. 48) The stage was set for the post-colonial perpetuation of a class structure which, although modified from traditional African social structures, depended upon a rural peasantry below and an urban elite above, with its supportive petty bourgeoisie. A class society developed throughout much of Africa that included remnants of traditional hierarchical rule. Its economic existence depended upon an intermediary relationship with Global Capital and international lending institutions, which also gave it justification as a nonproducing class.

Rwanda: 1964, 1990, 1994

In 1964, after the election of a republican government dominated by Hutu with some Tutsi cabinet members and administrators, a Tutsi guerrilla group invaded Rwanda. The nervous government of Gregoire Kayibanda saw the movement collapse, executed many Tutsi government officials, and encouraged local massacres of thousands of Tutsi. These actions were justified through discourse which stressed a corporate views of ethnicity: all Tutsi were "brothers" and therefore responsible for the attempted coup. With the more formidable invasion of the RPF in 1990, the same pattern was repeated. The Habyarimana government jailed more than 9,000 Rwandans, mostly Tutsi and others who were known to oppose the regime. Many prisoners died in prison from mistreatment and harsh conditions, but most were eventually released under protest from an incipient human rights movement within Rwanda and pressure from outside donors. The Hutu regime constantly articulated a scapegoat discourse in its media, premised on the notion that all Tutsi must support the invasion. Government propaganda overwhelmed arguments for universal understanding set forth by human rights groups, who stressed the commonality of all Rwandans. Thus, the same essentialist argument for an absolute difference between Hutu and Tutsi underlay the 1964 persecutions and reappeared a generation later in reaction to the RPF incursion of 1990.

Under the Hutu-dominated government of President Juvenal Habyarimana, Tutsi and other groups continued out of favor in Rwanda. Following Habyarimana's assassination in April 1994, ethnic massacres began against government "enemies," most of whom were Tutsi, other ethnic groups, and government opponents. Hutu militias entered rural villages on daily killing sprees, often taking money bribes not to kill beyond certain quotas. The extreme terror lasted for four months, until the Tutsi-led Rwanda Patriotic Front (RPF) took the capital, Kigali, and regained power. Experts estimate anywhere from 500,000 to 1 million died during that brief period. The perpetrators were Hutu militia groups, regular Rwandan army units, and occasionally neighbors and local enemies. One year later, mass graves littered the countryside, some so shallow that bodily remains were visible.

Under the new Tutsi-dominated government, human rights investigators were allowed into the country. The government began a human rights discourse with the goal of stabilizing their political power in a country fraught with factionalism. Although it professed interest in bringing those responsible for the massacres to justice by imploring the international community for help, human rights investigators were too few and hindered by lack of basic necessities for their work, such as transport to move through rural areas and translators for interviews. At that time the UN promised Rwandans that the mass killings would be referred to a new international tribunal to try cases of genocide, but by 1998 the International Criminal Court for genocide was still in the planning stages. With the Tutsi in power, mass killing began against the Hutu. This time the violence occurred chiefly in the eastern Congo, where a million refugees were living, mostly in inadequate camps surrounding the city of Goma. Eighty percent of the population in these camps were women and children. The killing began in July 1995, when the new Rwandan army used artillery on unarmed civilians, including women and children. Many Hutu were killed in the stampede to escape the falling shells. The refugees covered every alley, street, and square in Goma, until they were moved out of town to makeshift camps. Diseases such as cholera appeared only after a few days. Within a few weeks, over 50,000 would die from disease in the filthy camps. International assistance was behindhand. Food, potable water, and medical treatment were not available for months. By then, the camps were controlled by members of the old Hutu militia, the same groups that were responsible for the Rwandan genocide. Aid workers were restricted by threat, and refugees who wished to return to Rwanda were brought back or killed. The entire population of the camps were held hostage by the old political power, who saw the refugees as their only source of legitimacy. The former army chief of staff, General Augustin Bizimungu, resided in Goma, surrounded by his court of bodyguards, claiming that he was a man of peace rather than a Hutu extremist. One UN worker admitted being ambivalent about helping perpetrators of genocide, but justified her human rights efforts: "If we have to help the bad guys to help the good guys, then that is the choice we have to make" (Pace, 1995b, p. 44). But perhaps by 1998 it was not so clear who were the good guys and who the bad, as the Tutsi-led Rwandan army pursued its interventionism all the way to Kinshasa, the capital of Congo, where they were clearly not wanted (French, 1998f).

Politicizing Ethnicity

In Rwanda, the politicization of ethnic divisions has been a deliberate strategy of ruling elites throughout its post-colonial history. The cultivation of a corporate view of ethnicity remains the key to misplaced social anger, which would otherwise be directed toward more immediate economic problems and inequities. Prejudgment is essential for such ethnic generalizations of blame. The Hutu-dominated government of 1994 repeated referred to the Tutsi as "enemies of the state." More hateful language was repeatedly used against them in newspapers and radio broadcasts (Chretien, 1995). The corporate understanding of ethnicity was repeated after July 1994, when the new Tutsi government broadcast its rhetoric against the Hutu, a million of whom had fled the country to the Congo, Tanzania, and to a lesser extent Uganda and Burundi. The propaganda campaign against the Hutu continued for over two years, until, in October 1996, the Tutsi Rwandan Patriotic Army together with Laurent Kabila's liberation army against Mobutu of Zaire (Congo) destroyed the refugee camps. When the remaining refugees fled westward into the mountains of Congo, both armies pursued them. Thousands were killed, including women and children, in these search-and-destroy missions (Campbell, 1997).

What is striking about the events of 1994 to 1998 is the facility with which both governments were able to exploit the same propaganda strategy, even though their discourses reversed the target of culpability. The Tutsi-led government used the word *genocidaires* as a substitute for Hutu. The ability to turn the tables on particular groups depends upon the denial of the universal nature of human rights and is congruent with relativistic views of truth. As Catharine Newbury (1998) has observed of the Rwandan genocide, "[I]n such a polarizing atmosphere, historical reconstruction is itself highly contested. Here, with an intensity that surpasses the normal cliches, there is no single history; rather there are competing 'histories'" (p. 9). While the old maxim remains true, that history is written by the winners, there remains the problem of how to learn from our social past in order to build a better society for the future. Moving beyond the limitations of human particularities and recognizing that truths can be applied across cultural boundaries—which, like the borders of the African colonizers, are themselves products of the perceptions and needs of particular groups—are the first steps toward a tolerant pluralism in the 21st century.

During the decade before Rwanda gained its independence from Belgium, the colonial authorities and the Roman Catholic Church reversed its previous political support of the Tutsi chiefs and instead began policies that favored the Hutu majority. Their untimely reversal denied traditional Rwandan social interactions, practices that had been in place for centuries. During the elections after independence, the external orchestration of power plunged Rwanda into an intensified divisionism not unlike the developing friction between ethnic groupings in post-colonial Nigeria (see Chapter 8, in this volume). The eventual collapse of royal power, the exodus of many Tutsi to other countries, and the ethnic violence were directly related to colonial policies that ignored—either deliberately or through ethnocentric misperception—the realities of wise rule.

However, another view of Rwandan history transcends traditional ethnic rivalry to describe what may appear to most First World cultures as a more recognizably modern turn of history. In this view, Hutu leaders, together with the majority of rural poor and some Belgians and church human rights advocates, precipitated the revolution by rejecting the "double colonialism" of Tutsi and Belgian hegemony. A Hutu counterelite demanded equal access to education, office, and economic advancement, privileges that the Tutsi had enjoyed under colonial rule. Thus, the Rwandan revolution resulted from persistent rural poverty, the popular rejection of the self-aggrandizing power of local chiefs, and the contingencies of land tenure. Certainly, the success of Hutu candidates for office in the post-colonial elections of 1960 and 1961 lend support for this economic and social view of Rwandan history.

A more romantic view of Rwandan history held that before the arrival of the European imperialists, Tutsi, Hutu and Twa lived in relative harmony. With the arrival of colonial rule, deliberate policies that encouraged ethnic differences were introduced. The degree of social mobility that had existed during the pre-colonial period was also eliminated. Another version of Rwandan history has the ethnic divisionism purely the result of indigenous actions. Thus the Hutu majority was subdued in earlier times by the more aggressive and ambitious Tutsi, who then lorded it over the rural population, turning the Hutu into servants. The colonial rule of the Germans, then the Belgians, directly or indirectly increased ethnic tensions, but does not fully explain the degree of ethnic prejudice that has determined most of the social violence over the decades.

Although each version of history may appeal to the ethnic group which appears more the victim than complicit, in fact, both Tutsi and Hutu accepted the colonialist account of the diverse origins of each group: that the Tutsi were from a different racial stock, they came from outside the present borders of the country, and they were superior to the Hutu in both intelligence and organizing abilities (Newbury, 1998). The glorification of the Tutsi by reference to a distant past created a persistent nostalgia that exaggerated the governing qualities of the Tutsi and underestimated the capabilities of the Hutu and Twa peoples. The racist underpinnings of this mythic discourse would reverberate throughout the post-colonial period and reach tragic proportions in the 1990s. "Even the majority of Hutu swallowed this distorted account of the past, so great was their respect for European-style education. Thus people of both groups learned to think of the Tutsi as winners and the Hutu as losers in every great contest of the Rwandan past" (Forges, 1995, p. 45). But the originative picture of Rwandan history ignored the complex interactions and realities of 20th century social and political life in the country, just as it spawned numerous channels of ethnic hatred. The colonial explanation offers an oversimplified and essentialist perspective, ascribing Rwanda's problems to a single cause that is mystified by the obscurities of time and location. Under such circumstances, critical analysis is not forthcoming, and creative thinking for change is ignored.

Rwanda became a centralized, hierarchical monarchy, not unlike other states in central Africa, by the end of the 19th century. Ethnic distinctions were not significant. Instead, clan, lineage, and family connections were more significant, since most of the local population had not been fully incorporated into the Rwandan state. Many Hutu and Tutsi shared lifestyles, cultivating land and raising cattle. But colonial policies, and the Tutsi chiefs who administered them, placed particular demands upon Hutu farmers. Under this double standard, ethnic demarcations took on additional social meaning. In the 1930s, Belgian authorities standardized ethnic identities, giving them a salience not present in traditional Rwandan social life. Identity cards were issued specifying particular ethnic membership, a bureaucratic decision that would eventually determine an individual's economic and social success. The colonialist ideology of ethnic distinctiveness homogenized members whose groups were hitherto more diverse and cross-cultural in their daily lives than the political apparatus was willing to acknowledge. The qualities of the ethnic categories that were rendered politically significance—race, historical difference, and culture—melded so that they were perceived as one and the same for all members.

Although colonial administrators regularized and standardized ethnicity for purposes of indigenous control and administrative efficiency, Rwanda before the arrival of the Europeans was a society of unequal classes. However, killings of genocidal proportions were nonexistent. Whereas before colonialism, a Hutu might align himself with the Tutsi royal court, under the "dual colonialism" of the Germans/Belgians and Tutsi royalty, the social significance of ethnic categories gave rise to class awareness and resentment. During the decade before independence, Hutu elites became more articulate and organized in opposition to the political and economic status quo. The Hutu Manifesto appeared in 1957. As a human rights document, it demanded equal access to education, office, and employment, but it also included racial language reflecting colonial categories (Newbury, 1998). Tutsi notables of the royal court reacted to the Manifesto with equally essentialist rhetoric, justifying the inability of Tutsi and Hutu to work together as equals because of the great historical and racial differences between both groups. Under such circumstances, rural uprisings and sporadic killings increased as the year of independence approached, but such incidents targeted local chiefs and functionaries rather than all Tutsi.

During the electoral campaigns of 1960 and 1961, moderate Rwandans of all identities urged consideration for the poor of whatever background. After independence, successive Hutu-dominant governments perpetuated the colonialist categories learned in German and Belgian schools. By 1996, such corporate thinking led all Hutu to be perceived as *genocidaires* and all Tutsi as *monarchistes*. Interestingly, the shift from ethnic labeling to political and class-based labeling occurred after the worst period of violence and social upheaval. Tutsi and Hutu identities now went beyond ethnicity, and ethnic membership became associated with reactionary political organizations. Thus, all Tutsi were now part of the "evil" Rwandan Patriotic Front (RPF), and all Hutu were loyalists of the Habyarimana government. The Hutu government of the 1994 genocide claimed to represent all rural elements of Rwanda and to uphold the human rights ideals of the 1959 revolution—an ideology consonant with their republicanism (an anti-monarchical and anti-aristocratic position). In actuality, the government was controlled by a clique of wealthy Hutu called the "Akazu."

During the late 1980s, disaffection with the Hutu government increased, and conflict arose over class and regional differences. However, these conflicts were begun chiefly by Hutu farmers and herders who resented the government's nepotism and unfair practices; interethnic conflict was not apparent. Only after the RPF invasion of northern Rwanda in 1990 did the Habyarimana government accuse the Tutsi force of attempting to abandon the ideals of the 1959 revolution and to bring back the monarchical social structure. Also, the introduction of multiparty elections in 1990–1991 continued to inspire the binary opposition of Hutu and Tutsi (Wagner, 1998). However, most rural Rwandans of all groups resented the class premises of the Hutu government and did not favor the RPF for the same reason. Class polarization continued as political corruption and nepotism hindered the fair distribution of land development, youth unemployment increased, and inadequate social services for the poor majority became apparent.

THE INTERNATIONAL RESPONSE

In 1995, the 18th Franco-African Summit was held in Biarritz, France, attended by most of the African heads of state and French President Francois Mitterrand, whose reputation as a European friend of Africa has seldom been questioned by the First World press. Missing from the list of 27 heads of state were the presidents of Rwanda and Uganda. Conditions were not yet "amenable" for the presence of the Tutsi-installed Rwanda government. Uganda was not invited because of its close support for the Tutsi-dominated RPF. France was severely challenged by the African representatives for not inviting Rwanda. The Rwandan genocide and civil war motivated renewed discussions of regional security. Preventive diplomacy was universally recognized as a priority in sub-Saharan Africa, as was the creation of an African rapid intervention force. Questions remained as to who would authorize such a peacekeeping force (the UN or the OAU), how would it be organized, who would command it, where would it be headquartered, how would it be used, and, especially, how would it be financed? (Pace, 1995a) While the First World proved tragically slow in responding to the Rwandan genocides with its peacekeeping armies, Africa seemed unable to organize itself militarily for the regional enforcement of human rights. In the early 1990s, Africa's greatest scholars and advocates had envisioned such a peacekeeping force, but their failure to convince their heads of state allowed the massacres of 1994.

Ominously, confronted with Africa's inability to organize and fund peacekeeping forces—or to send even a unilateral force—Mitterand promised at the Biarritz Summit to ask France's European neighbors to contribute and saw an eventual role for the United States. The Africans were divided even over European participation. Gabon's president Omar Bongo wanted a francophone force, while Burkina Faso's Blaise Compaore felt that a francophone force would exclude Nigeria and Ghana. Mitterand left the Summit with a strong message associating human rights standards with democratic development, which he averred was the only long-term guarantee of regional security. His words were apt, as the major problem in Rwanda has been a lack of democracy and social equality, an obvious fact usually overlooked by the First World press, which prefers to focus on the "ethnic strife" of Rwanda, Nigeria, Congo, and other African states. However, would France push for real democracy when Mitterand, the "friend of Africa," uncritically sat at the table with such anti-democrats as Mobutu, Bongo, and Gnassingbe Eyadema of Togo. In fact, the discourse of human rights continued in a much more direct way across town, where a Biarritz "Counter-Summit" was held, sponsored by human rights groups and humanitarian agencies.

During the period of the major genocides, 1994 to 1995, *genocidaires* were identified in every area of Rwandan political and social life. Ethnic hatred was extended to include outside international organizations. Because it failed to respond in an acceptable period of time to the killings, the UN was labeled a *genocidaire*. In fact, the UN Assistance Mission to Rwanda (UNAMIR) did not respond at all during the most intense period of the massacres, the spring of 1994. Fear and violence continued to plague Rwandan society through the 1990s. Hutu ministers of state were ousted from office when they became too critical of the RPF governments lack of emphasis on human rights. One such prominent minister was assassinated on a Nairobi street. The exploitation of grief became a systemic government policy, promoting continued hatred for "the enemy" Hutu through prolonged occasions when mass reburials were undertaken in formal state ceremonies. Wearing full dress with bodyguards, Tutsi officials and generals watched as Hutu POWs dug large pits and filled them with body bags. The commonly heard proposition, that one Tutsi death was caused by one Hutu murderer, was constantly repeated in the mainstream media. Somber processions and crowds watched mass funerals throughout Kigali (Wagner, 1998). Rwanda learned that even death can have political uses.

Rwanda experienced a long history of winner-take-all political fighting and a tradition of eliminating the deposed or losers by liquidation, exile or dispossession. However, these harsh practices before independence in 1959 were largely between Tutsi aristocratic families and clans who struggled for state power (Newbury, 1988). Interethnic conflict only appeared with the post-colonial election system, where parties and movements soon rigidified along ethnic lines. The formula of winner-take-all political resolutions, harsh punishment for the defeated, and the manipulation of ethnic tensions by government powerholders produced the widespread murders of Rwanda's post-colonial period. To overcome this tradition, new state policies must be undertaken to manage ethnic tensions. However, as Newbury (1998) warns, "'managing' ethnic tensions requires transcending them and addressing other forms of social inequality as well" (p. 18). The means to go beyond ethnic divisionism in Rwanda may mean that its incipient human rights groups need to have greater access to the propaganda tools of the electronic media and the press, as well as to educational reform.

QUESTIONS FOR FURTHER THOUGHT

1. Are there other instances of governments or social powers that hide class differences and awareness of social inequality behind ethnic struggle? Why does the First World media tend to report African social struggle in terms of ethnic rather than economic conflict? How common is this misdirected anger in the First World?

2. European colonialists in Rwanda cultivated an ideology of ethnic difference by presenting Rwandan students with separate historical developments for each ethnic group and different qualities common to each group. To what extent could this stereotyping and oversimplication have hindered the peaceful and profitable interaction of African groups?

3. Given the history of Rwanda's public discourse on the fundamental differences between Tutsi and Hutu, what social and political means could be used today to change this alienating perspective in that country?

4. Is it ever possible for a government or authority to "manage" ethnic identities in such a way that freedom of thought is not restricted? Are there instances when school systems or authorities should present only one picture of a people, even if it is completely positive?

5. What are the advantages and disadvantages of universal thinking about the qualities, manners, and origins of human beings? Is the emphasis on the commonality of all ethnic groups better than an emphasis on difference and uniqueness? Why or why not?

11

HAITI: HUMAN RIGHTS ABANDONED

HAITI DURING AND AFTER ARISTIDE

While international justice moved slowly in Rwanda and the Balkans at the end of the 1990s, the Caribbean and Central America remained largely unregulated, its laws and codes of conduct legally recorded but not enforced. Except for a handful of NGOs, such as Human Rights Watch and the U.S.-based National Labor Committee, abusive conditions went largely unreported, with investigative journalism sadly lacking. While the United Nations at times found itself in the role of policeman guarding the interests of owners and factory management, as in Haiti in the mid-1990s, the special UN tribunals for genocide created for the mass killings in the Great Lakes area of Africa (see Chapter 10, in this volume) and in the former Yugoslavia were moving slowly; the first convictions for the Rwanda genocide were only handed down in September 1998 (McKinley, 1998; Neier, 1998). Indeed, the Rwanda War Crimes Tribunal registrar, Agwu Ukiwe Okali, was struggling to get First World governments to cooperate for the release of the accused hiding in their countries (Crossette, 1998c). This chapter will explore the human rights situation in Haiti during the years immediately after the fall of the

Duvalier dynasty in the early 1990s through 1998. The period is one of great significance for Haitian political life, but also one in which labor and social standards reached an all-time low. Accordingly, great contradictions exist for the average Haitian, whose celebration of electoral freedom was soon disappointed when the elected statesman was prevented from introducing reforms, then violently forced from office.

The social and political destiny of Haiti continues to be determined largely by a combination of local enterprisers and TNCs, whose large annual profits remain the first priority. This chapter will explore the discourse of human rights as it has been transformed—in many cases profoundly distorted—by the economic and military power of Global Capital, specifically by those North American corporations that own apparel assembly plants (maquiladoras) for international markets. The maquiladora sector of the Haitian economy remains a highly attractive source of cheap labor, with "business-friendly" attitudes among local authorities. Huge profits from the exploitative working conditions in Haiti make the nation a valuable component of North American corporate response to the "pro-business" conditions in Asia, where the same grossly exploitative conditions for labor and the environment exist.

UNIVERSAL STANDARDS FOR
WORKERS—AN IDEA YET TO BE DISCOVERED

From the perspective of human rights and social equality, the question of overcoming the competitive stalemate strategy of TNCs persists, since democracy will not be possible when corporate profits remain the only concern of both foreign and domestic powerholders. Here, the United Nations could certainly initiate universal wage scales, workplace standards, factory codes of conduct, environmental safeguards, union rights, child labor restrictions, and pension and health guarantees. Such regulations, enforced by international observers and supported by UN or multilateral peacekeeping forces, would prevent the harmful competitive trajectories of one region of the world against another, a competition that continues at the expense of Third World employees and their developing democracies. Heretofore, however, the international public sphere has been dominated by economic competitors within countries and regions, whose corporate interests have no motivation to cooperate with such worldwide standards. The solution can be plainly stated: "If *all* countries paid their workers a wage to live decently, then the companies would have to compete not by exploiting their fellow human beings and the natural environment, but by making better quality products." Thus far, the United Nations and other international organizations that focus on trade and business practices have not actualized, and rarely debate, such solutions. By analyzing the discourse of power within and outside Haiti, we will attempt to uncover the reasons why such solutions have not been taken seriously and are either evaded or ignored entirely by the mainstream media worldwide.

THE CORPORATE CODES OF CONDUCT

Each year, North American retail corporations publish their own business standards and codes of conduct for stockholders and the general public. Although the language of these corporate policies varies somewhat, they generally attempt to convey a principled understanding and forthright response to the needs of their workers; this includes detailed descriptions of universal standards for the workplace, living wages, and a healthy environment in their Third World factories. One such corporate retailer, Dayton Hudson (DH), takes a straightforward approach to its human rights concerns without the flourish common to other major retainers: DH "has a tradition of conducting its business in an ethical manner that reflects our respect for the public franchise under which we operate. As such we are concerned with the worldwide state of being of human rights and environmental degradation." DH insists that its sourcing vendors "share these same ethical principles" (qtd. in Kernaghan, 1996, p. 48). The company even does its bit for children by supporting the growth of workplace apprenticeship programs, so long, they assure the public, as the children are not exploited by dangerous job situations.

The language of the 1993 Annual Report of the Kmart Corporation (KC) takes a nostalgic turn, as if its factory workers were similar to the middle-class Yankee girls who initially worked the factories of early 19th century New England mill towns. It declares that "[g]iving back to the communities [KC] serves has long been the tradition of [KC]. Every [KC] store has associates who are members of *Good News Committees* to improve the quality of life in their home towns." The Sara Lee Corporation finds that a more sociological style fits the bill for public relations in its 1990 Annual Report: "One of our most important goals is to provide the highest quality of life in our industry. We do that by allowing employees to develop their full potential through employee training and mentor programs." Not to be outdone, the Walt Disney Corporation (WDC) assumes a more involved, caring role, befitting its interest in the world of children: "We look for opportunities to initiate, develop, administer and implement diverse programs for the benefit of the community which also perpetuate the traditions and ideals of [WDC]" (qtd. in Verhoogen, 1996, pp. 29, 31).

While the ethical discourse of the major North American clothing retailers are designed to pass inspection for most mainstream media reporting in the United States, investigative journalists and fact-finding teams—few and far between in the United States—have sought confirmation of corporate claims. When they do, they find a very different reality hidden behind the words. Although retailer representatives insist in interviews with human rights investigators that they do not tolerate labor abuses and claim not to know of such instances, when confronted with the evidence they adopt a public relations strategy of defensiveness. In this mode, they admit nothing but instead focus on warding off negative publicity (Herbert, 1995).

Such strategies usually work for the major media newspapers and networks. However, in 1994, human rights NGOs devised a plan to defeat the public relations circumlocutions of the TNCs. Two girls from a maquiladora plant in El Salvador toured the United States, sponsored by the National Labor Committee and other organizations. They spoke of workplace abuse, abysmal wages, long working hours, corporal punishment, rape by managers, forbidden unions, and unhealthy factory conditions. Their tour of several U.S. and Canadian cities included upper-middle-class neighborhoods, schools, churches, and community centers. As a result, consumers and local community leaders—ministers, rabbis, priests—were motivated to write the GAP Corporation (GAP, Banana Republic, GAP for Kids). Contrary to what retail executive, with airs of grave authority, routinely tell reporters—that their buyers don't care where their clothes come from—North American consumers do in fact care about the conditions under which their clothing is made. Charles Kernaghan, executive director of the National Labor Committee and organizer of the campaign for workers in the Caribbean and Central America, comments on the success of the tour: "This thing touched a chord. People are not interested in wearing clothes made by exploited workers and children" (qtd. in Herbert, 1995).

Hearing from young people who had endured working conditions comparable to the worst possible 19th century abuses in the First World, consumers were outraged and motivated to action. Under siege from their public, the GAP broke from the ranks of other TNCs and allowed an unprecedented inspection of their clothing factories by independent fact-finding teams. Commenting on the event, U.S. Labor Secretary Robert Reich admitted, with a great deal of unintentional understatement, "It is something of a watershed. The major retailers and manufacturers have been somewhat reluctant to police their contractors here and abroad. This raises the question for other big retailers who haven't moved in this direction—why not?" (qtd. in Herbert, 1998). Unhappily, nothing substantial developed from this well-publicized triumph for human rights. In fact, Mandarin International, the Korean factory management firm contracted with the GAP, was under no obligation to comply with their firing of union organizers. More importantly, the sweatshop victory had little effect on the practices of other TNCs in or outside of El Salvador.

Damage Control: The TNCs Huddle

Confronted with the GAP campaign, TNC retailers reacted swiftly. The National Retail Federation (NRF), the largest such organization in the United States, began a red-herring strategy designed to mislead and diffuse the negative fallout. The retailers were well aware that muckraking of their "offshore" maquilas could become a habit with consumers. In August 1995, the NRF called an emergency meeting in Washington, D.C. Among those attending were GAP, Eddie Bauer, J.C. Penney, and the governments of Haiti, Honduras, and El Salvador. J.C. Penney's corporate code of conduct reflected high moral principles for its "sourcing practices"—the conditions within its contractors' sweatshops. It forbade its North American store employees to speak about such matters and instructed its managers to refer only to its corporate news release on the topic. J.C. Penney had reason not to describe conditions in its maquila plants. At least four of its contractors in Haiti were openly ignoring Haiti's minimum wage law, which was grossly inadequate to begin with. Rather than pay the legal wage of 30 cents an hour, a standard so removed from reality that it could not cover living expenses in Haiti, J.C. Penney paid its Haitian workers as little as 11 cents per hour (Kernaghan, 1996). In fact, the newly elected President Aristide attempted to raise the minimum wage, only to face severe reaction from Haitian power elites and the TNCs. Such history is not the stuff of corporate ethical codes that profess sincerity.

Another North American business lobby, Caribbean/Latin American Action (C/LAA), held its 1995 conference in Miami for 2,000 U.S. and Latin American businesspeople. One major corporate participant, Kellwood, sought out "favorable business climate" on every continent of the Third World. In 1984, Kellwood opened a factory in Haiti under the Duvalier dictatorship. Seeking "pools of inexpensive labor" Kellwood "found Haiti an ideal hunting ground...the prevailing Haitian wage is only $2.65 a day, which is about as low a pay anywhere in the world" (Farnsworth, 1984, p. F4). The language of the *New York Times* report accurately, though perhaps unintentionally, reflected the predatory nature of such operations and the management ethics behind them. In the face of a much publicized competitive threat from Asia, any corporate practice could be justified on the grounds of "free market competition."

International outrage at the overthrow of Haiti's first elected head of state, President Aristide, resulted in an Organization of American States (OAS) embargo of the military junta that replaced him. Kellwood became one of the U.S. maquila companies to remain operating in Haiti during the embargo. The military repression after Aristide proved very profitable for Kellwood and other TNCs. Kellwood's third-quarter 1995 profits were up 26 percent at $14 million (Kernaghan, 1996, p. 32). This is not surprising, considering that it paid its Haitian workers 17 cents per hour, or slightly over half the legal minimum wage.

Kellwood is not an unusual company in Haiti; in fact, it is taken as the norm. Its executive vice president, James Jacobson, was appointed to the Board of Directors of the C/LAA at the 1995 Miami conference. Judy Bond, a family-owned business that makes and sells blouses, had sales of $39.9 million in 1993. At the C/LAA Miami conference, its president, Andrew Postal, spoke at a workshop called "Creating and Maintaining a Favorable Business Environment for Global Industries." What is quite apparent is that Postal's business environment had little in common with the natural environment. He reassured his wholesale buyers that Judy Bond's customers don't care that their clothing is made by people making 10 cents an hour in prison-like conditions. All Judy Bond customers care about is saving money—good quality merchandise at the lowest price. Interestingly, Postal seems to be speaking more about his own business ethics, projected onto his customers, than about reality. Consumer response to the NLC tour of the U.S. and Canada disproves Postal's assertion. Also, according to a consumer survey by Marymount University released in 1995, 78 percent of U.S. consumers said they would avoid retailers who were known to contract with sweatshops (Kernaghan, 1996, p. 33). Postal's workshop rhetoric can be deconstructed to mean that "customers won't think about the working conditions behind their merchandise if they don't know about them"—an obvious redundancy that nevertheless continues to be standard corporate public relations. Postal's truth assertions depends upon a facile cynicism all too common in the media and among authority figures in the First World: "Nobody cares. The bottom line is money and profit, so it is only a matter of doing it before someone else does it first."

In 1984, Postal opened in Haiti two factories under the name Brewton Fashions International. After the coup that overthrew Aristide, Postal publicly claimed that the elected government had not been "business-friendly" (qtd. in Kernaghan, 1998, p. 33). Like Kellwood, Postal kept operating in Haiti after the coup and despite the OAS embargo, until his plants were forced to close under pressure from international NGOs and the UN/OAS sanctions. Afterward, Postal appeared before the U.S. Senate Committee on Foreign Relations (March 9, 1995) to generate government interest in financing (with taxpayer money) business ventures in Haiti when the sanctions expire. Postal apparently believed that governments are harmful when they regulate human rights (such as Aristide's minimum wage standard) but necessary when they finance business—a direct contradiction of the notion of "free trade." Postal's efforts to find government money paid off. The U.S. government, like big business, was more interested in the discourse than the reality of free enterprise; it rewarded the TNCs through the Overseas Private Investment Corporation (OPIC), a quasi-government organization. For its part, Haiti has learned not to stray too far toward democratic goals. The Haitian-American Chamber of Commerce and Industry assures its North American members that the minimum wage in Haiti is fixed at 36 gourdes (30 cents an hour), which is below the level of other countries in the region.

The discourse of exploitation requires the perception of an outside threat. This predatory Other serves as a projection of the exploiters own negative ethics and state of mind. Postal tells everyone at the Miami conference that maquilas must be reopened in Haiti because the GATT (General Agreement On Tariffs and Trade) agreement eliminating quotas by 2004 "will unleash the Pacific Rim" and force U.S. business to "face the tide of Asian competition" (qtd. in Kernaghan, 1996, p. 36). It is therefore clear what the role of Haiti is to be. It must function as a frontline force against the Asian juggernaut. Postal's language remains traditionally racist in its depiction of "the yellow peril"—phrase that has become so associated with traditional jingoism that Postal's use of the term in public would prove counterproductive. Thus, instead of the yellow peril, the "Pacific Rim" will be "unleashed," and the "tide" of Asian business will inundate North America. Although new metaphors appear in Postal's rhetoric of self-justification, the incorporation of traditional racist notions of Asian people functions as a persuasive tool in what amounts to asking the U.S. government for a personal handout.

While North American business interests were jockeying for start-up money in Haiti during the human rights embargo, the U.S. Commerce office in Haiti was run by the newly appointed Sally Yearwood, a former C/LAA staffer and associate of Postal. At C/LAA, Yearwood was responsible for maintaining the loopholes that allowed U.S. maquilas to operate during the OAS embargo. As a newly appointed government official, she facilitated business contacts between Haiti and the United States. Her career move was yet another instance of government/corporate complicity in human rights issues made all the more ironic by the free enterprise/ small government rhetoric of the TNCs.

When Richard Morningstar, vice president of OPIC, insisted at the Miami Conference on worker rights compliance for every OPIC loan, his words met stinging resistance from corporate executives. One businessmen shouted, "I'm from a right to work state, and you mean I have to accept a union in Haiti?" (qtd. in Kernaghan, 1996, p. 37) Although their hearts were obviously somewhere other than with human rights for their workers, the conference members were wary after a recent NCL/60 Minutes television episode wherein working conditions in the U.S. maquilas were exposed. Accordingly, all agreed that corporations should have their own codes of conduct. The following parameters for corporate "commitments" were adopted:

"Creating and Maintaining a Favorable
Business Environment for Global Industries,"
a Miami conference workshop led by James Jacobson

Parameters:

1. Corporate codes of conduct were to be strictly voluntary—nothing was to be legally binding.
2. Corporate codes of conduct were a private sector solution to human rights concerns—there was to be no government involvement, standard setting, monitoring, or enforcement.
3. Human rights issues must never become a condition for future trade agreements, nor in any way condition a corporation's access to tariff or other trade benefit programs.

Instead of discussing the human rights of workers, hearing examples of abuse, interviewing workers themselves, or even questioning their own factory managers and contractors, the C/LAA members spent their time devising damage control for the future. Their parameters carefully rejected any accountability for human rights standards—the sort of work their own corporate lawyers could easily add to any private contract. Parameter 3, however, was perhaps the most important stipulation. It reminded the executives to be more vigilant in the future to prevent the sort of human rights stance that Richard Morningstar articulated for OPIC. Henceforth, the U.S. government will be expected to offer only start-up money and infrastructure repair in Haiti and other states in the region, but never again to propose human rights standards for their U.S. and Canadian business operations.

Despite their concern to prevent accountability, the corporate huddles may have been a tempest in a teapot, a means of relaxing business executives and CEOs frustrated by the unusual mainstream media publicity on worker rights and corporate control of the Third World. In fact, most human rights standards are not enforced in the region of C/LAAs interest. The minimum wage in Haiti is enforced only in some plants, and where it does apply, corporate management has devised ways of working around it, such as requiring more "piece work" per hour (Verhoogen, 1996). What makes the TNCs nervous is the prospect of government regulation, which they perceive as hindering their competition against an unleashed Pacific Rim. Beyond the thinking of such executives is the concept of universal labor rights and conditions. Given a much stronger international body, perhaps the United Nations, wages, workplace conditions, union rights, environmental protection, and so on could be assured throughout the world. Under such conditions, business competition would not be restricted, since every nation would enforce the same—or comparable—standards. However, this is not what the C/LAA, or any other TNC group, really wants. Not the virtues of Adam Smith's free enterprise, but a globalized form of mercantilism is desired (and usually attained), wherein TNCs are assisted by their governments and some international trade organizations to dominate a region or subregion by excluding in some fashion other TNCs. This requires compliant Third World governments whose own elites have been allowed a piece of the franchise for that purpose. Thus, in Nigeria, Mobutu's Zaire (Congo), Rwanda, and nearer to home, Haiti and numerous Latin American countries, local elites prevent the spread of rights to those below them. For example, when President Aristide increased the minimum wage, effective May 4, 1995, the TNCs simply increased their production quotas in Haiti to nullify his new standard (Excel Apparel Exports reported an increase of 133 percent since the new minimum wage applied in Haiti). Nevertheless, Aristide was perceived as too great a threat to the "business-friendly" reputation of Haiti, so the local elites were allowed to remove him through force.

For its part, the U.S. government has attempted through its bully pulpit to convince Aristide to drop the minimum wage. Lawrence Crandall, head of the U.S. Agency for International Development (USAID) mission to Haiti, claimed publicly that his organization "had no position" on the Haitian minimum wage; yet he actively pressured Aristide not to increase the minimum wage (Verhoogen, 1998). However, as in the case of the parameters for the corporate codes of conduct at the

Miami Conference, USAID's interest in rejecting a new Haitian minimum wage was more symbolic than substantive, since, as noted above, the idea of a minimum wage in an unregulated and "business-friendly" country is seldom actualized. The three-way cooperation between TNCs, national governments, and local Third World elites confirm what an early 20th century theorist of economic imperialism observed, "finance capital, expressing as it does capitalist monopoly organizations, cannot relinquish the policy of monopolizing 'spheres of influence,' of seizing sales markets, markets for raw materials, and spheres of capital investment. If one state capitalist trust fails to get hold of an unoccupied territory, it will be occupied by another" (Bukharin, 1929, p. 391). In order to understand the dynamics of power in Third World maquilas today, we need to look more closely at the social and laboring conditions in Haiti.

"THE SCREWDRIVER AND THE SUN": WORKING CONDITIONS IN HAITI

The average day of a worker at Quality Garments, a clothing contractor in the SONAPI Industrial Park of Port-au-Prince, is typical. She (assembly plant workers are 80 percent women and girls) makes as little as 15 gourdes per day, or 12 cents an hour, well below the legal minimum of 36 gourdes. Company production quotas are set so high that most workers cannot meet them. In Creole, workers describe this piece-rate system as working "pa kouray," literally "by courage" (Verhoogen, 1996, p. 1, n. 2). Despite the widespread practice Haitian law prohibits such piece-rate abuse, Article 2 of Aristide's decree states, "Where the employee works per piece or per task, the price paid for a unit of production (per piece, per dozen, per gross, per meter, etc.) must allow the employee who works 8 hours to earn at least the minimum salary" (*Le Moniteur*, 1995, p. 463). The average Quality Garments worker earns 25 gourdes (U.S. $1.67) per day. The work schedule is 8 to 10 hours, 6 days per week. Workers are also required to work Sundays—without overtime pay—when needed. Interviewed workers told NLC investigators that they had worked seven Sundays in a row, during the hottest season.

The working facility of Quality Garments is comparable to the worse 19th century standards. NLC investigators described one factory:

> The factory is hot, dimly lit, crowded. The air is heavy with dust and lint. There is no ventilation to speak of. Piles of material—scraps of pajamas, dresses, shirt hems—clutter every aisle and every; corner. The workers have sad, tired faces. They hunch over antiquated sewing machines, some more than 20 years old, sewing "Kelly Reed" dresses to be sold by Kmart and Mickey Mouse pajamas for the Walt Disney Company. (Verhoogen, 1996, p. 1)

Other U.S. contractors had comparable conditions, with no union rights and health benefits. Workers were routinely abused verbally. Many of the women and girls were reported raped by supervisors or assistants and had no means of redress. Workers were often shortchanged on pay days. John Whistler, the American director of Chancerelles S.A., a subsidiary of Fine Form, was asked by a NLC team if the supervisors presented a problem: "They empathize with the people too much" (Verhoogen, 1996, p. 5).

Haitian business and government are also closely allied and, like the public relations ploy of TNC codes of conduct, participate in the cover-up of labor abuses. Jean-Edouard Baker headed the Haitian Association of Industrialists (ADIH) and allegedly cooperated with Luckner Cambronne, Defense and Interior Minister under "Papa Doc" Duvalier, to sell Haitian blood to U.S. laboratories (Abbott, 1988). He also aggressively sold cadavers to U.S. medical schools, allegedly stealing them from funeral homes when Haitian hospitals were in short supply (Farmer, 1994). Baker chaired the Haitian Presidential Commission on Economic Growth and Modernization, which a USAID publication described as "leading the analytical process to improve the business and investment climate." When asked if Haitian businesses were paying the minimum wage, he affirmed that they were (Verhoogen, 1996, p. 11).

According to Michael Rothbaum, Chairman of the Board of the American Apparel Manufacturers Association (AAMA), Third World government attitudes toward businesses are the main concern of TNCs. In Haiti, all maquila export factories are tax exempt—in a country with one of the lowest per capita incomes in the world and a debt of $820 million in 1996. Beginning in 1996, the Haitian government subsidized half of all telephone, electric, and port charges for all new maquilas. Testifying before the U.S. International Trade Commission, Rothbaum explained the close relation of Third World Ministries of Labor to TNCs. Minimum wage, overtime rates, forced overtime, medical insurance, child labor, organized labor, and so on, "become factors of cost." Therefore, it is necessary to have a compliant labor ministry with little or no inspection. The language of human rights becomes heightened from the perspective of TNC public relations. According to Rothbaum, the endeavors of U.S. apparel corporations in the Caribbean were not only "remarkably successful" but also "so necessary and noble an effort" (qtd. in Kernaghan, 1996, p. 44). Such discourse—putting aside its purely cynical disregard for reality—presupposes the ultimately beneficial effects of business enterprise in "underdeveloped" areas. Such effects, however, remain unfounded. In fact, Haiti's per capita income has dropped as the presence of TNC maquilas have increased in the 1990s.

The overwhelming majority of Haitian employees have never heard of their companies' codes of conduct. When told of their corporation's code of conduct, women workers in Haiti have remarked, "Our code is 'the screwdriver and the sun.' To punish us they hit us on the head with the butt of a screwdriver or put us out into the blazing sun for the day, or even every day for a week" (Kernaghan, 1996, p. 40).

RECENT EVENTS AND FUTURE DIRECTIONS

Aristide won the December 1990 election largely because of grassroots support from an extensive network of local organizations called *Lavalas* (the flood). Although the opposition candidate, a former World Bank official, Marc Bazin, had U.S. backing and commanded vast resources and media, he received only 14 percent of the vote to Aristide's 67 percent. During the next several months, Aristide achieved significant progress for a country near economic ruin. He began by eliminating much of the corruption, drug trafficking, government atrocities, and enlarged state bureaucracy; for all of which he received international praise. With U.S. planning and support, the coup against Aristide occurred on September 30, 1991. When the OAS responded in protest with an embargo on Haiti, the United States reluctantly complied, but the Bush administration attacked Aristide's alleged atrocities while ignoring the major violence of the coup. The U.S. media passively reflected the Bush perspective, concentrating on Aristide's supposed wrongdoing. Within a few months, the United States broke the embargo by allowing U.S.-owned businesses to trade. By 1992, Marc Bazin was in power as Prime Minister, and trade with Haiti was nearly restored (Chomsky, 1994).

During the coup, the number of Haitian refugees to the United States increased after going down sharply during the Aristide administration. In direct violation of the UDHR, President Clinton returned refugees to Haiti, after criticizing Bush for the same action during the presidential election campaign. Those returned often faced death on the streets of Port-au-Prince. On October 15, 1994, Aristide was returned to power in Haiti by the United States, with strings attached. After promising a new minimum wage on May 1, 1995, he introduced a wage rate well below his original plan—36 gourdes verses from 45 to 75 gourdes. Even the highest figure was believed not enough for a family to live on, by Aristide's own estimate (Verhoogen, 1996).

Mainstream media coverage of the Haitian plight and U.S. involvement has been slight. When events are reported, they nearly always follow a Washington trajectory and view of reality. Katharine Kean's 1997 film about the daily terrorism in Haiti from 1985 to 1997, *Rezistans*, has thus far not been viewed on U.S. network or public television (*Rezistans*, 1997). One of the few screenings of the film was at the 1998 Human Rights Watch International Film Festival in New York, an important, though limited, source of discourse in human rights. Throughout Kean's film are interviews with Antoine Izmery, a wealthy, informed businessman who supported Aristide and sought to forge a progressive Haiti. When relatives and friends around him are killed by government forces, he remains optimistic, but when he himself is assassinated in a live scene, the reality of official terror in Haitian life is shockingly exposed in a sequence that could not be acted. Kean's message is clear—Haiti remains a country whose human rights violations are central to the continued security of its powerholders in business and government.

While the 1993 World conference on Human Rights at Vienna acknowledged "its dismay and condemnation that gross and systematic violations and situations that constitute serious obstacles to the full enjoyment of all human rights continue to occur in different parts of the world," in fact, very few concrete and specific remedies were proposed (qtd. in Leckie, 1998, p. 82). The Inter-American Commission on Human Rights has also declared the obligation of its members states to observe human rights. However, as Scott Leckie observes, "when people die of hunger or thirst, or when thousands of urban poor and rural dwellers are evicted from their homes, the world still tends to blame nameless economic or 'developmental' forces, or the simple inevitability of human deprivation, before placing the blame on the state" (1988, p. 82). In the case of Haiti, however, the state is very much complicit in the denial of ICESCR standards and values. Such denial is also reflected in the unwillingness of governments to support the Optional Protocol complaint procedure of ICESCR, a fact that reassures powerholders in business and government of impunity from human rights violations. Moreover, 57 UN member nations—with a combined population of 2.3 billion people—have yet to ratify ICESCR.

The UN Commission on Human Rights has also repeatedly temporized in its goal of providing mechanisms to address human rights violations. This is not because of lack of analysis or working principles on the part of the world community. For example, the Limburg Principles (June 1986) were presented by the Commission on Human Rights as a means of taking economic and social rights through effective enforcement procedures. Paragraph 72 stipulates that a government will violate ICESCR if "it willingly fails to meet a generally accepted international minimum standard of achievement, which is within its powers to meet" and if "it deliberately retards or halts the progressive realization of any rights, unless...it does so due to a lack of available resources or *force majeur*" (Limburg Principles, 1987, p. 131).

The work of numerous NGOs in Haiti and other Caribbean countries have demonstrated the low employee wages and high profits of the major retailers, and the unwillingness of the Haitian government to enforce its own labor and environmental laws. It only remains for effective grassroots pressure to be applied on First World governments to change long-standing policies that prioritize corporate profits over people. To do this may require fundamental change in the mainstream media so that the reality of human rights abuse is exposed to the public.

QUESTIONS FOR FURTHER THOUGHT

1. What efforts could be made to focus mainstream media attention on countries such as Haiti that are currently ignored or misrepresented?
2. The NLC's successful North American tour of El Salvador workers was a one-of-a-kind event. What long-term strategies could be used to draw U.S. attention to human rights abuse worldwide?
3. Corporate justifications for their human rights violations often represent First World consumers as indifferent or cynical about the lives of Third World workers. Do you feel that their outlook is generally true or untrue? Justify your answer with current examples.
4. How can citizens in democratic countries persuade governments to transform their foreign policy to give priority to human rights over corporate profits?
5. What steps could be taken to actualize the Limburg Principles for international governing institutions? What do you feel has been the greatest obstacle to their implementation?

12

INDONESIA REACHES
FOR HUMAN RIGHTS

William F. Schulz (1998), executive director of Amnesty International USA, recently commented on the problem of human rights in Indonesia to the Board of Directors of Levi Strauss: "If the current situation in Indonesia teaches us anything, it is that corruption, cronyism, intimidation of the press and manipulation of the political process lead to instability and unrest, and instability and unrest cannot help but be bad for business" (p. 22). Indonesia's recent upheavals, including the overthrow of Suharto, ethnic unrest, and the genocide of East Timor, was caused by the flagrant and prodigious corruption of the Suharto family and the close oligarchy surrounding that dynasty. Human rights has been profoundly affected by this circumstance, an instance of "comprador," or indigenous corporate development generating negative effects on the population of this culturally heterogeneous nation. This chapter will discuss the particular discourse of human rights within the context of recent developments in Southeast Asia, giving particular attention to the circumstances of ethnic tensions and cultural conflict within an area of the world where rapid economic development is displacing traditional cultures at an accelerated rate. Ethnic tensions in Malaysia between Malays, Chinese, and Indians have colored the political and business spectrum of that developing nation, while ethnic conflict in Cambodia and Burma (Myanmar) continue to tear the social fabric (Sodhy, 1997). In Tibet, the continued debate in the West as to the nature of that country's democratic traditions and the place of religious practice in its contemporary social and political life have accompanied the ongoing human rights violations of Tibetans by Chinese authorities. The issues of cross-cultural conflict, the recent introduction of "offshore" electronic and other assembly plants of TNCs, and the presence of repressive oligarchies and pro-business governments are all related to the continued problems with human rights enforcement in Southeast Asia. A general outlook for human rights in Indonesia will be offered and recommendations for improving the communication of human rights standards for the 21st century.

ETHNIC CONFLICT IN INDONESIA

Historical Background

Before the arrival of the Dutch in the last quarter of the 17th century, Minahasan culture was involved in extensive trade with neighboring societies. Production, distribution, and social power were interrelated, especially through religious practice and ritual (Buchholt, 1994). Trading and economic matters in general melded with the social context and were not separable, as with Western capitalism. Beginning with the United East India Company of the Dutch (1679–1798), cash crops were substituted for food crops and the European colonizers employed traditional trading minorities from the region to assist their trading and production ventures. Integration into the world market economy began in the nineteenth century under Dutch rule and continued down to the present. Violent conflicts between the indigenous majority and relatively elite "trading minorities" have continued throughout the 20th century, notably in 1965 and most recently in the 1980s and 1990s, when economic discontent resulted in anti-Chinese rioting. While European colonizers used preexisting trading networks to build their spice trade, the trading minorities, mostly people of Chinese origin, were incorporated into the Western network and order of law. Often the effect was to strengthen existing ethnic heterogeneities originally formed by differences of religion, language, and race. In order to maintain the colonial status quo, the Dutch, consciously or inadvertently, used the policy of "divide and conquer" by selecting alien minorities in Indonesia and other Southeast Asian societies to act as intermediaries between them and the indigenous majority. The connecting link not only facilitated trading operations—through familiarity with language and customs—but also functioned as a buffer zone to assure smooth colonial rule. The trading minorities were able to an extent to exploit this arrangement to their own advantage, thus creating their own monopolization of certain important economic sectors.

As "middlemen" of the Indonesian colonial power, the Chinese supplied the anticipated cash crop of spices to the Dutch, but also profited by supplying the

Indonesian majority with imported goods and credit. The ethnic hierarchy that developed, with Europeans at the top, followed by Chinese, then the Indonesian majority, reinforced traditional notions of the trading minorities as usurious and given to exclusivity. The ethnic tensions following colonial independence have been almost always caused by economic disappointment. The most common symptoms have been indebtedness, inflation, decline in monetary income, and hunger. Although the European color bar was legally removed, economic divisions along ethnic lines persisted. The social frustration was commonly manifested in group envy. Alien trading minorities were blamed for blocking the expansion of the trading sector as a source of profit for the Indonesian majority. Much of the criticism was justified, as the trading minorities used their traditional networks and credit systems to expand their economic dominance in the absence of the Dutch and to exclude the remaining population. The nationalistic side of this tension has included the perception that the alien minorities were "parasitic" and "disloyal" as regards their close association with the European colonizers (Buchholt, 1994). The result is that the Chinese population is further distinguished from the Indonesian majority, and thus stigmatized.

With independence, the ruling elites of the new nation-states of Southeast Asia exploited this existing divisiveness and enmity. New legal arrangements favored the Indonesian and Malay majorities of those two states. The so-called *bumiputra* ("sons of the soil") policy created partnerships between the government and indigenous majorities. More drastic measures included straightforward violations of human rights, such as forced deportation of Indians to Africa and police indifference to the plundering of alien minority stores. Following independence, indigenous elites have been motivated to use trading minorities to divert attention from their own complicity in failed economic policies and resulting negative conditions for the majority. This blaming also can serve to unite a heterogeneous population around a newly formed nation-state, whose borders may have been arbitrarily set by the departing European colonizers. Moreover, the negative side effects of rapid industrialization in traditional cultures may leave the general populace with a malaise of anonymity, individual isolation, and the loss of kinship structures and home setting. Scapegoating helps define an artificial nationalism and patriotism as remedies for such social angst. Also characteristic of indigenous elites is the use of the national budget for private appropriation and the division of the profits of trading minorities through taxes, bureaucratic corruption, and the granting of overpriced trading licenses (Evers, 1987). This hypocrisy usually goes unreported in the mainstream media, which are generally controlled by the ruling elites, and so is known usually only by the more educated in the country.

Other factors may motivate the indigenous majority to blame and attack the trading minorities in post-colonial societies. Horowitz (1985a) finds that sociopsychological factors influence such pogroms rather than initiatives by the ruling elites. Thus, trading minorities are perceived by the majority as superior in enterprising methods, attitudes, qualifications and skills. Such feelings of inferiority are often relieved by ethnic and religious prejudices that predate the colonial period. According to Horowitz, these traditional attitudes towards the other group motivate the ethnic struggle. No doubt more evidence and study is needed in the area of majority attitudes towards the traditional trading minorities. Economic interest may be the driving force behind these attacks, and recent studies show that ethnicity and social class are no longer completely identified (Evers, 1984). Trading minorities may antagonize the remaining population by ethnocentric methods of competition, such as eliminating potential competitors by using their own credit unions, trading organizatons, and family labor (Bonacich, 1973). From the perspective of the trading minorities, protective measures against the hostile machinations of the ruling elite may motivate their continued close cooperation and group counterstrategies for self-protection, such as commercialized kinship systems, religious and cultural revivalism and fundamentalism (Winder, 1967). Of course, such group homogeneity continues the vicious cycle of group resentment and suspicion.

Global Business Strategies in Southeast Asia

The development strategies of the major international financial agencies, the IMF and the World Bank (both nominally under UN authority), emphasize the "free" market economy as a remedy for all economic and social maladies and a solution for the side effects of modernization and development. This was the consistent rhetoric of President Clinton on his 1998 China Summit Trip (see Chapter 13, in this volume), a deregulated business strategy that lessens the role of government, which interferes with the free flow of goods and presents major obstacles to development (Evers, 1994). Indications of the unhindered forces of market expansion can be seen in Indonesia since 1982 and in the boom of export products in Malaysia and Thailand. In these countries, comprehensive deregulation of the environment, labor conditions, and wages and benefits, together with lenient tax structures fueled the rapid development until the quite recent collapse of the Asian markets in 1997. To an extent, this expansion has been the result of the increased economic integration of East and Southeast Asia. Taiwan, for example, is the largest foreign investor in Indonesia. This "South/South development" is the source of a certain pride among the populace of the countries involved (Sodhy, 1997).

In contrast to the view that liberal democracy has arisen only in nations that are market-oriented, not in all of them but only in them—also a basic premise of Clinton's speeches during the 1998 China Summit visit—is the view that trade is potentially damaging to society if it is allowed to continue unregulated and uncontained. The introduction of cash-crop economies and assembly plants can significantly endanger the cohesiveness and security of traditional rural Asian cultures. Sudden unrestricted imports damage local small businesses, and export modernization can negatively affect the environment and public health standards. From this perspective, a strong state is a necessary precondition to maintain effective control of the economy for the rational formation of an open market. Here, "rational" would be a policy that was most concerned with the human rights articulated by the ICCPR—civil and political rights such as adequate housing, education, health, and employment. In fact, the economic and social realities of Southeast Asia do not fit neatly into the binary opposition of strong versus weak government, which may be too much a Western reading into the region. Other terms, such as "post-colonial," "transitional," and even "hybrid strategic groups," have been employed to describe the Indonesian region (Evers, 1994, p. 240). All are equally inadequate. It is clear, however, that this region has developed differently than Western countries.

From the human rights perspective, no country in Southeast Asia has a market that adequately produces the free play of supply and demand. Large populations of poor exist who are unable to affect the market because they lack sufficient money. Political protest, religious fundamentalism, and ethnic strife are often the methods by which their frustrations are manifest. Perhaps most troubling for Southeast Asia is its extremely rapid economic and trade development without a corresponding political and social institutional development. "THE MARKET and THE STATE are drifting apart and frantic international negotiations (GATT, UN peacekeeping efforts, etc.) or UN institution-building have not been able to fill the gap so far" (original emphasis, Evers, 1994, p. 243). The danger of Global Capital in the Third World is perhaps that highly integrated regional markets with no meaningful political life will form on a more or less permanent basis. Such regions will represent quite lucrative investments for First World business and Third World elites, who will attempt to maintain the status quo (Lewis, 1998b). This prospect can only continue to affect human rights negatively.

The Indonesian Uprising

In July 1998, the Attorney General of Indonesia determined that the Suharto family fortune remained at about $30 billion, despite the collapse of the Indonesian currency (Fink, 1998). The political tumult that led to the overthrow of the Suharto regime in May 1998 had as one of its negative components the attack on the human rights of the traditional trading minorities throughout Indonesia. Clearly, the Indonesian government and military had an interest in fostering resentment against these ethnic groups as a means of scapegoating them for the generally deteriorating economic conditions. This strategy of fomenting displaced civil anger was extented to more general objects of concern and even terror. Allegations by human rights groups in Indonesia include rape, arson, and other terrorist public acts perpetrated by government-sponsored or led groups (Nairn, 1998a). Often these groups wore military uniforms. Suharto himself, though out of power, was apparently not out of contention as a future political force of influence, perhaps with members of his family poised to resume dominant positions of economic and even political power.

Suharto, aging and perhaps not physically able to run the country anymore, nonetheless has kept close ties with the powerful Indonesian military in the weeks following his step down. He was seen recently attending Islamic prayers in military mosques with high-ranking generals (Shenon). Four of his six children are members of the People's Consultative Assembly, the highest legislative body in Indonesia. Moreover, Suharto has attempted to buy political support with his family fortune wherever he can. After his ouster, he apparently still controlled his political party, Golkar, which has the majority of the legislators. Powerful forces within the government still seemed open to the possibility of Suharto's return. B. J. Habibie, Suharto's vice president and the current ruler, threatened to fire Sujono Atmonegoro, the Attorney General, after the latter announced his investigation into Suharto's personal wealth. While Suharto was buying influence from all factions, the revolution that overthrew him remained, in contrast, fractious and unable to unify. This situation may underscore Evers 1994 prediction that the new international world order may comprise regions with sophistocated financial and technological systems sitting atop underdeveloped political cultures.

In the case of Indonesia, its large population and diverse religious, ethnic, and linguistic character no doubt has impeded its ability to overcome both political and economic human rights violations. Also, officially incited attacks on trading minorities, covert and overt governmental terrorism, and confused reporting by a largely coopted press have contributed to the political confusion and lack of objective civic discourse in Indonesia. The inability of the student movement, the religious opposition, and rebellious farmers to unite contrasts with the 32-year reign of Suharto, who attempted at times to cultivate the image of a traditional king of Java. In 1966, Indonesia was a country of uneducated farmers with an annual percapita income of $70. Many saw their new leader as possessing *wahyu*, "the favor of the gods," or "a divine mandate" (Kristof, 1998, p. 6). This image, although lacking any relation to the realities of power in Indonesian society, brought a certain feeling of national unity around which the heterogeneous population could identify. It was perhaps looked upon with a great deal of ambivalence throughout the 32 years of the Suharto regime. Still, coming after the particularly bloody and disconcerting overthrow of the Sukarno government in 1966, the idea of a wise successor possessing, or at least proclaiming as doctrine, the wisdom of *wahyu* must have functioned as an effective method of control. According to anthropologist Clifford Geertz, the relatively gradual replacement of a failing and weak ruler by a stronger protege is a Javanese tradition (Kristof, 1998). Sukarno replaced Suharto peacefully amidst a violent revolution that took as many as half a million lives in the anti-Communist purges of the 1960s.

Although considered less violent than its predecessor, the 1998 uprising came as a much overdue response to economic injustice and rising prices of basic human need items such as fuel and electricity. After the death toll from rioting reached the hundreds, Suharto returned fuel prices to their original levels. In a direct way, the

UN's International Monetary Fund (IMF) precipitated the overthrow by insisting upon such economic strictures. Its austerity package was part of a deal that would allow Suharto a $40 billion "economic rescue package" (Mydans, 1998a, p. 1). The 70 percent rise in prices of fuel and electricity on May 4 was the last straw leading to the overthrow, as students and workers sensed the injustice of an international deal by a wealthy ruler that sidestepped domestic debate. Where was the *wahyu* of the President who could give his people washing machines, televisions, and other commodities in the lower food chain of Global Capital, but not job security, unemployment insurance, pensions, basic necessities, and retraining?

The human rights abuses that paralleled the protests and overthrow remain the most contested aspect of the 1998 events. An important army commander, Suharto's son-in-law, Lieutenant General Prabowo, kept the military under tight control. Under belated U.S. pressure, commander of the army General Wiranto demoted Prabowo for the "disappearances" of protestors and opposition leaders, and other terrorist activities. The U.S. Defense Intelligence Agency (DIA) had worked closely with Prabowo's KOPASSUS, a terrorist unit, training and supplying weapons, and distancing itself from Prabowo only after civil protest and government human rights abuses had become widely publicized (Nairn, 1998b). General Wiranto himself was in overall charge of these repressive units. His army intelligence unit, BIA, arrested and tortured labor activists. Although some senior government and military officials signed a public statement urging the President to resign, the unity of the military and its close association with the former leader remained important influences on the political direction of the overthrow. For example, a key officer of the Wiranto faction, Lieutenant General Yunus Yosfiah, recently told students that the army would not tolerate any campaigns for drastic political reform and was implicated in the 1975 murder of five foreign journalists in East Timor. He is now Information Minister in the new government. In significant ways, the Indonesian uprising may have been a restructuring of the status quo rather than a true revolution from the bottom.

Although misplaced anger was exploited and in many cases instigated by the tightly controlled military still loyal to the Suharto family, still, the widespread nature of the violence suggests long-standing resentment among the general population. Certainly, the 1998 violence against the ethnic Chinese "trading group" was less severe than earlier pogroms, which extend back to Dutch colonial rule in the 19th century. However, Chinese citizens were treated brutally, with many fleeing the country before more violence could occur. During one May week alone, dozens or more were burned to death in their homes. Others were stopped on the highways by rioters, pulled out of their cars, and killed.

The majority's resentment of the Chinese minority was perhaps more economically than ethnically based. Making up only 5 percent of the population, Chinese citizens account for three-quarters of Indonesian wealth. Chinese enterprisers control 80 percent of the 163 companies listed on the Jakarta Stock Exchange (Landler, 1998b). While most Chinese in Indonesia remain small shop owners and working-class people, indigenous Indonesians associate wealthy Chinese businessmen with the economic corruptions of the Suharto government. Considered the country's richest man, Liem Sioe Liong, born in China, won government contracts for cement and steel plants and obtained import monopolies on rice and sugar. Rioters stormed and burned his house in Jakarta, leaving the words "Suharto's dog" on the front fence. The words indicate political and economic resentment more than ethnic hatred. The relative mobility of the Chinese minority may also be cause for resentment among the majority. Chinese citizens with wealth and influence were able to flee relatively easily, not only the riots but also economic recessions and natural calamity, the latter all too common in Southeast Asia. Liem, in fact, was in Singapore when the attack occured, as was his son and heir, Anthony Salim, who runs the family business. Salim was a member of the Indonesian delegation to finance $80 billion in private debt. Another prominent Chinese family, the Riadys, fled to Hong Kong. James Riady, head of the Lippo Bank, remained a friend of President Bill Clinton and was a financial contributor to the U.S. Democratic party, a relationship that was scrutinized by the U.S. Congress. Such connections with international economic and political forces motivated much of the uprising.

According to human rights groups such as the government's own National Commission for Human Rights and the NGO Jakarta Social Institute, many of the rapes, executions, and arson cases that resulted in nearly 1,200 deaths during the May 13–15 civil strife were carried out in an organized manner by the military or other security forces. By its own admission, members of the military's special forces had kidnapped opposition activists weeks before the riots. What international NGOs speculated on, Indonesians in the streets were certain about. In July, 100 women demonstrated outside the Defense Ministry demanding that it take responsibility for the rapes. Their posters showed soldiers sexually violating women. Banners read, "Indonesia! Republic of Fear, Republic of Terror, Republic of Rape!" (Mydans, 1998d). The NGO Volunteers for Humanity reported threats against women's crisis center workers and victims who had called the center's hotline. Reverend Sandyawan Sumardi, head of the NGO Jakarta Social Institute, reported threats against his own life and against witnesses, family members, and hospital staff. Even the Internet was used to show fake photos claiming to be riot victims, a strategy designed to promote general fear and confusion. The ability to monitor phone conversations and use technology suggested to the NGO officials that government groups were behind the harassment and terror tactics (Mydans, 1998d).

HUMAN RIGHTS SOLUTIONS

International and domestic NGOs remained an important source for the promulgation of human rights education to the Indonesian populace during the 1998 protests. They spoke of garment and shoe factory workers who earned $1.50 per day for manufacturing Nike and other elite brand shoes that sell in the First World for

$100 per day or more; of university students who had been tortured by the police during crackdowns on political protests; of the rampant corruption, repression, and "crony capitalism" of the Suharto government (Surjadinata, 1998, p. 5). NGOs reported that, under the new Habibie government, many prominent political leaders remained imprisoned, such as Mochtar Pakpahan, a labor organizer; Sri Bintang Pamungkas, a former member of Parliament; and Xanana Gusmao, the chief East Timorese spokesman.

After Suharto's overthrow, grassroots indignation over his family activities continued. Under public pressure, two members of the Suharto extended family were ousted from their government positions and the Habibie government announced measures to curtail economic favoritism at the top. Street activists handed out photocopies listing in detail the Suharto holdings, which were valued at trillions of Indonesian rupiah. Newly liberated newspapers did the same. Also during the weeks following the overthrow, Suharto's second son, Bambang Trihatmodjo, was forced to resigned as head of the Bimantara Citra conglomerate, one of the country's largest corporations. He and Suharto's son-in-law also quit its board of directors. The new government also canceled tax breaks for a "national car" program run by another Suharto son, Hutomo Mandala Putra, a circumstance that had become symbolic of family nepotism. However, these events may have been only window dressing. Bambang Trihatmodjo retained a controlling share in the Bimantara Citra corporation. Other actions of the highly publicized reform policies of the transitional government, such as the cancellation of four port contracts owned by the Suharto family, and the investigation of contracts to process driver's licenses given to a company owned by Suharto's eldest daughter, Siti Hardiyanti Rukmana, may or may not prove substantive. Indonesias tropical rain forests continue to be burned at a dangerous rate, causing lung problems and accidents. The burning policies of large agribusiness firms have been directly related to government payoffs and cronyism under Suharto. As Emmy Hafild, director of the Indonesian Forum for the Environment, observed, "There are a few honest ministers and senior bureaucrats, but the big businessmen are far more powerful than they are. Corruption is the standard in our country. There is no rule of law" (Simons, 1998a, p. 112).

IMF officials targeted the corruption and nepotism of the Indonesian government, withholding $40 billion in funds originally approved in October 1997. Suharto apparently complied with those IMF austerity measures that negatively affected the populace, such as high prices for essential items, while temporizing on those that affected his personal wealth, such as corruption and nepotism. The resulting sense of unfairness led to the May overthrow. Adding to the civil discontent was the IMF's suspension of its aid package in February because of the slow implementation of reforms by the government. Economics and Finance Minister Ginandjar Kartasasmita pledged to abide by the IMF program, stating his commitment to eliminating food shortages, creating labor-intensive projects, and helping small companies. A major dilemma in the IMF-managed agenda for Indonesia was the continued commitment to austerity measures set on the people for the sake of what the chief fund official, Hubert Neiss called "macroeconomic parameters" (Mydans, 1998c, p. 10). As the economy continued to weaken, unemployment will go up while prices climb. Moreover, bankruptcies, bank closures, inflation, and food shortages for Indonesia's 210 million people would continue to cause widespread suffering. Adding to the sense of injustice was the continued disclosures by a newly unrestricted press of the extent of the Suharto corruption. The Jakarta Post in May reported numerous lucrative concessions that channeled profits to the Suharto family middlemen and away from state revenue.

The problem of human rights as Indonesia enters the 21st century turns upon the two factors: One the one hand, the demands of Global Capital—represented by the IMF austerity measures and TNC pressure to maintain weak labor organization—and on the other hand, the ecological, cultural, ethnic, and linguistic diversity of the country. Indonesia is the largest country comprising an archipeligo, which spreads across the sea for thousands of miles. Its religious and racial heterogeneity prevents easy roads to political mobilization at the grassroots level. The Java-centered government has historically neglected the other islands, some of which comprise large geographical areas with agrarian minority groups that have resisted Javanese polity. University students have been aware of the disunity of the movement, which is progressive for some factions, self-centered for others. Medan University students, for example, recently lamented the comparison of their own country's unfocused activism with the "people power" uprising in the Philippines that overthrew the dictator Ferdinand Marcos. Muchtar Efendi Harahap, a lecturer in sociology at Medan University, commented succinctly, "The problem in Indonesia is that not everyone is united." Still, the students took comfort in the broad consensus for change in Indonesia, reflecting on the shallowness of the government reactionary power: "If a thousand people are protesting, the army will kill them. If five thousand people are protesting, the army will leave them alone. If more than five thousand people are protesting, the army will join them" (Landler, 1998a, p. 8).

In July 1998, the Indonesian government was actively pursuing debt restructuring in the First World. Officials campaigned to persuade international banks to repackage up to $9 billion in debt. Finance Minister Ginandjar's main concern was "to stabilize the economy," which means courting IMF and other First World lenders, promising to alter Indonesian society to make it more attractive for foreign investors. This agenda will conflict with important domestic freedom issues, such as the legalization of trade unions, which the Habibie government has promised the populace. While Ginandjar sought to keep interest rates high to combat inflation and would allow his country's weakest banks to fail in order to support stronger banks, he also agreed to continue to liberalize social policies: "Indonesia has been portrayed as an outcast country because of our legal system and human rights issues. We are embarking on a new era that we hope will cause the Western people and the Western media to look more favorably on us" (O'Brien, 1998, p. A9). However, the collapse of the rupiah in 1997 has Western investors willing to keep Indonesia under pressure to remain pro-business in its orientation in order that its existing debt—$64 billion to $66 billion owed by Indonesian corporations, $54 billion to $55 billion owed by the state—will be repaid. However, by World Bank forecasts, half the country's population, 100 million people, will fall below the poverty line this year, and mass starvation is expected. These conditions violate the social and economic rights of the UN human rights covernants. While Ginandjar's lobbying efforts continued with bankers in New York, Washington, Frankfort, Paris, Tokyo, Seoul, and Singapore, these investors have cooled to similar debt restructuring in South Korea, which they consider on a sounder footing than Indonesia. Under this sort of outside pressure from Global Capital, and the undercover influence peddling of the Suharto family and associates, can the Habibie government's commitment to labor unions, the freeing of political dissenters, and the promise of free elections by 1999 be achieved in any real way? Only a strong, united, and long-term grassroots democracy movement can resist such systemic economic power.

The East Timor independence movement revived when Habibie offered special administrative status to that province, which had been abandoned by the Portugese colonizers but seized in 1975 by the Suharto government. East Timor experienced genocidal killing of 200,000 of its 800,000 people under the Suharto regime. Jose Ramos-Horta, the East Timor independence leader, said in June 1998 that he would accept an offered of limited autonomy and a 5-year delay on a referendum for the territory's independence. Habibie offered to remove army troops from East Timor and release all political prisoners, including Jose Xanana Gusmao, a prominent guerilla leader. He also met with Bishop Carlos Ximenes Belo of East Timor, who together with Ramos-Horta had won the 1996 Nobel Peace Prize. However, Habibie also ruled out independence for the territory. Ramos-Horta compared the changes needed in Indonesia to the liberalization agenda of Kim Dae Jung, a longtime dissident and opposition leader who became president of South Korea in 1998. Kim released all of his country's estimated 500 political prisoners. Ramos-Horta attributed recent violent incidents in East Timor against European envoys to the provocation by Indonesian government agents (Crossette, 1998a).

Indonesian military violence against the East Timorese continued into 1998. In November 1997, eight students were killed by troops as they demonstrated during the anniversary of the 1991 Santa Cruz massacre in Dili. Forty thousand troops guarded a population of only 800,000. With such examples of covert terror and agitation throughout the archipeligo, the progressive transformation of Indonesia seemed imperiled. U.S. aid continued to the Indonesian government despite the civil protests and breakdown, although the U.S. Congress did pass legislation blocking weapons to Indonesia in 1997. President Clinton offered a general prescription for future democratic progress in Indonesia, but avoided comment on the close association of the CIA and DIA with the repressive elements in the nation's military: "What we do believe is important is that the present government open a dialogue with all elements of society and that it lead to genuine political reform" (Mydans, 1998a, p. A6).

Perhaps the only hope for substantive democratic reform and social justice in Indonesia lies in the ability of recently released political opposition leaders to activate large constituencies that will keep pressure on the power structure. The overthrow of Suharto was precipitated in the Summer of 1996, when the Indonesian Democratic Party under Megawati Sukarno, the daughter of the former President, directly challenged the Suharto government. Although the party was destroyed, the political uprising that followed continued for two years. Establishing a power base for progress needs coalition building in a way Indonesia has not achieved before. Amien Rais, for example, led almost 30 million Muslim Indonesians, but did not use his power to help overthrow Suharto. The valiant student protestors remained without a grassroots base. Other opposition leaders, including Megawati Sukarno, appear unable to command large power bases. Hope perhaps lies in two recently released figures: Muchtar Pakpahan, head of the independent trade union, S.B.S.I., and Sri Bintang Pamungkas, founder of the United Democratic Party. Bintang announced a grassroots campaign for justice that will involve hundreds of villages in all 26 provinces. Pakpahan is capable of organizing labor movements on a broad front. As Indonesian newspaper agitate for the release of the remaining 200 political prisoners, other grassroots organizers like Budiman Sudjatmiko intend to revitalize his banned People's Democratic Party, perhaps the most progressive of the existing parties (Winters, 1998). Such efforts depend upon the continuing possibility of a free press that exposes abuses of power and a vital political movement that can overcome efforts at intimidation from a reactionary military.

One important strength of the recent political reform movement in Indonesia has been the liberation and revitalization of the press (Mydans, 1998b). Suharto's ban on three important progressive newspapers in 1994 helped precipitate the student protest movement that included the first protest against censorship in the Suharto era. One of these voices, the weekly news magazine *Tempo*, was republished on the Internet as *Tempo Interactive*, where it became the chief source of reliable information for activists (Harymurti, 1998). Young journalists formed the Independent Journalists Alliance, which has published events ignored by the coopted press. Such vigilance remains a positive force for change in a country that has, despite all the odds against it, overthrown its dictator through the peaceful spread of information. As Indonesia under Habibie began to withdraw its army from East Timor in August 1998, the promise of a more democratic future will perhaps continue (Shenon, 1998). Hal Hill (1996) has documented the impressive economic advance of Suharto's New Order Indonesia from the 1960s onward. Yet broad-based development must become the goal of all economic ventures in Indonesia so that all its people may obtain a standard of living consistent with the UN human rights covenants.

QUESTIONS FOR FURTHER THOUGHT

1. What can be done to transcend the vicious cycle of conflict between the traditional "trading minorities" and the Indonesian majority?

2. What can strengthen those Third World countries (NICs) who have developed economically but remain underdeveloped politically? Does the responsibility lie within these countries, with outside forces, or with both? Are these factors related?

3. Given the great cultural diversity of the Indonesians, what political perspectives would be best able to bring about a sustained progressive movement?

4. What can be done to put international pressure on the new Indonesian government for genuine democratic reforms?

5. Given the great profitability from the bountiful natural resources and inexpensive labor of Indonesia, what pressure can be exerted on Global Capital and indigenous enterprise to assure human rights standards for the environment and the people?

13

CHINA:
THE OPEN DOOR
AND HUMAN RIGHTS

Not until the 1980s had China (PRC) taken an active involvement in UN initiatives. Unable to enter the United Nations until 1971, it became a permanent member of the Security Council, where it generally withdrew from participation in votes, particularly regarding peacekeeping operations. As of 1980, it had ratified only six out of 190 UN treaties while joining only five IGOs in the UN system (Glahn, 1981). About the first decade of China's participation in the United Nations, Samuel Kim (1979) observes:

> None of the PRC delegates has ever served as chairman of any committee or subsidiary body of the General Assembly. In the Asian group meeting, China declines chairmanship even by the rotational system. China's support of the Third World countries generally takes the form of a partisan spectator who cheers, moralizes, and votes when necessary, rather than an active, not to say leading, player in the game of global politics. (p. 159)

China's rising interest in the United Nations since the early 1980s follows a general turn outward under Deng Xiaoping following the death of Mao Zedong. It became more articulate at the Security Council and General Assembly, joined most of the specialized agencies, including the capitalist oriented World Bank and IMF, and supported all UN peacekeeping actions. Today, all indications confirm that China will continue to pursue an outward, multilateralist course (Rochester, 1993). The causes that brought about its motivational turn are complex and include both internal changes and the pressure of international forces. Outwardly, the demise of other nominally Communist states, the rise of fellow Asian economies—particularly those economies with a traditional Chinese presence, such as Hong Kong, Singapore, and Malaysia—and increased solicitation from TNCs were probably all factors in the increased willingness of China to become global in its thought and practice. Inwardly, discontent among the populace who perceived their limited civil and personal freedoms relative to other countries, together with a growing awareness of the outside world through increased electronic communication and personal contacts were among the important causes. Finally, the recognition among the governing elite that China must become more open or fall behind motivated new approaches from the top. For the nation's hierarchy, no doubt economic improvement has been the dominant motivation. The desires of China's people are probably more complicated, but certainly include economic improvement, which may be perceived as causally connected to the attainment of human rights and social justice. In this regard, the Western rhetoric of rapproachment—leaving aside the issue of whether or not its rhetoric is sincere—may parallel the thinking of most Chinese.

Certainly, economic improvement has been the greatest concern on both sides during President Clinton's official visit to China in 1998. A look at the Clinton trip to China can help clarify the complex discourse of human rights that has placed China at the center of world scrutiny in the 1990s. To better understand the rhetoric of statemen, their overt and hidden agendas, and the levels if thought and emotion evoked by the people of China and America, it is necessary to look at the language of both U.S. official representatives and the spokespeople of China. Keeping in mind that the language of diplomacy involves as much body language and personalistic judgments as it does verbal statement, we will attempt to interpret the images of diplomacy as presented by its media coverage, chiefly television and newspapers.

THE CLINTON TRIP TO CHINA:
HELPING "THE FROG AT THE BOTTOM OF THE WELL"

Political Background

While many in the U.S. Congress perceive China as a security risk, other Clinton administration critics held hearings to determine whether China was exploiting liberalized U.S. commercial export laws to improve its spy satellites and nuclear missiles. Meanwhile, transnational corporate executives, set for disappointment at the degree to which China would open its doors for U.S. business investment, pressed the president for more commitment to trade. Government officials were also anxious over the growing trade deficit between the United States and China, with China selling more than it received from the United States. The Clinton administration, however, wished to distance itself somewhat from trade issues and the TNCs after recent domestic disclosures of Chinese money to campaign funds and allegations of technological theft. For its part, the White House wished to redeem its somewhat tarnished domestic image with a stateman-like 9-day summit visit, the longest of the Clinton administration. Plans were for the president to stress the nonpolitical side of China instead of human rights, which was initially perceived as too sensitive a topic for the visits. Meetings with villagers, small businessmen, and teachers were planned. Early in the visit, however, human rights and other political issues moved to the forefront when Clinton and Chinese president Jiang Zemin exchanged direct remarks over live Chinese television about the killing of protesters at Tiananmen Square in 1989. Sensing favorable reaction from the Chinese people and permission from its leaders, Clinton allowed human rights to move center stage early in the visit. As one U.S. journalist phrased it, "Human rights in China is a live political issue in Washington" (Faison, 1998a, p. 5). Wishing to keep a certain distance from big business's open-door aspirations, Clinton also wished to appease human rights advocates who charged his administration with ignoring human rights in China for the sake of future corporate profits. For its part, China wished to keep close relations with U.S. leaders to insure its membership in the World Trade Organization (WTO).

The Visit and Summit

Pressed by domestic and international human rights groups to articulate a clear stand on freedom of expression, legal violations, and recent alleged abuses in Tibet, the Clinton administration planned to mention political dissent and to meet with Chinese dissenters during the 9-day trip. At the same time, he would avoid taking an overtly trade approach to the summit, rejecting earlier plans to visit factory sites of U.S. businesses in China and deleting most remarks on the benefits of investment in his speeches. Aware of the underlying motives of the visit—to clear the way for accelerated TNC investment—the Clinton administration was also keenly aware of recent negative publicity connected with alleged donations to the Democratic campaign fund by Chinese business interests and charges that U.S. technology was illegally used for Chinese missile guidance systems. While the U.S. delegation was interested in pleasing transnational business interests, it was hamstrung by these other pressures. The Chinese, on the other hand, were more willing to talk of business investment than human rights. While it would seem that both countries were at cross-purposes, events surprised most U.S. strategists. Jiang Zemin, the Chinese president, allowed the wide dissemination of Clinton's remarks on human rights, even allowing live television coverage of a speech and question and answer period at the acknowledged center of student dissent in China, Beijing University. Some U.S. officials speculated that Jiang was using Clinton as a ventriloquist's dummy to raise controversial topics in China, enabling him then to defend his own position before the Chinese people. Another theory was that Jiang was making a major concession to the Clinton administration, knowing how much they wished to talk human rights and avoid seeming like a business booster club. This theory assumes that Jiang was well motivated to nego-tiated with the Americans. One unnamed senior U.S. official commented, "They recognized that the price of engagement with us was giving us axxess to their peo-ple. Jiang knew he needed to do that to make this a successful summit" (Broder, 1998a, p. A9).

Certainly, the Chinese party hierarchy was aware of the Clinton administra-tion's domestic vulnerability. Samuel R. Berger, the president's national security advisor, had met with Chinese officials weeks before the visit, making it clear to them that the U.S. president needed "a positive outcome" at the summit to keep his domestic critics in line (Broder, 1998a, p. A9). What Berger demanded and got was access to the Chinese people—and to Americans at home—through ample television, radio, and public appearances. For most Chinese, in China and in the United States, Clinton's personal contact with Chinese people was taken as an important gesture of respect. Along with that, however, many Chinese in America expressed viewed commonly associated with socialist member states of the United Nations: "Human rights are the ability to have food, clothing, education and shelter. Only after you have these can you think about things like democracy and freedom," Chunde Shi, an immigrant living in New York, remarked. Mang Xu, a Shanghai immigrant in New York observed, "Contact is better than confron-tation," but he went on to predict, If you open the economic door, then you'll open the political door." Jane Eng, a New York immigrant expressed a more subjective view of United States Chinese relations: "China is like a frog at the bottom of the well. It only knows what it can see. America is at the top; it can see the whole world. So people should have patience while China—with the help of the United States—figures out a way to get out" (Chen, 1998, p. B4).

Although many U.S. journalists, including David Chen himself, have attributed to cultural difference the prevalent Chinese attitude that economic and social rights should precede civil and political rights, in fact, the notion that those rights emphasized in the International Covenant on Economic, Social, and Cultural Rights (ICESCR) should take precedence over those of the International Covenant on Civil and Political Rights (ICCPR) are a common view of many, if not most, Third World nations and socialist countries. Even in the West, the famous pyramid of the psychologist Abraham Maslow is often cited to explain how "physiological needs," such as food, shelter, and safety, take precedence over "esteem needs" and "self-actualization," or the full expression of the individual. Accordingly, most Chinese may not be expressing so much cultural difference from the West as a uni-versal desire to have the basic needs satisfied first. From this perspective, President Clinton's success with promoting what the U.S. media has termed "human rights" in China will depend upon his ability to convince most Chinese that American business access through a new open-door policy will benefit Chinese life through the "positive" rights of ICESCR. At the beginning of his trip, the U.S. president stressed the ICCPR rights, so-called "negative" rights—freedom of speech, assembly, religion, and so on. However, if most Chinese people are keenly aware of what is expressed by the Maslow pyramid, that the physiological needs are the foundation for "higher" ideals such as freedom of expression and individual rights. Along with this, what may be the bottom line for most Chinese is what the U.S. president has avoided in his China speeches—the nature and practice of U.S. business involvement in China.

In a separate ceremony, U.S. Commerce Secretary William M. Daley and Zeng Peiyan, chair of the China State Planning Commission, gathered in Beijing at the Great Hall of the People to confirm a $1.6 billion trade and investment deal between the two countries. The Americans were disappointed. The impressive figure was largely stuffing. Banks and insurance companies were denied entrance to China's market, and companies like Boeing were unable to sell their planes. Although the poor showing was partially the result of an uncertain Asian economy, the Clinton administration had backed off somewhat from the plane deal, sensitive to domestic charges that it had helped U.S. aerospace corporations conduct business in China for campaign contributions (Zuckerman, 1998). Clinton is clearly distancing himself from U.S. business interests. In contrast to previous foreign visits, no executives accompanied him to China, and he avoided tours of U.S. plants in Beijing and Shanghai. One anonymous administration official admitted that the U.S. president felt vulnerable to accusations that the China trip and summit were driven primarily by business interests (Zuckerman, 1998). Such hesitancy is perhaps a sign that human rights advocacy has some effect on U.S. public opinion.

In part to take attention away from the business objectives of the summit, Clinton emphasized Chinese intolerance with political dissent, inviting prominent dissenters to speak with him and lecturing university students on the advantages of the marketplace of ideas. Playing the moral high ground is perhaps what Jane Eng had in mind with her image of the frogs at the bottom of the well, but Clinton risks being labeled a hypocrite when his message becomes too one-sided. Sensing a bit of cross-cultural lecturing, students began asking him about problems with human rights in his own country during the question and answer period at Beijing University. Clinton handled the questions well, perhaps anticipating such response, but he clearly was on narrow ground. After all, Jane Eng's image of the frog that needs the guidance of the being at the top of the well may be to an extent only a polite way of welcoming a visitor to a culture where social relations have important symbolic purpose.

By June 30, Clinton was clearly associating human rights, ecological awareness, and unregulated legal systems with business interests. Perhaps time away from an oppositional U.S. Congress and domestic criticism allowed him to find a way toward his own agenda, which was to cajole China into appropriate behavior for the era of Global Capital. To do this required a personable lecturing style and a careful articulation of what China needed for the next century. For this task, Clinton was famously equipped, with a speaker presence surpassing that of Ronald Reagan. Millions of Chinese saw over live television the great contrast in the speaking styles of both presidents. While Jiang read his speech stiffly with little eye contact, Clinton delivered his words confidently, with a vocabulary of facial expressions, vocal variety, and continuous eye contact. During the question and answer period with university students, he spoke casually, with his hand on his chin—not unlike the confident poses of ancient Chinese sages on woodcuts. When students asked him critical questioned about the U.S., Clinton responded with personal disclosures and detailed examples, finishing his answer with the remark—perhaps unheard of, at least with regard to China's national leaders—"That's a good question." In fact, Clinton's remarks in speeches, question and answer periods on television and call-in radio, and in interviews often included mini-lectures to the Chinese on how to express and respond to political and social opinion in public.

This version of statesmanship proved particularly effective with most Chinese. For a young businessman, Zhao Xingang, "This visit has opened the possibility that Chinese themselves will be able to openly debate such topics." He went on to praise President Jiang for allowing the U.S. president to appear uncensored on live television and call-in radio. For a publishing house worker, Song Jiantong, Clinton's informal style was most effective in a highly censored society: "Before we had only seen him in pictures. We didn't know he was so funny and easy going. He answered every question. We now have a better understanding of what United States democracy is about." For a member of the Chinese Academy of Medical Science, Xiu Ruizhaun, Clinton's open personality was a positive sign of future relationships: "Clinton has the right to talk about issues. It was a good beginning to see that he was not hostile to China" (Rosenthal, 1998, p. A13). Just how the Chinese people read the Party's willingness to allow Clinton to speak uncensored may be more difficult to determine. It is important to remember that total disinterested reporting is a nearly impossible objective. Certainly in the U.S. media, spokespeople of disfavored nations are underreported and often presented with unfavorable commentary, as with Fidel Castro when he visited New York City in the mid-1990s.

Clinton's personable lecturing approach sought to appease, if not satisfy, human rights advocates at home while he prepared China for transnational business involvement. On June 30, Clinton told the American Chamber of Commerce in Shanghai that corruption, environmental reglect, weak financial regulation and restrictive trade practices could prevent China's from entering the global economic system. Remarking, "China's economy still is burdened with complicated and overlapping barriers," he instanced inefficient state monopolies, weak legal and regulatory systems, wasteful and polluting energy patterns, closed markets and poor banking supervision. No doubt with the Chinese leadership in mind, he mildly threatened that Beijing needed to make "difficult decisions" to bring China into the WTO (qtd. in Broder, 1998b). Meeting with young Chinese entrepreneurs, on July 1, Clinton gave a more realistic assessment of how capitalism may change Chinese life. There will be more career choices and chances to run one's own business, but also less security as the government reduces payrolls at state-owned organizations. On a more political track, haunted by a high estimated trade deficit with China, U.S. Secretary of Commerce William M. Daley and others contended that Chinese tariffs and other trade barriers were limiting U.S. sales in China, while Chinese exports continued to grow rapidly. In contrast to Clinton's easy-going, almost advisory approach to the Chinese, Daley's language seemed a barely veiled threat, "There has been an acknowledgment that they understand that this has the potential to be a political issue, and that we do have a disagreement over the amount of the deficit" (Broder, 1998b, p. A12).

Clinton's human rights discourse on live call-in radio in Shanghai melded with preachments on business attitudes and behaviors: "I believe...that high levels of personal freedom are quite important to the success of a society in the information age, because you need people who feel free to explore their own convictions and then live out their own dreams, and that this will add to the stability of a society by enriching it" (Faison, 1998c, p. A12). The personal freedoms of the West are presented as necessary for the continued cohesion of society so important to traditional Chinese thought and practice. Although keeping his distance from U.S. TNCs—refusing to have any CEOs in his official entourage and allowing others to represent U.S. business at various trade talks during the visit—Clinton instead closely associated with Chinese enterprisers, toured new business districts, and met homeowners. Focusing on new business freedoms in China was not controversial back home and also underscored the message that the invisible hand of capitalistic growth will cure all Chinese ills, including human rights. This is a big assumption, made perhaps bigger by the embarrassing development that China's new economic freedom has recently produced a worrisome recession. As the Clinton tour passed new wide avenues of commercial neon in Shanghai, many of the new high-rises were empty from overdevelopment. Unemployment was also rising in the largest commercial cities. Undaunted, Clinton's speeches never mentioned these recent side effects of the "free" market.

Samuel Berger's pre-trip agreement with the Chinese to allow Clinton access to the Chinese people was unfolding as planned. In a further attempt to steer China towards more acceptance of political dissent and individual freedom, meetings with dissidents were arranged. Clinton met with seven "agents of change" in Shanghai. Included were a law professor, a consumer advocate, a physicist, an economist, and a bishop who had spent years in prison. Zhu Lanye, of the international department at the East China University of Politics and Law, told Clinton that China needed to train thousands more lawyers and persuade people to seek legal remedies to their grievances with the government or in the private economy. The Chinese legal profession, labeled "primitive" by Western, (particularly U.S.) standards, is consistent with the Eastern concentual approach to conflict, but hinders large business enterprises, which depend upon contract law, torts, and adversarial approaches. Clinton, following most legal scholars and experts in the West, has tried to associate Western-style legal practice with personal freedoms rather than with Western business practices, a strategy that allows him to avoid the sensitive bottom line of opening up China for U.S. business.

Not before the public eye, but referred to at the end of newspaper articles and on the op-ed pages of the larger U.S. newspapers was the sharp disagreement between the U.S. and China over missiles. The former wanted China to fully participate in the Missile Technology Control Regime, an agreement on missile technology exports, while the latter wanting the United States to sign an agreement not to use the "first strike" strategy in nuclear exchange. The U.S. delegation's objective was to get China to agree to the ban on exports without surrendering the first strike strategy. Since the U.S. military strategy of the first strike sits uneasily with human rights preachment, Clinton avoided mentioning it and U.S. mainstream media have obligingly focused elsewhere.

Clinton continued to associate economic liberalization and personal freedom, referring to both in strong language—they were "morally right" for the Chinese people. In doing so, he subtlely equated freedom and openness with the American ethic: "I think there's a genuine movement towards openness and freedom in China, which obviosuly as an American, and as an American president, I hope will continue and increase and which I believe is right—morally right—but I also think it's good for China." In what was perhaps an indirect Chinese way of challenging U.S. hegemony in the world, Clinton was asked whether the world needed a single leader to mediate disputes within and among nations. His response was consistent with the trip's overall message of openness, democracy, and tolerance, geopolitics as a round-table discussion: "The world needs a leader, but not in the sense of one country telling everyone else what to do. So it's a different sort of world leadership than in the past where it's just a question of who has the biggest army gets to send a list ofinstructions to another country and you think it will be done. That's not the way the world works now" (Broder, 1998c, p. A8). More educated Chinese may wonder about Clinton's assurance that might no longer makes right at the end of the 20th century. His examples were also a cause of concern. Haiti and Bosnia were advanced as instances of forging new alliances to exert influence rather than unilateral actions. But U.S. intervention and covert activity in Haiti and elsewhere in the Third World hardly seems merely "forging new alliances" (see Chapter 11, in this volume). Clinton's version of pax Americana sounded more like democracy in action than geopolitical power tactics: "And so the United States role I think is to try to create a structure where more likely than not the rights things will be done when problems arise—not to just do it all ourselves or tell other people what to do." Certainly, many in the Beijing University audience were skeptical or perplexed by Clinton's advisory persona during the trip, as instanced in one students question to him which commented specifically on his wide smile and whether truth lay behind it. At times, to be sure, it seemed as though the U.S. president were overstepping his bounds by selling the American Dream of individualism as foreign policy. His speech on a tour of a new house development project in Shanghai told homeowning families there that "All China benefits from more home owners because that means more jobs, a stronger econcomy, stronger families. And, of course, when people own their own homes, they are free to take new jobs without worrying about losing housing benefits. We also see around the world that homeowners take more responsibility for the communities in which they live" (Broder, 1998c, p. A8). The message, that lifting oneself up by the bootstraps without government assistance, would have gone over well at any U.S. Chamber of Commerce chicken-and-pea dinner.

With many reports about China's arrest of political dissidents appearing in the U.S. media, Clinton made mention of particular Chinese intolerance over the last decade. Although he expressed welcome that China had recently released several well-known dissidents, he called upon Beijing to release whole classes of prisoners. Particularly mentioning 150 people held on charges related to the 1989 Tiananmen Square demontrations, he also urged the release of prisoners held for other politically related actions. Clinton's moral high ground about the virtues of an open society were somewhat compromised by other news reports about the political records of U.S. client states. In a effort to throw off his countriy's authoritarian political past for the purpose of rebuilding in a more open way in the wake of the economic collapse in December 1997, South Korea's president, Kim Dae Jung, announced during Clinton's China trip the release and amnesty of political prisoners. Human rights groups estimate the number of incarcerated for political views in South Korea as about 500. In total, however, the general amnesty included 5.5 million South Koreans, from individuals who lost their jobs to those given excess traffic tickets for their ideological views. Among the prisoners released was Woo Yong Gak, the world's longest-serving political prisoner, who would not abandon his North Korean doctrines (Strom, 1998). Similar records exist of the closed nature of China's other political rival, Taiwan. Perhaps these states are what former U.S. Ambassador to the United Nations Jeanne Kirkpatrick distinguishes as "authoritarian" rather than "totalitarian" states (see Chapter 3, in this volume). Except for their size in relation to China, the difference escapes immediate discernment. Human rights violations continue throughout most of the capital-oriented societies in Asia, Africa, and Latin America. Clinton has never qualified his statements regarding human rights abuses in China with reference to these near neighbors of China, a stance that puts his human rights discourse into a limited political framework. His wish to cultivate an advisory rather than a political image in China becomes itself qualified.

As for China itself, which sought the "most favored nation" status in trade throughout most of the 1990s, its turn toward capitalism is not all the American

Dream road to openness and freedom the Clinton administration, and much of the U.S. mainstream press, would like to project. During the Asia Pacific Summit in Seattle, Washington in November 1993, as Clinton announced that the United States would be sending high-tech nuclear equipment to China despite the ban on such trade because of China's violation of missile and nuclear proliferation agreements, 81 women were burned to death because they were locked in a factory in Kwangdong province, called the economic miracle of China. A few weeks later, 60 workers were killed in a Hong Kong-owned factory. China's own Labor Ministry reported that 11,000 people had been killed in the first eight months of 1993, twice the rate of the previous year (Chomsky, 1994). Although reports of Chinese prison labor abuse can make the front pages of *The New York Times*, abuses in private factories have gone unreported in the U.S. media. The difference is that prison labor is associated with the old regime of government control, Kirkpatrick's "totalitarian" system, whereas abuses in private factories are "authoritarian," nongovernmental, and therefore acceptable. From another perspective, factory prisons compete with private factories, thus undermining private profits. As for Clinton's ignoring China's efforts toward nuclear and missile proliferation, his 1993 decision to send sophistocated satellites, supercomputers, and nuclear generators was the beginning of what became his scandal of compaign contribution funds from China.

Clinton also warned the Chinese about its disastrous ecological policies. With a nearly unregulated system of air and water pollution, China, with its large population, has become a major concern of environmentalists worldwide. Given the global ramifications of such a major pollutant, even the TNCs have been concerned. Too much pollution endangers owners—including their families—as well as workers, and worldwide pollution means there is no place to escape, even for those who can affort to vacation in remote parts of the world. The Clinton administration's decision to stress an environmentally correct ethos fits its dual criteria for the China summit: to help promote private investment in China and appear to support human rights efforts.

Less prominent, but still a subject of concern for the U.S. visitors was allegations that the Chinese government was practicing forced abortions to promote its one-child policy. Clinton arranged to speak about the emotive issues in private meetings with Jiang. Probed by U.S. journalists at the Hong Kong end-of-trip press conference, Clinton appeared to accept Jiang's response: "My view is that these reports are accurate, there may be an insufficient monitoring of what's being done beyond the capital and beyond the place where the orders are being handed out to the place where they are being—the policy is being implemented" (Reuters, 1998b, p. A5). He then mentioned his wife Hillary's efforts to raise this issue with the Chinese at the 1993 UN Women's Rights Conference in Beijing. Realizing that the forced abortion issue was a concern of U.S. groups from both the right and left, and wishing to give his final speech on foreign soil an upbeat tone, Clinton kept the issue out of the media as much as possible, responding only to queries from Western journalists after the trip.

RESULTS OF THE CHINA SUMMIT: HUMAN RIGHTS CENTER STAGE AND IN THE WINGS

Bolstered by the trip were the reputations of China President Jiang Zemin and Prime Minister Zhu Rongji, the latter praised frequently by President Clinton as a long range planner for China's economic growth. Also helped was President Clinton's reputation as an international statesman. Among the business community, Clinton's reputation was also advanced, as he achieved the goal of gaining the confidence of the Beijing leadership as regards the transition of China to a market-oriented society with closer ties—or dependency—upon U.S. and European trade. Some U.S. critics felt Clinton should have been harder on Beijing concerning human rights, offering the recent student-led downfall of President Suharto of Indonesia as a grim example and the democratic direction of Taiwan as a model (Eckholm, 1998a). Clinton perhaps felt that U.S. government, military, and business ties with the Suharto regime over two decades was a source of potential embarrassment, and Taiwan's democracy has left out native Taiwanese, whose suppression of culture has been systematic on Formosa.

In general, Clinton played it safe with the Chinese. He refused to meet with any outspoken opponents of the government during the trip, in his own words dealing with human rights "in a way most likely to yield progress." Instead he pressed Jiang to release political prisoners and avoided "a theatrical encounter with dissidents." Clinton assured the Chinese that "our human rights policy is not an excuse for some larger strategic motive...we believe it's best for [the Chinese] as a practical matter over the long run" (Broder, 1998d, p. A4). Understated in the wrap-up speech and during the nine-day trip was the determination of the U.S. visitors to promote private business interests, chiefly for the TNCs, and to use human rights and other issues to that end. Free speech becomes the same thing as a "free" market in such a reduction. Human needs are generated by the tide of capital that lifts all boats great and small, the famous invisible hand of Adam Smith. Issues such as freedom of the press and consumer rights under a corporate-controlled government and legal system do not fit into the picture. When Beijing students asked Clinton what were problems in his own country, Clinton could offer only drugs, crime, and racism, not pollution caused by industrial smokestacks grandfathered in under existing federal environmental laws, the great disparities between rich and poor in education, health, employment, and so on. Moreover, Clinton made no mention of the outlawing of labor unions in China or the violations of working conditions throughout China.

On the positive side, the Clinton China summit and trip gave the Beijing leadership more space to loosen control of civil and political rights, perhaps obliging

Asian rivals such as South Korea to release political prisoners and to loosen the society as well. With the Chinese people, Clinton's personable presence allowed them to see the United States in a way different from the official party line of their mainstream media, perhaps allowing space for less defensive behavior and more tolerance for dissent over the long run.

QUESTIONS FOR FURTHER THOUGHT

1. What other issues of human rights or social justice could President Clinton have raised with the Chinese during the trip?
2. Could other members of the official U.S. entourage to China have raised more sensitive problems or issues with the Beijing leadership? If so, who would be the most appropriate official for this?
3. Could more have been done to bring business, trade, and investment issues before the Chinese public? Based on your knowledge of the Chinese people, would they be concerned about the sudden expansion and conversion of China into a country of Global Capital?
4. China's desire to have the United States give up its "first strike" policy of nuclear missiles was played down by the U.S. media. What other specific issues raised by the Clinton China trip were misrepresented or downplayed? How should they have been represented?
5. What was the most effective strategy used by President Clinton regarding human rights in China? Do you feel he could have altered his approach for a more effective presentation of human rights issues?

Part IV

Global Issues
and Dilemmas

14

WOMEN AND INTERNATIONAL JUSTICE

CURRENT PROBLEMS AND AGENDAS

Approaches to women's rights in the international public sphere have been informed by long-standing negative views of women that have slighted both their traditional social lifestyles and newfound vocational roles. Among political theorists and international policymakers, the equation of femininity with "the communal essence" of non-Western cultures has become a common strategy for marginalizing Third World women (Robertson, 1992, p. 108). Even mainstream Western feminists have often essentialized women's culture as communal and affective as opposed to abstract and individualistic (Gilligan, 1982). Set in opposition to the rationalist individualism of dominant Western legal and social systems, Third World societies are typically understood as consensual and feminine. This binary opposition effectively presents women stereotypically as socially ineffective in the postcolonial era, a reductionism that hinders attitudinal change in both First and Third World societies. The view that women and women's culture are somehow beyond the legal boundaries and adversarial rationalism of trial law finds substance in the ambiguities of international law concerning women and in the tardiness with which legal systems worldwide have responded to abuses against women (Liebenberg, 1995).

Human rights for women has been undertaken in earnest by IGOs and individual states only within the past two decades, despite the fact that the equality of men and women has been articulated clearly in Article 1 of the United Nations Charter. "We the peoples of the UN determined...to reaffirm faith in fundamental human rights, in the dignity and worth of the human person, in the equal rights of men and women...." The Convention on the Elimination of All Forms of Discrimination against Women was made effective in 1980. As of June 1990, 103 states had ratified it (not including the U.S.). For centuries, women have been discriminated against and their persons violated with impunity. Many of the states that have ratified the UN Convention accept some forms of human rights abuse against women as part of their cultural beliefs and practice. The increased emphasis on women's rights during the 1990s will continue into the 21st century, as more and more women become advocates for change as they attain greater educational levels.

Although the case of gender discrimination and abuse comes with its own difficulties involving cross-cultural differences, social praxis, and definitions of social value and function, this fact does not make the women's rights movement unique in that regard. Most human rights initiatives face intercultural obstacles, some of which are quite similar to those confronting women's rights advocates. By far the greatest problem confronting the women's movement is common to all other human rights, social justice, and environmental movements in the international sphere—the problem of implementation. As Kathryn Damm (1991) notes, "[H]ow much of these conventions are merely rhetoric? The key to that question lies in implementation and publicity." Moreover, "The machinery for human rights implementation must not be restricted to those areas in which the majority has a direct political interest. Thus, all human rights violations must be treated equally, for a man beaten to death in Chile is just as dead as a man beaten to death in South Africa" (p. 100). This is typically true of women's human rights. Some nations and cultures have comparatively well-established advocacy networks and institutions, while others have very little or none at all. Even within cultures and states, class divisions can affect the degree to which women both advocate change and are influenced by change. These disparities inevitably hinder the efficacy of the movement.

Nonetheless, women have been continually overlooked in 20th century human rights discourse, despite the early recognition of their gender in the UN Charter. This chapter will explore more fully the progress of human rights discourse for women, noting both its similarities and differences with regard to other human rights discourse. It will also consider needed reforms and restructuring to assure the effectiveness of women's rights in the future.

NEGLECT: PAST AND PRESENT

The legacy of women as second-class citizens has evolved from an earlier tradition—quite recent in many cultures—of women as non- or second-class citizens.
The Judeo-Christian bible represents examples of this struggle to overcome inferior status, as when Hebrew women petitioned for the right to inheritance and
when women's testimony was not considered in a court of law nor in private life.
In the Gospels, the three Marys are not believed by Peter and the other disciples
when they bring news of the empty tomb. This tradition carries down to the beginning of the 21st century, when women in some cultures are still denied access to
rights considered basic for men and where forced marriages continue.

Very recently, Global Capital has created another impediment to women's
rights. The systematic use of women and girls to work in assembly plants and
other maquiladora factories has become common practice across the spectrum of
Third World cultures (see Chapter 6, in this volume). For example, in El Salvador
clothing assembly factories, young women and girls are given birth control pills
without doctor examination or consent. The management lies to them by claiming
they are anti-malaria pills. Although the workers know what the pills are, they take
them anyway for fear that they will be fired or punished harshly (Belle, 1995).
Local managers use women and girls as policy because they believe they will be
less likely to resist than men and will be more compliant. It is also clear that many
of the girls will work for less than even the low wages of male workers. The preference for women workers is widespread throughout the Caribbean, Latin America, Asia, and, most recently, Africa.

While women in the post-colonial period have entered nontraditional occupations in greater numbers· and have received generally higher levels of education,
health services, and other social benefits, the overall effect of rapid and unregulated industrialization on Third World societies has left poor women in an ambivalent position. Human rights discourse that addresses problems specific to women
must also consider problems women in newly entered occupations share with
men. While both women and men are exploited in maquila factories and other
forms of employment, the belief that women are less likely to complain than men
and are otherwise more exploitable places them in a special category. Recent
international discourse on women rights has sought to defined those areas where
women are uniquely discriminated against. Often, their special discrimination
happens alongside or within more general discrimination based on class, race, and
nationality. This overlapping has commonly resulted in unresponsive legal procedures and variable court judgments on rulings specific to women. Moreover, the
enforcement of many newly created laws and rights initiatives has miscarried
from lack of understanding or motivation by law enforcement officials. Recent
women's rights advocates have endeavored to clarify these and other obstacles to
progressive change.

INTERNATIONAL INITIATIVES AND NATIONAL RESPONSE

Refining the Law: A South African Example

Article 1 of the Declaration on the Elimination of Violence Against Women (DEVAW) uses language intended to amend ambiguities in international law resulting from the exceptional nature of crimes against women. It reads in part, "[T]he term 'violence against women' means any act of gender-based violence that results in, or is likely to result in, physical, sexual or psychological harm or suffering to women, including threats of such acts, coercion or arbitrary deprivation of liberty, whether occurring in public or in private life" (DEVAW, 1994). The language allows broad application, yet it is carefully worded to include specific kinds of abuse. Coming just before the Fourth World Conference on Women (Beijing Platform), DEVAW motivated one Beijing participant, the post-Apartheid government of South Africa, to reform its laws concerning victims of rape. In 1985, the Apartheid government reaffirmed the so-called "cautionary rule," which requires a judicial officer to regard the testimony of complainants in sexual offense cases with caution. In effect, women's testimony would be approached with skepticism. The attempt to overturn the cautionary rule is an indication of the new consciousness regarding women's rights.

In 1993, South Africa's Interim Constitution guaranteed the right to freedom and security of the person, including torture of all kinds, but without specifying protection against violence. However, Section 5 of the Prevention of Family Violence Act of 1993 provides that a husband may be convicted of raping his wife, a measure that legally nullified the "marital rape exemption" from South African law (Combrinck, 1998, p. 667). One year after the Beijing Platform, the South African Constitution (1996) was adopted, which specifies (section 12.1.c) the right "to be free from all forms of violence from public and private sources." This inclusion has far-reaching implications, but will affect the area of violence against women fundamentally. The new South African government also ratified the Convention on the Elimination of All Forms of Discrimination Against Women (CEDAW), which the former Apartheid government had refused to sign, despite its adoption by the UN General Assembly in 1979. In addition, the new South African Constitution guaranteed the right to equality and human dignity, using language specific to the UN Charter and subsequent UN human rights conventions. These new developments are a positive sign that progressive change can be undertaken at the national level.

Unhappily, most Third World and many First World countries have not approached the Beijing Platform with as much enthusiasm. Many governments remain politically insensitive to the particularities of women's issues. Although international documents such as the UN Bill of Rights (1948–1966), the European Convention for the Protection of Human Rights and Fundamental Freedoms (1950, 1953), and the American Convention on Human Rights (1969, 1978) require states to assume responsibility when their own actions violate their international obligations, nonetheless, such accountability has not been generally effective, since governments are not required to allow UN enforcement officials to intervene. Moreover, UN secretaries general have not thus far shown a willingness to press for intervention in disputed human rights cases, as the 1998 example of Kofi Annan in Mexico demonstrates (see Chapter 17, in this volume). Unless, "invited" to intercede by the national government, such international actions are rarely undertaken. Also, international courts have not typically considered cases of individuals under the threat of violence. Since women's rights concerns often arise on an individual basis, international courts have largely sidestepped women's most pressing issues. The new South Africa has pioneered legal actions designed to overcome such limitations in traditional Western legal procedures.

International law was not used significantly for human rights advancement during the Apartheid period in South Africa (Combrinck, 1998). However, with the new Constitution and a more progressive government, the 1996 Constitution provided that a court "must consider international law" when interpreting the Bill of Rights (South African Constitution, 1996, ch. 2, 39.1.b). Hence, the South African government is not limited by its own treaties with regard to human rights. Moreover, the state must take positive action when presented with violations of human rights. The ICCPR, for example, imposes duties on state parties to "respect and ensure" the rights of their citizens (Article 2.1). The obligations of the documents of the UN Bill of Rights go beyond mere negative obligations: "The obligation to respect rights and to prevent violations is not confined to a restriction of government action, but must to some degree extend to positive government action to overcome violations of rights by private actors" (Cook, 1994, pp. 237–238).

CEDAW formulated a series of recommendations for governments when interpreting violence against women. General Recommendation 19 states that gender discrimination encompasses "gender-based violence—that is, violence that is directed at a woman because she is a woman or that affects women disproportionately" (qtd. in Combrinck, 1998, p. 673). The most vigorous movement to articulate harms against women grew out of the Beijing Platform, which described its Program of Action as "an agenda for women's empowerment" (United Nations, 1995a). The Platform was not legally binding; instead, it asked states to develop implementation strategies for the Platform by 1995. Unhappily, South Africa's timely response was not generally followed by Third World governments.

Legal Change

Initiatives to improve the status of women were not confined to the United N.ations The Organization of American States (OAS) adopted the Inter-American Convention on the Prevention, Punishment and Eradication of Violence Against Women in 1994. The Convention became the first legally binding international treaty focusing specifically on violence against women. As with international rights covenants in other areas, however, structural change and implementation at the national level remained problematic, in no way following automatically from international agreement. In that regard, the South African example may be helpful to other states struggling with the gap between formal acknowledgment of human rights and the implementation of effective systems. The South African Department of Welfare has produced a report setting forth strategic objectives as responsibilities within each government department. Although responsibility for overseeing the entire project for women's rights remained unclear in the report, such structural systems may be adopted for other UN states.

Although many NGOs, including Human Rights Watch, have recommended the abolition of the cautionary rule, which permits the court "to exercise an excessive level of discretion in deciding whether to believe women who allege that they have been raped," debate on the subject continues (Singh, 1995). The right to be protected from sexual violence must be weighed against the right against false witness. In righting the wrong of a cultural tradition that has devalued women's testimony, a legal tradition that considers women's testimony of greater value than men's seems equally unjust. The test used to evaluate evidence should be the same as for other assault offenses. A cautionary rule should not be replaced by another cautionary rule—this one devaluing the testimony of the accused. Perhaps most effective is a responsive enforcement system that brings immediate counseling to the victim, and a committed and focused investigative branch that uses recent advances in technology to prove rape and assault charges. As yet, however, there are very few examples, national or international, of integrated and consistent justice system reform. In another area, educational programs on the right to protection under the law need to be coupled with sex education and health programs in school systems to raise cultural awareness and sensitivity towards everyday violence against women.

Understanding Violence Against Women

Women in the First World began speaking out about sexual violence and rape in the late 1960s and 1970s. These studies concluded that sexual violence was a significant ingredient in male power and control over women. Moreover, male violence against women is likely to be sexual in some form, either in rape, sexual assault, or other forms of contact (Hester, 1992; MacKinnon, 1982). Terminology began to be developed in the late 1970s and 1980s that reflected a deeper understanding and theorizing about men's violence against women. For the feminist theorists, the phrase "sexual violence" acknowledges that violence is a gendered phenomenon within the context of patriarchal social relations (Kelly, 1988). This view insists that "sexual violence is not a question of '*people* raping/battering/ abusing *people*.'" The way violence is used and acted out in relationships, encounters and institutions is specifically gendered and constructed by, as well as a reflection of, the power relations which constitute heteropatriarchy (Radford, Kelly, & Hester, 1996).

During the 1980s, a cross-cultural critique of these explorations was applied by women of color in the First World and in postcolonial cultures. This dialogue enriched the study of violence against women, as it recognized that sexual violence takes many forms and has variable meanings as it affects culture, class, sexual orientation, age, and subculture (Mama, 1989). Globally, women are at risk as refugees, as in the Hutu refugee camps of eastern Congo (see Chapter 10, in this volume). Sexual violence has been used by men during periods of war, civil conflict, and social dislocation to both control those perceived as below them in social status and as a channel for misplaced anger. Existing international structures remain ill-equipped to deal with women's rights under these circumstances, which are regarded as extraordinary, temporary, and confused by racial and ethnic divisionism (see McCollom & McWilliams, 1994).

One threat to feminist discourse, as to other socially and politically oriented projects, has been the post-structuralist understanding of power as diffuse, as infusing all social and personal relationships. "Being everywhere, but nowhere in particular, [power] dissolves in complex and confusing ways within the subjectivity of unique individuals" (Radford, 1996, p. 9). Hence, within postmodern discourse, it is quite possible to regard the category "women" as insubstantial or irrelevant. As Tania Modleski (1991) has shown in *Feminism Without Women*, this movement effectively rules out feminist projects, including human rights advocacy. Despite the post-structural devaluation of recognizable social institutions and their determinisms, central to international women's rights is the presupposition that women are oppressed (and some also privileged) by power structures of class, race, ethnicity, geography, and age, as well as gender. Many feminists recognize the importance of exploring the commonality and differences between women of various cultures and economic backgrounds as they are affected by sexual violence and male power in their lives (McCollom & McWilliams, 1994). In the 1990s, major gatherings of women from different UN member nations, such as the Beijing Convention, have made it possible to begin to explore the different understandings of women's rights, sexual violence and abuse, and social constructions of women's identities. Future efforts must be made to move beyond the recognition of cultural differences to establish common goal-oriented mechanisms for progressive change.

Important studies of the social processes by which women's experiences of sexual violence are rendered invalid have been undertaken by the British Sociological Association (BSA) Violence Against Women Study Group during the mid-1980s through the early 1990s. Its studies found that women tend to minimize violence from men. Their response is in turn supported by an institutional penchant to minimize such experience. Helpful in this regard has been the area of feminist theory that finds, creates, and redefines terminology reflecting women's experiences of rape and abuse. Concepts that soon became commonplace did not exist before the current wave of women's rights activism. Phrases such as "domestic violence," "sexual harassment," "child sexual abuse," and "date rape," along with "sexual violence," replaced such strong but vague phrases as "unspeakable outrages," descriptions that encouraged nondiscussion, denial, and hence the very minimalization that advocates sought to overcome.

The importance of the new terminology for human rights discourse has been explicated by Kelly and Radford (1996): "Whilst these behaviors undoubtedly existed...what women lacked were social definitions. Names provide social definitions, make visible what is invisible, define as unacceptable what was accepted; make sayable what was unspeakable" (p. 20). Giving names to the actions of men offers a rhetoric of analysis that challenges the traditional view that men's behavior was "natural." Such essentialist notions of masculine and feminine was first challenged by social construction theory. Instead of regarding men's behavior as "natural," and therefore determined, sexual violence was placed within a context of women's oppression by and resistance to male power structures. This new perspective took away the inevitability—hence, the "naturalness"—of male behavior, which was now perceived in terms of social control and dominance within cultural constructs. While social critics such as Camille Paglia still argue as if the violence men do to women is "natural" and inevitable, most theorists and advocates have striven to convince jurists, legislators, enforcement authorities, and the populace of the origins of such behavior in culture, not "nature."

While recognizing that it is impossible to legislate against all forms of abuse against women, thereby criminalizing a great deal of behavior in the relationships between men and women in many cultures, the BSA Study Group did acknowledge the importance of changing local and international legal systems to make the law more responsive to the realities of women's lives. For noncriminalized abuse against women, they recognize the necessity of women's collective resistance, since such abuse is all too frequent and ubiquitous. Thus, women's rights in the international sphere pursues a two-pronged attack—to change existing laws to reflect the realities of violence against women by both individual perpetrators and social systems, and to organize crossroots education and advocacy movements for social change.

A recent project to reform the legal system is the BSA's Rape in Marriage Campaign. It has worked for a less exclusionary definition of rape, one that would resist the decriminalization of spousal rape and introduce a more inclusive understanding of rape. "The two central planks of the campaign were achieving legal recognition that women's consent cannot be presumed and that sexual violence should be defined in relation to the form of the assault, not the relationship between the man and the woman" (Kelly, 1996, p. 32). Such efforts reveal the extent to which women's experience of violence from men is dependent upon prevailing ideologies and institutional structures, such as definitions of marriage and the family, dominant constructions of masculinity and femininity, and conceptions of the boundaries between private and public space. In the latter case, legal and enforcement systems often view men who rape their wives as "no threat to the community," as a private rather than a public matter. Here an early slogan of the women's movement becomes operative: "the personal is the political." Recent feminist challenges to the binary opposition "public and private" counters culturally ingrained notions such as "a home is a man's castle" and men's "rightful ownership" of their wives.

What such feminist projects assume is that predominant constructions of masculine and feminine influence but cannot determine self-image, beliefs, and behavior. Presupposed is the alterability of such ideologies and their resulting behaviors. Needed is further exploration of the avenues of change that must be undertaken in non-Western cultures. This involves cross-cultural dialogue and activism along with localized advocacy and education programs. Much of this work has begun in recent years through efforts of international cooperation and communication at the Beijing Convention. That meeting tried to overcome the barriers towards intercultural cooperation raised by essentialist notions of separate cultures and postcolonial suspicions of First World motives to push neocolonializing ideologies. In the latter case, influential post-colonial critics such as Edward Said and Homi Bhabha have attempted to move beyond these binaries to recommend new levels of intercultural understanding and cooperation. In *Culture and Imperialism,* Said (1993), attempts to break down the absolute boundary line between colonial and anti-colonial that risks becoming an exercise in unproductive anger. He advocates a strongly anti-nationalist but also anti-imperialist vision, replacing the "politics of blame" with cross-cultural empathy, while searching for "new alignments...across borders, types, nations, and essences" (pp. xxiv–xxv). Similarly, Bhabha has attempted to show how colonized and colonizer have always shared identifications of hybridity that have made the absolute division between them unrealistic (Young, 1990). Especially in the 1990s, women have demonstrated their commonality across First World and Third World divisions in the ability to organize and maintain international movements and grassroots organizations for women's rights.

Population Control and Women's Status

One successful movement has combined international and local projects to reduce birth rates in Third World countries. Although the global population control movement has faced its share of criticism, chiefly from nationalist Third World advocates who regard First World efforts to curb growth rates of people of color a hidden attempt to diminish their political significance, or even to foster a kind of nonviolent elimination of populations along racial lines, nevertheless, the worldwide project to control birth rates among poor women has generally met with unexpected success. The consequences of diminished birth rates in poor countries has always had positive effects on the status of women. Not surprisingly, the chief advocates and workers in this effort have been First and Third World women.

Bangladesh, one of the most impoverished countries in the world, is one such success story. There women's life expectancy has been below men, chiefly due to risky pregnancies and malnutrition, conditions that often affect each other. Nevertheless, the high birthrate of 4.9 children per woman in 1990 has been reduced to 3.3 children. The dramatic reduction surprised regional experts, who believed that the rate would drop only after poverty and illiteracy were eliminated. Two organizations responsible for the reduction are the Grameen Bank of Dhaka, which began a program of small loans for women to begin business project, and the Bangladesh Rural Advancement Committee (BRAC), which organized a program of rural clinics in villages throughout the country.

Since 1976, the Grameen project has given more than $2 billion in loan amounts averaging $180 to 2.1 million women. Mohammed Abul Hossain, a Grameen loan officer, commented, "We find that when women start borrowing it benefits the whole family. Her children become important, the family's welfare becomes important" (Zwingle, 1998, p. 41). Financial independence also brings greater freedom for women, especially evident in traditional settings such as rural villages, where much of Third World populations still live. Sharifa Akhtar Shikha, a student at Bangladesh's Jagannath University, commented on her mother's receiving a Grameen loan: "For the future…[s]he will be independent and have more income. And she'll be happy also" (Zwingle, 1998, p. 42). In fact, Grameen families are twice as likely to have family planning than the national average. Such programs demonstrate that financial independence for women leads to other decisions about their lives.

Mergina Khatun, a village health worker funded by BRAC, commented on the desire among women for birth control methods: "Many more women want contraceptives now. They see that if a mother has fewer children, she can give them better care. And her health will be better" (Zwingle, 1998, p. 42). Contraception for many poor women not only offers a choice of when and if to have children, but also can improve their health, since many women suffer lingering illness as a result of poor diet and constant pregnancies.

Over the past 20 years, Kenya has shown a substantial decrease in the birthrate, a result of massive education campaigns, more clinics, and inexpensive contraceptives. Still, Africa as a whole has the highest birthrate in the world. Overcoming negative attitudes towards birth control inevitably involves changing male notions of virility, the faithfulness of wives, and religious tradition. The assumption of many family planners was that women would communicate what they had learned about contraceptive methods to their husbands, but this proved overoptimistic. For that reason, male clinics were introduced in Kenya, Ghana, and many South American countries. Many men responded favorably to the information. Objections along traditional religious lines were often rebutted by husbands as well as wives. When told that contraception went against biblical law, one husband responded that God gave him an obligation to help his wife. To a traditional Muslim leader who proclaimed that contraception went against the will of God, one woman in Bangladesh remarked that God commanded all to be responsible to their families. Rather than proving a hindrance, theological justifications were often used to support progressive change. Contraceptives, health care, and education have proven to significantly reduce the birthrate of poor women, allowing them more discretionary power in their lives.

COOPERATIVE EFFORTS FOR
WOMEN'S RIGHTS IN THE NEW CENTURY

The globalization of corporate power has introduced new problems for theorist of women's rights. Its creation of new jobs for women has come with a price. While Third World women are offered their own wages and therefore some degree of economic independence—a first for most—they are also exploited by the same concentrations of economic power, which continue to transform the rural landscapes of the Third World. The ambivalent status of women under these recent conditions needs further study and negotiation by women's organizations and grassroots groups. Undoubtedly, new alliances need to be forged with the international labor movement, itself undergoing profound transformation at the advent of the new century. First World feminists need to merge gender and class priorities, just as labor theorists need to acknowledge feminist realities. Until now, both movements have not seen the advantages of cooperative advocacy. This is reflected in the dearth of scholarship that values both areas of social justice. Benjamin R. Barber (1998), director of the Walt Whitman Center for the Culture and Politics of Democracy, takes perhaps a more realistic approach to the advancement of international worker rights than does Schulz (1998), who still clings to the belief that TNCs will voluntarily prioritize worker well-being and social justice (see Chapter 16, in this volume):

> Government can act here as a jawboning partner—as it did in the Apparel Industry Partnership against child labor in foreign plants; as a provider of inducements, through tax breaks for corporations that agree to responsible work practices...and as an enforcer, by negotiating effective workplace standards, meaningful protection for labor organization and citizen-friendly policies for international institutions like the WTO and the IMF that depend on U.S. cooperation. (p. 14)

Moving national and international governments in that direction may be a difficult task, given the reluctance of elected officials to sever connections with the interests of big business and financial institutions. Women's rights progress, along with most other human rights movements, continue to depend upon the more efficacious methods of the NGOs. However, during the 1990s, IGO initiatives have found new enthusiasts in the women's movement. The renewed vitality that was demonstrated at the 1993 Beijing Convention drew from the Convention on the

Elimination of All Forms of Discrimination Against Women (CEDAW), which went into force in 1981. Its preamble recognizes that changes in the traditional roles of women and men in both society and family are needed. Among the most disputed statements of the document, it remains pivotal to bringing real change to the status of women. The Convention also requires governments to submit periodic reports on the progress of their efforts to improve women's rights, allowing them to prioritize their projects in the hope that they will pursue their agendas in a goal-oriented fashion: "The reports should not be confined to mere lists of legal instruments adopted in the country…but should also include information indicating how these legal instruments are reflected in the actual economic, political and social realities and general conditions existing in their countries" (Illic & Corti, 1997, p. 308). Thus, the CEDAW understands the dependence of women's rights upon social, economic, and cultural conditions, not solely upon first-generation political rights, which were formally granted to women decades before.

Article 1 of the CEDAW has refined the understanding of discrimination against women to include "any distinction, exclusion or restriction made on the basis of sex which has the effect or purpose of impairing or nullifying the recognition, enjoyment or exercise of women…on a basis of equality" (Illic & Corti, 1997, p. 313). This important recognition rejects narrower definitions of women's rights that include only contractual agreements. It centers the struggle on dominant social structures and ideologies that have *the effect* of excluding women, not merely the intent, which has been notoriously hard to prove. Other CEDAW refinements include the recognition that gender-based violence is a form of control over women, and that many traditional attitudes towards women place them subordinate to men both overtly and indirectly.

Without grassroots movements and focused efforts at the regional and global levels, efforts to improve the status of women will remain confined to formal agreements between states. Vitally important for progressive development is the maintenance of cooperative efforts among all these levels. Without a consistent movement to unify the international public sphere for change—the recognition that labor rights, women's rights, family planning rights, and legal rights must work together—equality between the genders will remain an elusive ideal.

QUESTIONS FOR FURTHER THOUGHT

1. What additional measures need to be taken to assure that the special experience of women facing sexual violence are not overlooked by legal systems? How can international courts focus more fully on women's issues?
2. What additional positive steps need to be taken by nation states to comply with the CEDAW and the Beijing Platform's Program of Action? What can the U.S. government in particular do to implement these rights more fully?

3. In what ways do women's rights need to be given special consideration in cases of rape and spousal rape? What alternative forms of justice are possible?
4. Very little attention has been given to reforming police departments and regulatory agencies responsible for investigating crimes against women. What programs need to be introduced to change the attitudes of such institutions?
5. How can the international women's rights movement move more quickly to ally itself with other international human rights movements? Should alliances first begin at the local, regional, or global levels? Why?

15

HUMAN RIGHTS
AND LABOR JUSTICE

This chapter turns from the theoretical analysis of human rights issues to their application. Since the conditions of labor and the rights of workers have been recognized from the beginning as salient features of human rights efforts, predating in fact the UN Charter of 1945, the history of international response to abuses in the workplace covers most of the twentieth century. Its UN special agency, the International Labour Organization (ILO), was established more than a generation before the United Nations, and has influenced other UN human rights agencies and covenant language. Before looking at detailed instances of labor violations, it is necessary to review briefly the standards and practices through which labor conditions and worker rights are determined by intergovernmental institutions and NGOs.

"DEAL, DISTRIBUTIVE JUSTICE"

Chapter 2 of this volume discusses the UN's social and economic rights history, beginning with the covenants of 1966, which came into effect in 1976. These rights seem to demand a form of ideal, distributive justice. A glance at a few fundamental articles in this regard will suffice:

All peoples have the right to self-determination. By virtue of that right they freely determine their political status and freely pursue their economic, social and cultural development. (Article 1.1, ICESCR)

Everyone has the right to a standard of living adequate for the health and well-being of himself and his family. (Artilce 25, UDHR)

Everyone has the right to education. Article 26, UDHR)

These and many other provisions suggest that everyone should have equal control over resources, and by extension, working conditions. This goal has been pursued by international bodies along two broad avenues: the classical liberal, so-called "free market" approach, and the socialist, "state-centered" approach. Through most of its history, the UN has been divided between Member State groups representing either of these two camps. Although the Cold War era between Western capitalism and Eastern Communism has passed, the vestiges of both approaches remain, continuing the binary geopolitics of that period.

Arguments against strong state control are well known in the West. A brief list of the more cogent arguments follow:

1. Powerful state control can interfere with individual freedoms and political pluralism.
2. Establishing such a distributive state in the current economic and political climate would evoke strong resistence from powerful groups who profit from the alternative system (the recent examples of Haiti and Chile come to mind).
3. As Bard-Anders Andreassen and others (1988) have claimed, "Abrupt, overambitious attempts at large-scale redistribution might produce disincentives to production and attendant dislocations to the point where the position of the least advantaged might in fact be lowered instead of raised toward the full-scale implementaiton of socioeconomic rights" (Eide, 1993, p. 163).
4. Ideal distributive justice hinders capital accumulation and reinvestment, which delays the condition for improved economic and social rights for all.
5. State central planning hinders the sort of creativity and innovation need for capital accumulation and reinvestment.
6. Other priorities, such as national security interests, arms races (India and Pakistan, Israel and certain Arab states, the United States and "global hot spots," etc.), and militarization will make such comprehensive undertakings difficult.
7. Finally, at present, more attention is given to national and nationalistic priorities than to global cooperation.

Many if not all of these points can be debated, and some merely express the negative state of international affairs and economic conditions today rather than arguments in favor of maintaining the status quo. They nonetheless have great influence on human rights advocates, government representatives, and the general public. The proposed alternatives to strong state regulation range from purely libertarian "free market" capitalism, wherein complete privatization is presumed to do the double duty of maximizing investment capital and sufficiently raising the standards of everyone, to proposals for a minimum threshold for human rights realization (Bard-Anders Andreassen, 1988), whereby the state would guarantee nutrition, employment, acceptable infant mortality rates, life expectancy, income, and so on. Even such compromises have been attacked as impractical and too constraining of individual freedom by conservative "classic liberal" and libertarian groups. One further problem involves the great disparity between First World and Third World economies and cultures. Under this circumstance, Eide (1992) proposes that "all governments should establish a nationwide system of identifying local needs and opportunities for the enjoyment of economic and social rights, and in doing so, they should identify the particular needs of groups which have the greatest difficulties in the enjoyment of these rights" (p. 164). Left undiscussed by Eide, and in fact by most of the discussants of these issues, are the realities of power distribution, which make even—or perhaps especially—Third World governments unwilling to attend to such needs and opportunities for their most deprived groups, which in many cases involves large majorities of the populace.

Even assuming a fairly sincere Third World government with a degree of democratic motivation, one that gives some attention to minimum threshold human rights, biases seem inevitable when great economic disparities exist, and when capital investment flows at its own dictates. Most Third World settings, for instance, experience a systematic bias in favor of urban over rural development. Accordingly, the rural poor usually suffer most from the nonfulfillment of economic and social rights. This is also commonly the case with employment conditions and labor rights. In many Third World societies, urban areas have become swollen with economic refugees from disintegrated rural areas. These new urban poor are former rural farmers who now experience unregulated employment situations in unfamiliar and often hostile settings. Facing alien situations within their own countries, these new workers are often unable to find redress from local authorities, who are often culturally different from them. Frequently cut off at the other end—their rural villages depopulated or no longer viable—the new urban workers become people without a culture confronting bleak new lifestyles of underemployment and exploitation. New workers such as these are cogently represented in Ousman Sembene's Senegal films (see Chapter 7, in this volume); often young women, they find themselves alienated from their village elders or priests, and rejected by their families and neighbors. In short, the "alienated man," the subject of Western social novels and problem plays of the late 19th and early 20th centuries, are recreated today in many Third World societies.

The oldest and by far the most important organization devoted to international labor conditions is the International Labour Organization (ILO). Although now a specialized agency of the United Nations, it was established by the Treaty of Versailles in 1919 to abolish the "injustice, hardship, and privation" of workers and to work towards "fair and humane conditions of labour" (Leary, 1992, p. 582). The European powers who formed it had mixed motivations. In part, there was a conscious response to the perceived threat from Leninism and socialism after World War I. The ILO was the only major intergovernmental body to survive the League of Nations. Since human rights are the concern of the ILO as well as other agencies of the United Nations, comparisons are useful. Over the years, the ILO has gained a reputation for being more focused and more effective. Since the UN human rights instruments and agencies have a more general mandate, often resulting in the compartmentalization of human rights, it is not surprising that the ILO appears more focused. While the ILO's organizational structure has influenced those of the other UN human rights agencies—the reporting system being one example—ILO practice differs in important ways. Worker and employer representatives participate fully in ILO activities, including drafting of conventions, an instance of the successful integration of nongovernmental actors into the human rights process. This feature, called "tripartism," allows for actors who, when truly independent, are generally less politically motivated than governmental representatives. Although the ILO continues to use the normative approach to reported labor violations, as do other UN agencies, more and more it emphasizes technical cooperation, research, and diplomatic contacts to leverage and promote human rights. This strategy can effect progressive change in certain situations, but is limited to employment situations that require a degree of technical assistance. Often, transnational corporate development in the Third World does not require technical and research assistance, and therefore would not be influenced by such pressures.

One shortcoming of the ILO method is that NGOs, elsewhere effective, are relatively absent from the process. The ILO has been unable or unwilling to find means through which NGOs can consult and supply information. For their part, NGOs have not made themselves familiar with ILO procedures, as they lack an active role in its processes. Moreover, human rights activists have often ignored working conditions, and few articles on labor conditions appear in human rights journals. Finally, the UN Committee on Economic, Social and Cultural Rights needs to draw upon ILO expertise in legislation and labor practice to help define Articles 6-9 of their Covenant (ICESCR).

Through its conventions, the ILO has made specific Article 7 of ICESCR, which offers the "right of everyone to just and favorable conditions of work." These include detailed norms for employment security, wage fixing machinery, protection of wages, hours of work, weekly rest, and paid leave. By 1991, the ILO had passed 171 conventions and 178 recommendations on freedom of association (for unions), job discrimination, work hours, occupational safety and health, labor inspection, social security, and so on. In practice, however, the ILO is less impressive. Although its technical assistance program establishes close relationships with Third World governments, offering them advice on labor standards as well as technology, its own trained specialists are often given only a superficial orientation to human rights standards. In the field, ILO actors sometimes ignore human rights norms in employment or give them low priority. Even worse, the ILO has not chosen to use its technical and research assistance to leverage change for human rights. It has never withdrawn technical assistance for a state's failure to implement human rights or labor standards (Leary, 1992).

At its annual conference, the ILO provides a great deal of advice for drafting fair labor legislation and for setting standards for specific occupations. These methods are consultative only, not judgmental. Generally, the ILO has not used its knowledge as power for change, preferring instead persuasive methods at conventions and often ignoring human rights in the field. Part of the problem may lie in how it regards itself as an institutiom. Its stress on good will and building long-term confidence between itself and Third World governments may prevent it from becoming more activist. Moreover, these governments may realize that the ILO isn't the only source for technical assistance, since TNCs are also capable of offering certain assistance and will not demand labor standards and regulations.

THIRD WORLD LABOR CONDITIONS

Many colonialized regions passed through periods of successful labor organization; West Africa was typical. During the turbulent decades of the 1930s and 1940s, Ghana established organizations offering a modicum of security to its urban workers. The depression, land shortages, declining cocoa farm yields, and export crop disease left many of the lower rural classes in southern Ghana without employment, particularly farmers, *abusa* sharecroppers, and farm laborers. Especially without power and increasingly cut off from traditional bonded roles were *abusa* sharecroppers (descendents of slaves), women, indebted peasant farmers, hired laborers, and pawns. With fewer cocoa fields to harvest, these groups sought nonagricultural work in the cities, a migration that put pressure on existing workers in the commercial, administrative, and mining centers of the colony (Grier, 1987). Consequently, the latter, hired on a daily rate basis, began demanding more job security and long-term hiring as well as better working conditions. Strikes, work slowdowns, and downing of tools increased significantly between 1935 and 1938. These actions prompted the British colonial apparatus to reform its criminal codes, which had treated strikers as felons. A Labor Department was created and the rights to unionize (1940) and to strike (1941) were given. Ghana's labor activism was directly connected to the rural crisis in that workers already employed in railroads, harbors, and mines saw their daily rate jobs further threatened by the increased influx of rural poor. These more established workers began to look upon their wage labor as long term, since the rural crisis made clear that they would be unable to return to their previous agricultural life. "While they were by no means landless, they could no longer look completely to the land to sustain them in sickness, unemployment, and old age" (Grier, 1987, p. 43). This development can be seen as a general trend in 20th century Third World societies. When first and second-generation wage earners become identified with their new occupations, labor organization usually follows.

Not all Third World societies develop along the same lines, however. In South Africa, labor conditions have been affected by the overriding agendas of the white apartheid government through the 1980s and early 1990s. The black rural areas of South Africa, the so-called Bantustans, had by the 1980s, become destitute and administratively disintegrated. "With faltering agricultural production and massive overpopulation, the Bantustans provide meager security and virutally no sustenance; remittances from the wage economy rather than marginal agricultural production, sustain these massive African rural populations" (Greenberg & Giliomee, 1987, p. 309). When the administrative labor control within these areas failed, workers themselves initiated their own employment searches. Accordingly, the South African government was forced to find alternative means of control within the apartheid system. Economically, the Bantustans no longer serve their original function—to cheapen labor and thus facilitate the extraction of surplus value. Whereas in Ghana earlier in the century, workers organized from a perceived threat to the flooded labor market, the surplus of labor in South Africa led to alternative government controls within a repressive system.

Many Africans in rural areas of South Africa had no labor market. In this mostly unsupervised and unregulated system, squatters were relatively free to find work on the margins of the legal labor market. The manufacturing sector of South Africa showed little interest in recruitment in the Bantustans. Moreover, the legal labor market has been fragmented by gender segregation and exclusions. Often, mothers and fathers found themselves separated by hundreds of miles—often experiencing a three-way separation from their children as well—in order to adapt to the government's segmentation of labor. Moreover, government practice confined urban job recruitment to men. Women were at the bottom of the job hierarchy, almost always in rural areas (Greenberg & Giliomee, 1987). African laborers in these circumstances were highly controlled along racial, gender, and tribal lines by a apartheid state which nonetheless was unable to develop efficient labor supplies as it had originally intended. In any case, labor organization was impossible under conditions of systemic segmentation.

The newly independent Ghana of the late 1950s experienced the now typical situation of foreign direct investment (FDI) by a transnational corporation (TNC). Foreign capital (the U.S. aluminum firms of Kaiser and Reynolds) would build a dam on the Volta river to generate power and the private sector would own the smelter. The original plan that Ghana would take a 40 percent stake in the project never materialized. Ghana supplied the cheap labor but did not assume that the smelter would use up the majority of the dam's power (65 percent). Valco, the corporation set up by the foreign firms, received tax benefits from Ghana, but it operated as an enclave industry (Sklair, 1995). Moreover, according to the agreement, nationalization was impossible. By 1980 only 5 percent of Ghana's people had electricity. The TNCs involved got far more from the scheme than did Ghana, whose labor situation did not expand or improve in quality. Elsewhere, the effect of TNCs in low-wage countries is often to create intense pressure to keep down wages. Also, in Third World export-oriented zones (EOZs), the workers' right to organize is not possible due to the collaboration of native governments and TNCs (Edgren, 1982). The International Confederation of Free Trade Unions, the non-Communist bloc transnational labor movement, gave a pessimistic report (1983) on the suppression of trade unions in EOZs (Sklair, 1995).

The EOZs also are responsible for gender division in labor. The vast majority of workers, from the *maquilas* along the Mexican–United States border to South East Asia, are women between 16 and 24 years old. Women are preferred by TNC and local corporations because they are perceived as more docile and less likely to organize and resist (Ruiz & Tiano, 1987). In both foreign and domestic corporate employment in Third World EOZs, it appears that the foreignness of the product and its technology, rather than the foreignness of the corporation, leads to neglect of labor conditions (Vaitsos, 1974). The three-way collaboration between local "comprador" bourgeoisie, TNCs, and Third World governments creates an easily controlled labor population that is to some degree cut off from its traditional culture and thus easily exploited. A good example of this condition is found in EOZs in El Salvador and Haiti at the end of the 1990s.

Workers' Plight in El Salvador and Haiti

An unauthorized film of the working conditions in an EOZ factory of a major U.S. clothing manufacturer has received very limited screening in the First World. Its onsight cameras and private, follow-up interviews with the girls reveal that their exploitation was systematic, long-term, and comprehensive, affecting all areas of their lives. *Zoned for Slavery* (1995), by filmmaker David Belle, demonstrates how U.S. companies exploit the assembly export industry that U.S. foreign policy has proffered to Central America and the Caribbean as a major means of development. The majority of the workers are girls averaging 14 or 15 years of age, with some boys as young as 12 years old. Working for 30 cents per hour, they are forced to finish extremely long shifts (one mother waits the next morning for her daughter to come back from a shift that began the morning before), and are beaten if they take more than 5 minutes for breaks. Worker Rosa Martinez finds that her life is hopeless and she does not see the day when she will be able to attend school. The profits from this exploited labor is tremendous. Thirty thousand U.S. dollars worth of GAP t-shirts are made by workers in one day for the combined wages of just $185. Moreover, there are no corporate taxes and no tariffs for the companies in the El Salvador assembly plants.

The labor violations extend to the treatment of the girls in the assembly plants. They are beaten if they take more than 5-minute breaks, are spoken to harshly by supervisors, and are unable to protest without fear of being fired. Sexual abuse and violence are common. The girls are forced to take birth control pills, which are distributed to them as "anti-malaria" pills. Every worker knows what the pills are but are afraid to refuse them. The pills are intended as a cost-saving means of avoiding maternity leave. When girls do become pregnant, they are often forced to take an inexpensive abortion injection that also causes serious side effects. Belle (1995) shows large amounts of used birth control wrappers at th edge of the factory park. The families of workers have been uprooted from the countryside by business development schemes to become squatters by the factories, with the result that they lack their traditional base of legal, church, and community support. These and other abuses are systemic in many Latin American EOZs.

In Haiti, workers are forced into long hours in dangerous and uncomfortable facilities that assemble brand-name clothing for First World markets. These and other abuses clearly violate ILO rights and regulations as well as other UN human rights conventions. Still, very little attention has been given to this problem from the perspectives of health science, human rights, ecology, women's rights, and business practice. Undemocratic business oligarchies in Haiti and El Salvador discourage reform. Moreover, First World mainstream media is often reluctant to publish investigative reporting of corporate activity, especially in the Third World. When the media does respond, there is often a noncritical approach that sides with corporate power (Dowie, 1998). While human rights NGO advocates often document such labor practices in poorer countries, their publicity capabilities are significantly weakened by lack of access to First World mainstream media; by an indifferent film industry (see Chapter 7, in this volume), which ignores the realities of Third World conditions in favor of formulas that politically and aesthetically reassure the status quo; and by a "public" television and radio system heavily financed by corporate donations.

Worst yet, in some areas of the Third World slavery is still practiced. Under such circumstances, labor organizing becomes secondary to the immediate action of international authorities, which should be immediate and unequivocal, since slavery has been condemned unconditionally by international agreements before the founding of the United Nations. Unhappily, IGOs and individual nations have been slow to respond to what would seem to be an urgent and relatively uncomplicated violation of human rights. Geopolitical priorities and lack of documentation are perhaps major causes of this current neglect. Many of the present slave-practicing sites are rural, remote, and outside the political "hot spots" of current First World spheres of influence.

One recently reported account of slavery, near Bouafle, Ivory Coast, describes agricultural labor on corn and cotton plantations. Documentation of this and similar events can occasionally appear in the International section of *The New York TImes*, perhaps in part because no powerful international agricultural corporations seem involved. Information about current slavery often comes from the runaway slaves themselves, who have fled to their native villages (often in bordering countries), where they report their stories. One young man's account of his plight evokes images of 19th century slavery practice:

> Under the stern gaze of an overseer, he and other workers there had to weed row and row of the crops planted in ther dark, rich soil with their simple hoes and carry countless sacks of harvested crops the three miles back to the farmhouse. When they were thirsty they had to fetch water from a distant well....The only break came in the evening, when they were allowed to return to their camp for the only meal of the day—invariably a thin corn porridge—and then were locked inside their mud-walled pillbox shelter, where they were kept under guard until sunrise. (French, 1998b)

As the most prosperous West African state, the Ivory Coast depends heavily upon poorly paid immigrants for agricultural labor. Its independence movement was spurred by the forced labor policies of the French colonialists, who were intent on building a cash-crop economy of cocoa and coffee. Most of the forced labor today are from neighboring Mali and Burkina Faso, which has suffered economically, forcing children to leave their families in hope of making a better future. Many escape the plantations and flee to the Mali embassy, where they are sent home. The Mali consul, Fassiriman Dembele, has been responsible for broadcasting their plight to the world, which has heretofore ignored the slave conditions in the Ivory Coast (French, 1998b). Government authorities have been slow to recognize the problem, perhaps because their are two million Malis in the Ivory Coast working in many occupations and because the economy is so dependent on foreign labor for its booming economy.

Working conditions in the Third World have not always precluded effective change, especially when workers were organized and First World demand for their crops and products were high. In pre-Peron Argentina, railway workers comprised a strongly identified occupational community, whose self-image was as an elite with particular noneconomic attributes (Horowitz, 1985b). In Guatemala during the 20th century dictatorships, railway workers (*ferrocarrileros*), shared a cultural identity as Ladinos (*mestizos*, mixed European and Native American) in a country whose majority was Mayan Indians that had been recently dispossessed from their landholdings to make way for coffee plantations. Thus, the *ferrocarrileros* were able to approach the powerful consolidation of the International Railways of Central America (IRCA) in a unified fashion for successful bargaining (McLeod, 1997). By contrast, the Mayan Indians, forced off their lands and unorganized, were directed into agricultural labor for the coffee cash crop. In both countries, workers who clearly identified with their occupational group were able to organize around specific goals against a clearly discerned oppressor.

In 1930s Cuba, cane-cutters, railway, factory, skilled and unskilled workers were of diverse racial and ethnic origins. Nevertheless, they succeeded in organizing a wide revolt against powerful foreign and domestic interests. The achievement is more remarkable because of their solidarity across occupational and cultural lines. Even Communist and other labor organizers admitted that the spontaneous uprising took them by surprise, as they hastily sent organizers to help local actions (Braga, 1997). Its initial organizers, however, were mainly local union leaders. The workers' success was in part the result of careful timing. When the Machado dictatorship fell in August 1933, the Sergeants Rebellion, with a disunited army led by Fulgencio Batista, was not organized sufficiently to respond to calls for support from managers. The Cuban labor movement was motivated in part by nationalist sentiments, perhaps to a greater extent than in Argentina and Guatemala. These sentiments, perhaps better described as anti-colonialist, were directed chiefly against the foreign owners, U.S. and Canadian corporations and banks, who controlled three quarters of Cuba's sugar crop production (Perez, 1986). The foreign-owned mills preferred to place native English speakers in top-level management and key technical positions. The individual mills, spread throughout the island in rural areas, operated without governmental regulation—although with the occational assistance of the Rural Guard—and determined who would live and work within the mill proper and in the harvesting fields.

Since immigrants from Haiti and Jamaica were willing to plant and harvest sugar cane for less pay and were reluctant to join unions, the Cuban sugar companies benefited from transient labor. Despite these obstacles, and the occasional presence of the U.S. Marines, who assisted sugar owners during the labor disputes following the 1916 elections, the Railway Brotherhood struck in solidarity with Cuba Cane mill workers in 1924. Although Communist, anarchosyndicalists, and representatives of the new Grau San Martin government were disseminating information and ideas to strike committees, local union representatives remained in charge of the grassroots movement (Braga, 1997). With no means of transportation to ports, the sugar companies were forced to negotiate. Key concessions were granted, including the right to strike, the reinstatement of strikers, and guaranteed regular payments every two weeks (Braga, 1997).

More recently, efforts in many Third World countries to undermine organized labor have greatly succeeded, as the current examples of Salvadoran and Haitian clothing workers demonstrate. These EOZ workers are under age, female, cut off from their own cultural support groups and land, and remain unorganized. Close collaboration between oligarchic governments, large international business, and First World foreign policies are largely responsible for these conditions. Often the rhetoric of privatization is used to help eliminate worker resistance. For example, in 1990s Argentina the Peronist President Carols Saul Menem wanted to sell the nationalized railroads back to private corporations. In 1948, the British-owned railways were nationalized after years of struggle by highly organized Argentinian railway workers. When Juan Peron attempted to "rationalize" production, railway workers opposed him successfully. In 1955, the military government that overthrew Peron tried to eliminate labor regulations, but they abandoned their efforts when faced with railway worker opposition. Menem's efforts to privatize the railways were part of his general effort to privatize all national industries. In the 1990s, Menem has increased worker layoffs (Tuozzo, 1997). Typical of current Third World rulers, Menem used the rhetoric of privatization, and the promise of greater workplace rationalization and efficiency to justify his actions, with no mention of the boom opportunity of increased profits for investors. Ironically, much the same argument had been used to justify nationalization decades before. Recognizing that Menem's interpretation of *peronismo* preferred labor productivity and corporate profits to justice in the workplace, current Argentinian labor activity has waited for IMF-style economic austerity policies to incite a renewed labor rights movement (Snodgrass, 1997).

With the onrush of Third World privatization, due in part to political open-door policies, and the increased productivity of Third World workers, aided also by technological improvements and efficient methods of communication, the power of organized labor in the Third World has greatly diminished. Whereas, earlier in the 20th century, increased high-volume production actually aided labor rights, since work stoppages threatened daily production significantly, today, routine producers are in competition with every other routine producer around the world (Reich, 1992). The result is that workers are given substandard wages in countries with no labor regulations or with regulations that are not enforced. Nearly all of these countries have signed the UN human rights covenants and ILO conventions.

The Discourse of Enforcement

In the era of Global Capital, one key to labor justice success is strengthened international enforcement. International cooperation must increase to meet the standards of dignity necessary to enhance life rather than cheapen it. Many, perhaps nearly all, signitories to human rights documents violate their own standards, often routinely and systematically. In the Third World, these violations are typical. Success at the international level will also require the continued involvement of NGOs—a group that is happily growing in number today and is at least as involved in the discourse of human rights as are the major international bodies such as the UN. But while both public and private international organizations are necessary for social justice, they are by no means sufficient. Above all, local motivation and focus are necessary for progressive change in human rights. Those labor forces that saw themselves as fully proletarianized—as fully dependent on one source of labor and identified with that struggle—were generally more willing to resist the formidable forces of reprivatization, foreign capital interference, and national oligarchy. For example, in 1970s Peru, miners' unions (at Toguepala, for example) that were more fully proletarianized participated in national politics more consistently than miners' unions that were not. On the other hand, most members of the Centromin miners' union planned to work in the mines only temporarily, after which they could use their skills and savings to become self-employed in agriculture or other areas. They were less willing to sacrifice through work stoppages over the long term than were miners less divided between traditional agriculture and mining (DeWind, 1997).

Similarly, in Chile during the same period, the Popular Unity government misinterpreted the radical nature of the miners, who proved unwilling to sacrifice their hard-won wages and benefits for the economizing measures of the Allende government. "[T]hey were unwilling to lose economic benefits especially when a government 'of the workers' was in power" (Swanger, 1997, p. 292). Although Chilean miners preferred nationalization to privatization—employment under foreign companies—leftist intellectuals had not considered the hybridity of many Latin American union members, who did not fit into orthodox Marxist categories of worker and peasant. Here, the self-identity of the worker is key. Organizers must be willing to look more closely at the particularities of culture and the economic profile of workers before progressive movements can become viable over the long term. The message is clear. The discourse of labor rights must involve workers themselves at every level, from local work stoppages to governmental policy. Efforts to turn around Global Capital will be difficult in the coming decades, requiring, rather than one form of activism, the concerted effort of advocates, workers, and governmental representatives. Persistence will be needed, but also the assistance of the First World mainstream media, as the recent partially successful efforts to improve the working conditions of Nike factories in Indonesia have demonstrated (Cushman, 1998; Kieschnick, 1998).

QUESTIONS FOR FURTHER THOUGHT

1. How might First World workers unite with Third World workers to allow for fairer wages and standards in the workplace?
2. What methods could the ILO use to improve its success rate with Third World countries and international corporations that violated labor standards?
3. Do you agree with the author that attention to the particular culture of the workers in Third World sites are necessary for success? How might First World NGOs and governmental organizatons go about identifying the relevant life conditions of the workers?
4. Why does the First World media often ignore labor rights issues in the Third World and even to a degree in the First World? How can this be changed?
5. How can international corporations be persuaded to change policies of underpayment, factory abuse, long shifts, and other violations of human rights instruments? Which would be more effective, constraint or persuasion?

16

TNCs:
THE IDEOLOGY
OF GLOBAL CAPITAL

While First World labor unions have struggled to survive in the post-industrial world, and Third World unions have remained persecuted or outlawed by elites willing to sacrifice human rights for personal aggrandizement, Global Capital has become essential to most Third World economies (Brecher & Costello, 1998). The extent of this trading dependency is vividly illustrated in the case of post-Gulf War Iraq. The First World trading boycott of Iran since the Gulf War of 1991 has seriously threatened the lives of that country's people, despite efforts by Kofi Annan to broker limited "oil for food" deals (Capaccio, 1998). The 1990s boycott of Haiti by the OAS showed little effect only because of the exceptionalism of the United States, which continued to allow its TNCs to trade despite the boycott. The message has been restated continually during and after the Cold War era: Third World human rights continue to be economically and politically dependent upon First World TNCs and the foreign policies of their cooperating governments.

Third World states have repeatedly complied with the dictates of TNCs and various international investment organizations, such as the UN's World Bank and IMF. Their dependency has extended to such internal projects of social engineering—a term that should by no means be limited to totalitarian Communist governments—as so-called "land reform" and "liberalization" of land tenure schemes, which result in the mass dispossession of rural peoples from their traditional means of subsistence (Bethell, 1998; Twentieth Century Fund, 1998). Quite often, young Maquiladora workers commute to their newly built factories from wayside lands where their parents "squat" because they have been dispossessed of their lands by huge transnational business ventures, often undertaken by the same corporations that supply the daughters with their low-wage jobs.

On the other hand, TNCs are not dependent on Third World views of self-determination, as the recent example of Haiti shows, where North American TNCs can hold back long enough from civil strife even to bargain with their First World governments for business venture subsidies at taxpayers' expense. Moreover, TNCs in Haiti operate freely outside the order of law by refusing to follow minimum wage laws, and so on (see Chapter 11, in this volume). The state of imbalance between Global Capital and Third World populations greatly contributes to the worldwide human rights dilemma. Nevertheless, First World academics and policymakers continue to write about human rights IGOs and NGOs as though corporations and financial institutions had no influence on social justice problems. Often highly critical of such multilateral organizations as the United Nations, and generally ignoring the prodigious fact-gathering of hundreds of well-established NGOs, these experts often concentrate on the presumed negativities of the UN General Assembly, where Third World countries have a majority, than on the Security Council, whose permanent five dominate UN policies (see, for example, Righter, 1995). For such thinkers, TNCs and international financial institutions have little causal connection with human rights. This chapter will examine the power and influence of Global Capital, together with their assisting national and international governments, as they affect human rights standards throughout the world.

HUMAN RIGHTS DISCOURSE AND THE IMF:
"THE LAW HAS A DIFFERENT STANDARD"

In April 1998, U.S. Congressman Bernie Sander questioned Timothy Geithner, the Assistant Secretary for International Affairs for the Treasury Department, about who the IMF represents. Quoting a *New York Times*' description of the IMF and the World Bank as "the overlords of Africa," and pointing out that over half the world's population—90 countries—live under IMF regulations, Sanders (1998) asked a probing line of questions untypical of the House Banking Subcommittee:

> It is disconcerting to learn...that from 1982 through 1990, debtor countries in the South paid their creditors in the North $6.5 billion in interest and another $6 billion in principle payments every month, as much as the entire Third World spends on

education and health....Yet the debtor countries were 60 percent greater in 1990 than in 1982. In other words, after all of their basic programs, they were more in debt than when the IMF got to them in the first place. Does that sound like a successful load program? (p. 34)

Sanders then quoted the assistant secretary's own words: "The United States pursues the advancement of human rights through a variety of diplomatic channels and international institutions. As provided in legislation, the United States executive director has opposed IMF financing to countries about which the United States has human-rights concerns or countries harboring war criminals." He followed this quote with the U.S. State Department's annual human rights report for 1996: "Despite a surface adherence to democratic forms, the Indonesian political system remains strongly authoritarian....The government continued to commit serious human-rights abuses....The authorities maintain their tight grip on the political process, which denies citizens the ability to change their government democratically." Finally, Sanders quoted the Sanders–Frank Amendment of 1994: "The Secretary of Treasury directs the United States Executive Directors of the international financial institutions to use the voice and vote of the United States to urge the respective institutions to adopt policies to encourage borrowing countries to guarantee internationally recognized worker rights and to include the status of such rights as an integral part of the institution's policy dialogue with each borrowing country." When Sanders reminded Geithner that the IMF provided billions of dollars to Indonesia's Suharto government, the Assistant Secretary could only comment, "The law has a different standard than the standard of the report" (1998, p. 34).

Geithner's reply at Bernie Sanders's House hearing points out the connection of U.S. foreign policy and international financial institutions. While the State Department, perhaps for its own reality-based purposes, reports accurately the tyrannies of Third World "client" countries of the United States, its interdepartmental directives take a very different trajectory. Geithner was accurate when he testified, "[T]he law has a different standard than the standard in the human-rights report, and that is not something that we are responsible for" (p. 35). The "different standard" to which the Treasury Department official refers is the double standard of human rights policy. Before Suharto's fall in 1998, brought about by a hard-fought grassroots uprising (see Chapter 12, in this volume), President Clinton praised him cogently as "our kind of guy." Motivated first by the interests of Global Capital and geopolitical ideology, U.S. foreign policy and international investment organizations give human rights and other democratic values low priority. As we have seen in other chapters, this low priority often translates into policies that directly counter human rights and social justice concerns.

THE GAME PLAN OF PRIORITIES

Influential policymakers in the North follow a discourse that supports the placement of profit and geopolitical power over human rights. Zbigniew Brzezinski, National Security Advisor under President Jimmy Carter, has perceived current world history as "a strategic game" in which "global anarchy" will be avoided only when the United States maintains "the hegemony it commands" (Gwertzman, 1998, p. 30). Reviewing his 1997 book, *The Grand Chessboard: American Primacy and Its Geostrategic Imperatives*, Bernard Gwertzman uncritically supports its unilateral paranoia, commenting, "The fear of anarchy is of great moment to Brzezinski, perhaps because anarchy is something that Americans can visualize and become concerned enough about to generate some political interest" (p. 30). Brzezinski presupposes a huge U.S. military designed to "stabilize" the ensuing chaos of a world order not managed by Washington. His use of phrases such as "American hegemony" and "America's global primacy," assume a world controlled by one culture for the benefit of that culture. Such policymakers have evolved from cold warriors to unilateralists who shun pluralism, tolerance for diversity, and alternative systems. The world is envisioned as a great chessboard whereon Washington's dominance must be maintained lest all the chess pieces tumble away into chaos:

> The disruptive consequences of population explosion, poverty-driven migration, radicalizing urbanization, ethnic and religious hostilities, and the proliferation of weapons of mass destruction would become unmanageable if the existing and underlying nation-state-based framework were itself to fragment. Without sustained and directed American involvement, before long the forces of global disorder could come to dominate the world scene. (Brzezinski, 1997, p. 89)

However, the chaos that Brzezinki specifies has resulted more from unregulated corporate expansion and free-market policies than from the vague "nation-state-based framework" he mentions. For example, the unregulated growth of Third World cities and the increase of "poverty-driven migration" is related to policies of land dispossession and free-market priorities that ignore social and political rights, policies by local business elates and TNCs that Brzezinski himself supports (Horowitz, 1985b). In fact, he has very little directly to say about Global Capital, taking it as a given for world dominance.

To be sure, there is light at the end of the tunnel for this policymaker, even room for a kind of multicultural tolerance, but this is a long way off, not to be taken too seriously in terms of U.S. world domination:

> In brief, the U.S. policy goal must be unapologetically twofold: to perpetuate America's own dominant position for at least a generation and preferably longer still; and to create a geopolitical framework that can absorb the inevitable shocks and strains of social-political change while evolving into the geopolitical core of shared responsibility for peaceful global management. (p. 215)

How this geopolitical core regulated by a dominant global power is to evolve into a multilateral system is not explained, despite the messages of history, which repeatedly tell us that power does not willingly surrender its power and that world empires built on dominance do not become exceptions. Brzezinski's U.S. exceptionalism, however, is consistent with the ethnocentric orientation of so many empires of the past: "to save the world from itself, we must take away its freedom and do it our way."

Such thinking ignores the need—obvious to most Americans—for greater cross-cultural trust and cooperation. Brzezinski, however, is anything if not consistent. His other books also reduce the world to a game for control: *Game Plan: A Geostrategic Framework for the Conduct of the U.S.–Soviet Contest* (1986); *Out of Control: Global Turmoil on the Eve of the Twenty-First Century* (1993). The low priority given human rights and international cooperation is evident throughout his works. In *Game Plan*, for example, the United Nations is mentioned once and then only parenthetically. His cynicism is not unique, however. Many prominent Washington political analysts have published along quite similar lines. The image of global anarchy facing a sleeping or innocent America is featured in such discourse as Richard N. Haass's *The Reluctant Sheriff: The United States After the Cold War* (1997); Samuel P. Huntington's *The Clash of Civilizations and the Remaking of World Order* (1996); and Fareed Zakaria's *From Wealth to Power: The Unusual Origins of America's World Role* (1998). Each of these studies perpetuates dominant American myths—America's innocence in a power-hungry world; America's reluctance to use force; the world's cultures as inherently clashing; and the barbarism of the Third World. Positive and affirming worldviews do not serve the purposes of the Washington status quo, which must justify an oversized military budget, huge CIA, DIA, and various hidden budgets of "national security." These thinkers take exception to Francis Fukuyama's overly optimistic position in, *The End of History and the Last Man* (1992). However, Fukuyama assumes a similarly exceptionalist U.S. worldview that underestimates the negative effects of Global Capital on democratic development and self-determination issues.

The hard-liners of U.S. unilateralism share with more moderate voices in Washington the view that the United States must urgently find a cause through which its people can give homage in the post-Cold War era. For example, Robert Reich in *The Work of Nations: Preparing Ourselves for 21st-Century Capitalism* (1992) finds that U.S. workers must sacrifice for the sake of global corporate competitiveness to avoid being swallowed whole by a multicultural world. This paranoia follows closely the intense nationalism of Brzezinski, Huntington, and Haass. Assumed is that confronting a world of sovereign nations who have their own views of self-determination and right to development is necessarily diminishing to the United States: "Given these trends, without the external pressure of Soviet Communism holding us together, America may simply explode into a microcosm of the entire world" (p. 321). As an economist, Reich finds his cause through direct competition with such newly emergent economic giants as Japan: "The purpose of having a Japanese challenge is to give us a reason once again to join together" (p. 322). The Cold War becomes a period of nostalgia—perhaps a halcyon era (!)—to which America must return. Like Huntington and Brzezinski, Reich sees a dominant ideology that channels the thinking of U.S. citizens as the only way to avoid worldwide social and economic chaos:

> Here we face a principle basic to civic life: Individuals comprising a society will sacrifice their personal well-being to the greater good only if they feel connected to that society in such a way that "the greater good" has substantive meaning for them. If, absent the Soviet menace, the identity of America seems somewhat vaguer, its purpose somehow less compelling than before, Americans will be more reluctant to make the sacrifice. (p. 317)

Just why Americans, or any other citizens of the world, should need an international cause to avoid cataclysm is not explained but only assumed by Reich. *The Work of Nations* is more interested in U.S. corporate global dominance than in explorations of the American psyche. From the perspective of human rights discourse, compelling moral causes should be directed towards agendas that support worldwide cooperation, intercultural tolerance, regional/global regulatory organizations, and universal moves towards disarmament. Only multilateral projects that prioritize human rights and social well-being will lead to lasting peace with justice. On the other hand, paradigms of unilateral domination, of the strong (the United States) against the weak (everyone else, including, in the view of Brzezinski, even Western Europe), abandon human rights in favor of a self-serving nationalism.

THE MAI: WITH LITTLE PUBLIC SCRUTINY

The global free-trade establishment, including multinational businesses, corporate law firms, and trade officials of both Republican and Democratic parties, continued negotiations after the establishment of the World Trade Organization in 1995. With very little media reporting, the new pact would establish corporate freedoms beyond the reduction of tariffs in a wide range of areas, including protection of intellectual property and deregulation of financial services. The outcome was the Multilateral Agreement on Investment (MAI), which presented an exclusive bill of rights for corporations and wealthy investors. In many cases, these corporate privileges were at the expense of individual human rights and rights to self-determination. Under pressure from other UN member states, the Clinton Administration changed its strategy. It would first get an investment agreement from the group of industrialized nations comprising the Organization for Economic Cooperation and Development (OECD). The idea was that the developed countries would be more willing to reduce controls over global investment, including inevitably human rights standards, than would developing states.

The U.S.-based Council for International Business, comprising more than 300 TNCs and international law firms, helped to draft the MAI language. The draft language would give international investors the legal status of sovereign nations. It would require that nearly the entire economy of a country be open to foreign investment and allow TNCs to sue governments for monetary compensation, even for human rights regulations. Alan Tonelson, research fellow at the U.S. Business and Industrial Council, a trading organization of small to medium-sized businesses, observed, "This agreement gives big corporations an extraordinary set of new rights *vis-à-vis* political authorities around the world. The more people learn about this, the more scared they get. And they should, because it is a dangerous and audacious power grab that must be stopped" (qtd. in Moberg, 1998, p. 26).

In effect, average citizens would absorb a greater share of the risk of venture capital, which would operate with less and less government regulation around the world. Largely because human rights NGOs drew public attention to the Paris negotiations of MAI, the signing was delayed in May 1998. To become legal in the United States, it must pass the Senate by a two-thirds majority. With the inevitable public exposure in mind, business negotiators attempted to make the MAI more palatable to the public by strategies that would obscure its abandonment of social obligation. With that in mind, NGOs and grassroots advocates needed to draw public attention to the pact, under the assumption that the mainstream media would not be interested.

Other items of the final draft—available only because it was leaked to public-interest groups—would be the elimination of all "performance requirements" for TNCs. That is, local employment stipulations, targets for sales, and research in a given country. The movement of capital would be unrestricted—long-term investment in Third World countries would not be required. Governments must compensate investors if regulations—such as minimum wage and environmental laws—delay or reduce potential profits. Compensation to TNCs would be paid by Third World governments for contingencies such as revolutions, civil protest demonstrations, and labor strikes. These last stipulations would offer Third World governments the excuse to crack down more thoroughly on organized labor (see Chapter 15, in this volume). The MAI is far more comprehensive in its expanded rights for investors and corporations than previous trade agreements, such as NAFTA and GATT. TNCs could sue governments at international trade tribunal, venues that are usually stacked with free-traders. Petroleum and tobacco corporations have already tried to sue the U.S. and Canadian governments for their attempts to apply health standards to their products. Under MAI, such practices would greatly increase, severely encouraging international deregulation and limiting human rights enforcement at the national level.

The list of human rights standards threatened by MAI is staggering: In the United States alone, "the community renewal act, local economic development initiatives, unilateral state and local actions against human-rights violators, set-asides for minorities, women, small businesses, rules promoting socially responsible investment by public pension funds, and government promotion of recycling" (Moberg, 1998, p. 26). It must be assumed that the social damage would be much more severe in Third World countries. Governments of political elites would be given another go-ahead signal to continue national policies of self-aggrandizement at the expense of the general populace. Aside from human rights NGOs and possible grassroots movements—the latter always an uncertain eventuality—hope for critical public exposure of MAI lies in the legislative process in democracies. In the United States, this discourse would eventually arise in the United States Senate. Legislative debate of the pact would inevitably draw some degree of public exposure, but how much is greatly dependent upon the willingness of mainstream U.S. journalism to feature the debate. Since the U.S. media is greatly influenced by corporate interests—through advertising and "nonprofit" funding, hope for the human rights cause can by no means be assured.

BUSINESS ETHICS IN THE TRANSNATIONAL WORLD:
PETER DRUCKER

Peter Drucker remains a business writer for the "post-modern" age, an epithet he himself helped define. For decades, his thinking on the social responsibility of corporations has justified transnational dominance in a world increasingly divided into North and South largely by economic definition. Following Adam Smith's basic assumption that industrialists and traders should strive for the betterment of society in general, Drucker affirmed that "[m]anagement" was "an integrated discipline of human values and conduct, or social order and intellectual inquiry...a liberal art." Moreover, "Free enterprise cannot be justified only as being good for business. It can be justified only as being good for society" (qtd. in Lewis, 1998a, p. 5).

However, while the early Drucker imparted a high social role for the business manager, his later views of corporate motives and behavior became more cautious. He was wary of the accelerated trend among corporations to maximize profits by firing workers, and viewed the increasing habit of hostile takeovers as a significant failure of corporate capitalism. Although he did not abandon the notion of a free market, Drucker began to develop serious reservations about the social benefits of capitalism. He found hope in the enterprising spirit of the nonprofit organization, which must supply the social benefits that Global Capital cannot do. He remained far more vague, however, about Third World economic and social justice. Nonprofit organizations may prove ineffective, even nonexistent, in societies of extreme poverty and economic disparity. Drucker saw sound legal structures as a prerequisite for democratic development in the Third World, but his stress on the civil life of Third World nations was underdeveloped.

Drucker's approach to business always prioritized human well-being. Corporations should focus on the long-term progress of its employees. Helping individuals would eventually help business; both goals were causally related. "Development...was the development of people. Resources do not develop themselves; they can be developed only by people. The key resource for the enterprise and for the nation is people" (Catherwood, 1970, p. 241). In the 1990s, Drucker began to question whether transnational corporations were sufficient to protect workers' well-being. Needed was *Rechtsstaat* (the Justice State), or human rights, which he defined as chiefly political rights as defined in the ICCPR: "a social and political order which effectively protects the person and the property of citizens against arbitrary interference from above...freedom to choose their religion; to choose their professions or their vocations; to form autonomous social institutions and to read, speak, write and think, free of dictation by any power whether party, church, or state" (Drucker, 1995, p. 333).

Noting the failure of the free market to deliver its economic promises, especially in former Communist eastern Europe, Drucker prescribed a solution wholly outside the realm of business management:

> At the least, governments will have to learn that it is futile, folly and predictably a waste of money, to invest—whether through a World Bank Loan or through a Stabilization Credit—unless the recipient country establishes a truly independent and truly effective *legal* system. Otherwise the money will only make the wrong people rich: political bosses; generals; con-artists. Instead of enriching the recipient country it will impoverish it. The same lesson needs to be learned by businesses....The experience of the last decade is crystal-clear: the Free Market will not produce a functioning and growing economy unless it is embedded in a functioning civil society, with effective Human Rights a minimum requirement. (1995, pp. 336–337)

For Drucker, the rule of law and the guarantee of those rights prescribed by the United Nations "first generation" rights of ICCPR can eventually lead to democracy in the Third World. While democracy is not always the result, it cannot be achieved without ICCPR standards. They are necessary but not sufficient for social justice and democratic conditions. Moreover, first-generation political rights are necessary for the second-generation social and economic rights of ICESCR, although there is no guarantee that one will lead to the other. Drucker apparently rules out social-oriented state systems that would first guarantee ICESCR rights before achieving ICCPR, and perhaps social-democratic systems that would work towards both at the same time.

Drucker (1995) specifically disagrees with policymakers such as Brzezinski, Haass, and Huntington, who would increase U.S. aggressive postures worldwide to give America a national purpose: "It is often said today that the Democracies have lost their bearings with the collapse of Communism.... To be sure: the old policies, priorities, and criteria do not make sense now that there is no longer a 'public enemy.' But there is a new policy, a new priority, a new necessity: the promotion of civil society as a goal of international policy" (p. 337). Drucker reaffirms the need for the ICCPR guarantees of a civil society with a pointed reference to Fukuyama's hastily optimistic view of the end of history through democratic Global Capital: "A civil society is not a panacea. It is not the 'end of history.' It does not by itself guarantee democracy, and not even peace. It is however prerequisite to these, and equally to economic development. Only if Civil Society worldwide becomes their goal can the Democracies win the peace" (p. 337).

By prescribing first-generation human rights before economic development in the Third World, Peter Drucker prioritized the needs of people over corporate success (1995). This was a significant change from his earlier perspective, which tied worker well-being to the well-being of the corporation. Unhappily, Drucker has not attempted a more detailed understanding of how Third World governments can be motivated to redirect their interests to place human rights and economic development above corporate development. Nor has he explored more recent approaches to Third World democracy, such as the right to self-determination, self-development, and the connection between social and economic rights and civil and political rights.

THIRD WORLD COOPERATION FOR HUMAN RIGHTS

Presupposed by most international business executives and mainstream foreign policy experts is the belief that the rising tide of Global Capital will lift all ships, that transnational investment will, despite some initial social displacement and cross-cultural adjustment problems, benefit all classes over the long term. Such a belief is, of course, self-serving and rarely questioned by its practitioners, as the meetings of North American retail clothing manufacturers in Haiti suggests (see Chapter 11, in this volume). William Schulz (1998), executive director of Amnesty International USA, used evidence from recent history to challenge this presupposition in an open letter to Levi Strauss:

> It is no doubt true that an emergent middle class may provide the impetus for democratic reforms, but if economic growth alone were enough to turn the human rights trick, there would have been little need to bring international pressure to bear to end apartheid in South Africa. Absent active dissent inside a country and persistent pressure from the international community, economic growth by itself will not lead people to the Promised Land. (p. 22)

The active dissent and international pressure necessary for realizable social and economic justice supports the contention that social and economic rights, those articulated in ICESCR, depend on the more traditional civil and political rights of ICCPR (see Chapter 2, in this volume). Schulz's open letter attempts to convince corporations that it is in the best interests of international business to promote human rights for their workers and for their host societies at large:

> [W]ithout transparency, a free flow of information, respect for contracts and reliance on the rule of law, any business enterprise is inherently put in jeopardy. If the current situation in Indonesia teaches us anything, it is that corruption, cronyism, intimidation of the press and manipulation of the political process lead to instability and unrest, and instability and unrest cannot help but be bad for business. (p. 22)

Schulz, like Drucker before him, may be too optimistic when he depends upon Global Capital to support progressive social change. His own example of South Africa shows that a prosperous industrialized middle class does not necessarily lead to general social justice. How then can he expect boards of directors to bring about systemic social change? Moreover, Global Capital, especially U.S. transnationals, think in terms of quarterly earnings, not long-term developments. That Levi Strauss, Nike, and Eddie Bauer would voluntarily make the leap to long-term human rights concerns is not historically demonstrable.

The more reasonable approach to social justice is to support internal dissent, the free exchange of ideas, independent trade unions, and international organizations at different levels that would compel Global Capital to change its priorities. Recent attempts to change the minds and habits of CEOs through reasoned discourse alone have resulted in trifling success at best. Michael Moore's attempt to change Phil Knight, CEO of Nike Corporation, in his film *The Big One* (1998) is an instance.

On the other hand, the use of the boycott can have both an economic and symbolic effect on international corporate practice. Recently, student activists from the University of North Carolina, Chapel Hill, have protested Nike's labor abuses in its Southeast Asian factories and forced open discussion of their university's support of Nike through its athletic program (Dalrymple, 1998). Three professors team-taught a course entitled Economics, Ethics and Impacts of the Global Economy. The movement spread to St. John's and other universities. Harvard students forced its university to reject a PepsiCo contract with its dining halls, an action that convinced that corporation to divest from Burma in 1997 (Titelbaum & Morgan, 1998).

Although the power of the Global Capital establishment is extensive, there are democratic solutions to its sway, methods that do not rely on traditional 20th century totalitarian authority. One such approach was originally anticipated by the 19th century economist Frederick List. The present-day Listian formula would use Third World national governments and subregional and regional economic organizations to assure that all business practices would conform to universal standards of human rights and social justice. Michael Lind (1998) has encapsulated such an approach: "National governments should be

able to regulate the terms on which their nations engage with the world economy.... National programs of redistribution and promotion of human capital
can genuinely increase social equality within the nation-state. Immiseration and
class war are not inevitable" (p. 32). This national and regional approach can
begin in the First World as well, when wiser leaders—or leaders compelled by
their electorates—could use their control over access to common markets (for
example, through the European Union and NAFTA) to force government dictators and First World corporations into offering their Third World workers
human rights, decent social and economic standards, and political rights. "Until
they are ready to join the high-wage club, developing nations should form their
own regional economic blocs, liberalizing trade among themselves while collectively bargaining with the rich nations over terms of trade and investment"
(Lind, 1998, p. 31).

The Listian approach has been easier to plan than to achieve, as Nelson Mandela
and other African leaders have discovered during the 1990s when they attempted
to establish regional economic and peacekeeping agreements in sub-Saharan
Africa (see Chapter 17, in this volume). What is needed for the achievement of
human rights in the Third World is not only attention to civil and political rights,
as Drucker and Schulz advocate, but also the viable and long-term commitment to
self-determination and self-development. To achieve this goal in any meaningful
way may require a combination of the Listian concept of strong regional cooperation among Third World states and a vigorous civil and political life within each
nation to force Global Capital into a human rights agenda. South Africa is one
nation independent and politically aware enough to begin such an approach. Other
regions have agreements that have not yet been pursued with conviction, such as
the five-nation Mercosur, the South American common market. In the 21st century, other Third World nations together may build upon this beginning to create
a globally equitable and interactive system that can control both the hegemony of
Global Capital and nationalistic domination.

QUESTIONS FOR FURTHER THOUGHT

1. The Sanders–Frank Amendment of 1994 reads, "The Secretary of Treasury directs the U.S. Executive Directors of the international financial
   institutions to use the voice and vote of the United States to urge the
   respective institutions to adopt policies to encourage borrowing countries
   to guarantee internationally recognized worker rights and to include the
   status of such rights as an integral part of the institution's policy dialogue
   with each borrowing country." What measures need to be taken to insure
   that these requirements are carried out?

2. For Brzezinski, the U.S. policy goal must "perpetuate America's own
   dominant position" in order "to absorb the inevitable shocks and strains of

social-political change." Can such domination lead to his desired goal of "shared responsibility for peaceful global management"? What are sound alternative possibilities for worldwide progressive change?

3. How true is it that America is reluctant to use force in the world, and to what degree are the world's many nations and cultures dangerously "out-of-control," as Brzezinski, Huntington, and Haass contend? What purpose does the propagation of American innocence serve?

4. According to Reich, Brzezinski, and other mainstream thinkers, the United States needs a cause to holds itself and the rest of the world together. Do you agree or disagree?

5. Which foreign policy system do you feel works best? The policing of the world by one dominant power to assure that power's agenda, the prioritizing of human rights and self-determination for all countries and cultures, or another system? Support your answer with contemporary examples.

17

MULTILATERALISM AND HUMAN RIGHTS: KOFI ANNAN AND NELSON MANDELA

"WE ARE THE INDISPENSABLE NATION"

Proclaiming itself "the world's policeman," and designing a huge military budget that dwarfed the budget of its nearest competitor, Russia, in fact U.S. foreign policy operated in ways inappropriate for a signatory of human rights covenants. The State Department saw itself as more able than other nations or multilateral organizations to perceive right from wrong in the international public sphere. This perception has not gone unvoiced by its adherents. In 1998, Secretary of State Madeleine Albright defined the U.S. government's attitude towards the rest of the world quite accurately: "We are the indispensable nation. We stand tall. We see further into the future" (Traub, 1998, p. 80). Such thinking remains critical to U.S. unilateralism, a view dependent upon an aggressive exceptionalism that trumps all universal notions of international justice.

In the 1990s, the post-Cold War era can no longer be characterized as "the West and the rest"—a polarizing position to begin with—but in fact must be regarded, in the eyes of U.S. foreign policy, as "the U.S. and the rest." This outright willingness to dominate world opinion and international action at the expense of international judicial and legislative authorities has come at a time when U.S. economic dominance is no longer supreme, as it once was before the OPEC oil crisis in the early 1970s. The increasing willingness of the United States to use military force to bypass international legal procedures and due process—instanced by the Clinton administration's hasty and illegal use of cruise missiles to bomb civilian targets in the Sudan and Afghanistan in August 1998—may perhaps be a result of a world superpower's fear that it may be surrendering its economic preeminence.

The arrogance of U.S. foreign policy in the international human rights sphere is not new in the 1990s. Since the founding of the United Nations, Secretary Generals have been at odds with the West's greatest power. The typical attitude of U.S. Ambassadors to the UN Commission on Human Rights (UNCHR) under both Republican and Democratic administrations is typified in the tenure of Geraldine Ferraro, the Clinton administration appointee to that office from 1994 to 1996. She remained one of the few delegates to oppose numerous popular initiatives championed by African and other Third World member states. Ferraro expressed indifference to efforts within the UNCHR to broaden its representation to include more non-white member states—in fact, 53 percent of its membership were from First World nations. Even more, Ferraro reversed the U.S. position on the right to development in 1994. She justified her rejection of the popular resolution (debated at the United Nations for decades by a minority of member states) by labeling it a "diversion" and a waste of "scarce resources that could better be used to protect all human rights" (qtd. in Barrett & Steinberg, 1998, p. 42). Only two other member states (Japan and the U.K.) voted with her on rejection of the right to development, a freedom which is undergirded by the concept that economic rights are as important as civil rights.

In 1995, Ferraro led a second attempt to defeat the right to development resolution at the UNCHR. In the face of near universal support of the right, she finally conceded in 1996, but only after forcing through a rejection of the important evaluation mechanism for enforcement with an ineffective "voluntary progress report" by each member state. Afterward, she continued to speak out against the right to development concept in language that directly blamed developing countries for their own lack of progress: "If governments are not prepared to provide the internal conditions needed for all human rights, it should come as no surprise if the right to development continued to be unfulfilled" (qtd. in Barrett & Steinberg, 1998, p. 42). Regarded as a New York progressive by most of the U.S. mainstream press, her performance on the UNCHR was nonetheless well within the acceptable parameters of behavior for U.S. foreign policy officials.

The reluctance of the United States and its closest foreign policy allies to favor a wider interpretation of human rights is directly related to its retrogressive position on economic and social rights in such countries as Haiti and China, to name only two covered in this book. In the cases of China and Haiti, the United States has tolerated clear violations of labor practices by domestic business and especially its own TNCs. The right of association and to have independent trade unions remain problematic in China today. For example, two independent trade unionists in Shenzhen were imprisoned for subversion in 1996 for disseminating information on workers' rights (Schulz, 1998). Also, China continues to hand down capital punishment for crimes such as bicycle theft. A relatively underdeveloped country of 1.2 billion people is perhaps too tempting for Global Capital to bother about labor rights, hence President Clinton's decision to avoid labor violations in his condemnation of Chinese repression (see Chapter 13, in this volume). The unilateral decision to tolerate the Chinese government but continue to boycott and otherwise subvert Cuba has more to do with pressure from TNCs than with ideological consistency. Although both countries are at least nominally Communist, China, with its much larger population and no history of North American sugar company exploitation, represents a far greater potential for corporate development than Cuba, which remains under a U.S.-led boycott.

In the case of sub-Saharan Africa, President Clinton has proclaimed a new era of economic development for a region much neglected in recent decades for geopolitical reasons. That he can make such a grand tour and broad claim unilaterally speaks tellingly of the United States as a world power at the dawn of the millennium. If Madeleine Albright perceives her country as bigger, better, and all-knowing in world affairs, President Clinton has fashioned U.S. trading policy as the economic salvation of Africa. In fact, the discourse of transnational corporate economics was apparent in the descriptive language of U.S. mainstream journalism during the Africa trip. For *Time* magazine, Clinton was transformed into a TNC executive as he greeted African crowds: "Dressed in a dark suit among a gathering of Africa's new leaders at Entebbe in Uganda, he conveyed the dignified persona of the world's unchallenged leader—or top CEO" (McGeary, 1998, p. 49). The media accurately placed the U.S. presidency in the role of corporate spokesperson to the world, an identity that sits uneasily beside more democratic identities. With the hubris of 19th century European colonialists, the president talked to Africans of "partnerships" but always on his own terms.

The question of whether unilateralism American style will dominate international discourse in the 21st century, and of how this possibility and its alternatives could affect human rights, depends upon the strength of multilateral notions stemming from the tradition of the League of Nations and more clearly in the United Nations Charter and Bill of Human Rights. That the multilateral vision has the greater moral force seems a certainty. Yet the major actors of multilateralism are currently less powerful today than the proponents and powerholders of unilateralism. Hope for an improved international public sphere lies with those few advocates of international cooperation who currently command worldwide respect. United Nations Secretary General Kofi Annan has been among these, but his attempts to make his office an engaging force in the international scene is hindered by the particularism and exceptionalism of lingering nationalistic sentiments, eth-

nic and religious divisionism, and Global Capital. The success of his plan to realize a truly multilateral peacekeeping and human rights enforcement system
remains problematic.

KOFI ANNAN AND THE NARROW WALK

Although he has referred to himself as a soft-spoken, gentle lamb, Kofi Annan has
become a persistent negotiator for global peacekeeping and an advocate for
strength through the multilateral approach, despite the essential powerlessness of
his office and the heavily bureaucratized nature of the United Nations. His success
in avoiding military conflict between the U.S., the U.K., and Iraq in February 1998
was an unprecedented achievement for multilateralism, gaining universal acco-
lades, even from the U.S. foreign policy establishment. In some respects, 1998 has
shown encouraging signs of international cooperation. In September, the new UN
Rwanda tribunal of genocide and war crimes, after a slow start, sentenced a former
prime minister of Rwanda to life imprisonment for actions leading to the mass
killings of 1994. Jean Kambanda became the first person in history to be convicted
of the crime of genocide, an offense first defined legally in the 1948 Genocide
Convention (McKinley, 1998). The trial and conviction required the cooperation
of countries into which the accused had fled. Kambanda's arrest in Nairobi, Kenya
became the first such action. The tribunals of Rwanda and Yugoslavia were *ad hoc*
institutions, but the new International Criminal Court for War Crimes, also
founded in 1998, established the long-term significance of what might be called
the new multilateralism.

As UN Secretary General, Annan must have been reassured by these progressive developments, yet his dependence on the United States continued to be a
handicap that hindered his effectiveness. He faced the disheartening task of solic-
iting dues from the world's major unilateral power while attempting to recast the
role of his own institution, giving it an identity that would challenge the major
powerholding nations. By taking seriously the UN Charter's principle that human
rights transcend national sovereignty, Annan became a major player in the geopolitical dynamic of the late 1990s. Heading an institution that endured decades of
weak and accommodating secretary generals, from U Thant through
Boutros-Ghali, Annan strove not so much to develop a confrontational style with
the United States as the world's single superpower, but to establish an independent
peacekeeping and human rights program. The United Nations' new assertiveness
would eventually capture international attention and enlist member states in its
initiatives.

Annan's call for a vigorous multilateralism would expand beyond the Union
Nations's "golden age" under Dag Hammarskjold, when the Cold War face-off
between East and West allowed a modicum of independent action for the world's
international institution. Encountering the post-Cold War age of unilateral domi-

nance, of the unquestioned triumph of Global Capital with its awesome military backing, Annan, unlike Hammarskjold, could not occupy the little space between two world factions, but somehow had to construct an alternative way, one that eventually would establish a viable multilateralism. Annan's multilateralism would command the allegiance and material backing of the majority of countries, at last making possible Immanuel Kant's call for tolerant interconnectedness between all nations. While Kant articulated the notion of a cosmopolitan community for peacekeeping purposes, he fell short of advocating a single worldwide institution to administer such a necessary task, finding the idea of a single working democratic organization politically naive and unworkable. Instead, he foresaw a confederation of nations under a collective security agreement or nonaggression pact (Kant, 1970). By contrast, Annan's plan would build upon 20th century international configurations that have increasingly prioritized individual human rights over national sovereignty.

Moving beyond the UN Charter and 1948 UNDHR, the European Convention for the Protection of Human Rights and Fundamental Freedoms (1950) directly articulated in its preamble the establishment of a means for "collective enforcement" of human rights. In addition, it accepted a radical legal innovation: the right of individual citizens to begin direct proceedings against their own governments before the European Commission on Human Rights. Another bold innovation makes provision in the Treaty of European Union (the Maastricht Treaty) for both a European Union citizenship and an ombudsman to whom citizens may appeal directly against their governments. Other regions of the world have not be slow to follow the European lead. The American Convention on Human Rights (1978) has both a commission and a court, although it is seldom used, and the OAU created the African Charter of Human and People's Rights (1981), which has a functioning commission on human rights. As David Held has remarked, "what all these charters highlight is further evidence of a gradual shift from the principle that state sovereignty must be safeguarded irrespective of its consequences for individuals, groups and organizations" (1995, p. 103). Nevertheless, this challenge to the power of individual states remains at the incipient stage, and, as we have learned through the examples of Nigeria, Congo, and Rwanda (Chapters 10–12, in this volume), Third World nations have been either unwilling to organize their own peacekeeping and regulating forces (as during the Rwanda and Congo crises) or unable to challenge unilateral and TNC authority (as during the Haiti and Nicaragua crises).

While institutional structures have evolved sufficiently to accommodated permanent cooperative mechanisms, the dynamic of the North/South power arrangement has prevented multilateral efficacy. Aware of the present power vacuum of multilateralism, the secretary general must walk a narrow path between principle and power. To do this he has on his side a considerable personal capacity to present his position across a wide spectrum of cultures and political orientations.

The Annan Style

On February 22, 1998, the secretary general smoked cigars with Saddam Hussein while they negotiated access to military sites in Iraq. After two hours, Annan persuaded the Iraqi leader to accept what Hussein had proclaimed would never be acceptable—unlimited access to eight sites heretofore designated off-limits to UN inspection teams. With U.S. warships off the coast, Annan singled-handedly succeeded in avoiding a second Gulf War while offering nothing more than a few largely symbolic concessions. As James Traub commented, "It might well have been the most dramatic achievement by a Secretary General since the era of Dag Hammarskjold" (1998, p. 46). The question of whether a heavy U.S. military presence helped or hindered Annan's negotiations with Saddam remains open, despite the near universal acceptance that it did in U.S. mainstream journalism.

Annan's brilliant demonstration of multilateral diplomacy, averting war and saving the Clinton Administration from itself, was received with ambivalence in Washington. Senator Trent Lott likened Annan to Neville Chamberlain, and the secretary general's plea before Congress for UN back dues of $1 billion was not granted. Perhaps before human rights could be effectively and universally enforced, the UN's peacekeeping role had to be more fully established. Annan's ambition to establish an effective peacekeeping role for the United Nations succeeded everywhere but in Washington. While the great powers at the United Nations want a person who is "more secretary than general" in order to keep control through their permanent Security Council membership and veto power, the smaller states, particularly in the Third World, have traditionally argued a more substantive role for the secretary general. During an official trip to China in 1955, Hammarskjold articulated an authority that derived not merely from the UN Member Nations but from the UN Charter itself, a perspective that became known as the Peking Formula (PF). Annan has become the first UN head to attempt a full realization of the PF.

In the recent past, the post-Cold War power of the United States has overshadowed United Nations attempts at multilateral discourse. Boutros-Ghali, Annan's predecessor and fellow African, was denied an anticipated second term on the strength of President Clinton's threat of veto, an incident that revealed the ascendancy of U.S. unilateralism. Initially, Annan was liked by the U.S. foreign policy establishment because of his presumed compliant nature and willingness to undertake "reform" of the UN bureaucracy. Clearly, Annan's personal gifts included an ability to negotiate, but his style was regarded as low-key and unimaginative. Jean-Pierre Halbwachs, UN comptroller, characterized his skills: "He has this uncanny ability to get people to shift their position without feeling threatened or without any tension" (see Traub, 1998, p. 47). Moreover, Annan came to office owing personal favors to the main voice of U.S. unilateralism at the United Nations, Madeleine Albright, who promoted his candidacy against opposition.

Once in office, however, Annan pushed for a strong and multilateral United Nations, one possessing real independence in the PF sense. He continually urged those member states who had contributed UN peacekeeping troops to Yugoslavia to reconsider the limited mandate of that force. He complained that the United Nations had asked for 34,000 troops and got 7,600. In the case of the Rwanda genocide crisis of 1994, President Clinton had prevented even a nugatory force of 5,000 African troops—not his own—to be sent. Clearly, U.S. unilateralism demanded peacekeeping on its own terms. The U.S. cruise missile attacks on civilian target in the Sudan and Afghanistan in 1998, supported in the United Nations only by the United States and a reluctant Britain, were flagrant violations of international law on two counts—one, because of unilateral aggression, and two, because of the clear civilian targets (Ahmad, 1998; Weiner, 1998). The United States arrogantly rebuffed a move within the United Nations to send a fact-finding team to search the ruins in Khartoum, Sudan for signs of elements similar to the presumed chemical weapon VX. Peter Burleigh, deputy U.S. representative to the United Nations answered: "I don't see what the purpose of a fact-finding study would be. We have credible information that fully justifies the strike we made on that one facility in Khartoum" (see Myers, 1998, p. 1). The vigilantism of the U.S. response to the African embassy bombings was not remarked upon in the U.S. mainstream press. Opinion polls of U.S. citizens, who were not presented with any oppositional viewpoint, ran to 80 percent in favor of the illegal attacks. Certainly, Annan was faced with a formidable opposition to multilateralism through the U.S. media, government, and military.

Annan's February 1998 negotiation with Saddam prevented violent strikes and possibly war, but it was nearly canceled under U.S. pressure. Although France had proposed another inspection team, the United States refused to accepted any inspection effort besides the UN Special Commission (Unscom). U.S. opposition grew strongest just before Annan's trip to Baghdad. Annan's decision to retain a level of diplomatic independence, despite pressure from the Security Council permanent five to dictate his bargaining points, was a direct challenge to unilateralism. The language of his defense included a direct reference to the PF: "I had a constitutional duty to avert this kind of tragedy if I can" (see Traub, 1998, p.49). Traub has commented that Annan's problem was how to deal with the U.S. ambition to become the world's policeman. But he ignores the more important role of U.S. foreign policy—to serve the interests of transnational business by supporting Third World governments that favor TNCs and by maintaining not just a policing role but one that promotes a "free-market" system oriented towards U.S. interests.

This form of intolerant unilateralism is widely supported in the United States, where UN actions are often perceived as threatening the property rights and global dominance of the U.S. economy. Thus, Trent Lott attacked President Clinton for "subcontracting" U.S. foreign policy to the United Nations after Annan's February trip, and Republican Congressman Roscoe Bartlett's proposal to end UN membership rests on his belief that multilateralism will lead to a weaker United

States. Presupposed is the widely held notion of U.S. exceptionalism, the double standard by which the United States separates its own actions from those of the rest of the world. The exceptionalist view in world affairs has been succinctly expressed by John Bolton, Assistant Secretary of State in the Bush administration. Contrasting the "good" multilateralism of the 1991 Gulf War, when the United States led the United Nations to its position, and the "bad" multilateralism of Annan's negotiation with Iraq, he lamented that the Clinton administration acts as if the UN "had a life or existence outside of what the United States wants it to do" (qtd. in Traub, 1998, p. 80).

Overcoming such global loftiness is not easy for the UN leader. Annan appears to have enough capacity for diplomatic engagement to get the world's lone superpower to comply to multilateral actions, but only for short periods. He has never directly challenged U.S. officials verbally. While his actions are notably independent at times, his discourse remains accommodating. In fact, he takes care to apply a dual approach that conforms to the double standards of U.S. exceptionalism. Although he is capable of reproving Taha Yassin Ramadan, the Iraqi vice president, during a UN oil-for-food meeting ("You should try to moderate your language"), thus far he has not undertaken a confrontational discourse with Washington officials, despite the fact that the time limit for payment of member dues is fast approaching for the United States, which acts as though it paid the entire UN bill. In some respects, the success of his diplomatic engagement with Saddam has placed even greater pressure on the secretary general to either continue to walk a narrow line of compliance with U.S. wishes or to strike out on his own and establish a more confrontational posture with Washington. After winning concessions from Saddam in February 1998, he was expected to deliver more in the future with very little thanks from the unilateralists. Annan was perhaps wary of straying to far from accommodation, since his direct predecessor, Boutros-Ghali lost his second term by questioning the double standard of U.S. exceptionalism in supporting a Bosnian but not a Rwandan peacekeeping force.

Annan was not finished with the Baghdad negotiations. In August 1998, Saddam challenged U.S. authority behind the Chair of Unscom, Australia's Richard Butler, by demanding another Chair and a new arms commission moved to Geneva or Vienna rather than New York to distance itself from Washington. In the event, Annan postponed a trip to Portugal, where he intended to meet with East Timor resistance leaders. While Saddam charged that U.S. spies were everywhere in his country and Butler temporarily called off site inspections during the standoff, Annan urged the Security Council towards a moderate course, perhaps aware that the next scheduled reassessment of the inspections and sanctions was only two months away. Annan's words were conciliatory and free from vilification: The Council should remember "the ultimate objective of the exercise, which is to insure that Iraq is effectively disarmed and that the Iraqi people are enabled to take their place among the community of nations, free of sanctions" (Agence France-Presse, 1998, p. 8).

As the stalemate continued, Annan sent his special envoy for meetings with Saddam while he met with the East Timorese in Portugal. This time, the Clinton Administration did not threaten military action, a silent admission of Annan's previous success at diplomacy. However, U.S. academics and officials churned the waters for military action. Ruth Wedgwood, an expert for the U.S. Council on Foreign Relations, pushed a hawkish position: "In international politics, multilateral diplomacy without a unilateral commitment to enforcement is unlikely to be effective" (qtd. in Crossette, 1998d, p. A3). Others, rather speculatively, drew a connection between Iraqi resistance to U.S. influence and the threat of renewed Arab terrorism around the world. In these exceptionalist views, nothing short of total compliance with U.S. policies will prevent worldwide terrorism, and only unilateral military force is effective. On the other side, the Arab League accused Butler of exceeding his authority with weapons inspections and demanded his dismissal. On August 13, Washington reversed its martial posture and favored Annan's personal diplomacy, a silent concession to multilateralism (Erlanger, 1998).

Meanwhile, Annan became an active mediator between Portugal, Indonesia, and East Timor. He met with Timorese independence advocates, Bishop Carlos Ximenes Belo and Jose Ramos-Horta, both sharers of the 1996 Nobel Peace Prize. The effort to resolve East Timor's status was the first diplomatic break in 20 years. Annan facilitated indepth discussions of the three-way conflict between Portugal, as East Timor's former colonial ruler, Indonesia, which seized it, and the East Timorese, who sought self-determination.

Annan, however, was less engaging in Mexico during an official UN visit. The U.S. mainstream media reported that he had "delicately defused" a diplomatic crisis with Mexico, when in fact he had backed down from his human rights commitment by refusing to meet directly with the Chiapas resistance groups, the Zapatistas. Instead, he repeatedly praised President Zedillo's four-year strategy of violence against resistant Indian villages. Disappointed were human rights groups, which had repeatedly requested the United Nations to mediate the dispute. Annan was clearly unprepared for a strong multilateral approach in Mexico. His few offhand comments about UN involvement were immediately attacked by the Mexican government, which has refused international mediation. UN entourage officials replied apologetically, claiming they could not intervene in an internal conflict without that government's approval. In fact, the Mexican government had forced Bishop Garcia out of the role of mediator a few months before he openly sought international help.

Annan's response during the Mexico visit fell short of the independent role he sought for the United Nations and the multilateral approach to human rights: "It takes two to tango. I would urge the other parties to work in a sustained and persistent manner with the government to seek a peaceful and political solution" (qtd. in Preston, 1998). In fact, Annan's advice would have been more appropriate for the Zedillo government, which continued to use brutal force to suppress the resistance movement of land reform and social and economic rights.

MANDELA AND REGIONAL MULTILATERALISM

Fashioning a self-determined response to the dictates of global power is the first president of post-Apartheid South Africa, Nelson Mandela. Unlike Annan, who depends financially and politically upon the world's most dominant unilateral nation, and who owes personal favors to its officials, Mandela achieved political success largely without help from First World powers. His 18-year term as a political prisoner on a desert island, where he slept on the floor of a small cell, impressed on him the importance of human rights standards and enforcement. Mandela has taken particular interest in building a regional multilateral approach to African problems, hoping thereby to bring Africans self-determination for the first time since the colonial era. As the Chair and most important member of the 14-nation Southern African Development Community, Mandela has sought peaceful means of resolving regional conflict and human rights violations. His opposition to military involvement in the Congo/Rwanda power struggle (see Chapter 9, in this volume) has been challenged by other sub-Saharan states, notably Zimbabwe and Angola, who has already involved themselves in the fighting. Mandela's efforts to bring Laurent Kabila and the Presidents of Rwanda, Uganda, Angola and Zimbabwe to Pretoria for peace negotiations has met with resistance (Onishi, 1998). Nonetheless, his engaging diplomacy and broad respect among African nations holds promise for a nascent multilateralism, which is understood as an African alternative to U.S. unilateralism.

The Clinton Visit: Unilateral Charisma

President Clinton's 12-day tour of sub-Saharan Africa in March 1998 was thus far the longest foreign trip of his Presidency. It intended to promote the African Growth and Opportunity Act (AGOA) pending before the U.S. Congress. Basically a free-trade agreement that would allow the Overseas Private Investment Corporation to support private "development" on the continent, it offered certain concessions to African states: duty-free and quota-free exports to the United States for 10 years. However, most human rights and other NGOs opposed the act, since the price for a poor Africa was too high. Participating countries would be requires to follow the harsh and inhumane demands of the IMF: cuts in corporate taxes, reduced government spending, privatization of valuable assets such as mines, forests, harbors, and oil wells. TNCs and other wealthy foreign investors would be poised to buy these sell-offs at very profitable rates. According to Randall Robinson, president of the human rights NGO TransAfrica, studies of other IMF structural adjustment programs in Africa have shown disastrous effects in the health, education, and nutrition areas (Herbert, 1998).

Mandela has voiced strong opposition to the U.S. strategy, characterizing AGOA as clearly "not acceptable." However, as in the case of the Congo/Rwanda conflict, Mandela found himself alone. Most sub-Saharan states accepted the new agreement and ignored the possible consequences. Confronting extreme poverty and high unemployment among their populations, they continued to place their hope in the economic power and unilateral charisma of the United States and its huge TNCs. For Mandela, however, establishing a strong regional system of multilateralism remained the only hope for prioritizing social and economic human rights standards. In this effort, he had the respect, if not always the following, of other sub-Saharan governments.

Nowhere was Mandela's independent stance better illustrated than during the Clinton visit to South Africa. While other African states presented enthusiastic receptions for the U.S. president—in Ghana, Clinton was nearly trampled by over-enthusiastic crowds—South African crowds remained restrained. Clinton's reception among South African legislators was only correct; hand shakes were offered only when he initiated. Since the post-Apartheid government began in 1994, Mandela's country has held the world's attention, receiving many world leaders and advocates. Its attitude toward the Clinton trip was consciously blasé—a leading Cape Town newspaper ran the headline, "Bill Who?" For Mandela the visit offered the opportunity to confront the world's most powerful advocate of unilateralism (Apple, 1998). For Clinton, the Africa trip had already been the occasion for apologetics. In Rwanda, he publicly expressed regret that he had prevented UN peacekeeping forces from ending the 1994 genocide. However, iIn South Africa, Clinton would sit in silence to receive a lecture from the most respected human rights advocate in the world.

In Cape Town, the 79-year-old Mandela vigorously defended South Africa's right to remain friendly with Cuba, Libya, and Iran, suggesting further that the United States also should make peace with these and other states: "The United States, as the leader of the world, should set an example to all of us" by saying to its enemies "Let's sit down and talk peace." Then the standing of the United States would be "tremendously enhanced" (qtd. in Apple, 1998, p. A1). Mandela's use of analogy was brilliant diplomatic discourse. He compared his own movement's hard decision to sit down with its former enemies to form a new South African government of freedom with Washington's hard decision to cooperate with its former enemies to bring about a new era of multilateral peace:

> It was very repugnant to think that we could sit down and talk with those people, but we had to subject our plan to our brains and to say: without these enemies of ours, we can never bring about a peaceful transformation to this country. And that is what we did. The reason why the world has opened its arms to South Africans is because we are able to sit down with our enemies and to say, let us stop slaughtering one another. Let's talk peace. We will comply with the provisions of the United Nations Charter. And the United States, as the leader of the world, should set an example to all of us to help eliminating tensions throughout the world. (Associated Press, 1998)

Mandela's moral authority allowed the rare opportunity for Washington officials to listen in silence and to take no offense. The contrast with Kofi Annan, another African among white world leaders, could not have been more startling.

Throughout the Africa Trip, Clinton expressed his wish for full "partnerships," rather than unequal relationships, with the continent's emerging states. Mandela, and Africans generally, have heard such egalitarian discourse before, always heralding the inequality of colonial or neocolonial arrangements. Mandela's brilliant move was to set the 90-minute meeting and joint news conference with the U.S. president on Robben Island, where Mandela spent 18 years as a political prisoner. The lonely spot has now become hollowed ground for most South Africans and human rights advocates worldwide. While communication satellites flashed photos of both leaders looking through the bars of Mandela's former cell, each man responded according to his perspective. Clinton's praise of Mandela included a cautionary element: Mandela had endured his suffering "not in anger, but in hope, passion and determination to put things right." The effect of the physical setting, however, diminished any message from the Clinton side, as both presidents walked to the quarry, where Mandela had been forced to break stones for hours on end until his back became so weak that he was given a cot to lie in place of the bare floor. Mandela's former prison cell became a metaphor of the human rights struggle, which must endure the injustice of national power and the indifference of the international public sphere. Clinton's presence in the tiny room told the world that the struggle was not over yet.

Mandela's language was typically casual and friendly as both men walked with hands on each other's shoulders. "When I come here I call back into memory that great saga in which the authorities, who were pitiless, insensitive and cruel, nevertheless failed in their evil intentions." Aware that his opposition to AGOA would not help its passage in the U.S. Senate, Mandela repeated his rejection: "This is a matter over which we have serious reservations." His commitment to self-determination, however, was most clearly expressed when he justified trading with Washington's foes: "I do that because our moral authority dictates that we should not abandon those who helped us in the darkest hour of the history of this country. Not only did they support us in rhetoric, they gave us the resources for us to conduct the struggle, and the will." Mandela politely substituted citizens of his own country for what was obviously intended as the official U.S. foreign policy attitude: "Those South Africans who have berated me for being loyal to our friends—literally, they can go and throw themselves in a pool. I'm not going to betray the trust of those who helped us." Although Mandela did not mention Washington's support of apartheid South Africa through military sales and its refusal to participate in the protest boycott, he praised Cuba and other countries for being consistent allies of human rights.

A comparison of the multilateral approaches of Nelson Mandela and Kofi Annan shows a similar desire to develop peacekeeping forces that support and enforce human rights standards. The diplomatic styles of both men show an emphasis on informality, intimacy, and soft-spoken understanding over inflexible and institutional discourse. Their differences lie in the relative independence and emphasis on self-determination of Mandela's approach, and the concern to please both the weak and the strong in Annan's method. Annan labors under largely negative attitudes towards his office among many First World member states, and a UN polity with too much responsibility and proceduralism and too little power. Mandela's towering moral presence, relative independence from U.S. unilateralism and TNCs, and regional and worldwide respectability make him the more effective advocate of multilateralism.

QUESTIONS FOR FURTHER THOUGHT

1. Is it possible to consider your country bigger, better, and wiser than any other country, as Madeleine Albright does, and still retain a foreign policy with democratic goals? What attitude towards the rest of the world should a powerful country take to assure democratic decision making?
2. Is it necessary for the United Nations to establish an effective peacekeeping role before it can develop a significant human rights agenda? What steps need to be taken to create a more effective UN human rights effort?
3. What are the main differences in the approaches to human rights of Kofi Annan and Nelson Mandela? Which method will hold the best possibilities for progress in the next century?
4. What are the dangers in the attitude of exceptionalism when it is tied to nationalistic feeling? Have the United States and other First World global powers rejected multilateral approaches in favor of unilateral dominance? Give examples for or against.
5. Could Mandela's idea of a strong regional multilateral approach to international problem solving and human rights be connected with similar global efforts during the next century? Is a multitiered system of subregional, regional, and global multilateral organizations be a possible direction for future human progress? What are the advantages and disadvantages?

18

HUMAN RIGHTS ACCOUNTABILITY: ARRESTING A FORMER DICTATOR

THE ABSENCE OF ACCOUNTABILITY

The year 1998 witnessed continued civil unrest from chronic social injustice throughout Latin America. In Bolivia, workers in the manufacturing, education, and health sectors, together with campesino coca producers began an open-ended general strike on April 1 in which four were killed and many injured by "anti-drug" police, regular police, and the army. President Hugo Banzer Suarez considered declaring a state of siege. In Peru, thousands demonstrated in opposition to the regime of Alberto Fujimori, crying, "Democracy yes, abuses no!" (*Update*, 427, 1998, p. 2). The Lima Bar Association along with Peru's political opposition intended to bring charges before the Inter-American Human Rights Commission against the Fujimori government for overriding decisions of Peru's judicial system. Activists rallied in Mexico City to begin a national "peaceful mobilization" protesting the Mexican government's actions against the Zapatista National Liberation Army in Chiapas state. A mass protest was planned by the National Indigenous Congress and human rights organizations in Zocalo, Mexico. These examples demonstrated not only gaps of credibility within these countries, but also the persistent social inequalities that motivate protest against a civil fabric frayed by ongoing disregard for the standards articulated in the UN Bill of Rights. Latin America remains a region where democracy is fleeting and small economic elites survive as political elites.

Civil protest and human rights monitoring are dangerous activities throughout Latin America. In April 1998, Bishop Juan Gerardi was brutally killed two days after publishing an exhaustive report on human rights violations in Guatemala. The report concluded that the Guatemalan armed forces were responsible for 80 percent of the 150,000 deaths and 50,000 disappearances that occured during the war (Rohter, 1998). The government has refused to conduct a proper investigation into the bishop's death. In Brazil, two national leaders of the Movement of Landless Rural Workers were murdered on March 26 by two landowners because they were negotiating campsites for families banished from corporate property (MST, 1998). In Argentina, the offices of the Argentine Association of Relatives of the Detained and Disappeared for Political Reasons (*Familiares*) were ransacked. Although the human rights group has had such violence eight times since 1984, the Argentinian police have done nothing to solve the crimes. Computers were stolen that had replaced those stolen the year before. Only the CPUs, where the information is stored, were stolen, not other equipment (*Update*, 425, 1998). At least 15 people were hurt in Santo Domingo, Dominican Republic, when they demanded drinking water and an end to the energy blackouts that often last 18 hours a day. A community leader and local journalist were also injured by police.

When organized resistence is successful, the fruits of victory are often snatched away. For example, a Taiwanese-owned garment factory in Nicaragua was closed after workers won official recognition for their union. The Chentex Corporation announced its plant closing in the "free trade zone" and its move to Mexico. Its management sent a letter to the new union demanding, "to instruct your leaders to suspend these actions, which only discourage investment in our country and endanger workers' stability" (*Update*, 425, 1998, p. 5). Chentex assembles garments for the U.S. retailers Wal-Mart, Kmart, J.C. Penney, and Gloria Vanderbilt. It had been under investigation by the U.S.-based National Labor Committee (NLC). Another Taiwanese company reconsidered plans to open its factory in Nicaragua as a result of the union recognition. What constantly frustrates the NLC and other human rights NGOs in the Third World is the absence of international regulation, a condition that promotes the social irresponsibility of TNCs such as Chentex and many others. When Third World societies remain hunting grounds for the most exploitative labor, environment, and political conditions—situations that are "business friendly" in their social obliviousness—accountability remains elusive. Consistent laws that would prevent corporations like Chentex from abandoning a sight when its workers become organized need to be proposed at regional and international levels, but such initiatives must come from grassroots movements and NGOs in both the First and Third Worlds.

This chapter will evaluate the discourse of accountability for human rights in the era of globalization, when national political elites and transnational corporate power outreach democratic agendas. Although TNCs and their contractors have been permitted absolute mobility to escape social obligations, new movements involving IGOs, NGOs, and national government judicial structures are beginning to respond to an increasing number of international agreements that demand stricter accountability and positive action. A startling instance in 1998 was the arrest of a prominent former Latin American dictator in London under the direction of a Spanish investigative judge.

EXTRADITION

In October 1998, Baltasar Garzon, a Spanish judge who had gained recognition for his persistent pursuit of Argentinian junta generals accused of human rights crimes, issued an international arrest warrant for General Augusto Pinochet, former President of Chile (Simons, 1998b). The news shook the international public sphere, making the front page of *The New York Times*. Apprised by Interpol, the international police agency, that Pinochet was in London for a medical operation, Garzon requested extradition to Spain of Pinochet, Chilean citizen and "Senator for Life," for trial on charges of violations against humanity. Initially, Garzon's charges centered only upon the torture and deaths of Spanish citizens living in Chile. A few days later, however, the charges were extended to include citizens from other countries, including Chile, whose human rights had been violated. Garzon's request was based on the European Convention on Terrorism, which requires member states to assist one another in matters related to human rights violations. His action resonated throughout the international community.

However, it was not the first time that a former head of state was held for crimes related to his political office. In September 1998, a former Rwandan head of state was convicted of genocide at the UN Genocide Tribunal for that country. Jean Kambanda became the first person in history to be convicted of the crime of genocide, an offense first defined legally in the 1948 Genocide Convention. Still, Pinochet had been a much more powerful political figure than Kambana. In fact, Pinochet still held considerable political power in Chile in what has been described as a "behind-the-scenes" capacity; in fact, Pinochet's role was more onstage than off. What was happening in 1998—the 50th anniversary of the UNDHR—was a positive, though belated, response to international human rights legislation. The Pinochet request for extradition, however belatedly, promised to actualize that legislation ("Arresting a Dictator," 1998).

The initial response from Chile was immediate outrage from the political establishment and shock from the Chilean populace. Chilean television was obsessed with the news. Various political figures, celebrities, even opposition leaders, whose voices had been suppressed for years, were interviewed. A former general under Allende, Pinochet had seized power with CIA assistance by illegally over-throwing and killing Salvador Allende in 1973. He immediately repressed politi-cal opposition and curtailed freedom of speech. At least 3,000 Chileans were shot in the streets or "disappeared" during his regime, and internal movements for social equality were ended.

Pinochet's title of Senator for Life came with a lifetime immunity from prose-cution. This privilege was only granted by the Chilean government, not an inter-national body. Garzon's action represented a new level of globalized assertiveness for the judiciary, one that took seriously human rights agreements developed over half a century. The protests of the Chilean government demanding Pinochet's release from Scotland Yard authority put pressure on the Labor government of Tony Blair, which had criticized the Conservatives for allowing two previous vis-its of Pinochet for military contract negotiations. Blair was under considerable political pressure both to release and to hold Pinochet. His government remained ambivalent, caught between election pledges and fear of losing trade and diplo-matic relations with Chile. Some of the trade was for military weaponry. Thus, the Labor government found itself in a potentially embarrassing situation. Labor's foreign secretary, Robin Cook, distanced himself from the issue by telling the Chilean foreign minister that the arrest was an entirely judicial action and there-fore the British government could not intervene (Krauss, 1998a). Pinochet's law-yer threatened to go to Britain's highest court while the Labor government sought out national and international response to the event.

Two days later, Judge Garzon sent British authorities a list of 78 people of var-ious nationalities kidnapped in Chile and sent to Argentina, where they disap-peared between 1976 and 1983 under an agreement between several South American states called "Operation Condor," which was devised to eliminate polit-ical enemies of those countries. The implications of Garzon's judicial activism was immediately recognized by legal scholars, who generally supported his posi-tion. Despite the Geneva Conventions signed after World War II, which required all signatories to respond to crimes against humanity by denying safe haven to promoters of genocide and other political crimes, most governments have not met their responsibilities. Ruth Wedgwood of Yale Law School noted that "[e]xtradi-tion law has changed radically in the last 10 or 15 years. Torture and diappearance are considered such gross crimes that they are often held to be subject to interna-tional jurisdiction" (qtd. in Krauss, 1998a, p. 12). However, torture, disappear-ance, and other human rights crimes did not begin over the last decade or so. What has changed is not the nature or amount of the crime but a new priority given such violations by a more activist international public sphere, one willing to take on dominant economic and political structures.

Many lawyers and scholars hold that in international law there can be no immu-nity for those responsible for crimes against humanity, whether or not they are political leaders. Diane F. Orentlicher, director of the War Crimes Research Office of American University, recognized the implications of Garzon's action and the response of the British police. It showed through action rather than words that those who commit crimes against humanity, as defined in the UN Bill of Rights, the Geneva Conventions, and other international accords. "The central point of all of this is that crimes against humanity transcend the concerns of the countries where the abuses are committed. In theory, there should be no safe haven for world-class criminals, but the central problem has been [that] the enforcement of the law depends on the mobilization of the world's conscience" (qtd. in Krauss, 1998a, p. 12). Clearly, the world's conscience has been helped by the conviction of a Spanish judge. Whether the legal principle will bear fruit very much depends upon the fortitude of politicians in Britain, the willingness of international lawyers and scholars to continue to support human rights law, and the pressure that a motivated public can direct upon the politicians responsible for institutional mechanisms of justice.

Although initially taken off guard, the opposition to the arrest has been mounting. President Frei of Chile has already called Pinochet's extradition warrant a violation of diplomatic immunity, and some British politicians are concerned about retaliations against British citizens in Chile. The legal struggle quickly became political, as politicians in both countries sought the mood of their constituencies and acted accordingly. Thus far, both the British and Spanish governments have ignored the Chilean protests. The time period for the British was 40 days, during which home secretary Jack Straw would decide whether or not to honor the request for extradition.

The arrest of Pinochet broke new ground in holding former political leaders responsible for human rights violations despite being granted immunity by their own countries. Jean Kambanda, the convicted former prime minister of Rwanda, had not previously been granted immunity by his country. What has been recognized is that human rights courts from one country can find a citizen from another country responsible for crimes. In the Pinochet case, one country requested an alleged perpetrator from a second country through a third country. Here, unilateralism has been replaced by a multilateral approach to human rights enforcement, offering a new dimension to the globalization era—activist transnational human rights justice.

BALTASAR GARZON

The Spanish judge asserting a new human rights accountability had come to lead a life of caution. Baltasar Garzon has received constant death threats, walks with body guards, and must work amidst tight security at the National Court offices in Madrid. To charges that he has undertaken high-profile cases for self-promotion, he responds in interviews that he is committed to uncovering crimes in high places, which are too easily overlooked. Moreover, by talking with the media about his cases, he can often prevent important cases from being ignored or denied by mainstream journalism. Clearly, Garzon is not the typical successful jurist.

In Spain, Garzon gained his reputation as an aggressive investigator of sensitive issues, including drug trafficking, Basque terrorism, and government corruption (Simons, 1998b). He became involved in South American human rights issues only in 1996, after Spanish legal associations approached him about the torture, killings, and disappearances of Spanish citizens in Argentina during the Junta of 1976 to 1983. The Spanish Senate had denounced the crimes as state terrorism, but to no effect. Garzon's response was characteristically forthright: "According to the law, these crimes must be investigated and hundreds of assassinations cannot remain unpunished" (qtd. in Simons, 1998, p. 1).

Working as an investigative magistrate rather than a judge on the bench, Garzon concluded after months of legal research that the Argentinian perpetrators could be brought to account under international law, specifically the Geneva Conventions, which opposed serious human rights violations anywhere in the world. International legal scholarship had encouraged his global perspective, as did the recent attempts of First World states to bring trials and punishments in Rwanda and the Balkans. In the end he charged 110 Argentinian military and police officers. At least 11 senior military officers were issued international arrest warrants, including the former President, General Leopoldo Galtieri. Countries part of Interpol would be obliged to arrest the perpetrators if they left Argentina. In the same Spanish court as Garzon, another judge began to investigate the torture and killings of Spanish citizens during the Pinochet regime in Chile. Garzon became involved in both countries, but now the cases have broadened to include victims of nationalities other than Spain. Other members of the Chilean High Command were also charged with crimes against humanity, genocide, and terrorism.

THE CONTROVERSY WIDENS

The extraterritorial investigations were called invalid by the governments of Argentina and Chile, which had given wide immunity to those charged. In Spain and Britain also, negative reaction came from high places. Spain's present prime minister, Jose Maria Aznar, disapproved of the charges, as did Margaret Thatcher, former prime minister of Britain. Both conservative politicians justified their remarks on self-serving grounds—Aznar felt it would be bad for business between Spain and the South American countries involved; Thatcher felt that Pinochet had been "a good friend" to Britain during the Falkland War (Cowell, 1998c). However, the discourse widened, as the British all-party Human Rights Group pressed for a trial of Pinochet in the U.K. if the Spanish request for extradition failed.

When the British police refused Garzon's initial request to hold Pinochet after his medical operation, Garzon issued an arrest warrant linking the general to the case of a Chilean citizen, Edgardo Henriquez, who was kidnaped and tortured in Argentina, then handed over to the Chilean secret police as part of Operation Condor. A few days later, Garzon expanded the warrant to include 80 more victims of Operation Condor. The request for extradition needed to be approved by Spain's minister of justice, then prime minister Aznar and his cabinet. These formalities, together with the delayed response in Britain, added uncertainty to the controversy.

In Chile, about 200 demonstrators protested the arrest warrant in front of the residence of the British ambassador in Santiago, throwing fruit and eggs; later, a British flag was burned in front of the Spanish ambassador's residence, but the group retired quickly upon seeing police arrive with a water cannon. Chilean television showed relatively uncensored debate between left and right-wing groups over the arrest. Most Chilean politicians opposed the arrest, even those who had opposed Pinochet's regime, an indication that the issue could swing to one of nationalism rather than human rights. However, Gladys Marin, running for president on the Communist party ticket in the forthcoming elections, expressed support for the arrest on television. "I couldn't be more happy. This government has been unwilling to bring this genocidal criminal to justice over the last eight years, so it is up to the Spanish to do it" (qtd. in Krauss, 1998b, p. A8). Her sentiment was shared by the many Chilean families of the deceased and "disappeared," who had been attempting to bring legal action against the Pinochet government for years. The other presidential contenders were not so positive. The leading candidate on the left, Ricardo Lagos of the Socialist party, claimed noninvolvement in judicial matters while scolding Pinochet for letting himself be placed in such a vulnerable position abroad. The two conservative presidential contestants opposed the arrest, while some rightists urged diplomatic separation from Britain.

Over the next few days, small groups of protestors on both sides visited the British embassy peacefully. Anti-Pinochet activists left flowers at the embassy and pro-Pinochet protestors shouted and waved Chilean flags. Generally, however, Chile's response was surprisingly calm. Mireya Garcia, secretary general of the Group of the Families of the Detained and Disappeared, remarked, "After 25 years of absolute impunity for violations of human rights, it takes a while for the people to absorb this news and understand its importance and dimension" (qtd. in Krauss, 1998b, p. A8). Perhaps the out-of-the-blue legal action came too unexpectedly. Pinochet was not only the most well-known former ruler subject to the new international human rights activism, but he was still a powerful figure in Chilean national politics and a well-known advocate of privatization in the South American region.

The mainstream Chilean news media began an exceptional coverage of the Pinochet arrest. Its usual highly selective and censored broadcasts were replaced by a relatively well-rounded discussion of the event. While Chile has enjoyed free elections since Pinochet stepped down in 1990, its political life was nonetheless signficantly influenced by a military presence. Chileans saw news coverage of anti-Pinochet exiles celebrating and were even exposed to the reactions of a very personable Fidel Castro, heretofore treated as an evil Communist dictator. However, the level of denial was still quite high in a society that had been encouraged to forget its past political sins by a media that had preferred to emphasize Chile's relative economic prosperity in the 1990s, a positive development that had affected only Chile's middle classes. The son of Pinochet, Augusto Pinochet Hiriart revealed the level of denial within Chilean society when he remarked with some annoyance on television, "Countries have lost wars and committed real genocide, but that is not what happened here" (qtd. In Krauss, 1998b, p. A8).

Pinochet's son was willing to relativize his father's crimes so that he became a victim of unjust selectivity and overreaction. The fact that the mechanism for accountability was international, not regional or national, made General Pinochet's arrest seem all the more unjust to many Chileans. Also prominent within the Chilean mainstream media is the belief that economic prosperity both justifies and supercedes all claims to human rights standards. Left unstated is the issue—more wide-reaching than even the alleged political rights violations—that the social inequities rife in Chile, and in South American societies in general, contradicts the all-healing power of economic prosperity. Under Allende, the indifference and negativity of Chile's middle class presented the greatest obstacle to his proposed programs of social justice. Its willingness to let the military control the political scene, and its indifference to foreign manipulation of national politics—in the form of the U.S. CIA—was in large measure responsible for the 17 years of repression under Pinochet, who only a year before his rise had been a relatively low-level army general.

In Britain, the protests were much more in one direction. The Labor government faced the vehement response of Chilean emigres, who gathered outside the up-market London clinic where Pinochet received his back operation. They demanded Pinochet's extradition and some held up photos of many of the "disappeared" during the years 1973 to 1990. Prime Minister Blair found himself a European politicians atypically facing the implications of the human rights agreements crafted over the past half century. Chile was no Rwanda or Yugoslavia, but an economically influential state whom Britain had come to regard as its trading and diplomatic ally. Along with Spain, other European countries wished to move Britain center stage as an international human rights enforcer. Linking the Pinochet arrest with the actions of the International Criminal Tribunal for the former Yugoslavia in the Hague, Jacques Poos Luxembourg commented angrily: "What goes for General Pinochet also goes for all the Mladics and Karadzics who are still in hiding and will be, one day or another, arrested and judged for their crimes" (qtd. in Cowell, 1998a, p. A8). British and Spanish politicians were thrust into a new era of international human rights, involuntarily becoming main actors in the transition to a more vigorous and legally based global system of accountability.

SECOND THOUGHTS: BACK INTO THE CLOSET

Garzon would not back down but instead widened the charges against Pinochet, including the genocide, torture, and terrorism relating to 94 people (Cowell, 1998b). Britain became divided along traditional lines of Conservative and Labor—the former valuing Chile's economic buying power, not the least of which were lucrative arms deals negotiated in part by none other than Pinochet himself, while the latter pondered the ethical implications of Britain's foreign policy if the Blair government would release the former despot. One side claimed the Pinochet arrest by the London police showed a just response to a brutal dictator, while the other side called it the behavior of "a very arrogant government" (qtd. in Cowell, 1998a).

Perhaps predictably, given the prodigious implications of the arrest, second thoughts began to develop after the first week of the arrest. Spanish prosecutors turned against Garzon by formally opposing the arrest, despite the condemnation of Pinochet's military rule by the Spanish government, which labeled it "repugnant." Eduardo Fungairino, chief prosecutor of Spain's High Court, claimed that Spain had no legal jurisdiction (Reuters, 1998d). In Chile, the debate intensified as the arrest was increasingly perceived as an issue of political and social identity. Left and right became more demarcated as violence increased. Many conservative politicians accused the socialists of secretly promoting the arrest. Many more Chilean leaders and opinion makers expressed fears that prolonged factionalism would result from the issue, which they preferred to keep in the closet of history. Indeed, the discourse was for no more discourse, but instead a silent forgetfulness. Andres Zaldivar, president of the Senate and a candidate for president, admitted, "I'm not afraid of a coup or an interruption of democracy, but I see the possibility of the country entering into a period of serious tensions, polarization and constant demonstrations" (qtd. in Krauss, 1998c, p. A3).

Zaldivar voiced a discourse common to Chileans—that the "emerging democracy" of the country was jeopardized by the issue and its consequent disclosures. Among the conservatives, who had sought to distance themselves from the military dictatorship, there was a reactive drift right as it sensed more support and unity for a pro-Pinochet stand. The government kept up its diplomatic resistence, claiming foreigners had no right to try Chileans. Both the Chilean and British governments discovered a new argument, a way out of their involuntary human rights commitment, by claiming that the aging General's health was too poor to withstand a trial. Thus, Jack Straw announced his option to deny the extradition on "humanitarian grounds," a point of irony when the nature of the charges against Pinochet are considered. Ricardo Israel, chair of the political science department at the University of Chile, added support for this tactic: "If Pinochet dies in custody, many Chileans will look for someone to blame and you could see uncontrolled waves of violence" (qtd. in Krauss, 1998c, p. A3). What developed was an intensification of political discussion at the grassroots level, in the news media, and on the streets of Chile and Britain, just as the governments involved attempted to circumvent discussion, dodge legal commitments to human rights agreements, and deny the significance of the extradition request.

BROADER IMPLICATIONS:
THE CONCEPT OF "A UNIVERSAL CRIME"

Much of First World journalism echoed what had become the Chilean right's standard justification for Pinochet's amnesty. The *Washington Post* editorial of October 20 was typical: "But he also saw to the rescue of his country from a chaos to which he was only one contributor, and to its controlled evolution into a prosperous Latin democracy" ("Arresting a Dictator," 1998, p. A18). Putting aside the fact that such a statement could also apply to any number of the world's dictators (including Adolf Hitler's contribution to German prosperity) the editorial is also remarkable in its assumption that Chile is prosperous and democratic. However, the other side was also consolidating its position. Peter Mandelson, Britain's trade minister, ardently supported the arrest: "I think the idea that such a brutal dictator as Pinochet should be claiming diplomatic immunity is, for most people, pretty gut-wrenching stuff" (qtd. in Reid, 1998, p. A13).

The tendency to view human rights violations by political systems as the legal responsibility of individuals has grown throughout the 1990s. This has been in part due to the willingness of unilateral powers such as the United States to pursue across international borders alleged perpetrators of terrorist acts against them. Garzon's contention that he has the authority to try Latin American dictators and political henchmen is consistent with the U.S. government's argument that it can try terrorists, hijackers, and other crimes against its citizens. What has only begun to be recognized is the next legal step—that human rights culpability can apply to more than single terrorist acts. Samuel Buffone, a Washington lawyer who represents victims of Pinochet's regime, comments, "What is really innovative and important here is that a Spanish court is looking at international acts of terrorism, systemic human rights abuses and genocide, and is asserting jurisdiction on that basis" (qtd. in Pear, 1998). Even politicians, although honored former "statesman" of their country, can become the modern-day equivalent of pirates if their actions in office significantly violate human rights.

Several legal questions follow from the Pinochet arrest—the fact that the case is legally complicated also means that it is potentially precedent-breaking in several areas of international law. Does Pinochet have immunity because of his status as a former head of state or because of his present title as "Senator for Life"? Are other countries bound by Chile's granting him amnesty? Can Spain or any other country try him for actions in Chile? These and other issues would be decided by the outcome of the case. Lori Damrosch, international law expert at Columbia University, observed, "[Chile's granting amnesty to Pinochet] doesn't carry any weight outside Chile. It's not binding on any other country. All these ex-dictators must have an understanding that they are somewhat at risk when they leave their own countries" (Pear, 1998, p. A8). Thomas Buergenthal, international law scholar at George Washington University, noted that Pinochet was not accredited to Britain when he traveled there on his diplomatic passport for a back operation. Thus his diplomatic immunity was not valid there.

The European Convention on Terrorism and other human rights agreements both regional and global supported Pinochet's arrest, as did the 1961 Vienna Convention on Diplomatic Relations, which states that diplomatic immunity was not created to insulate people against prosecution for crimes against humanity or other heinous acts. International law has increasingly assigned personal responsibility for widespread political atrocities. Jonathan Charney, editor of *The American Journal of International Law*, noted that genocide, torture, and cruel and unusual punishment are considered universal crimes (Pear, 1998). The fact that political acts can be considered universal crimes grounds the debate of human rights accountability. Without a universal understanding of human rights standards, nation states would typically rally around their perpetrators and prevent the work of justice.

The acknowledgement of crimes that are universal would encourage the enforcement of anti-genocide and other international laws. The Chilean power structure and perhaps great numbers of the middle class have demonstrated their preference for denial of the past over historical reality. Certain historical truths would embarrass the present political system, revealing its unjust provenance. For Gernaro Arriagada, a one-time opposition leader of the Pinochet government, the closet of history now seems more appealing: "Part of the achievement of our transition back to democracy has been to take all of the demons of this history and put them into some kind of closet. This case brings them all back out again. What right does some Spanish judge have to do that?" (Golden, 1998, Sec. 4, p. 6). Demons, however, have an old habit of escaping confinement. The "out-of-sight-out-of-mind" mentality that Chile and other Latin American states have made in recent decades are for the sake of "transitions to democracy," as Arriagada euphemistically terms his country's unwillingness to bring justice to its political victims. His discourse for human rights introduces the red herring of economic prosperity, for which the denial of social repression is somehow necessary and sufficient: "If these transitions to democracy were just about trials, we could leave them to the judges. But these transitions are about achieving a great number of goals, including political goals, economic goals—and also human rights goals" (Golden, 1998, Sec. 4, p. 6). Put more plainly, Arriagada and others have made political compromises with past oppressors in order to stay in power themselves. Presidential candidate Zaldivar sees the issue as too much reality affecting the fragility of the "democratic transition," wherein the Pinochet arrest would lead to "tensions, polarization and constant demonstrations" (Krauss, 1998c, p. A3). One wonders just how much of a "transition" can occur within a society that refuses to face its own injustice, and whether such injustices are not continuing today in other ways.

The red herring argument was echoed internationally by Britain's Margaret Thatcher: "The people of Chile...have determined how they should come to terms with their past. An essential part of that process has been the settlement of the status of General Pinochet, and it is not for Spain, Britain or any other country to interfere in what is an internal matter for Chile" (Golden, 1998, Sec. 4, p. 6). Buttressing these efforts to circumvent past oppression are references to the absoluteness of national sovereignty; a presumed national "prosperity," which, however, has only affected a portion of the population; and a comparison to other regional states, who have also managed to ignore their own unjust pasts.

In Washington, 36 U.S. Representatives petitioned President Clinton to release documents vital to the human rights case against Pinochet. Clinton, eager to sign on Chile to his second-phase NAFTA fast-track before it was rejected by Congress, had a vested interest in the red-herring of Chile's "economic miracles," following what was called the "free market fascism" of Pinochet's 17-year rule. Congressmen George Miller and John Conyers reminded Clinton that "Absent our firm response, terrorists will continue to believe they can act with impunity" (Vest, 1998, p. 58). The 4,000 or more *desaparecidos* (disappeared) of Pinochet's regime were victimized around the world by the DINA, Chile's secret police, including two allegedly killed in Washington itself. Also, the U.S. involvement in the establishment of the regional network of terrorism dubbed Operation Condor has been closely documented (Dinges & Landau, 1980). To the argument that political repression is justified if its leads to economic prosperity, Larry Birns, director of the Council on Hemispheric Affairs, remarked:

> It came out clearly in the [Senator Frank] Church hearings that it was the aim of U.S. policy to economically asphyziate Chile under Allende—not only was there a successful concerted effort to make certain that no bank would lend Chile money, but the CIA was also paying off truckers to strike. Under Pinochet's labor laws—which are still in force—the trade unions suffered incredibly, losing their rights to strike, to collectively bargain, to have a reliable financial base. Whatever Chilean "economic miracle" there is was built on the backs of the poor. (Vest, 1998, p. 61)

The attempt to smother all political dissent and organized opposition were well documented in Patricio Guzman's renowned film, *The Battle of Chile* (1976). In his recent sequel, *Chile, Obstinate Memory* (1998), Guzman considers the silence over two generations upon which Chile's power structure depends for its survival. Clearly, Chile's preference for social amnesia was not created without help from a compliant news media and obliging social institutions. The problem of eliciting and then developing a strong public voice in domestic and foreign policy affairs in the era of transnational power has been well documented by Eric Alterman (1998), who ascribes the disenfranchisement of the public to, among other main factors, the attempts of Global Capital to champion free trade at the expense of working-class interests. While Alterman addressed recent U.S. political history, much of the reality he describes applies also to Chile and other Third World societies, where the mainstream media's constant repetition of "economic miracles" belies the reality of social disparity and political repression. What is needed for a new human rights accountability is a responsive general populace that demands access to international discourse throughthe media.

QUESTIONS FOR FURTHER THOUGHT

1. What should the British government do in response to the charges that General Pinochet has been granted amnesty by Chile and therefore should be released?
2. What crimes should be regarded as "universal," in that they are considered so severe that international justice should intervene?
3. Are there risks of the misuse of international intervention for genocide and other political crimes? How might some of these charges be misapplied?
4. What measures can be taken to prevent the misuse of international intervention for crimes against humanity, genocide, and torture?
5. How might governments be further encouraged to enforce the human rights agreements they have signed over the years since the Geneva Conventions and the UN Bill of Rights? Which organizations could best facilitate human rights commitments regionally and globally?

19

CONCLUSION: EMPOWERING HUMAN RIGHTS

TWO SIGNIFICANT ACCOMPLISHMENTS

At the end of the 20th century, hopeful circumstances offer the prospect of human rights advancement. In both civil/political "first generation"rights, and economic/cultural "second generation"rights, events undertaken in the first half of the 1990s have opened a productive and exciting period for social justice issues. The effectuality of the international public sphere was confirmed by the unprecedented rise of the NGOs at the Vienna Human Rights Convention in 1993. There for the first time, the NGO presence took on substantive form through the sheer number of participants and their demonstrated unity. More than that, the great accomplishment of the NGOs at Vienna was the forging of operative definitions that would associate human development (other preferred terms included "economic self-determination" and "economic redistribution") with the more traditional agendas of human rights.

The second significant accomplishment of the decade has been the more recent strengthening and expansion of the concept of international human rights justice. With the creation at Rome of the UN's International Criminal Court in 1998, opposed by the United States but supported by over 120 member states, the idea that national leaders and their subordinates could be tried by international bodies for crimes against humanity, genocide, crimes against women, and other categories, has opened new legal dimensions for human rights. Currently, the UN-sponsored tribunals in Yugoslavia and Rwanda have brought jurists from many nations, including the United States, to try national leaders for similar actions when in office. Judgments and convictions have been made.

Most controversial, but perhaps also most significant, has been the detention of the former Chilean dictator Augusto Pinochet in London under orders from a Spanish investigative judge who previously pursued Argentinean junta generals for war crimes. The first ruling of the British courts (British High Court, October 28) was in Pinochet's favor, citing sovereign immunity and even "the divine right of kings"under British law; however, the Crown Prosecution Service, representing Spain at the second, House of Lords hearings, cited the Nuremberg principles against immunity for crimes against humanity and won the appeal.

Political and economic rights are being conjoined, clarifying norms that have been only implied or stated broadly for decades in international agreements. Hence, the question raised in the Introduction of this book, whether or to what extent universal notions of human rights have a purchase in the new century that will no doubt challenge the viability of universal standards, has been answered in part by the insistence of international bodies on the commensurability of political and economic rights in all cultures. Relativistic references by national power structures have been consistently rejected by both nongovernmental and governmental world bodies, who have shown their willingness to use interventionism as an affirmative response to human rights abuse. Like the increasing willingness in First World societies to intervene when instances of child and spouse abuse are revealed, the new trend to enforce international standards on offending state governments and their private collaborators derives from the recognition that absolute sovereignty, whether on the national or the familial levels, is inconsistent with the norms of a revitalized international public sphere. This chapter will review recent developments in these two areas of human rights—the right to human development and the legal enforcement of crimes against humanity—with the intent of clarifying the direction and effectivity of the new discourse.

ECONOMIC DEVELOPMENT AND HUMAN RIGHTS

Nongovernmental organizations have insisted in the 1990s that economic systems with their capital formations are causally related to human rights. Human rights achievement has been widely perceived as a necessary step in economic redistribution. Philip Alston (1995) commented that, since the crucial link was made in the early 1990s, the vocabulary of human rights has received a clarity and focus that earlier mention of "basic needs"and "human well-being"did not possess.

"[Human rights] are no longer a vague and undefined entitlement to a favour of some kind to be bestowed upon them by a benevolent government, if and when they can afford it" (p. 10).

Substantive Approaches to Human Rights

The more specific language of human rights and its connectivity with economic well-being has given social justice discourse a consistent and reliable basis for monitoring and advocacy. While human rights is now conceived as enabling economic well-being, the reverse is also true, that economic redistribution in developing countries can enhance human rights significantly. Furthermore, the negatives are also true, that the lack of human rights standards—for working conditions, the minimum wage, and so on—can inhibit democratic economic development; and that the lack of economic well-being for Third World majorities encourages human rights abuse.

The grounding of social justice in economic well-being has received its share of anticipated criticism from "free market"advocates and unilateral government policy makers (see Chapter 16, in this volume). Such free-market theorists as Brzezinski, Huntington, Haass, and Reich presuppose that confronting a world of independent nations who affirm self-determination and the right to economic and cultural development is necessarily diminishing to the United States. The new post-Cold War era seems a fearful place to such global unilateralists. At times this paranoia can reach pathological proportions: "Given these trends, without the external pressure of Soviet Communism holding us together, America may simply explode into a microcosm of the entire world" (Reich, 1992, p. 321; see also Chapter 16, in this volume). Moreover, the forces of Global Capital seek to unite with local political and economic elites to assure that human rights and social equality are kept within bounds.

The intense urge towards global privatization, reaching feverish proportions during the 1990s, especially in former Communist states, must be a source of concern for human rights advocacy. For example, in Mongolia, which abandoned its Communist government in 1991, corruption, unregulated business practices, and Russian mafia influence have combined to give that nation a high unemployment rate and the widespread loss of the order of law. In October 1998, Sanjaasuren Zorig, the newly elected prime minister and a founder of the pro-democracy movement, was murdered, probably by business cartels or the mafia (Eckholm, 1998b). The usual practice of human rights organizations has been to monitor government structures in their search for human rights abuse, but the civil (private) sector is as much a source of violations. In this regard, Bruce Robbins (1997) worries that the increasing influence of international NGOs, rapidly increased to over 10,000 by the late 1990s, will not have an entirely positive effect. There are, after all, immense differences in NGOs, and their recent predominance in the international public sphere is partially the result of the "privatization"campaigns by the

United States, its client states, and most powerful allies. Moreover, progress at the Vienna conference failed to open to public observation the "private"operations of the World Bank and IMF. What needs to be remembered is that the abuses of power, in both its public and private forms, has saliency in human rights.

> Though both unequal power and cultural difference exist in friction with the universality of human rights, the two differ in at least one crucial respect. The assertion of cultural difference is often understood as an all-or-nothing proposition that offers no substance for further debate. The assertion of unequal power, on the other hand, opens out into a continuing discussion with more than two sides, indeed, with a profusion of tactical and principled complications to attend to. It relativizes the universal on a common ground of assumptions—from within universality itself, as it were. (Robbins, 1997, p. 228)

By making commensurate values of social and economic justice, equality, and human rights, the new international discourse moves beyond particularism and exceptionalism, but, because it attends to the particularities of localized power, it at the same time relativizes universal notions. One hegemony's assertion of unequal power "opens out into a continuing discussion,"whereas absolutizing claims to cultural difference typically "offers no substance for further debate." It is to those ends that the 1993 Vienna Declaration on Human Rights and related agreements recommended a clear interventionist role for both individual states and intergovernmental organizations. It was at Vienna that the 5,000 representatives of 900 NGOs helped to end the impasse between First World universalists and Third World relativists (Baxi, 1994). Vienna clearly pointed to social equality as the chief indicator of human rights norms. This standard will continue to be applied, most certainly with greater clarity and force, into the 21st century. Thus, the questions posed in the Introduction of this book relating to "the appropriate degrees of universality needed to apply human rights standards in an effective way" can be answered in part by linking economic and social equality with international human rights through a vigorous universalist standard that critiques unilateralist and self-serving ends. What are the motives of dominant power and how do they support or reject democratic agendas?

The universalizing side of the balance has an additional function as global whistle blower to powerful First World states with requests for extraterritorial rights against poorer nations. The unilateral U.S. invasion of Panama and forced extradition of head of state Manuel Noriega to the United States was undertaken in violation of international law and human rights agreements. Early in the century, Western requests for extraterritorial rights in Manchu China were not concerned with universally applicable human rights standards. Nor was the indifference of the U.S. mainstream media once U.S. citizen Michael Fay was canned as punishment in Singapore. Most U.S. media criticism was not universalistic, but rather nationalistic (and perhaps racist) in its outrage "that Singapore should presume to cane an American rather than that it should cane *anyone at all* irrespective of nationality"(Perera, 1994, p. 122). The *realpolitik* of international power commonly undertakes a dubious human rights agenda, using human rights issues highly selectively, even within the same country, as evident in President Clinton's 1998 visit to China, where human rights violations in foreign Special Enterprise Zones were ignored in favor of state (i.e., Communist) interference with freedom of the press issues.

Beyond the Pragmatic:
Human Rights as Interventional and Culturally Detachable

By linking human rights to economic development and social equality, arguments by self-serving power interests on both the local and global levels can more easily be rebutted. What cuts across cultures and economic power arrangements are the norms involved in human dignity, well-being, freedom, and equality. The UN General Assembly has reconfirmed the universality of human rights by passing a resolution—introduced by Cuba in 1985, opposed by many Western powers but passed in 1991—which asserts the principles of nonselectivity, impartiality, and objectivity in human rights advocacy (Robbins, 1997). Unilateral claims to extra-territoriality, or simply the avoidance syndrome of world powers when practicing vigilanteism, as the United States did in 1998 with unauthorized missile strikes against civilian targets in Sudan and Afghanistan, are exceptionalist approaches to foreign policy grounded in conceptions of unique privilege. Madeleine Albright's chilling words in 1998 proclaimed U.S. exceptionalism in it most arrogant and predatory form: "We are the indispensable nation. We stand tall. We see further into the future"(qtd. in Traub, 1998, p. 80). The arrogance of world power can be exposed through universalistic concepts that cut across the cultural constructs of nations and power systems. Anything short of universal principles gives way to pragmatic accommodationism and half-measures. Indeed, the UN Bill of rights agreements were intended as interventionist legislation, not as culturally complementary adjuncts to particular social structures.

President Clinton's arguments against China's repression of the freedoms of speech and assembly claimed human rights normativity, yet his selectivity and disregard of abuses in the Chinese Special Enterprise Zones of his own TNCs goes against the joining of human rights to economic equality and the right to development. Still, his interventional urge was firmly grounded in the human rights discourse of the United Nations and several regional agreements. In the Introduction of this volume, the worth of universal norms for human rights was considered as a means of opening to international public discourse "the goal of unlimited possibility and...a horizon of broadening options." In the chapters we have examined (for instance, on China, Indonesia, Haiti, Nigeria, Congo, Rwanda), powerful transnational economic forces working with local political and economic elites have sought to limit these options and possibilities through reference to exceptionalist notions of dominant culture and through appeals to cultural incommensurability, usually with absolutist notions of national sovereignty. In the truth claims of universalist notions, however, human rights violations remain human rights violations, and accountability gains substantive status.

The interventionist role of human rights assumes the detachability, or translatability, of culture (see the Introduction, in this volume). Far from being incommensurable, cultures have within them the ability to recognize analogous conditions, behaviors, and circumstances in other cultures. Cross-cultural perception in human rights is evident in the degree to which the myriad cultures of the world's member states have ratified intergovernmental human rights statements, and in the willingness of thousands of NGOs from both the First and Third Worlds to pursue like-minded goals and standards of accountability, as we have seen in Chapter 4 (NGOs). When Singapore responds to U.S. media attacks on its punishment of Michael Fay by pointing out flaws in the U.S. criminal justice system, it is acknowledging universality. As Leon Perera (1994) points out, "If values embodied in our domestic political arrangements can be defended without recourse to arguments about incommensurable cultural differences, but rather using purely political ideas, isn't this an admission that the choice of values can be made on the basis of transcultural criteria?"(p. 132). Going further, the reinvigorated international human rights movement of the 1990s lends support to the challenge set forth in the Introduction, that "[s]ocial criticism in any given age requires a stepping back from the particularities of historic determiners, where perspectives wider than the pragmatic can be applied."

Universal Values and Decentralization—A Contradiction?

Our examination of various world settings suggests that universal normativity for human rights is not exclusive or in contradiction of the particularities of human rights directives. As Pheng Cheah (1997) has noted, "The open-ended nature of the human rights enterprise is expressed in the exhortatory nature of the *Declaration* which involves a pledge by all signing nations to achieve a nonexhaustive common standard"(p. 242). He offers of evidence of this open-endedness the great increase in the number of human rights organizations and their ongoing debate from a host of perspectives.

Deriving the local and particular from universal human rights standards has been effected throughout the post-World War II era. Currently in Pakistan, for instance, various local NGOs have worked with the national government to undertake various working systems of socioeconomic development in rural areas. Two key criteria, local participation and decentralization, were evident: "that responsibility for all aspects of development programs should be shared by local people and institutions; and a belief that decentralized organizational structure is one of the most effective means of facilitating this" (Bennett, 1998, p. 55).

Of the 10,000 NGOs existent in the late 1990s, some 4,000 work primarily with development issues. They generally give priority to the human resource development components, which trains villagers in local projects (Perkins, 1998). Local initiatives support universal notions of self-determination, human dignity, and ecology through local processes of collective empowerment. Self-reliance thus becomes a powerful tool for social transformation, beyond the meliorative projects often imposed by external development institutions. Human resource development begins through decentralizing programs that are nonetheless grounding in the universal concepts of fair economic distribution, human dignity (in the workplace, for example), and ecological soundness.

Common to many Western relativists as well as universalists is the assumption that Western universalizing notions are the only ones applicable to human rights. Quite often, however, indigenous traditions, most extending to the pre-colonial era, prove insightful, indeed, are necessary to fully understand and overcome many Third World conditions. Throughout much of the world, Western legalism leaves human rights abuse unexplained. For example, Western versions of human rights ignores Africa's current crisis. "That equality must mean more than technical legal inequality is obvious to Africans who have experienced colonialism (where equality only applied to settlers) and neocolonialism (where money makes some more equal than others" (Penna & Campbell, 1998, p. 12). For social justice, dignity, and well-being in Africa, Okoye (1990) understands that local values must complement Western values to achieve universal norms of human rights: "For justice, as we know it, is not limited to what happens in the law courts but extends to the whole web of relationships between person and person, between group and group"(p. 175). This communitarian perception of human rights efficacy is based on a decentralizing norm that responds to local concerns, including economic, cultural, and environmental needs in a consensual manner.

Campbell and Penna (1998) point out that many Third World communitarian notions of human rights, such as those expressed by Okoye, can not only be used to clarify local problems, but also find resonance in many Western notions of communitarianism, which have been ignored or lost in the globalization project. By studying the historic evolution of rights issues in particular cultures—women's status, social equality, access to a bountiful, nonpolluting environment, and so on—human rights discourse can break the stalemate of relativist/universalist dichotomies. Local approaches have saliency for any historical understanding of human rights development. For example, since much of the despoliation of Third World landscapes has resulted from recent external alterations of traditional ecological systems, local control over development policies can assure environmental rights.

The fact that traditional cultures across the Third World have respected many of the basic norms of human rights agreements should aid rather than hinder human rights projects, endowing universal principles with local interpretations. The detachable nature of culture allows for the play between the particular and the universal. Moreover, as Kwame Appiah (1992) advises, since it is too late for cultures to escape each other in a globalized, shrinking world, "we might instead seek to turn to our advantage the mutual interdependencies that history has thrust upon us"(p. 26). Both symbol and substance can be gained by learning from the evolutionary histories that different cultural traditions bring to human rights. Recognizing the wisdom of other cultures is to know that particular cultural traditions are not hermetically sealed bastions of meaning, but open repositories available to the diligent.

That governments worldwide would function better decentralized with more participatory structures is a truth that can be applied to issues besides human rights. Moreover, most non-Western traditional societies function through community-based, participatory, and decentralized systems with a minimal level of legal transaction. These cultures were, and many still are, consensually based rather than grounded in individualism as in the West, particularly in the U.S. As Penna and Campbell (1998) advise, when knowledge is becoming increasingly more interdisciplinary, the time has come to expand limited concepts of rights deriving from only the legal and political. To this we could add that integrating human rights with sustainable human development makes purely legalistic approaches to rights outdated, minimalist, and often retrogressive in their uses. Since certain rights may be culturally bound while others may connect more universally, it is important to study more closely local cultures to understand which rights concepts would be more fruitful under which contexts. Assuredly, a better understanding of cultural context in human rights can further defend international human rights against the "cultural imperialism"arguments of authoritarian regimes.

REASON TO TREMBLE: THE NEW ACCOUNTABILITY

November 25, 1998, witnessed perhaps the most important judgment for international civil and political rights in the 50-year history of their existence. Peter Kornbluh's (1998) description captures the moment:

> The decision by the five lords—televised live around the world—constituted one of the most dramatic human rights rulings of modern times. One by one the lords offered their opinions on theappeal to overturn the lower court ruling. The first two upheld the ruling to free Pinochet; the second two said it should be overturned. When the fifth judge, Lord Hoffmann, stood up and said, "I too would allow this appeal," pandemonium ensued in Europe and the Americas."(p. 22)

For synchronicity, it was also Augusto Pinochet's birthday. Although international agreements condemned nefarious acts of heads of state and their practitioners since the Nuremberg Trials and the UDHR, the new judicial activism was based on legal agreements in the 1990s. In the case of Pinochet's detention, direct motivation came from the new European Convention on Terrorism. Chilean president Eduardo Frei proclaimed loudly, "Chileans should be judged only by Chilean courts." In rebuttal, Chilean congressman Juan Pablo Letelier—whose father was murdered in 1976 in Washington, D.C., just one mile from the White House from a car bomb set by Pinochet's police—answered "Immunity does not equal impunity"(qtd. in "Prisoner Pinochet," 1998, p. 3). The long-standing legal impasse, whether heads of state and their officials are immune from criminal prosecution, was resolved during the events of late 1998. What remained was the far more important challenge—to motivate and enlist the international public sphere. Legal rebuttal aside, it has always been wide public sentiment that actualizes human rights.

The significance of the decision was not lost in the European community. During October and November, several European states filed criminal and civil suits against Pinochet, adding force to the Spanish and British actions. Spain's influential newspaper *El Mundo* observed, "The basis is beginning to be set for what can and should be justice without borders" (Crossette, 1998e, Sec. 4, p. 1). But universal justice beyond national boundaries has been realized through the public acceptance of other legal principles as well. Jose Miguel Vivanco, director of the Americas division of Human Rights Watch, points to the underlying significance of the legal judgments of Spain and Britain: extrajudicial executions and torture can no longer be considered legitimate actions of heads of state, and therefore do not qualify for foreign immunity. The Pinochet case has established these key principles.

Vivanco's observations may be too limiting, however. He dismisses the question of whether a powerful world leader, an American president for instance, could be indicted by a foreign court, since such cases were exceptional and were intended only for perpetrators of war crimes or crimes against humanity who have not been judged by their own courts (Crossette, 1998e). But who is to say at what point justice beyond borders should stop? The fact that the Law Lord's decision was met with silence from the White House while most of Europe and much of the rest of the world spoke out (a leading Paris newspaper ran the headline, "Tremble, Tyrants!") indicates less certainty among the world leadership on that question. The U.S. has typically refused to honor decisions of the International Court of Justice (the World Court), which was formed to adjudicate between nations rather than individuals. Washington's language of discourse, repeated uncritically by its mainstream media, commonly disparage World Court decisions, as evidenced by a recent *New York Times* paraphrase of U.S. officials: "The...World Court has been used to score policy points such as opposition to an American embargo on Nicaragua during the Sandinista years, or in favor of the outlawing of nuclear weapons"(Crossette, 1998e, Sec. 4, p. 3). But to dismiss international legal decision making by trivializing its deliberations—"to score policy points"—is a tactic that will prove increasingly less effective in the new era of global accountability, when more and bolder international courts and tribunals will aim at high-ranking individual as well as national perpetrators.

What They All Did

During the first weeks of Pinochet's detention in London, general uncertainty and shock prevented the world's governments from discerning its significance. Chile's largely negative initial reaction came more as indignant shock after years of market-induced amnesia. For years, its political, economic, and media elites avoided all commentary on the years of Operation Condor and the general state terrorism of the time. Also, the resolve of the British Labor government to agree to the Spanish extradition request was at first uncertain. Even the Spanish government seemed to back away from the unprecedented action of its investigative judges. The British were no doubt in part testing Washington's position, as there had been reports in their press of the Clinton administration's behind-the-scenes efforts to prevent the extradition ("Prisoner Pinochet," 1998). However, as the weeks passed, second thoughts began to awaken moral consciences across Europe and Latin America. Chile exhumed mass graves of Pinochet's so-called Caravan of Death; stories of torture and sexual abominations were widely reported in Chile's media; and the Chilean government finally promised its own prosecution.

The conspiracy of silence around Chile's Senator for Life broke. As two-thirds of Chileans favored Pinochet's punishment in opinion polls, Juan Guzman, a prominent Chilean judge, accepted several murder cases against the former dictator. Guzman's justification epitomized the new respect for human rights law: "For all the power Mr. Pinochet has, we have jurisdiction over him granted by the law" (qtd. in Cooper, 1998, p. 26). More importantly, the reawakening was not confined to intellectuals and jurists. Chileans came to resent the sight of Pinochet's former political opponents rushing to his defense after the first announcement of the London arrest. The grassroots of the mainstream parties began to understand that national borders were less significant than human rights.

Chile's transformation came about by the legal actions of foreign countries and the subsequent mobilization of public opinion across the new global village. No longer can Latin American governments count on human rights being among their *desaparecido* (the official terms for those individuals who "disappeared"as opponents of the government). But the arrest that stunned the world was not the result of unilateral action. From its inception, it required international, intercultural, and bipartisan cooperation, enlistments premised on universal principles of human rights. Spain's Progressive Association of Prosecutors filed complaints of genocide and terrorism against Argentinean and Chilean military leaders in 1996; petitions for the criminal investgations were presented by the United Left, one of Spain's leading parties; the progressive Judge Baltasar Garzon took the assignments; the conservative Judge M. G. Castellon received the particular case against Pinochet; perhaps most significantly, Joan Garces, leader of a pro-Allende Spanish NGO and former political advisor of President Allende, transformed the case into what became a human rights class-action lawsuit, covering not just Spanish citizens but all victims of the Pinochet regime. It was because Spanish law allowed universal jurisdiction for offenses such as genocide, illegal detention, and terrorism that Garces was able to find a means to prosecute Pinochet (Kornbluh, 1998).

Within the Britain Labor government, the urge to reverse its nation's relative indifference to human rights agreements allowed for the quick response and subsequent legal decisions to extradite Pinochet. As in Spain, the political structure was greatly motivated by a wide spectrum of public opinion. But earlier in the year, Tony Blair's Labor government performed an unprecedented action that would become equally significant for human rights. At the Rome treaty conference for the first permanent international court on crimes against humanity, Britain broke ranks with the other UN Security Council permanent members by backing a proposal by Singapore that would prevent the permanent postponement of crimes against humanity cases; instead, the Security Council could halt investigations only temporarily if circumstances such as civil war prevented immediate action. Moreover, the Singapore proposal would require the unanimous vote of all five permanent members. Under the proposal favored by the United States, the Council would simply not refer a case to the international prosecutor, thereby permanently preventing legal action. Jelena Pejic, coordinator of the Lawyers' Committee for Human Rights Work on the international criminal court, remarked, "What the British did was very important, extremely important. It has loosened the Security Council's ranks"(qtd. in Crossette, 1997, p. 23).

The British action strengthened the new international court by giving it independence from politicizing moves by the Security Council and other bodies. In the history of the world, there have been only *ad hoc* tribunals for war crimes—such as the tribunals for the Balkans, Rwanda, the Nuremberg Trials, and the tribunal against Japanese war crimes. The Rome planning conference also greatly clarified and expanded the definition of crimes against humanity. Added to the list were crimes against women. Controversial issues included attacks on civilians, mass starvation, the use of nuclear weapons, and land mines as war crimes. Human rights NGOs argued for the widest possible humanitarian conventions and against the self-serving interests of the world powers with large, active militaries. Once again, NGOs played the most active and decisive role in the legal disputation. They were especially engaging in the crimes against women category.

Enough Accumulated Experience

The formation of the new International Criminal Court must be seen as a harbinger for the new discourse of human rights in the 21st century. At the Rome conference, advocates for the universality of human rights generally overcame resistance from world power advocates who sought the narrowest interpretation of crimes and the least independence for the new court. Canadian Justice Louise Arbour, chief prosecutor of the war crimes tribunals in the Balkans and Rwanda, observed that there is finally enough accumulated experience to demonstrate that, when international crimes are recognized as universally repugnant, national and inter-governmental legal systems do not get in the way of prosecution (Crossette, 1997). When the world's accumulated experience in human rights discourse reached a critical mass, as it did during the 1990s, formal structures changed to accommodate new levels of understanding. But the progressive evolution of human rights discourse will not develop further without the lasting vigilance and cooperation of the world's peoples. To achieve these ends, thinking that ventures beyond traditional boundaries of nation state and culture must be actualized.

Detaching Culture for New Visions

Conflict can be resolved through the deliberative capacities of the international public sphere. With Cheah's (1997) notion of the "nonexhaustive common standard," allowance for infinite variation within universal principles of human rights can be realized. Intercultural deliberation between the periphery and the global center does not exist in a vacuum of distinct cultures, but has the capacity to move beyond hermetically sealed particularities to new levels of discourse. Jurgen Habermas's (1992) later reflections on the public sphere make this point:

> the source of legitimacy is not the predetermined will of individuals, but rather the process of its formation, that is, deliberation itself.....A legitimate decision does not represent the will of all, but is one that results from the deliberation of all. It is the process by which everyone's will is formed that confers its legitimacy on the outcome, rather than the sum of already formed wills. (p. 446)

The democratic deliberation of all cultures will form new goals and visions that are not the unique claims of any one culture but representative of all cultures in the new century.

QUESTIONS FOR FURTHER THOUGHT

1. What are current examples of human rights violations that also involve problems of human development?
2. In what ways are the UN Bill of Rights covenants interventionist agreements rather than merely advisory complements to national laws and practices? What are the major factors that have prevented UN member states from taking seriously these rights?
3. What are the advantages and disadvantages of stepping back from the particularities of human rights abuses for a wider perspective? How can arguing wider perspectives work for and against human rights?

4. In what specific ways can decentralization and participatory projects be helped by references to universal standards of human rights?
5. What other national leaders could be considered for class-action suits similar to the one against Augusto Pinochet? What should be the criteria for such legal judgments?

Appendix:
Abbreviations

AAMA	American Apparel Manufacturers Association
ACC	Administrative Committee on Coordination
ACDESS	African Centre for Development and Strategic Studies
ADB	African Development Bank
ADIH	Haitian Association of Industrialists
AEC	African Economic Community
AGOA	African Growth and Opportunity Act
AI	Amnesty International
AIM	American Indian Movement
Beijing Platform	Fourth World Conference on Women
BRAC	Bangladesh Rural Advancement Committee
BSA	British Sociological Association
CEDAW	Convention on the Elimination of All Forms of Discrimination Against Women
CERD	Convention on the Elimination of All Forms of Racial Discrimination
C/LAA	Caribbean/Latin American Action
DEVAW	(UN) Declaration on the Elimination of Violence Against Women
DH	Dayton Hudson (Corporation)
DIA	(U.S.) Defense Intelligence Agency
DRD	Declaration on the Right to Development
ECA	Economic Commission for Africa
ECOSOC	(UN) Economic and Social Council
EOZ	Export-oriented zones
FDI	foreign direct investment
GATT	General Agreement on Tariffs and Trade
GNP	Gross National Product
IBRD	World Bank
ICC	Intergovernmental Council for Communication
ICCPR	International Covenant on Civil and Political Rights
ICESCR	International Covenant on Economic, Social and Cultural Rights
IGO	intergovernmental organization

ILO	International Labor Organization
IMF	International Monetary Fund
IRCA	International Railways of Central America
KC	Kmart Corporation
MAI	Multilateral Agreement on Investment
NAFTA	North American Free Trade Movement
NAM	Non-Aligned Movement
NBA	National Association of Broadcasters
NGO	Non-Governmental Organization
NIC	Newly Industrialized Country
NIEO	New International Economic Order
NLC	National Labor Committee
NRF	National Retail Federation
OAS	Organization of American States
OAU	Organization for African Unity
ODA	official development assistance
OECD	Organization for Economic Cooperation and Development
OPIC	Overseas Private Investment Corporation
PAC	Political action committee
PF	Peking Formula
PRC	Peoples Republic of China
SAP	structural adjustment program
RPF	Rwandan Patriotic Front
TNC	Transnational Corporation
UNCHR	UN Commission on Human Rights
UNCTAD	(UN) Conference on Trade and Development
UNDP	United Nations Development Program
UNHR	Universal Declaration of Human Rights
UNDP	United Nations Development Program
UNESCO	UN Educational, Scientific and Cultural Organization
UNICEF	UN Children's Fund
UNAMIR	UN Assistance Mission to Rwanda
UNPAAERD	UN Program of Action for African Economic Recovery and Development
Unscom	UN Special Commission
US	United States of America
USAID	U.S. Agency for International Development
WCIP	World Council of Indigenous Peoples
WDC	Walt Disney Corporation
WFP	(UN) World Food Program
WHO	(UN) World Health Organization
WTO	World Trade Organization

References

Abbott, E. (1988). *Haiti: The Duvaliers and their legacy.* New York: McGraw-Hill.

Adedeji, A. (1993). Marginalization and marginality: Context, issues and viewpoints. In A. Adedeji (Ed.), *Africa within the world: Beyond dispossession and dependence* (pp. 1–14). London: Zed Books.

Agence France-Presse. (1998, August 9). From Iraq chief, strident words on sanctions. *New York Times*, p. 8.

Ahmad, E. (1998). Missile diplomacy. *The Nation*, 29.

Ai, Z. S. (1991, December). *On the situation of radio, movies and television.* Paper presented at the Central Academy of the Chinese Communist Party, Beijing, China.

Alston, P. (1992a). The Commission on Human Rights. In P. Alston (Ed.), *The United Nations and human rights: A critical appraisal* (pp. 126–210). Oxford, England: Clarendon Press.

Alston, P. (1992b). Critical appraisal of the UN human rights regime. In P. Alston (Ed.), *The United Nations and human rights: A critical appraisal* (pp. 1–22). Oxford, England: Clarendon Press.

Alston, P. (1995, August). The rights framework and development assistance. *Development Bulletin, 34*, 3–19.

Alston, P. (1997). The purposes of reporting. In United Nations (Ed.), *Manual on United Nations reporting* (pp. 19–24). Geneva: United Nations.

Alterman, E. (1998). *Who speaks for America?: Why democracy matters in foreign policy.* Ithaca, NY: Cornell University Press.

Amnesty in America. (1998, November 16). *The Nation*, 7.

Amnesty International (1998). *Rights for all.* London: Author.

Anderson, A. (1992, Spring). Cryptonormativism and double gestures: The politics of post-structuralism. *Cultural Critique, 21*, 63–95.

Andreassen, B., et al. (1988). Human rights performance in developing countries: The case for a Minimum threshold approach. In B. Andreassen & A. Eide (Eds.), *Human rights in developing countries* (pp. 144–168). Copenhagen: Akademisk Forlag.

Angelika Filmbill. (1998, February/March). New York: Sony Pictures Entertainment.

An-Na'im, A. (1992). Toward a cross-cultural approach to defining International standards of human rights: The meaning of cruel, inhuman, or degrading treatment or punishment. In A. An-Na'im (Ed.), *Human rights in cross-cultural perspective: A quest for consensus* (pp. 19–43). Philadelphia: University of Pennsylvania Press.

Ansah, P. (1992, May). *Broadcasting—the African experience.* Paper presented at URTNA Symposium, Dakar, Senegal.

Aperture (1995). *Cuba: Image and imagination.* New York: Author.

Appiah, K. A. (1992). *In my father's house: Africa in the philosophy of culture.* New York: Oxford University Press.

Apple, R.W. (1998, March 28). From Mandela, a gentle admonishment. *New York Times,* pp. A1, A5.

Arresting a dictator [Editorial]. (1998, October 20). *Washington Post,* p. A18.

Assefa, H. (1996). Ethnic conflict in the horn of Africa: Myth and reality. In K. Rupesinghe & A. Valery (Eds.), *Ethnicity and power in the contemporary world* (pp. 32–51). New York: United Nations University Press.

Associated Press. (1998, March 28). Two presidents, two strong commitments to Africa. *New York Times,* p. A5.

Avery, N. et al. (1993). *Cracking the codex.* London: National Food Alliance.

Azzam, F. (1997). Non-governmental organizations and the UN World Conference on Human Rights. *Review of the International Commission of Jurists, 50,* 89–100.

Baehr, P. R., & Gordenker, L. (1994). *The United Nations in the 1990s* (2nd ed.). New York: St. Martin's Press.

Barrett, W., & Steinberg, D. (1998, September 8). The UN-gerry. *The Village Voice, 43,* pp. 41–42.

Bauer, J. (1997). *Report on the United Nations Commission on Human Rights,* 52nd session, March 18 to April 26, 1996 [Online]. Available: http://www.hri.ca/unifo/unchr96/highc.shtml

Baxi, U. (1994). *Mambrino's helmet: Human rights for a changing world.* New Delhi: Anand.

Beatty, J. (1998). *The world according to Peter Drucker.* New York: Free Press.

Becker, C. B. (1997). Toward an ethical theory for comparative political communication based on the coherence between universal human rights and cultural relativism. In A. Gonzalez & D. V. Tanno (Eds.), *Politics, communication, and culture* (pp. 76–86). Thousand Oaks, CA: Sage.

Belle, D. (1995). *Zoned for slavery* [Film]. (Available from Brecht Forum, 122 W. 27th St., New York, NY)

Bennett, J. (1998, September). Development alternatives: NGO-government partnership in Pakistan. *Development, 41,* 54–57.

Bethell, T. (1998). *The noblest triumph: Property and prosperity through the ages.* New York: St. Martin's Press.

Bhabha, H. (1994). *The location of culture.* London and New York: Routledge.

Bielski, V. (1997). Shell game. In P. Phillips (Ed.), *Censored 1997: The news that didn't make the news.* New York: Seven Stories Press.

Bohlen, C. (1997, December 14). Catholic bishops finish survey of challenges to the Americas. *New York Times,* p. 26.

Bonacich, E. (1973). A theory of middlemen minorities. *American Sociological Review, 38,* 583–594.

Bonner, R. (1998, July 13). Envoy rejects accusations Americans acted selfishly. *New York Times,* p. A9

Boven, van T. (1997). The international system of human rights: An overview. In *Manual on United Nations reporting* (pp. 3–16). Geneva: United Nations.

Braga, M. M. (1997). To relieve the misery: Sugar mill workers and the 1933 Cuban revolution. In J. C. Brown (Ed.), *Workers' control in Latin America, 1930–1979* (pp. 16–44). Chapel Hill, NC, and London: University of North Carolina Press.

Brecher, J., & Costello, T. (1998, September 21). Labor's day: The challenge ahead. *The Nation*, 11–17.

Broder, J. M. (1998a, June 30). Jiang held his cards to the final moment. *New York Times*, p. A9

Broder, J. M. (1998b, July 1). Clinton tells of hopes and risks on trade. *New York Times*, p. A12.

Broder, J. M. (1998c, July 2). Clinton in China reaches out for new understanding. *New York Times*, p. A8.

Broder, J. M. (1998d, July 4). Clinton Foresees Democratic era in China and says current leaders could lead the way. *New York Times*, p. A4.

Brzezinski, Z. (1986). *Game plan: A geostrategic framework for the conduct of the U.S.-Soviet contest*. New York: Basic Books.

Brzezinski, Z. (1993). *Out of control: Global turmoil on the eve of the twenty-first century*. New York: Scribners.

Brzezinski, Z. (1997). *The grand chessboard: American primacy and its geostrategic imperatives*. New York: Basic Books.

Buchholt, H. (1994). The "great transformation" in Minahasa, Indonesia. In H.-D. Evers & H. Schrader (Eds.), *The moral economy of trade: Ethnicity and developing markets* (pp. 95–103). London and New York: Routledge.

Buell, F. (1994). *National culture and the new global system*. Baltimore, MD, and London: Johns Hopkins University Press.

Bukharin, N. (1929). *Imperialism and world economy*. In I. Howe (Ed.), *Essential works of socialism*. New York: Bantam.

Burgerman, S. D. (1998). Mobilizing principles: The role of transnational activists in promoting human rights principles. *Human Rights Quarterly, 20*, 905–923.

Buskin, R. (1997). *Princess Diana: Her life story, 1961–1997*. New York: Publications International.

Callaghy, T. M. (1987). Absolutism, Bonapartism, and the formation of ruling classes: Zaire in comparative perspective. In I. L. Markovitz (Ed.), *Studies in power and class in Africa* (pp. 95–117). New York and Oxford: Oxford University Press.

Campbell, S. (1997, September 22). What Kabila is hiding. *Washington Post*, p. A19.

Canby, P. (1998, Spring). Where the wild things are. *The Lingua Franca Book Review*, 4–26.

Capaccio, G. (1998, November). Iraq's children. *The Progressive, 62*, 23–28.

Carnegie Commission (1998). *Preventing deadly conflict*. New York: Author.

Catherwood, F. (1970). Peter Drucker: Contribution to economic development. In T. Bonapart & J. E. Flaherty, (Eds.), *Peter Drucker: Contributions to business enterprise* (pp. 239–249). New York: New York University Press.

The Center for World Indigenous Studies (1998). *Fourth World Documentation Project Archives* [Online]. Available: http://www/halcyon.com/FWDP/cwisinfo.html

Chandler, D. (1996). *Killing fields* (C. Riley & D. Niven, Photo Eds.). Santa Fe, NM: Twin Palms.

Chang, H-C., & Holt, G. R. (1997). Intercultural training for expatriates: Reconsidering power and politics. In A. Gonzalez & D. T. Tanno (Eds.), *Politics, communication, and culture* (pp. 207–230). Thousand Oaks, CA: Sage.

Cheah, P. (1997, Winter). Posit(ion)ing human rights in the current global conjuncture. *Public Culture, 22,* 233–266.

Chen, D. W. (1998, June 30). Chinese immigrants hail Clinton trip, citing mutual benefit. *New York Times,* p. B1.

Chen, J., & Amienyi, O. P. (1997, October). *Cultural imperialism: The impact of American media on Chinese youth.* Paper presented at the 20th National Third World Studies Conference, Omaha, NE.

Chinmoy, S. (1997). *Diana, Princess of Wales: Empress of the world.* New York: McKeever.

Chomsky, N., & Herman, E. S. (1979). *Third World fascism and the Washington connection.* Boston: South End Press.

Chomsky, N. (1993). *The prosperous few and the restless many.* Berkeley, CA: Odonian Press.

Chomsky, N. (1994). *Secrets, lies and democracy.* Tucson, AZ: Odonian Press.

Chretien, J. P. (1995). *Rwanda: Les medias du genocide.* Paris: Karthala.

Churchill, W. (1992). *Fantasies of the master race: Literature, cinema, and the colonization of American Indians.* Monroe, ME: Common Courage Press.

Cohen, R. (1998a, July 18). Anxiety rises as Nigeria awaits ruler's word. *New York Times,* p. A5.

Cohen, R. (1998b, July 19). Anger shaking a dead Nigerian's town to its foundations. *New York Times,* p. 3.

Cohen, R. (1998c, July 25). A Nigerian revisits his place in history. *New York Times,* p. A4.

Cohen, R. (1998d, July 27). A book party promotes Nigerian elite's hold on power. *New York Times,* p. A4.

Cohen, R. (1998e, July 30). Marble mogul caters to the Nigerian capital's elite. *New York Times,* p. 5.

Combrinck, H. (1998). Positive state duties to protect women from violence: Recent South African developments. *Human Rights Quarterly, 20,* 666–690.

Cook, R. (1994). State accountability under the Convention on the Elimination of All Forms of Dsicrimination against Women. In R. Cook (Ed.), *Human rights of women: National and international perspectives* (pp. 123–134). Philadelphia: University of Pennsylvania Press.

Cooper, F. (1981, June/September). Africa and the world economy. *African Studies Review, 24,* 44-63.

Cooper, M. (1998, December 21). Payback time for Pinochetistas. *The Nation,* 24–26.

Corntassel, J. J., & Primeau, T. H. (1995). Indigenous "sovereignty" and international law: Revised strategies for pursuing "self-determination." *Human Rights Quarterly, 13,* 343–365.

Cowell, A. (1998a, October 19). Arrest raises new issues on tracking rights crimes. *New York Times,* p. A8.

Cowell, A. (1998b, October 20). Spain widers charges for Pinochet. *New York Times,* p. A14.

Cowell, A. (1998c, October 23). Britain: Thatcher backs Pinochet. *New York Times,* p. A8.

Crossette, B. (1997, December 14). Legal experts agree on an outline for a global criminal court. *New York Times*, p. 23.

Crossette, B. (1998a, July 25). The Congo massacres: The UN steps aside. *New York Times*, p. A4.

Crossette, B. (1998b, August 6). Indonesia agrees to an autonomy plan for East Timor. *New York Times*, p. A3.

Crossette, B. (1998c, August 8). U.S. judge orders a Rwandan to surrender for trial on genocide. *New York Times*, p. A3.

Crossette, B. (1998d, August 10). U.N. chief tries again to get Iraq to allow arms searches. *New York Times*, p. A3.

Crossette, B. (1998e, November 29). Dictators (and some lawyers) tremble. *New York Times*, Sec. 4, pp. 1–3.

Cushman, J. H. (1998, May 13). Nike pledges to end child labor and apply U.S. rules abroad. *New York Times*, Business Day section, p. 4.

Dalrymple, M. (1998, October 5). University of North Carolina, Chapel Hill. *The Nation*, 13–14.

Damm, K. (1991). Human rights—How can the conventions be promoted and enforced? In W. Hoffman (Ed.), *A new world order: Can it bring security to the world's people?* (pp. 96–101). Washington, DC: World Federalist Association.

Dare, S. (1998, May 18). Guerrilla journalism in Nigeria. *The Nation*, 10.

Davidson, B. (1993). For a politics of restitution. In A. Adedeji (Ed.), *Africa within the world: Beyond dispossession and dependence* (pp. 17–27). London: Zed Books.

Davies, N. (1997). *Diana: The people's princess*. New York: Citadel Stars Books.

Davies, T. (1808). *Memoirs of the life of david garrick* (Vols. 1-2; S. Jones, Ed.). London and New York: Benjamin Blom.

Davis, L. L. (1997, Spring). Prime time in Ecuador: National, regional television outdraws U.S. programming. *Journal of American Culture, 20*, 9–18.

DePalma, A. (1998). Canada pacts gives a tribe self-rule for the first time. *New York Times*, pp. A1, A10.

DEVAW (1994). Declaration on the Elimination of Violence Against Women, UN GAOR, 48th sess., art. 1, UN Doc. A/Res/48/104.

DeWind, J. (1997). Continuing to be peasants: Labor militancy among Peruvian miners. In J. C. Brown (Ed.), *Workers' control in Latin America, 1930–1979* (pp. 244–269). Chapel Hill, NC, and London: University of North Carolina Press.

Dillard, A. (1998, Winter). The wreck of time: Taling our century's measure. *Harper's*, 51–56.

Dinges, J., & Landau, S. (1980). *Assassination on embassy row*. New York: Pantheon.

Dirlik, A. (1994). *After the revolution: Waking to global capitalism*. Hanover, NH, and London: Wesleyan University Press.

Donnelly, J. (1984). Cultural relativism and universal human rights. *Human Rights Quarterly, 6*, 400–419.

Donnelly, J. (1986). International human rights: A regime analysis. *International Organization, 40*, 599–642.

Dowie, M. (1998, July 6). What's wrong with *The New York Times*'s science reporting. *The Nation*, 13–19.

Drilling and killing [Editorial]. (1998, November 16). *The Nation*, 6–7.

Drucker, P. (1995). *Managing in a time of great change*. New York: Truman Talley.

Duvall, R. D., & Stohl, M. (1988). Governance by terror. In M. Stohl (Ed.), *The politics of terrorism* (3rd ed, pp. 201–212). New York: Dekker.

Dworkin, R. (1984). *Taking rights seriously.* London: Duckworth Press.

Eckholm, E. (1998a, July 4). Visit by Clinton leaves Chinese feeling elated. *New York Times*, P. A4.

Eckholm, E. (1998b, November 29). The youngest place on earth. *New York Times Magazine*, pp. 116–119.

Edgren, G. (1982). *Export processing zones: Spearheads of industrialization or sweatshops in the sun.* Geneva: ILO Mimeo.

Egan, T. (1998, March 8). New prosperity brings new conflict to Indian country. *New York Times*, pp. 1, 24.

Eide, A. (1992). Realization of social and economic rights and the minimum threshold approach. In R. P. Claude & B. H. Weston (Eds.), *Human rights in the world community* (pp. 158–167). Philadelphia: University of Pennsylvania Press.

England, M. W. (1964). *Garrick's Jubilee.* Columbus, OH: Ohio State University Press.

Entman, R. (1989). *Democracy without citizens: Media and the decay of American politics.* New York and Oxford: Oxford University Press.

Erlanger, S. (1997, November 2). China's president draws applause at Harvard talks. *New York Times*, pp. 1–14.

Erlander, S. (1998, August 14). U.S. retreats from vow to use force if Iraq blocks inspectors. *New York Times*, p. A3.

Evers, H. D. (1984). Urban landownership, ethnicity, and class in Southeast Asian cities. *International Journal of Urban and Regional Research, 8*(4), 481–496.

Evers, H. D. (1987). The bureaucratization of Southeast Asia. *Comparative Studies in Sociology and History, 29*(4), 666–685.

Evers, H. D. (1994). Trade, market expansion and political pluralism: Southeast Asia and Europe compared. In H. D. Evers & H. Schrader (Eds.), *The moral economy of trade: Ethnicity and developing markets* (pp. 136–149). London and New York: Routledge.

Faison, S. (1997, November 2). U.S. refrain on human rights strikes no chords with Jiang. *New York Times*, p. 14.

Faison, S. (1998a, June 28). China and America: Friends in need of hearing aids. *New York Times*, p. 5.

Faison, S. (1998b, June 30). President arrives in Shanghai; Focus on Talk with citizens. *New York Times*, p. A1.

Faison, S. (1998c, July 1). Clinton enjoys radio stint: No violence, drugs or sex. *New York Times*, p. A12.

Falk, R. (1992). *Explorations at the edge of time: The prospects for world order.* Philadelphia: Temple University Press.

Farmer, P. (1994). *The uses of Haiti.* Monroe, ME: Common Courage Press.

Farnsworth, C. (1984, June 17). Haiti's allure for U.S. business. *New York Times*, p. F4.

Fischer, B., & Hawes, L. (1971). An interact system model: Generating a grounded theory of small groups. *Quarterly Journal of Speech, 57*, 444–453.

Forges, A. D. (1995). The ideology of genocide. *ISSUE: A Journal of Opinion, 23*(2), 44–47.

Foster, J. B. (1998, March). *Capitalism and the media.* Paper presented at the Socialist Scholars Conference, New York.

Fox, R. (1994, September 17). Mother Theresa's care for the dying. *The Lancet, 344,* 807–808.

Franke, R. W. (1987). Power class and traditional knowledge in Sahel food production. In I. L. Markovitz (Ed.), *Studies in power and class in Africa* (pp. 257–286). New York and Oxford: Oxford University Press.

French, H. W. (1998a, April 4). Nigeria, in free fall, seethes under general. *New York Times,* pp. 1, A5.

French, H. W. (1998b, June 23). Age-old curse of slavery alive in the Ivory Coast. *New York Times,* p. A4.

French, H. W. (1998c, July 8). An awkward ally: Diplomats, in promoting democracy, seemed to shun the prime democrat. *New York Times,* p. A10.

French, H. W. (1998d, August 4). New Congo ruler facing rebellion by former allies. *New York Times,* pp. A1, A6.

French, H. W. (1998e, August 14). Rebels closing in on blacked-out Congo capital. *New York Times,* p. 1A.

French, H. W. (1998f, August 19). Top fear in Congo conflict: Wider regional violence. *New York Times,* p. A3.

Friedman, M. (1998). *Cuba: The special period.* Madison, WI: Samuel Book.

Fukuyama, F. (1992). *The end of history and the last man.* New York: Free Press.

Fuss, D. (1989). *Essentially speaking: Feminism, nature, and difference.* New York and London: Routledge.

Geneva 1977: A report on the hemispheric movement of indigenous peoples. (1978). In Akwesasne (Ed.), *Basic call to consciousness* (pp. 3–13). Summertown, TN: Book Publishing.

George, S. (1993). Uses and abuses of African debt. In A. Adedeji (Ed.), *Africa within the world: Beyond dispossession and dependence.* London: Zed Books.

Gilligan, C. (1982). *In a different voice: Psychological theory and women's development.* Cambridge, MA: Harvard University Press.

Glahn, G. V. (1981). *Law among nations* (4th ed.). New York: Macmillan.

Golden, T. (1998, October 25). Arresting a dictator is one thing. Then it gets tough. *New York Times,* Sec. 4, p. 6.

Greenberg, S. B., & Giliomee, H. (1987). Managing class structures in South Africa: Bantustans and the underbelly of privilege. In I. L. Markovitz (Ed.), *Studies in power and class in Africa* (pp. 308–321). New York: Oxford University Press.

Grier, B. (1987). Contradiction, crisis, and class conflict: The state and capitalist development in Ghana prior to 1948. In I. L. Markovitz (Ed.), *Studies in power and class in Africa* (pp. 27–49). New York: Oxford University Press.

Guzman, P. (Director). (1976). *The battle of Chile* [Film].

Guzman, P. (Director). (1998). *Chile, obstinate memory* [Film].

Gwertzman, B. (1998, October 26). Endgame: Zbigniew Brzezinski's latest blueprint for American foreign policy. *New York Times Book Review,* p. 30.

Haas, M. (1994). *Improving human rights.* Westport, CT: Praeger.

Haass, R. N. (1997). *The reluctant sheriff: The U.S. after the Cold War.* New York: Council on Foreign Relations.

Habermas, J. (1992). Further reflections on the public sphere. In C. Calhoun (Ed.), *Habermas and the public sphere* (pp. 421–461). Cambridge, MA: MIT Press.

Harries, R. (1991). Human rights in theological perspective. In R. Blackburn & J. Taylor (Eds.), *Human rights for the 1990's: Legal, political and ethical issues* (pp. 1–13). London and New York: Mansell.

Harvey, S. (1998, October). Doing it my way—broadcasting regulation in capitalist cultures: The case of "fairness" and "impartiality." *Media, Culture & Society, 20,* 535–556.

Harymurti, B. (1998, June 15-22). The press and freedom. *The Nation,* 15

Held, D. (1995). *Democracy and the global order: From the modern state to cosmopolitan governance.* Stanford, CA: Stanford University Press.

Herbert, B. (1995, December 22). A sweatshop victory. *New York Times,* p. A9.

Herbert, B. (1998, June 7). At what cost? *New York Times,* Section 4, p. 15.

Herman, E. S., & Chomsky, N. (1979). *The Washington connection and Third World fascism.* Boston: South End Press.

Herman, E. (1998, March). *Capitalism and the media.* Paper presented at the Socialist Scholars Conference, New York.

Herman, E. (1988). *Manufacturing consent.* New York: Pantheon.

Herskovits, M. J. (1964). *Cultural dynamics.* New York: Alfred A. Knopf.

Hester, M. (!992). *Lewd women and wicked witches: A study of the dynamics of male dominance.* London: Routledge

High Commissioner for Human Rights: Report [Online]. (1997, December). Available: http://www.unhchr.ch.org

High Commissioner for the promotion and protection of all human rights, G. A. Res. 48/141, UN GAOR, 48th Sess., UN Doc. A/Res/48/141, 1993.

Hill, H. (1996). *The Indonesian economy since 1966.* Cambridge, England: Cambridge University Press.

Hitchens, C. (1995). *The missionary position: Mother Teresa in theory and practice.* London and New York: Verso.

Holdt, J. (1985). *American pictures.* Copenhagen, Denmark: American Pictures Foundation.

hooks, b. (1992). *Black looks: Race and representation.* Boston: South End Press.

Horowitz, D. L. (1985a). *Ethnic groups in conflict.* Berkeley, CA: University of California Press.

Horowitz, J. (1985b). Occupational community and the creation of a self-styled elite: Argentina, 1973–1976. *Americas, 42,* 55–81.

Illic, Z., & Corti, I. (1997). The Convention on the Elimination of All Forms of Discrimination Against Women. In *Manual on human rights reporting* (pp. 305–366). Geneva: United Nations.

Iman in Somalia. (1998, April 25). In *In the news.* New York: Entertainment TV.

Iriye, A. (1997). *Cultural internationalism and world order.* Baltimore, MD, and London: Johns Hopkins University Press.

Irwin, H. (1993). Intercultural communication and identity: Beyond the anthropology of manners. *Australian Journal of Communication, 20*(3), 72–80.

Iturbide, G. (1996). *Images of the spirit.* New York: Aperture.

Jaquet, J. (1998, June 8). The media nation: TV. *The Nation,* 23–28.

Jewell, K. S. (1993). *From mammy to Miss America and beyond: Cultural images and the shaping of U.S. social policy.* New York: Routledge.

Kamminga, M. T., & Rodley, N. S. (1984). Direct intervention at the UN: NGO participation in the Commission on Human Rights and its Sub-commission. In H. Hannum

(Ed.), *Guide to international human rights practice* (pp. 186–199). Philadelphia: University of Pennsylvania Press.

Kant, I. (1970). *Kant's political writings* (H. Reiss, Ed.). Cambridge, England: Cambridge University Press.

Kaufman, M. T. (1998, July 8). Moshood K. O. Abiola: From wealth to troubled politics to flawed symbol. *New York Times*, p. A10.

Kean, K. (Dir.). *Rezistans* [Film]. (1997). (Available from the Film Society of Lincoln Center, 165 W. 65th St., New York, NY)

Kelly, L. (1988). *Surviving sexual violence*. Cambridge, England: Polity Press.

Kelly, L., & Radford, J. (1996). "Nothing really happened": The invalidation of women's experiences of sexual violence. In M. Hester, L. Kelly, & J. Radford (Eds.), *Women, violence and male power* (pp. 19–33). Buckingham, UK: Open University Press.

Kernaghan, C. (1996). Behind closed doors. In National Labor Committee (Ed.), *The U.S. in Haiti*. New York: National Labor Committee Education Fund.

Kibreab, G. (1985). *African refugees: Reflections on the African refugee problem*. Trenton, NJ: Africa World Press.

Kim, S. S. (1979). *China, the United Nations and world order*. Princeton, NJ: Princeton University Press.

King, M. L., Jr. (1964). *Why we can't wait*. New York: New American Library.

Kirkpatrick, J. (1979, Novermber). Dictatorships and double standards. *Commentary, 68*, 34–45.

Klee, H.-D. (1993). Mass media and democracy. In A. Adedeji (Ed.), *Africa within the world: Beyond dispossession and dependence* (pp. 179–183). London and New York: Zed Books.

Kornbluh, P. (1998, December 21). Prisoner Pinochet: The dictator and the quest for justice. *The Nation*, 11–24.

Kothari, S., & Sethi, H. (Eds.) (1989). *Rethinking human rights*. Delhi: Lokoyan.

Krauss, C. (1998a, October 18). Britain arrest Pinochet to face charges by Spain. *New York Times*, p. 1, 4, 7.

Krauss, C. (1998b, October 19). Most Chileans react moderately to arrest. *New York Times*, p. A8.

Krauss, C. (1998c, October 24). Threats over Pinochet case inflaming tensions in Chile. *New York Times*, p. A3

Kratochvil, A. (1997). *Broken dreams: 20 years of war in eastern Europe*. New York: Monacelli Press.

Kristof, N. D. (1998, May 17). Suharto, a king of Java past, confronts Indonesia's future. *New York Times*, p. 6.

Landler, M. (1998a, May 10). Unrest deepens in Indonesia, But Suharto offers defiance. *New York Times*, p. 8.

Landler, M. (1998b, May 16). The target of violence in a time of wrath. *New York Times*, p. A6

Langley, W. E. (Ed.). (1992). *Human rights: Sixty major global instruments*. London and Jefferson, NC: McFarland.

Latif, A. (1994, April 23). About the times. *Straits Times*, p. 2.

Lazreg, M. (1979). Human rights, state and ideology: An historical perspective. In A. Pollis & P.Schwab (Eds.), *Human rights: Cultural and ideological perspectives* (pp. 32–43). New York: Praeger.

Le Moniteur: Journal Officiel de la Republique d'Haiti (1995, May 4), p. 463.

Leary, V. A. (1992). Lessons from the experience of the Internaitonal Labour Organization. In P. Alston (Ed.), *The United Nations and human rights: A critical appraisal* (pp. 580–619). Oxford, England: Clarendon Press.

Leckie, S. (1998, February). Another step towards indivisibility: Identifying the key features of violations of economic, social and cultural rights. *Human Rights Quarterly, 20,* 81–124.

Lee, S. (Director). (1992). *Malcolm X* [Film]. (Available from Warner Studios)

Levin, L. (1981). *Human rights: Questions and answers.* Paris: UNESCO Publishing.

Lewis, M. (1998a, January 11). The man who invented management. *New York Times Book Review,* p. 9.

Lewis, M. (1998b, May 31). The world's biggest going-out-of-business sale. *New York Times Magazine,* p. 34–69.

Liebenberg, S. (Ed.), (1995). *The constitution of South Africa from a gender perspective.* Cape Town: David Philip.

Lind, M. (1998, October 5). Marx, Smith—or List?: An early thinker on free-trade problems. *The Nation,* 30–32.

The Limburg Principles on the implementation of the International Covenant on Economic, Social and Cultural Rights. (1987). *Human Rights Quarterly, 9,* 122–135.

MacKinnon, C. (1982). Feminism, marxism, method and the state: An agenda for theory. *Signs, 7,* 515.

MacNeil, W. P. (1997, Spring). Enjoy your rights! Three cases from the postcolonial commonwealth. *Public Culture, 23,* 377–394.

Mama, A. (1989). *The hidden struggle: Statutory and voluntary sector responses to violence against black women in the home.* London: London Race and Housing Research Unit.

Mamdani, M. (1992, Summer). Africa: Democratic theory and democratic struggles. *Dissent,* 312–389.

Manley, M. (1991). *The poverty of nations: Reflections on underdevelopment and the world economy.* London: Pluto Press.

March, J. G., & Olsen, J. P. (1989). *Rediscovering institutions: The organizational basis of politics.* New York: Free Press.

Masur, R. (1998, June 8). The world stage. *The Nation,* 30.

McCollom, H., & McWilliams, M. (1994). War against women. *Trouble and Strife, 28,* 12–19.

McGeary, J. (1998, April 6). Into Africa: Will Clinton's trip change the way Americans view Africa, and rewrite the terms of U.S. policy? *Time,* 49.

McKinley, J. C. (1998, September 5). Ex-Rwandan premier gets life in prison on charges of genocide in '94 massacres. *New York Times,* p. A8.

McLeod, M. C. (1997). Maintaining unity: Railway workers and the Guatemalan revolution. In J. C. Brown (Ed.), *Workers' control in Latin America, 1930–1979* (pp. 98–127). Chapel Hill, NC, and London: University of North Carolina Press.

Meiselas, S. (1981). *Nicaragua: June 1978–July 1979.* New York: Pantheon.

Meiselas, S. (1997). *Kurdistan: In the shadow of history.* New York: Random House.

Metz, H. (1998, April). Susan Meiselas. *The Progressive, 62,* 36–39.

Miller, J. (1998, February 15, 1998). Preaching to the converted. *New York Times Book Review*, p. 39.

Miller, M. C. (1998, November). *Defending ourselves against the twenty-first century.* Paper presented at the National Communication Association Convention, New York.

Moberg, D. (1998). Power grab: Big business wants to tighten its hold with a new global trade pact. *The Progressive, 62*, 24–26.

Modleski, T. (1991). *Feminism without women: Culture and criticism in a "Postfeminist" age.* New York: Routledge.

Moore, M. (Director). (1998). *The big one* [Film]. (Available from Image Entertainment)

MST (1998, March 27). Movement of Landless Rural Workers (Brazil). Human rights section.

Mydans, S. (1998a, May 16). Suharto reverses hike in fuel price demanded by I.M.F. *New York Times*, pp. A1, A6.

Mydans, S. (1998b, May 30). Suharto fortune drawing new fire. *New York Times*, pp. A1, A4.

Mydans, S. (1998c, May 31). Reeling Indonesia gets fiscal break. *New York Times*, pp. 1, 10.

Mydans, S. (1998d, July 20). New threats reported as rapes in Indonesia are investigated. *New York Times*, p. A9.

Myers, L. (1998, August 25). U.S. says Iraq aided production of chemical weapons in Sudan. *New York Times*, p. 1.

Nafziger, E. W. *(1985, November).* Stagnation, inequality, and urban discrepencies in Africa. Paper presented at the African Studies Association Conference, New Orleans, LA.

Nairn, A. (1998a, June 8). Indonesia's disappeared. *The Nation*, 14.

Nairn, A. (1998b, June 15). Our men in Jakarta. *The Nation*, 12–14.

Neier, A. (1998). *War crimes: brutality, genocide, terror, and the struggle for justice* New York: Times Books.

Newbury, C. (1998, January-February). Ethnicity and the politics of history in Rwanda. *Africa Today, 45*(1), 7–24.

Newbury, C. (1988). *The cohesion of oppression: Clientship and ethnicity in Rwanda, 1860–1960.* New York: Columbia University Press.

Nickel, J. (1987). *Making sense of human rights.* Berkeley, CA: University of California Press.

Nouwen, H. (1986). *Reaching out: The three movements of the spiritual life.* Garden City, NY: Image Books.

Noyce, P. (Director). (1992). *Patriot games* [Film]. (Available from Paramount Studios)

Noyce, P. (Director). (1994). *Clear and present danger* [Film]. (Available from Paramount Studios)

O'Brien, T. L. (1998, July 9). Indonesians visit U.S. seeking help with debt. *New York Times*, p. A9.

O'Donovan, D. (1992). The Economic and Social Council. In P. Alston (Ed.), *The United Nations and human rights: A critical appraisal* (pp. 301–310). Oxford, England: Clarendon Press.

Okigbo, P. (1993). The future haunted by the past. In A. Adedeji (Ed.), *Africa within the world: Beyond dispossession and dependence* (pp. 28–38). London: Zed Books.

Okoye, M. (1990). The African concept of human rights: Development, quality and justice. In G. W. Shepherd & M. Anikpo (Eds.), *Emerging human rights* (pp. 76–88). New York: Greenwood Press.

Onishi, N. (1998, August 22). Mandella says Congo's neighbors will hold talks on revolt. *New York Times*, p. A5.

Pace, S. (1995a, January-February). Francois Mitterrand's adieu a l'Afrique. *Africa Report, 40*, 42–43.

Pace, S. (1995b, January-February). Rwanda: Scenes from a nightmare. *Africa Report, 40*, 40–44.

Parker, A. (Director). (1988). *Mississippi burning* [Film]. (Available from Image Entertainment)

Payer, C. (1982). *The World Bank: A critical analysis*. New York: Monthly Review Press.

Pear, R. (1998, October 19). Officials accused of atrocities losing places to hide, scholars say. *New York Times*, p. A8.

Penna, D. R., & Campbell, P. J. (1998). Human rights and culture: Beyond universality and relativism. *Third World Quarterly, 19*(1), 7–27.

Perera, L. (1994). The Michael Fay controversy: What was at stake? *Commentary, 12*, 115–135.

Perez, L. A. (1986). *Cuba under the Platt amendment, 1902–1934*. Pittsburgh, PA: University of Pittsburgh Press.

Perkins, P. E. (1998, September). The potential of community-based alternatives to globalization. *Development, 41*, 61–67.

Pollis, A. (1992). Human rights in liberal, socialist, and Third World perspective. In R. P. Claude & B. H. Weston (Eds.), *Human rights in the world community: Issues and action* (2nd ed., (pp. 146–158)). Philadelphia: University of Pennsylvania Press.

Pratt, C. (1998, November). *Implications of press freedom for human rights: Lessons from Sub-Saharan Africa*. Paper presented at the National Communication Association Conference, New York.

Preston, J. (1998, July 24). By appealing to rebels, U.N. chief makes peace with Mexico. *New York Times*, p. A5.

Prisoner Pinochet [Editorial]. (1998, November 9). *The Nation*, 3.

Quinn, J. (1992). The General Assembly into the 1990s. In P. Alston (Ed.), *The United Nations and human rights: A critical appraisal* (pp. 55–106). Oxford, England: Clarendon Press.

Radford, J., Kelly, L., & Hester, M. (1996). Introduction. In M. Hester, L. Kelly, & J. Radford (Eds.), *Women, violence, and male power* (pp. 1–16). Buckingham, UK: Open University Press.

Ramberg, B. (1986). The Supreme Court and public interest in broadcasting. *Communications and the Law, 8*(6), 11–30.

Ramcharan, B. G. 1989). *The concept and present status of the international protection of human rights: Forty years after the Universal Declaration*. Dordrecht, Boston, London: Martinus Nijhoff.

Rasheed, S. (1993). Africa at the doorstep of the doorstep of the twenty-first century: Can the crisis turn to opportunity? In A. Adedeji (Ed.), *Africa within the world: Beyond dispossession and dependence* (pp. 41–58). London: Zed Books.

Reich, R. B. (1992). *The work of nations: Preparing ourselves for 21st century capitalism.* New York: Vintage Books.

Reid, T. R. (1998, October 20). Pinochet vows to fight extradition. *Washington Post*, p. A8.

Reuters. (1998a, July 1). U.N. chief holds talks with ruler of Nigeria. *New York Times*, p. 3.

Reuters. (1998b, July 4). In upbeat farewell, Clinton hails Jiang and sees democracy for China. *New York Times*, p. 4.

Reuters. (1998c, July 8). Ex-U.S. official, in Paris, again assails Washington's failure to intervene in Rwanda in '94. *New York Times*, p. 8

Reuters. (1998d, October 24). Prosecutors oppose extradition. *New York Times*, p. A3.

Righter, R. (1995). *Utopia lost: The United Nations and world order.* New York: Twentieth Century Fund Books.

Riis, J. (1890). *How the other half lives.* New York: Scribner.

Robbins, B. (1997, Winter). Sad stories in the international public sphere: Richard Rorty on culture and human rights. *Public Culture, 22*, 209–232.

Robertson, R. (1992). *Globalization: Social theory and global culture.* London: Sage.

Robinson, M. (1998) Message from the High Commissioner for Human Rights. In United Nations Development Program (Ed.), *Integrating human rights with sustainable human development* (pp. vi–vii). Washington, DC: Communications Development.

Rochester, J. M. (1993). *Waiting for the millennium: The United Nations and the future of world order.* Columbia, SC: University of South Carolina Press.

Rohter, L. (1998, October 23). Guatemala cover-up charged in killing of bishop. *New York Times*, p. A6.

Rosenthall, E. (1998, July 1). Chinese say Clinton makes them feel more free, but for how long? *New York Times*, p. A13.

Rothschild, M. (1998, July). Robert Fisk. *The Progressive*, 36–41.

Roxborough, I. (1979). *Theories of underdevelopment.* Atlantic Highlands, NJ: Humanities Press.

Ruiz, V., & Tiano, S. (1987). *Women on the U.S.-Mexico border: Responses to change.* Boston: Allen & Unwin.

Said, E. (1993). *Cultural imperialism.* New York: Knopf.

Sanders, B. (1998, July). Who does the IMF represent? *The Progressive, 62*, 34–35.

Sayles, J. (Director). (1987). *Matewan* [Film]. (Available from Hallmark Home Entertainment)

Sayles, J. (Director). (1998). *Men with guns* [Film]. (Available from Sony Pictures Classics)

Sembene, O. (Director). (1962). *Borom sarret* [Film].

Sembene, O. (1972). *The money order with white genesis.* London: Heinemann.

Sembene, O. (Director). (1974). *Xala* [Film].

Sembene, O. (Director). (1992). *Guelwaar* [Film].

Schemo, D. J. (1998, June 7). The perils in reporting on rights in Colombia. *New York Times*, p. 9.

Schulz, W. F. (1998, July 6). China, human rights and the wait for a duck. *The Nation*, 22–23.

Shenon, P. (1998, July 2). Suharto rebuilds his political base to shield fortune. *New York Times*, p. 1.

Shaw, T. M. (1993). Africa in the New World Order: Marginal and/or central? In A. Adedeji (Ed.), *Africa within the world: Beyond dispossession and dependence* (pp. 78–93). London: Zed Books.

Sklair, L. (1995). *Sociology of the global system*. Baltimore, MD: Johns Hopkins University Press.

Simons, L. M. (1998a, August). Indonesia's plague of fire. *National Geographic*, 100–119.

Simons, M. (1998b, October 19). Pinochet's Spanish Pursuer: Magistrate of explosive cases. *New York Times*, pp. 1, 8.

Singh, P. (1995). Protection from violence is a right. In S. Liebenberg (Ed.), *The constitution of South Africa from a gender perspective* (pp. 23–39). London and New York: Routledge.

Smith, J., Pagnucco, R., & Lopex, G. A. (1998) Globalizing human rights: The work of transnational human rights NGOs in the 1990's. *Human Rights Quarterly, 20*, 379–412.

Snitow, A. (1990). A gender diary. In M. Hirsch & E. F. Keller (Eds.), *Conflicts in feminism* (pp. 43–55). New York: Routledge.

Snodgrass, M. (1997). Topics not suitable for propaganda: Working-class resistance under Peronism. In J. C. Brown (Ed.), *Workers' rights in Latin America, 1930–1979* (pp. 159–188). Chapel Hill, NC, and London: University of North Carolina Press.

Sodhy, P. (1997, October 10). The Malaysian-Cambodian nexus in the 1990s: A growing Third World relationship. Paper presented at the Third World Studies Conference, Omaha, NE.

Sontag, S. (1977). *On photography*. New York: Farrar, Straus, Giroux.

Sotsisowah. (1981). Our strategy for survival. In Akwesasne (Ed.), *Basic call to consciousness* (pp. 112–119). Summertown, TN: Book Publishing.

South African Constitution (1993). Constitution Act 200.

South Commission (1990). *The challenge to the south*. Oxford, England: Oxford University Press.

Spivak, G. C. (1990). Strategy, identity, writing. *The post-colonial critic*. New York: Routledge.

Spivak, G. C. (1988). Subaltern studies: Deconstructing historiography. In G. C. Spivak (Ed.), *In other worlds: Essays in cultural politics*. New York: Routledge.

Stauber, J., & Rampton, S. (1997). Deforming consent: The PR industry's secret war on activists. In P. Phiilip (Ed.), *Censored 1997: The news that didn't make the news* (pp. 36–38). New York: Seven Stories Press.

Stevenson, R. L. (1988). *Communication, development, and the Third World: The global politics of information*. White Plains, NY: Longman.

Stone, O. (Director). *Salvador* [Film].

Strom, S. (1998, July 2.) South Korea's president to free even the unrepentant political prisoners. *New York Times*, p. A6.

Surjadinata, M. B. (1998, June). Time to pray for the people of Indonesia. *United Church News*, p. 5.

Swanger, J. (1997). Defending the nation's interest: Chilean miners and the copper nationalization. In J. C. Brown (Ed.), *Workers' rights in Latin America, 1930–1979* (pp. 270–300). Chapel Hill, NC, and London: University of North Carolina Press.

Teson, F. R. (1992). International human rights and cultural relativism. In R. P. Claude & B. H. Weston, (Eds.), *Human rights in the world community: Issues and action* (2nd ed., pp. 42–54). Philadelphia: University of Pennsylvania Press.

Titelbaum, M., & Morgan, D. (1998, October 5). Harvard University. *The Nation*, 12–13.

Traub, J. (1998, March 29). Kofi Annan's next test. *New York Times Magazine*, 44–81.

Tuozzo, M. C. (1997). As you sow, so shall you reap: Argentine labor and the railway nationalization. In J. C. Brown (Ed.), *Workers' rights in Latin America, 1930–1979* (pp. 128–158). Chapel Hill, NC, and London: University of North Carolina Press.

Twentieth Century Fund. (1998, January 30). *Evaluating NAFTA: Its impact so far on the United States* [Online]. Available: http://www.tcf.org

UNESCO (1949). *Human rights: Comments and interpretations*. London: Allan Wingate.

UNESCO (1980). *The McBridge Report*. New York: United Nations Press.

United Nations. (1991). *African recovery*. New York: Author.

United Nations. (1992). *Report of the United Nations Conference on Environment and Development*, Rio de Janeiro. New York: Author.

United Nations. (1993). *Human rights: The International Bill of Human Rights*. New York: Author.

United Nations. (1994). *The world social situation in the 1990's*. New York: Author.

United Nations. (1995a). *Report on the Fourth World Conference on Women*. New York: Author.

United Nations. (1995b). *The United Nations and human rights, 1948–1995*. New York: Author

United Nations. (1995c). *World Summit for Social Development*. New York: Author.

United Nations. (1997). *The world conferences: Developing priorities for the 21st century*. New York: Author.

United Nations (1998). *Integrating human rights with sustainable human development*. New York: Author

Update, 425 (1998, March 22). Weekly News Update on the Americas. Nicaragua Solidarity Network of Greater New York.

Update, 427 (1998, April 5). Weekly News Update on the Americas. Nicaragua Solidarity Network of Greater New York.

Vaitsos, C. (1974). Employment effects of foreign direct investments in development countries. In E. Edwards (Ed.), *Employment in developing nations* (pp. 331–350). New York: Columbia University Press.

Varis, T. (1984). The internaitonal flow of information. *Journal of Communications, 34*(1), 143–152.

Vatikiotis, M., & Delfs, R. (1993, June 17). Cultural divide. *Far Eastern Economic Review, 156*, 20, 22.

Verhoogen, E. (1996). The U.S. in Haiti: How to get rich on 11 cents an hour. In National Labor Committee (Ed.), *The U.S. in Haiti* (pp. 1–29). New York: National Labor Committee Education Fund.

Vest, J. (1998, November 3). Human rights "miracle." *The Village Voice*, pp. 58, 61.

Wagner, M. D. (1998). All the *Bourmestre*'s men: Making sense of genocide in Rwanda. *Africa Today, 45*(1), 25–36.

Wallis, W. (1998, July 31). Uncertainty rises in Congo as Rwandan troops depart. *New York Times*, p. A19

Wang, J., & Chang, T.-K. (1996). From class ideology to state manager: TV programming and foreign imports in China, 1970–1990. *Journal of Broadcasting and Electronic Media, 40*(2), 196–207.

Weiner, T. (1998, September 21). Decision to strike targets in Sudan based on faulty evidence. *New York Times*, p. 1.

Werber, H. (1983, February 23). Popularity of U.S. Series stalks the halls at Euro-telecom front. *Variety*, 38.

West. C. (1993). *Prophetic thought in postmodern times*. Monroe, ME: Common Courage Press.

Weston, B. H. (1989). Human rights. In R. P. Claude & B. H. Weston, (Eds.), *Human rights in the world community: Issues and action* (pp. 12–28). Philadelphia: University of Pennsylvania Press.

Whitelaw, N. (1998). *Diana, The people's princess: The story of Diana*. New York: Morgan Reynolds.

Whitman, W. (1973). *Song of myself*. In S. Bradley & H. W. Blodgett (Eds.), *Leaves of grass* (pp. 58–59). New York: Norton.

Winder, R. B. (1967). The Lebanese in West Africa. In L. A. Fallers (Ed.), *Immigrants and associations* (pp. 28–53). The Hague and Paris: Mouton.

Winters, J. A. (1998, June 15). Mobilizing the people. *The Nation*, 14–15.

Young, R. (1990). *White mythologies: Writing history and the West*. New York: Routledge.

Zakaria, F. (1996, April 7). Divining Russia. *New York Times Book Review*, p. 6.

Zakaria, F. (1998). *From wealth and power: The unusual origins of America's world role*. Princeton, NJ: Princeton University Press.

Zemeckis, R. (Director). (1994). *Forrest Gump* [Film]. (Available from Paramount Studios)

Zinn. H. (1998). *The twentieth century: A people's history*. New York: HarperPerennial.

Zuckerman, L. (1998, June 30). $1.6 billion in deals can't mask U.S. disappointment. *New York Times*, p. A10.

Zvobgo, J. M. (1979). A Third World view. In D. P. Kommers & G. D. Loescher (Eds.), *Human rights and American foreign policy* (pp. 90–107). Notre Dame, IN: University of Notre Dame Press.

Zwingle, E. (1998, October). Women and population. *National Geographic, 4*, 36–55.

Author Index

Subject Index

About the Author

William Over teaches English and Speech at St. John's University and is interested in cultural and cross-cultural studies, particularly as they pertain to human rights and social justice issues. Recent articles include "New York's African Theatre: Shakespeare Reinterpreted" (in B. Reynolds and D. Hedrick [Eds.], *Shakespeare Without Class: Dissidence, Intervention, Countertradition,* 1999) and "I, With So Much Strength and Argument Resisted: Difference Made Plain in *The Masque of Blackness*" (in J. Wainwright and M. al-Mussawi [Eds.], *Jailbreaks and Recreations: Resentencing the Other in Colonial and Postcolonial Discourse,* 1999).